The Psychoanalytic Study of the Child

VOLUME THIRTY-SIX

New Haven
Yale University Press
1981

Designed by Sally Harris
and set in Baskerville type.
Printed in the United States of America by
Vail-Ballou Press, Inc., Binghamton, N.Y.

Library of Congress catalog card number: 45-11304
International standard book number: 0-300-02762-1
10 9 8 7 6 5 4 3 2 1

Contents

PROBLEMS OF INSIGHT

CLINICAL CONTRIBUTIONS TO PSYCHOANALYTIC
THEORY

APPLICATIONS OF PSYCHOANALYSIS

In Memoriam
Marianne Kris
1900–1980

We deeply mourn the death of our beloved friend and colleague Marianne Kris, who was an editor of *The Psychoanalytic Study of the Child* since 1958. One of our future volumes will be dedicated to her.

The following three tributes were read at a memorial meeting held in New York on December 7, 1980.

ALBERT J. SOLNIT, M.D.

We have gathered together to honor and to say good-bye to Marianne Kris whose influence remains an abiding presence for each of us. As a mother, grandmother, friend, colleague, physician, psychoanalyst, teacher, and scholar she has left with us a rich and enduring legacy. By the way she lived her life and through the vital balance of human warmth, optimism, and searching intelligence that she gave to each of her relationships, she has made available loving and guiding resources that nurture and inspire us. This was her gift, an immortality that is available but not imposed, one that liberates and does not burden.

Marianne Kris was born in Vienna on May 27, 1900. A graduate of the University of Vienna, she had a close association with medicine and psychoanalysis from the days of her childhood in Vienna. Her father, a pediatrician, was a close friend and collaborator of Sigmund Freud. Dr. Oskar Rie was the pediatrician for the Freud children and had been an associate of Freud's in an outpatient neurology clinic for children. Dr. Rie also participated in the weekly Tarock card game.

At the age of 8 Marianne Kris told her father she intended to become a doctor. As it was told, Dr. Rie promised his daughter Marianne that he would support her plan if she still desired it by the time she was 14 years old and after she had begun gymnasium. Already one could see Marianne Kris's determination and problem-solving capacities. It is said that her parents also thought she was a bit stubborn! And it was also clear that she enjoyed the pioneer role—the zest of a challenge in which her playful optimism and serious intellectual commitment put her at the forefront of new knowledge and new methods for exploring how the human mind worked and developed, how the child and adult related and mutually influenced each other.

Marianne Kris received her M.D. from the University of Vienna in 1925. Thereupon, she moved to Berlin for psychiatric and psychoanalytic training under the leadership of Franz Alexander. She returned to Vienna in 1927. It was a very good year! Ernst and Marianne Kris married in 1927. Fleeing from the Nazis, they moved to England with Anna and Tony in 1938 and to the United States in 1940. There they were associated with the New York Psychoanalytic Institute, the American Psychoanalytic Association, and later with the Western New England Institute for Psychoanalysis and the Psychoanalytic Institute at Columbia University. Marianne Kris also became a Charter Member and Life Fellow of the American Academy of Child Psychiatry.

Beginning her association with Milton Senn and Sally Provence at the New York Hospital and Cornell University Medical College, Marianne joined Ernst in moving to Yale's Child Study Center in 1953. In 1958, after Ernst's death in 1957, Marianne became one of the Managing Editors of *The Psychoanalytic Study of the Child*. In the early 1970s, Marianne Kris gave the Annual Sigmund Freud Lecture at the New York Psychoanalytic Institute. The lecture, "The Psychoanalytic Study of the Family," was based on her careful and extraordinarily creative research on the simultaneous psychoanalyses of all members of one family.

Throughout her career as a medical teacher, university researcher and scholarly editor, Marianne Kris demonstrated her remarkable capacities to be constructively critical, to maintain highest standards, and to be fair and generous. One of her former students and later colleagues put it this way: "I have never known anyone in psychoanalysis and particularly child analysis who was so genuine and so little inclined to elitism. She was the most generous and warm spirit and I shall miss a dear friend." For our colleagues on the Editorial Board of *The Psychoanalytic Study of the Child* I can say, we shall miss Marianne's good judgment, her wisdom, and her fairness.

Marianne Kris taught extensively and wrote sparingly. Her teaching and writing have had a steady, continuing influence. Those who study the most difficult and complex scientific process and methodology, that of prediction, turn repeatedly to her report, "The Use of Prediction in a Longitudinal Study."[1] Her theoretical questions and insights were always embedded in clinical observations and interactions. In her essay, "Child Analysis,"[2] she lucidly interwove theoretical, technical, and clinical dimensions of child psychoanalysis within its developmental setting. As did her clinical teaching, these writings demonstrated rigorous scientific thinking, carefully integrated clinical observations, intuitive questioning, and theoretical formulations.

Always, she was aware of the complexities of the developing child and his world, enabling her to help child and family or to guide a younger colleague as he or she learned to observe, understand, communicate, and form an alliance with his child patient. An exquisite, friendly sensitivity to patients, parents, and students was a hallmark of Marianne Kris's work. Students and colleagues quickly learned that her warmth, astuteness, patience, and generosity were accompanied by demands for clinical understanding, dedication, and thoroughness. The understanding and care of the patient came first, second, and third. Sally Provence has pointed out that it was Marianne Kris's "gifted capacity for translating psychoanalytic knowledge into practical suggestions that facilitated the work of many teachers, pediatricians, social workers, and psychologists, as well as the other early childhood specialists and child analysts with whom she worked."

As a companion and collaborator she was gracious, energetic, and modest. In her teaching and collaborative scientific work

1. In: *The Psychoanalytic Study of the Child,* 12:175–189, 1957.
2. In: *Psychoanalysis Today,* ed. S. Lorand. New York: Int. Univ. Press, 1944.

her students and co-workers felt the effervescence of her lovely, warming sense of humor, her youthful resiliency, and her singular sense of fairness.

In 1965 Marianne Kris became the first president of the Association for Child Psychoanalysis. It is correct to say that she was both the creator and first leader of this international organization of more than 400 child psychoanalysts. Marianne Kris had long felt that there was the need for a scientific forum for child psychoanalysis. The existing forums, especially in the United States, were too restrictive and restricted. Initially, the leaders of the American Psychoanalytic Association asked Marianne Kris, whom they respected and loved, to create such a forum within the American Psychoanalytic Association. Two years later when the fear of nonmedical psychoanalysts led the Council of the American Psychoanalytic Association to defeat such a plan, Marianne Kris said, with a huge sigh of relief, "Now we are free to get on with our plan in our own way." Her way was that rare amalgam of standards of excellence, flexibly developed and administered without the burdens of political ambitions or distortions. Because Marianne Kris was so nonpolitical and nonrevolutionary the Association for Child Psychoanalysis was born, peacefully and healthfully. It had a lusty infancy and has become 15 years old this year. In celebrating the 10th anniversary of its birth at the 11th annual meeting in Kansas City in March 1976, Peter Neubauer said, "Dr. Kris is never self-serving and therefore she serves unerringly."

To give, at this time of parting, a sample of Marianne Kris's quality I quote some of our remarks and her responses to encomiums given by Peter Neubauer, Charles Feigelson, and myself at that time. Peter Neubauer spoke of the closeness of her friends, collaborators, and students. Charles Feigelson spoke of her clinical and teaching brilliance, and I spoke of Marianne's and Ernst's work at the Child Study Center at Yale. In my comments I said, "First of all, we had an introduction into the way in which psychoanalysts play with children in a nursery school at the same time as they are becoming systematic observers of them. In fact, sometimes when Marianne and Ernst were in the nursery school, we learned how to play with children by the way they played with them. They were very good with tricycles and blocks! Occasionally we worried a little bit about Marianne's zest in game playing. Once she got into a game, the game often became so interesting and worthwhile that it took on a new dimension. One of the games we worried about most was her driving to New Haven from Stamford. I don't know how many traffic tickets she got for speeding, but I am sure that in many cases she charmed the state trooper out of giving her a ticket. She drove with excellent skill and in a funlike way—just as it was fun for Marianne and Ernst to teach a child how to use a new piece of equipment in the gym or how to ride a tricycle. All this provided a balance to the view of not only what analysts thought, but what they did when they were in action, so to speak, in a longitudinal way. Now you must not think from this that playfulness and engaging in speeding were the outstanding characteristics. High standards were the primary frame of reference. If you deviated from those standards, you were reminded with kindness but firmness of what were the limits of speculation and what were the limits of our understanding."

She responded to our remarks as follows:

Thank you all three very much for what you said. You gave me good food for my narcissism.

I am glad, Peter, that we belong to one family.

I am sorry, Al, I have to correct one fact. I could not charm the trooper out of giving me a ticket, and I had to go to court.

Although you say, Charlie, that you did not idealize me, I think you did. I must say I enjoyed the supervision with you very much and learned at least as much too.

[She then added:] Since you mentioned my interest in child analysis and my teaching has been of value, I should like to say a word about the three to whom I owe the most in my development as a child analyst; two of them well known to all of us; the third especially so to me. As Peter has said, the latter was my father, whose occupation was concerned with helping children. He was a pediatrician. The second was my father's close friend, the founder of psychoanalysis. Identifications with the combined father images led me to our field.

The third person who influenced me so much was Anna Freud. I had the good fortune to have her as a teacher during my early training years, and even later as a model in various situations of learning. Together with Edward Bibring she led a seminar for younger analysts, who called it "If I Were King." Nevertheless, it functioned in a very democratic way. Ernst Kris and Edith Buxbaum each presented a case of an adult patient, while every member of the seminar became King in turn, having to state which data he or she would have selected for the interpretation. The conclusion eventually drawn was that "Many Roads Lead to Rome."

A second group chaired by Anna Freud in which I participated was the Seminar on Child Analysis. At first very small, it grew larger each year. I think it started as supervision with Editha Sterba, who was soon joined by Jenny Waelder, Anny Katan, Edith Buxbaum, and later on by many others. Jenny Waelder's well-known "Analysis of a Case of Night Terror" was presented there.

It pleases me that the Association for Child Analysis bears the imprint and continues the tradition of the three people who had such an impact on me. As you know, Anna Freud had long supported the idea of starting an association like ours.

With her gracious intelligence, playful humor, deft hands, and lively spirit, Marianne Kris was an astute observer of life. She was wonderful as a seamstress, mending clothes and making drapes. She was a fun-loving life player with unflagging loyalty to her family, friends, patients, students, and colleagues. As a mother and grandmother, she was devoted and joyful.

The flagging of physical energy and the discomfort caused by aging or physical ailments were quietly and realistically, at times with a gentle sense of humor, confronted without a loss of resiliency, interest, and concern for others. Perhaps one cannot further differentiate this wonderful woman and her creativity and generosity for she was always more than the sum of these qualities. Her talent and enjoyment in helping others have established a lasting influence for she was a person "of beauty and a joy forever."

PETER B. NEUBAUER, M.D.

As we are gathered here together at the memorial meeting for Marianne Kris, we are experiencing a deep sense of loss and of mourning. Yet, we shall not surrender to this feeling because we cannot but celebrate her life as we mourn her death.

Over the past years she had to struggle with illness, but she never complained; her response to the question, "How are you?" never went further than "I had some problems, but I am feeling better" or "I am all right again." She often said that she might not live much longer, and she said it with that tone which reflects reality. There was never sadness or self-pity or regret. When I once said to her how remarkable it was that she minimized her reactions to her illness, but that she could speak so freely about her death, for me obviously too often, she replied in her characteristic way, "Because I accept my death, I can do it."

She was too interested in continuing to live as before and in giving meaning to her life as she saw it, rather than challenging its limits. So she went to London for she wished so much not to miss the International Psychoanalytic Seminar at the Hampstead Clinic, and we cannot help but think that she had to return to Freud's home, her spiritual home, and to die there next to her closest friend, Anna Freud.

It is now more than 30 years since Marianne Kris joined the staff of the Child Development Center at the time it was established. She was our teacher, supervisor, program planner. She had brought with her the experience from Vienna and from London to coordinate psychoanalytic therapy with an educational nursery school and to focus on early childhood. Over the years she taught a large number of analysts, teachers, social workers, and psychologists how to understand the child, his normal development, and his pathological conflicts.

Her clinical conferences and supervisory sessions are unforgettable. While others may address themselves to the broad sweep of dynamic constellations, she would invariably listen to every clinical detail, pay attention to the sequences, and then explore their meaning; thereby the richness of the material revealed itself. This capacity to pay attention was matched by her talent to formulate interpretive statements to patients in one phrase that allied the unconscious meaning, the esteem of the defense, and, at the same time, support of the ego. And there was always respect for the patient. Whoever had been privileged to hear Marianne Kris's formulations was aware that she was a master endowed with unusual gifts.

As a training analyst, a member of the faculty of the New York

Psychoanalytic Institute, and a supervisor at various other child analytic institutes—the Columbia and the New York University analytic programs—she was sought after, and often enough students went to her or were assigned to her because they had unusual difficulties in their work. Marianne Kris would try where others were inclined to give up. When others were critical, she would rather err by trying harder and longer to overcome resistances or limitations.

Marianne Kris was primarily a teacher and a clinician, but with increasing frequency she initiated and participated in psychoanalytic studies and the development of new programs. Against many difficulties she formed the Association of Child Psychoanalysis to provide a forum to share experiences, to present papers, and to organize regional study groups. As Harold Blum said at a meeting of a study group, "Dr. Kris was always the pioneer, always gracious, and always facilitating." Indeed, one of her great pleasures was to encourage others to investigate psychoanalytic issues and to present their findings.

She was a member of the Board of Psychoanalytic Research and Development Fund created by her brother-in-law, Herman Nunberg. She helped to select topics and regularly took part in many discussion groups. There was a wide-ranging interest. In addition to participating in other studies, she was a member of groups which addressed themselves to infant development, the influence of sibling relationships on development, and reconstruction. Later, she was part of the steering committee which organized the international psychoanalytic seminars held at the Hampstead Child-Therapy Clinic.

Her function and her role in these study groups were always the same. She always asked that we start by presenting case material. She listened attentively, interested in what each colleague had to contribute, and when she spoke, she would either clarify for us the dynamic meaning of an event, a fantasy, a mode of behavior; or she would interrupt our spirited engagement in theoretical speculations and guide us to the clinical data, always demanding that we find the clinical evidence for our assumptions. This orientation toward exploring the complexity of the psychic life and the life story of the patient made her look for the as yet unknown, and to learn from each case about the territory as yet uncharted. This may have been the reason why she was not interested in repeating what had been said before, what her previous findings were, how one had formulated the analytic task in the past—in spite of her long and close participation in the evolvement of psychoanalysis in Vienna, London, and here, as well as her closeness to Ernst Kris's work and that of Hartmann, Kris, and Loewenstein.

She may have been too self-effacing; she never used her talents to give herself significance, but, as I suggest, she was too engaged in the present and the future to dwell on the past.

Sometimes, in these meetings, she could be insistent, or quietly but forcefully stubborn, in maintaining her position, when she found herself under pressure to deviate from her convictions. I suppose it was the same stubbornness she had shown early in her life when she had to prove to her father that she had made the choice to enter medical school and had to convince him to let her do it; or when she asked a professor in Berlin who criticized Freud, whether he had read his work.

How can I find a few words to speak about her friendship? She gave us the feeling of total safety; there was always her trust that needed neither confirmation nor testing. Where she was, there also was our home.

Marianne Kris always knew what she wanted, and did what she wanted to do. She filled her life with what gave it meaning; until the last moment she lived her life with ease and in peace. This gives us comfort and elevates our spirit.

SAMUEL RITVO, M.D.

I ask your indulgence to bring my remarks from a personal point of view. At first I thought this would not be appropriate, then I realized that everyone whose life was touched by Marianne Kris, whether as beneficiary of her physicianly psychoanalytic skills, or whether as friend or colleague, felt they had been personally enriched by a rare human experience. When I arrived in New York in 1943, one year out of medical school and knowing very little about psychoanalysis and nothing about psychoanalysts, it was one of the great good fortunes of my life and the good fortune of my family that I found my way to Marianne Kris not long after she and her family had arrived in this country. To have had her as analyst, teacher, colleague, and friend for 37 years brought blessings and gifts beyond counting.

To have had her as teacher and colleague at the Yale Child Study Center after the years in New York gave me the opportunity to see how she contributed her unique gifts and talents to a complex collaborative research effort—first when she joined her husband Ernst in the longitudinal study and later in the psychoanalytic family study which she initiated and led. In these settings her exquisite sensitivity to the analytic material, her ability to discern nuances of meaning, her rootedness in the daily lives of people as well as her responsiveness to the echoes of the past, her tact and skill in how she would talk to them, were all an inspiration to us. But her insight was by no means sheer intuition. It was based on a rigorous, disciplined, scholarly understanding of psychoanalysis, as well as on long and thoughtful immersion in the psychoanalytic situation and method.

The children were, of course, a focus in both studies. Here her understanding of how the child thinks and feels and of the nature of the internal and external world he constructs was a revelation to her colleagues.

Whenever younger colleagues had the opportunity to discuss their work with Marianne Kris, they came away doubly enriched—first by new insights into the subtleties of the psychoanalytic dialogue, and second by her interest in their development as psychoanalysts and by her empathy for their efforts and difficulties.

These skills and personal qualities made her a superb guide and counselor to parents, able to translate psychoanalytic understanding and insights into helpful practical guides to troubled parents without making them feel guilty or incompetent. They felt rather that they had a sympathetic and resourceful ally in their difficult task.

Marianne Kris's life could be taken as an exemplar for the life of a psychoanalyst in that "impossible profession." Her warmth, her gentleness, her natural and direct interest in other human beings gave her great satisfaction in entering constructively into the lives of people the way an analyst needs to do, without compromising the basic principles of psychoanalysis which are not points of honor or ends in themselves, but ultimately in the best interests of the patient. She had an unflagging interest in the institutions of psychoanalysis which are essential for its educational functions, its progress as a scientific endeavor, and its professional responsibilities. Her vision, her energy, and her leadership were the prime forces in creating the Association for Child Psychoanalysis. Her contributions to the New York Psychoanalytic Society and Institute and to a number of others were legion. Her devotion to her family and friends gave them the comfort of her love and gave her such deep satisfaction. All this she carried out with the utmost simplicity and with utter lack of pretension. Her humor, infectious laughter, and quick gestures remained youthful to the end. We are all grateful that she was able to live and work so joyously until the very last moment of her life just as she wished.

It is a great loss, she leaves a large gap. But in its many fulfillments, in its gifts to others which live on, it was a life to be celebrated, not mourned.

PROBLEMS OF DEVELOPMENT
Contributions in Honor of Dorothy Burlingham

Application of the Metapsychological Profile to the Assessment of Deaf Children

PAUL M. BRINICH, Ph.D.

THE METAPSYCHOLOGICAL PROFILE DEVELOPED BY ANNA FREUD (1965) and her coworkers at the Hampstead Child-Therapy Clinic has been applied to different age groups (A. Freud et al., 1965; Laufer, 1965; Meers, 1966; W. E. Freud, 1967, 1972), to different diagnostic groups (Michaels and Stiver, 1965; Thomas, 1966), and to children with organically based handicaps (Burlingham, 1975).

The utility of the Metapsychological Profile lies in the fact that it attempts to bring together in an organized framework many different facets of an individual personality. The framework is one which stresses intrapsychic structure and functioning rather than overt symptomatology. As such, it yields a much more dynamic and true-to-life picture of the personality than the more usual nosological categories such as the Diagnostic and Statistical Manuals promulgated by the American Psychiatric Association.

Any diagnostician who has struggled to fit an individual patient into one of the various Procrustean beds provided by the

Assistant Professor in the Department of Psychiatry of Case Western Reserve School of Medicine and Staff Clinical Psychologist at Cleveland Metropolitan General Hospital.

This paper grew out of work done while the author was Director of Training of the Center on Deafness, Department of Psychiatry, University of California, San Francisco. The Center receives significant financial support from the National Institute for Handicapped Research and from the Department of Mental Health of the State of California.

nosologists will breathe a sigh of relief when given the opportunity to describe his patient in Profile terms. However tedious the process of completing a Profile may at times become, it does encourage the diagnostician to think about the dynamic relationships between the various intrapsychic "parts" of his patient.

Experience has shown that the Metapsychological Profile also provides psychoanalytic psychologists with a spur for the elaboration of basic psychoanalytic knowledge. An excellent example of such an application appears in Burlingham's (1975) modification of the Profile for use with blind babies. This modification clearly demonstrates (1) the effect of blindness upon the psychological organization of a young child, and (2) the integral part played by vision in normal early development.

In this paper I attempt to organize several diagnostic sessions with a latency-age deaf child, whom I shall call Arthur Smith, around the Profile headings. When one applies what is by now a familiar tool used by many child psychoanalysts to a new kind of patient, some peculiarities emerge which highlight characteristics both of the tool and of the deaf child. Thus, in my introductory comments to each section of the Profile, I emphasize the special information and considerations that are peculiarly necessary for the assessment of deaf children—that is, the areas in which the tool needs to be adapted and expanded. It is my hope that the peculiarities that emerge not only will stimulate our thinking about a particular deaf child but will go beyond to highlight aspects of the psychological development of prelingually deaf people and to illustrate the parts which language and communication—as distinct from speech and hearing—play in that development.

PROFILE OF A DEAF CHILD

I. REASONS FOR REFERRAL

Most deaf children (and also deaf adults) have been referred to many different medical specialists, clinics, social service agencies, and educational facilities. The deaf children and their parents have usually experienced a great deal of frustration in these contacts as the diagnosis was gradually established and as rec-

ommendations for treatment (often contradictory recommendations) were presented to the parents by the "experts."

I have often found it useful to consider the deaf child and his
parents as a family which has been doubly traumatized—first by
the child's handicap, and second by the various and often contradictory interventions proposed. This traumatization means
that the diagnostician needs to spend a good deal of time discussing past frustrations with the parents. It also means that the
diagnostician may find it difficult to pull together the reports of
the various agencies' previous contacts with the family. Yet, such
a consolidation of information is crucial in the assessment and
treatment of a deaf child, as it is with any handicapped child.

Frustrations related to multiple agency contacts played a part
in the background of Arthur Smith. He was referred for assessment by his school, his audiologist, and his parents. Arthur's
teachers had tried to pressure Arthur's parents into seeking help
for their adopted son since he was 4 years old. Now, 7 years later
the school administrators were threatening to exclude Arthur
from school. They described a boy who was incapable of conforming to the normal restrictions of the classroom. He had
difficulties in maintaining attention, learning, and remembering
school material, and he was constantly in trouble with both
teachers and peers because of his provocative behavior and his
aggressive outbursts.

Arthur's parents saw things quite differently, however. They
believed that Arthur's difficulties were entirely the fault of his
school; they accused the teachers and administrators of being
unwilling to accommodate sufficiently to Arthur. The Smiths
made it quite clear that they would not have sought help for
Arthur without pressure from the school; they maintained
throughout the diagnostic period that Arthur presented no
problems at home. However, Mrs. Smith did respond to my
statement that I was exhausted after a diagnostic session with
Arthur by telling me, "You ought to try him 24 hours a day!"

II. DESCRIPTION OF CHILD

The description of the deaf child should include an audiogram
which describes the child's hearing loss in terms of its amplitude

at different frequencies, both with and without the child's hearing aids. Different "shapes" of audiograms have vastly different implications for the ability of the child to make use of his residual hearing for the perception of human speech. The "type" of hearing loss, i.e., "conductive" versus "sensorineural," also is crucial information because the former can often benefit markedly from surgical intervention and prostheses, while the latter can usually get no benefits from surgery and only limited benefits from hearing aids.

The age of onset of deafness is another very important factor in this section, for a child who has had some experience with sound in communication prior to becoming deaf is a vastly different child from one whose hearing has always been impaired.

The etiology of the child's deafness is also important, for many of the causes of childhood deafness are associated with other damage to the body (e.g., rubella in the first trimester of pregnancy often affects the heart, vision, and the central nervous system, as well as the auditory nerve). In fact, as new medical techniques enable more and more handicapped children to survive their infancy, the population in schools for the deaf is gradually becoming one that includes a very large proportion of multihandicapped children.

The etiology of the handicap is also significant insofar as it may be related to one or the other of the parents of the child or to their families. Recent studies (Moores, 1978) suggest that about 30 percent of all childhood deafness may be genetic in origin; the defect, while usually recessive, is sometimes "blamed" upon one side of the child's family or the other, with predictably disastrous effects upon the parents' marriage.

Arthur's case illustrates the importance of audiological information in the assessment of a deaf child. The audiologist outlined the functional implications of Arthur's hearing loss and, at the same time, emphasized the role that denial played in the attitude of Arthur's adoptive mother toward his handicap.

Arthur had a profound hearing loss. Recent audiological testing had shown no measurable responses in Arthur's right ear and very minimal responses in his left ear (70 dB loss at 125 Hz, 80 dB loss at 250 Hz, 110 dB loss at 500 Hz, and no measurable responses above 500 Hz). When his hearing was checked with his hearing aids, Arthur was able to detect sounds somewhat better (sound field responses showed a 30 dB loss at 250 Hz, 45 dB loss at 500 Hz, 45 dB loss at 1000 Hz, 55 dB loss at 1500 Hz, and no measurable responses above 1500 Hz); however, Arthur's audiologist still summarized his evaluation of Arthur by saying, "The fact is that he cannot process auditorily, and neither hearing aids, speech ability if he possessed it, nor mother's love can erase his deafness."

As far as the etiology of Arthur's deafness was concerned, his case is atypical in that he was adopted after the diagnosis of deafness. Thus neither parent "blamed" the other for the defect. Arthur's adoptive parents reported that they knew nothing of the etiology of Arthur's deafness. Careful medical investigation revealed no other physical anomalies at the time Arthur was referred to me for assessment.

Arthur was an attractive, slender, tow-headed boy of average height for his 11 years. From his behavior during the diagnostic assessment it appeared that Arthur was quick to make new acquaintances; he managed to communicate a surprising amount of information via a combination of mimicry, gestures, and some not very well-developed sign language. He was very curious and eager to understand how things worked. At the same time he was very provocative and quickly began testing the limits in the diagnostic setting by trying to play with typewriters and other office equipment.

In my diagnostic work with Arthur I used a variety of communication techniques: speech, sign language, gesture, mime, writing, and drawing. Despite this multimodal approach, there were many times when I did not feel confident that Arthur understood me as well as many times when I did not understand Arthur. These problems in communication certainly colored the diagnostic picture; they led Arthur to use provocative actions rather than words, and they made it difficult for me to assess the degree to which verbal interpretation of the provocative behavior might have helped Arthur to limit it.

III. FAMILY BACKGROUND AND PERSONAL HISTORY

I will confine my comments under this heading to (1) events surrounding the diagnosis of the handicap; (2) the resources available to the family; and (3) the presence or absence of other, healthy children in the family.

It is important to learn when and by whom the diagnosis was made. Deafness results in relatively subtle disturbances in the behavior and interactions of the deaf infant, and many parents of congenitally deaf children report that their own early concerns about their child were repeatedly dismissed by pediatricians and other experts until a point when the child's speech development was quite obviously retarded (i.e., often until 18 months of age or even older).

Parents of deaf children often report that they were told of their child's deafness by someone who expected them to comprehend and to accept the diagnosis as a simple matter of fact. Diagnosticians often are unwilling to deal with the shock, the feelings of loss, the anger, and the mourning which hearing parents of a deaf child usually experience at the time of diagnosis. It is therefore important to discover how the parents were told of their child's deafness and what resources were made available to them to help them deal with their profound reactions to this news. I have found in several cases that parents of a deaf child who was now in his teens had never been able to discuss with anyone their reactions to the diagnosis of deafness. This is a sad reflection upon the professionals involved with the family at the time of diagnosis.

A further consideration of which the diagnostician working with a deaf child must be aware is the extent to which the child's parents have been able to find and to make use of special medical and educational resources relevant to their child's deafness. As with other handicaps, there is a strong tendency on the part of parents to deny as much as possible the reality of the deafness. Perhaps because of the "invisibility" of deafness, this denial seems particularly prevalent in parents and educators of the deaf. Offered a choice between an educational program that promises to make their deaf child "just like" a hearing child and an educational program that is founded on the use of special techniques (such as sign language) which make their deaf child obviously different from hearing children, there are few parents who would not be tempted to opt for the former.

The diagnostician should also attempt to find out what special resources the individual deaf child and his parents bring to their interactions. Personal resources—such as flexibility, or the ability to "read" nonverbal cues, or excellent intelligence—will all help to modify the impact of the handicap.

Finally, it is also important for the diagnostician to take into account the presence or absence in the family of other, healthy children. In my experience, parents who have experienced themselves as successful parents with other children are in a better position to respond to the special needs of a handicapped child than are parents for whom the handicapped child is their first child, or who have had another handicapped child precede the deaf child.

Arthur was reportedly born at 35 weeks gestation and weighed 4 lbs. 9 oz. at birth. He was given up for adoption at birth; Mr. and Mrs. Smith reported that they knew very little about Arthur's biological parents. Arthur was placed for adoption at about 1 month of age but was returned to the adoption agency when, at the age of 5 months, he was found to be deaf. The etiology of Arthur's deafness remains unknown, as do the details of his first half year of life.

Arthur was adopted by the Smiths when he was 6 months old. They had specifically requested a deaf child because they believed that they could do a better job raising a deaf child than the parents of the deaf children whom Mrs. Smith taught (she was a professional educator of the deaf). Arthur was the fourth child in the family; the other three children, all hearing, were natural children of Mr. and Mrs. Smith and were between 5 to 10 years older than Arthur.

The Smiths recalled Arthur being easily upset as a child. The family made two moves while Arthur was young, and he found these very hard to take. The first move occurred when he was 1½ years old, and the second when he was 2½ years old; Mrs. Smith recalled that Arthur suffered through weeks of disturbed sleep and a great deal of anxiety after each move. She herself wondered if Arthur was afraid of being "rejected" and linked this to the fact that he had been rejected twice before.

Arthur began school at age 3; he was placed in a program for hearing-impaired children which emphasized the development of speech, giving this a higher priority than the development of meaningful communication.[1]

The first school placement did not work well; after little more than a year the school suggested that the Smiths obtain a psychiatric evaluation of their son because of behavioral problems which were already visible in Arthur. Unfortunately the Smiths did not follow through on the recommendation but instead decided that Arthur's problems were the result of the school's inability to adapt to his special needs. The Smiths moved Arthur into a new special education program for the deaf when he was 5 years old, but the new school quickly reported the same difficulties with Arthur as had been obvious in the first school.

Mr. and Mrs. Smith were particularly aware of what was going on in school because Mrs. Smith was herself a teacher in Arthur's school. This was unfortunate, for this emphasized an already strong symbiotic trend in Mrs. Smith. While the school administration consistently recommended that Arthur be transferred to a school which would provide Arthur with both oral and manual communication, the Smiths rejected this advice because such a move would prevent Mrs. Smith from being able to keep an eye on what happened to her son.

IV. POSSIBLY SIGNIFICANT ENVIRONMENTAL INFLUENCES

A. For the Timing of the Referral

A handicap such as deafness has different effects upon the child and his family at every developmental step. In most cases

1. This is an important distinction since most deaf children in the United States and Western Europe have been enrolled in special education programs which attempt to teach speech before the children have learned the purpose of speech, i.e., communication. This bias in educational philosophy goes back to an international congress on education of the deaf which was held in Milan in 1880. There it was decided that all deaf children should be educated by "oral" training and that manual communication should be used only if oral training failed. There has been a dramatic shift away from this position in the United States during the past 10 to 15 years as educators have found that deaf children who can communicate via sign language are in a much better position to learn to use what oral skills they are able to develop than are children who receive oral training with no previous experience of linguistic communication (Meadow, 1975).

the deaf child will be referred for assessment at a time when his handicap is interfering in some overwhelming way with his development, thereby putting him in severe conflict with his environment.

Arthur's disturbance had been obvious to outside observers for many years, though his parents consistently insisted that the problem lay in Arthur's school and not in Arthur himself or in their handling of him. At the point of referral the school was demanding that Arthur be removed and seemed willing to make this move despite the parents' objections. This increased external pressure motivated Arthur's referral for evaluation.

B. For the Causation of the Disturbance

In an outline of the environmental factors which may have contributed to the creation of a child's disturbance, it is important to bear in mind that a deaf child's environment is significantly different from that of other children. Deafness creates unusual frustrations for the child and puts unusual demands upon both him and his parents. Among these are the various medical procedures, prostheses, special educational regimens, and so forth, which may have been experienced by the child not as helps but as traumatizing events.

As a twice-adopted (and thus twice-rejected) child Arthur certainly experienced important discontinuities in his early care, which produced a special sensitivity to changes in him. Mrs. Smith described clearly how upset Arthur had become when the family had moved house.

Arthur's deafness was, of course, involved in his being returned to the adoption agency after his first adoption. His deafness was also involved in his second adoption, for not only had the Smiths specifically requested a deaf child, but they believed that they would be able to help this deaf child become like a hearing child. This simultaneous acceptance of and denial of Arthur's handicap led the Smiths to a series of inconsistent and mutually contradictory attitudes and expectations. On the one hand, the Smiths expected Arthur's teachers to make special efforts to overcome the communicative deficit associated with Arthur's deafness; on the other hand, the Smiths insisted that Arthur was able to communicate with them easily with little or no adaptation of their own communicative efforts. They simply spoke to Arthur loudly and clearly, believing that he comprehended much more of their speech than he did.

In addition to the frustrations implied by such contradictory expectations, Arthur also had to deal with a mother who was exceptionally intrusive in her demands for communicative contact with her deaf child. Mrs. Smith would grab Arthur's chin and turn his face toward her when she wanted to speak to him; this behavior was evident when Arthur was 2½ years old, and Mrs. Smith was still doing this with her son 8 years later. When Arthur responded to his mother's intrusions by trying to turn away, Mrs. Smith simply redoubled her efforts.

Mrs. Smith was also unable to tolerate long separations from Arthur. She was most comfortable when Arthur was enrolled in her own class (against the advice of her fellow teachers). She believed that she was unable to learn to use simultaneous oral and manual (sign language) communication and therefore resisted all advice that Arthur should be given such bimodal input. She feared that once Arthur learned to use sign language and was in regular contact with other signing people, he would not want to communicate with her. This fear that she might lose Arthur was very likely related to the fact that Arthur was an adopted child; i.e., that he "belonged" to someone else.

Finally, Mr. Smith's inability to limit either his wife's intrusiveness or her possessiveness in her interactions with Arthur was another environmental contribution to the creation of Arthur's disturbance.

C. Possible Favorable and Stabilizing Factors Contributing to Present Development

Here, too, it is important to consider the medical, educational, social, and personal resources available to the deaf child and to his family. Even technological advances may play a part as hearing aids are developed which can be adjusted carefully to match the "shape" and amplitude of a specific child's hearing loss and as other devices become available which allow the deaf child to circumvent the blocked auditory channel via vibrotactile sensations (Edmondson, 1974).

Several factors can be seen as favorable and stabilizing contributors to Arthur's development. First, Arthur was of better than average intelligence. Second, he made good use of his talent for mimicry in his attempts to communicate with others. Third, the Smiths were a stable family who, with all their faults, were very committed to each other. They fought vigorously to get what they believed was proper treatment for their son. Fourth, the Smiths had three other physically intact children who were important to them; they did not have to prove their ability to be parents with Arthur.

V. ASSESSMENTS OF DEVELOPMENT

A. Drive Development

1. *Libido.* Insofar as libidinal development has a foundation in biological maturation, it will not be affected by deafness. However, both ego and society attempt to bring the expression of libidinal impulses under the sway of the reality principle very early in life. Unfortunately, the secondary process thinking that is essential to the reality principle is very much affected by the communicative deficits often associated with deafness.

Here a consideration of the contrast between deaf children of deaf parents (where early communication developed via sign language) and deaf children of hearing parents (where such early, abstract, linguistically mediated communication was absent) is most helpful. Those few analysts who are able to communicate with deaf people directly via sign language have suggested that the development of deaf children of deaf parents closely approximates that of hearing children of hearing parents (Rainer, 1976; Rainer et al., 1969). Thus it appears that it is not deafness per se but the communicative handicap so often (and unnecessarily) associated with it which leads to the developmental deviations often reported in studies of deaf people.

It is, of course, true that the distribution of libido and the investment of libido in objects will be profoundly affected both by parental attitudes toward the handicapped child (i.e., whether they emphasize the child's value or his defect), and by the extent to which disturbances in the ability to communicate affect the deaf child's object relationships.

a. Phase development. Arthur's provocative, demanding,

constantly testing behavior was strongly suggestive of a fixation at the anal phase of development. Not surprisingly, the process of communication itself was prominent in Arthur's struggles as he repeatedly provoked me and then looked away, putting himself out of contact.

Despite the fact that part of Arthur's development remained stuck at the anal phase, he had managed to continue his development further. His active interest in the world and his at times extremely intrusive approach to people and their activities certainly suggested that libidinal development had proceeded as far as the phallic phase.

There were, however, few suggestions that Arthur had ever been engaged in the conflicts characteristic of the oedipal phase. The only example of behavior during the diagnostic sessions that might possibly have been related to the oedipal phase was an occasion when Arthur took my appointment book from my desk. He turned to the back of the book to see if his own name was among the addresses, then wanted to know about the other people in the book—did I see them for appointments too? (Later in treatment Arthur did begin describing one of my women colleagues as my "sweetheart" and tried to tease me about this. However, even at this point the rivalry and jealousy characteristic of the oedipal phase never came into clear focus.)

Arthur had achieved some latency-phase functioning at the time of the referral. His interest in adults other than his parents and his growing concern about his school performance were two indicators of this. However, this level was rarely maintained for any significant period of time. Instead Arthur regularly regressed and sought his libidinal gratifications in the torturing struggles of the anal phase.

The fact that the behavior associated with this regression also served to preserve Arthur's autonomy in a battle with his extremely controlling, intrusive, and frustrating mother complicated my assessment of Arthur. For it seemed possible that some of his "anal" behavior was a relatively healthy—or at least expectable—response to a pathological environment. I emphasize the *some*, however, because I believe it would be a mistake to underplay the amount of pleasure that Arthur was able to squeeze from these constant struggles.

b. Libido distribution. Arthur appeared to have achieved a reasonable balance between self and object cathexis. Of course, one must not overlook the fact that Arthur perceived his own body as defective and was clearly concerned about this. It was not clear, however, whether this concern retained a narcissistic character, as in the "exceptions" described by Freud (1916) and Jacobson (1959), or whether it was associated with a withdrawal of cathexis from the body. The latter did not seem likely, given Arthur's very competent control of his bodily movements and his excellent grooming and care of his body.

Parental ambivalence and resulting inconsistency in setting limits appeared to have left Arthur with an unrealistic, grandiose image of himself. The range of Arthur's object cathexis was clearly very limited, generally not extending beyond his small family circle. This limitation was probably the result of (1) his parents' wish to maintain unusually close, exclusive ties with Arthur; and (2) the limitations in contact with other people imposed upon Arthur by his communicative deficits.

2. *Aggression.* While deaf children are not different from hearing children in the quantity, quality, or direction of their aggressive impulses, they do tend to express these impulses in action more frequently than do hearing children. Here Anny Katan's (1961) paper on the importance of verbalization in early development outlines the issues better than I could hope to do.

One speculative point I might make, however, relates to the part played by the perceptual apparatus in the stimulation of a child's aggressive impulses and in the direction of those impulses away from the body and toward the environment. A.-M. Sandler (1963), Burlingham (1964), and Fraiberg and Freedman (1961) have described how blind infants seem in danger of a kind of passive withdrawal from, or failure to engage with, the world around them. Hearing, like sight, calls the infant's attention to things outside of and at some distance from his own body. Anecdotal reports of the early behavior of deaf infants (Schlesinger and Meadow, 1972) suggest that they, like the blind, may be more passive vis-à-vis the world around them than normal children and may be in need of special efforts by the caretakers to elicit their active engagement in their environment.

Arthur's use of aggression reflected the anal fixation described earlier in that aggression often appeared in the context of a struggle with his parents or other authority figures. To the extent that Arthur was attempting to escape his mother's over-controlling and overintrusive relationship with him, his expressions of aggression might have been adaptive, as they tended to put some distance between him and his parents. These struggles spilled over into other relationships, such as those at school, however, and made it very difficult for Arthur to take advantage of his educational opportunities. There were, of course, some positive aspects to Arthur's use of aggression; his competitive spirit and determination to master the tasks he set himself will no doubt be an important asset in his future development.

In its more sublimated forms Arthur's aggression was usually given vocal and mimetic expression; he was a master at creating sarcastic caricatures of his victims. From time to time, however, some unsublimated aggression was directed against others or against himself; on more than one occasion during the assessment period an aggressive act directed at me (e.g., a paper airplane thrown at me) was followed by an "accidental" self-inflicted injury (e.g., a bump on the head). Despite Arthur's attempts at sublimation and displacement, I soon found that I always had to be on my guard against a quick little punch, followed by a silly laugh with which Arthur attempted to deny and disown his aggressive actions.

B. Ego Development

1. *Ego apparatus.* This section of the Profile requires a careful description of the child's physical status (past and present). It is particularly important that the extent of any handicaps and their functional implications be carefully described.

Arthur's ego apparatus appeared to be intact, with the exception of his hearing loss which was described earlier. No evidence of the neurological and heart defects which often accompany deafness caused by rubella (the suspected etiological agent in Arthur's deafness) were found despite careful medical examination.

2. *Ego functions.* Deafness may be associated with many different limitations in ego functions. Motor functions may be

poorly developed because of restrictions imposed by the deaf child's parents in an effort to protect the child from unheard dangers. Problems in the normal development of speech are often associated with problems in the development of reciprocal communication (unless, of course, the deaf child is offered communication via sign language). Problems in communication, in turn, often lead to problems in the development of many other ego functions, such as memory, synthesis, reality testing, and secondary thought processes. These problems may be either on a primary or on a secondary level; i.e., they may reflect real (primary) failures in the development of a particular function (e.g., the ability to remember a past event) or problems encountered when the deaf child tries to communicate about the internal states which are the basis for these ego functions (secondary interference). It is very important that the diagnostician of a deaf child keep this distinction in mind. There have been a great number of cases reported in which a deaf child's poor speech development resulted in a diagnosis of mental retardation despite what was later found to be normal intellectual potential.

Arthur's ego functions were at widely varying levels of development. From my observations of Arthur and from psychological testing it seemed that he was of at least average intelligence; his scores on the Performance section of the Wechsler Intelligence Scale for Children (Revised) were:

Picture Completion	14
Picture Arrangement	12
Block Design	12
Object Assembly	14
Coding	4
Mazes	7

WISC-R Performance IQ = 102

In addition, there was little question that Arthur's memory, reality testing, and control of motility were within normal limits. Nevertheless, it was not possible to administer the Verbal section of the WISC-R to Arthur because of problems encountered in communicating the verbal tasks to him. This difficulty emphasizes the fact that Arthur's speech, language, and communication (the distinctions between these three are often crucial in the assessment of deaf children) were very poorly developed. Arthur's speech was almost totally unintelligible even given my familiarity with "deaf speech," and his written language did not go beyond two-word combinations of stereotyped vocabulary.

These deficits in speech and language left Arthur with only a repertoire of mime and perhaps 200 signs which varied in their level of abstraction to serve his communicative needs. Arthur did not appear to have any better command of syntax in his use of signs than was evident in his spoken or written communication. In addition, he was only rarely able to use his rudimentary sign language skills because both his parents and his teachers avoided using signs.

Cognitive development generally precedes linguistic development, and thus linguistic deficits need not necessarily lead to cognitive deficits (Furth, 1966; Sinclair-de-Zwart, 1969; Moores, 1978). Nevertheless, there are some concepts, especially those involving probability and temporality (and, hence, links between cause and effect), which are very difficult to master without a linguistic medium of exchange (Blank, 1974). In addition, socialization depends heavily upon language for the communication of the whys and wherefores of social rules (Meadow, 1975).

Arthur had very serious developmental deficits in terms of speech, language, and general communicative skills. These were associated with a rudimentary sense of time and an uncertain appreciation of cause and effect that made secondary process thinking, in the usual sense of the word, a very unstable acquisition. Here I must emphasize that Arthur was not functioning via unmodified primary process thinking; were this true, I would be describing a psychotic child rather than a child whose deafness has led to a series of developmental deviations. However, Arthur's secondary process thinking was certainly not at the level expected of an 11-year-old child.

In addition to, and related to, the deficits in speech, language, communication, and secondary process thinking described above, Arthur also showed problems in concentration, attention span, and short-term memory. These were certainly strongly affected by Arthur's insistence upon approaching both the psychological testing sessions and the general observational sessions strictly on his own, anally tinged terms.

Before leaving this section devoted to ego functions I must mention, however briefly, something about Arthur's affective states and responses. Affects of pride, pleasure, pain, surprise, curiosity, defiance, triumph, and anger all had a place in Arthur's repertoire. Affects such as sadness, shame, and hopelessness were notably absent—but not, I think, because they were outside of Arthur's experience. Rather, they were highly defended and observable only very briefly and occasionally.

3. *Defense organization.* Just as problems in communication lead to problems in the development of other ego functions, so problems in communication affect the development and use of defenses by the deaf child. If the deaf child, because of problems in communication, remains relatively ignorant of the relationship between events in the external world and the internal world of the people around him, his defensive strategies will reflect that ignorance. Some defenses, such as denial and externalization, may appear to be particularly prominent; here again, however, the diagnostician must differentiate between a child who *denies* the effect of his actions upon others and the child who *does not understand* the effect of his actions upon others. It is equally important to differentiate between a child who does not use fantasy for purposes of denial and a child whose fantasy life remains relatively inaccessible to the outside world because of problems in communication.

Arthur's defenses consisted mainly of denial, externalization, reversal, and the conversion of passive experiences into active ones. In our sessions Arthur showed me how other things were hurt or damaged or defective, not he. Other things were angry or sad, not Arthur (who, when he had such feelings, giggled in a silly manner). And other people were bossed around, not Arthur. Arthur's difficulties with control led to his demand that he decide when our sessions started and stopped. He also occasionally ran ahead of me into my office and sat in my chair; from that position he announced that *he* was the boss or teacher and thus avoided the passive role which he feared. An underlying anxiety motivating much of Arthur's defensive activity was, I believe, a fear that he would be rejected by his parents. This fear was undoubtably founded in the two circumstances of Arthur's deafness and his adoption.

Other defenses may have been present and active in Arthur, but it is worth noting that many defenses—such as denial in fantasy, isolation, and intellectualization—are generally judged from verbal material, a modality which was of limited use for Arthur. Thus Arthur's communicative deficits may have prevented him from telling me about his use of figures from science fiction films, with which his parents reported Arthur was preoccupied in his play at home.

C. Superego Development

Many authors have commented on what is sometimes described as the etiquette-book morality of deaf adults (Levine, 1960). Again, deficits in communication leave their mark as the deaf child often receives only the "yes" or "no" of parental approvals or prohibitions; he does not comprehend the reasons for the "yes" or "no." Thus there is a special danger that the superego will become particularly rigid.

There is also the opposite danger—that the deaf child will reject such proscriptions entirely. Such rejection may be based upon problems in communication which make the prohibitions seem completely unpredictable; or it may be based upon a view of oneself as one of the "exceptions" described by Freud (1916) and Jacobson (1959). In this case, the narcissistic injury of the handicap is converted into a kind of grandiosity which exempts the handicapped person from the usual social rules.

Arthur's behavior, while provocative and disruptive to those around him, contained many indications that he had developed some sort of superego. He was aware of many of the usual social rules of behavior, which he had taken over from observation of his parents' behavior. He also showed some anxiety when confronted with tasks that taxed his cognitive abilities; he seemed to feel badly when he could not succeed and quickly began to try to divert attention from his failure. Arthur's parents described how, when he had done something bad and was upset, he sometimes hung a "For Sale" sign on his bedroom door.

These suggestions of the existence of ego ideals and of self-critical trends in Arthur were not, however, adequate to prevent his continued expression of anal-sadistic trends. In addition, guilt, the hallmark of the superego, was not obvious during my assessment of Arthur. To a large extent Arthur's behavior suggested a reexternalization of superego functions; he had created a battle between his own instinctual impulses and the environment which was more palatable to him than an internal conflict between id and superego.

It is perhaps worth mentioning that during this assessment no evidence appeared of the kind of "split" between separate sets of parents (and derivatively between separate sets of ego ideals) which is sometimes seen in adopted children (Brinich, 1980).

VI. GENETIC ASSESSMENTS

At this point in the Profile we can return to familiar ground. It now remains for us to integrate our observations regarding the deaf child into psychoanalytic formulations which express our comprehension of the fixation points, the regressions, and the conflicts which the child brings to the assessment. There is no special metapsychology for deaf children or for any other group of children. If we have carefully taken account of the child's handicap in the earlier sections of the Profile, the metapsychological view expressed in this section and in that on dynamic and structural assessments will include the handicap as an integral part of the child.

There were many events in Arthur's history which might well have contributed to the creation of his disturbance. Among these are the early disruptions in mothering associated with his adoption and readoption; the presence of an adoptive mother who was unusually intrusive and possessive of Arthur; and an early and sustained battle between Arthur and his parents regarding his autonomy, especially regarding the production of speech.

From Arthur's behavior in this diagnostic assessment it seemed that the major trouble spot (in terms of libidinal fixation and regression) was centered in the anal phase. Arthur's difficulties here were expressed not in symbolic equivalents but in his object relations, which retained the character of tortured battles for autonomous control. It was clear that Arthur derived pleasure from such battles. Unfortunately Arthur's problems with communication (and the involvement of communication in this anal struggle) made it impossible to use verbal fantasy activity as a further indicator of fixations and regressions. And Arthur's other potential avenue of expression, play, also appeared to be restricted as a result of his preference for engaging in anal struggles with the people around him.

VII. ASSESSMENT OF CONFLICTS: DYNAMIC AND STRUCTURAL ASSESSMENTS

The conflict which appeared to be central to Arthur's current functioning was one between himself and his object world; Arthur seemed bent on showing that he would be in charge of his own actions and those of the people around him. This external (or rather, reexternalized) conflict was paralleled by an internal conflict of ambivalence toward his love objects. In addition, some of Arthur's behavior could be seen as a normal response to a pathological environment (i.e., Arthur's resistance to the intrusive and possessive trends in his adoptive mother).

However reactive they may have been in their formation, at the time of diagnostic assessment Arthur's conflicts posed a clear threat to his ability to form successful new relationships. It was partly concern about this interference with Arthur's ability to form new relationships, and with his ability to use such relationships for educational and social ends, that led to my recommendation for treatment.

A second problem which I saw in Arthur's behavior at the time of referral centered around what appeared to be narcissistic injuries associated both with his deafness and with his adoption. It seemed that Arthur had great difficulty in maintaining an image of himself as a wanted child. This led to repeated testing of his adoptive parents' love for him, testing which took the form of provocations which (unfortunately, but not surprisingly) fit in with the conflicts regarding autonomy outlined above.

At the point of referral Arthur was clearly in a "no win" position. If his parents responded to his provocative behavior by ignoring him, Arthur saw this as an indication that they did not love him and he would escalate the provocation. If they attempted to prohibit his behavior, Arthur fought back to assert his own autonomy and control.

A third problem, related to the issues of autonomy, ambivalence, and narcissistic injury, was that of communication. While Arthur had developed excellent mimetic skills, his use of sign language for communication was not adequate to meet the communicative needs of a child of his age. This deficit reflected the attitudes of Arthur's parents toward sign language, with which Arthur had probably identified himself. To sign was to be different and to be rejected. Arthur's poor sign language skills represented a compromise between ego capacities which were searching for an expressive outlet and ego ideals which denigrated signed communication.

VIII. ASSESSMENT OF SOME GENERAL CHARACTERISTICS

The frustration tolerance of many deaf children is notoriously low, as is their sublimation potential. These characteristics are consequences of the communicative deficit which is largely responsible for the deviations in ego and superego development which I have outlined earlier. These limitations require special consideration in the planning of treatment.

Arthur's frustration tolerance was low by almost any measure, and his inner conflicts were frequently expressed in impulsive activity. At the same time, Arthur was not without sublimation potential. He was particularly interested in how machines work and in what men do when they work.

Faced with an anxiety-provoking situation (i.e., one in which he feared rejection or loss of love) Arthur would quickly attempt to take control of the situation. At times this led Arthur to attempts at mastery; at other times he created diversions which removed him from the situation. This relatively active stance toward the world led me to believe that, in Arthur, the progressive forces outweighed the regressive forces.

IX. DIAGNOSIS

This section of the Profile requires no special modification for the deaf child, but a cautionary note is in order. Deafness is different for each child and thus has a different impact on the communicative abilities of each child. In addition, each deaf child is provided with different medical, social, educational, and personal resources which may modify the impact of deafness upon his development. It is my experience that while many deaf children can be placed in Anna Freud's fifth category—"there are primary deficiencies of an organic nature or early deprivations which distort development and structuralization and produce retarded, defective, and nontypical personalities" (1965, p. 147)—it is important not to overlook the fact that some deaf children incorporate into this picture conflicts which fit into Anna Freud's third category—"there is permanent drive regression to previously established fixation points which leads to conflicts of a neurotic type and gives rise to infantile neuroses and character disorders" (p. 147).

Because of this mixed diagnostic picture, it is frequently the case that a combination of educational and psychoanalytic interventions will be required in the treatment of deaf children.

In this diagnostic assessment Arthur appeared to be exhibiting—in some ways—a permanent drive regression to a previously established fixation point; this regression appeared to be related to conflicts of a neurotic type. Furthermore, these conflicts had, at the time of assessment, already made a significant impact upon Arthur's character formation. However, such a formulation does not take into account the impact of Arthur's deafness and of the communication deficits associated with it.

It was clear that Arthur's deafness had led to a deviation in development which left him without some of the ego functions which are extremely useful in establishing the supremacy of the ego over both id and superego. Thus it appeared that the analysis of conflicts would not be sufficient to get Arthur back onto the developmental track. Such analysis was necessary, but it had to be complemented with efforts to increase Arthur's level of ego functioning, particularly in the area of language. This was, in fact, a prerequisite to the analysis of conflicts, for such analysis requires a relatively unimpeded flow of communication between therapist and patient; this was certainly not possible in Arthur at the time of referral.

Because Arthur's difficulties in the areas of autonomy, ambivalence, narcissism, and communication interlocked with active conflicts in his parents, it was clear that work with his parents would be a necessary adjunct to Arthur's treatment.

DISCUSSION

In the descriptive material outlined above, I have indicated some of the ways in which the diagnostic evaluation of a deaf child demands the elaboration or extension of the Metapsychological Profile. In what follows I would like to focus on the impact of deafness on the psychological *development* of children. For this purpose I again draw on a concept introduced by Anna Freud (1965)—that of developmental lines—which is particularly suited to highlight the effect of a factor such as deafness on the various areas and steps in the development of children. While a complete description of the effect of congenital deafness is beyond the scope of this paper, an examination of some of the tasks required of the child to progress on the separate but interrelated developmental lines draws special attention to the degree to which communication difficulties based in deafness interfere with normal development.

DEVELOPMENTAL LINES

From Dependency to Emotional Self-Reliance and Adult Object Relationships

During the phase of "biological unity" the hearing mother and her deaf child find themselves occasionally out of tune as the child does not respond to the mother's auditory stimuli in the way the mother expects. It is this subtle but important disruption of the normal mother-infant relationship and reciprocity which usually leads to the diagnosis of deafness.

The mother of a deaf child does not gradually appear and disappear in the child's perceptual field as she ministers to her child. Instead, the mother is present only when she can be seen or when she is in bodily contact with the child. The sounds which the hearing child uses to anticipate his mother's appearance and which allow him to remain aware of her presence in a darkened room are unavailable to the deaf child. Thus the deaf child's achievement of libidinal object constancy involves some special problems not faced by the hearing child.

Other difficulties become apparent if one looks at the final stages of this developmental line. The deaf adolescent often has special problems in shedding his tie to his parents, who have functioned throughout his life as mediators and interpreters of the hearing world around him. The deaf child is thus poorly equipped to strike out on his own, away from his parents.

As far as could be seen, much of Arthur's behavior at the time of referral still reflected the ambivalence characteristic of the preoedipal, anal-sadistic phase. At the same time there were some clear indications of latency developments such as his interest in adults other than his parents and his wish to help other adults in their work (e.g., assisting a local auto mechanic). An interesting theoretical question might be: how much of the ambivalence seen in Arthur was actually related to a hypothesized fixation at the anal-sadistic phase in Arthur's development and how much was related to his parents' ambivalence and their proclivity for externalization? It may be that some of the ambivalence seen in Arthur was his response to, his living out of, the self image his parents had provided to him. Further, some of his "oppositional" or "testing" behavior may in fact have been healthy attempts to carve out some areas of independence from an overly intrusive and overly possessive mother.

From Egocentricity to Companionship

This developmental line, like the first, highlights the importance of communication in the development of children. Without smooth communication between himself and his peers and parents, the deaf child has great difficulty in developing internal representations of those people which allow him to interact with them as "partners and objects in their own right" (Anna Freud, 1965, p. 78).

It was difficult to say whether or not Arthur was on an age-appropriate level on this developmental line. Arthur's relationships with his older siblings were limited both by difficulties in communication and by Arthur's special status in the family. To his siblings Arthur seemed to be a rather amusing but tolerable nuisance. They did not appear to resent the fact that Arthur was the focus for a great deal of parental attention; on the other hand, they did not usually include Arthur in their own activities. For his part Arthur made only occasional efforts to engage his siblings; usually these attempts were frustrated by communication difficulties and Arthur then returned to more solitary activities.

Arthur certainly managed to include me as a partner in his activities throughout the assessment sessions and in subsequent treatment. This argued in favor of his ability to respond to other people as partners and objects in their own right. However, in his progress along this developmental line the deaf child encounters a special obstacle that is very similar to one he encountered in his movement toward adult object relationships: in order to interact with someone as a partner, it is necessary to have built up some internal models of both one's own and the partner's thoughts, feelings, and motivations. The creation of such models is dependent upon smooth communication between the deaf child and other people (peers and adults). It thus seems likely that if Arthur in fact was able to respond to other people as partners, they were partners with quite a restricted set of expected thoughts, feelings, and motivations (as seen from Arthur's point of view).

From Irresponsibility to Responsibility in Body Management

Insofar as deafness interferes with communication and therefore interferes with the comprehension of the relationships between cause and effect, the deaf child will experience some unique difficulties along this developmental line. In addition, if prosthetic devices such as hearing aids are used, the deaf child may be asked to take responsibility for the management of these devices at a very early age because he is in the best position to monitor the functioning of his hearing aids: whether they are properly adjusted, whether the batteries are adequate, whether the ear mold is comfortable.

Arthur appeared to be at an age-appropriate level on this developmental line. While he sometimes threatened to do dangerous things, it was clear that he recognized them as dangerous and could limit his behavior accordingly. He was also apparently reliable in his use of his hearing aids—a particular and constant body-management issue for most deaf children.

From Suckling to Rational Eating; and
from Wetting and Soiling to Bladder and Bowel Control

Deafness does not seem to interfere markedly with development along either of these developmental lines, although it is clear that insofar as deafness interferes with communication between the deaf child and his parents, some of the steps along these lines will not be elaborated in the same way by the deaf child as they are in the growing social sensitivities of the hearing child.

It is worth mentioning, however, that the battles experienced by the hearing child around the achievement of bladder and bowel control are often displaced, in the developmental history of the deaf child, to battles around the production and comprehension of speech.

Speech—or, more generally, communication—becomes contaminated with this instinctual battle. What is usually a relatively "neutral" ego function becomes the focus of a great deal of instinctual conflict and suffers greatly in the process. As a result the deaf child often ends up with a double obstacle to his use of speech: (1) his deafness, and (2) the conflicts around autonomy and control which invade the realm of speech and hearing.

From the Body to the Toy and from Play to Work

While Anna Freud does not specifically address the issues of language and communication in her description of this developmental line, it is obvious that many of the steps along this developmental line assume the child's ability to communicate easily with others (e.g., in agreeing upon the rules of various cooperative or competitive games). Insofar as games can be seen along a continuum which demands organization and foresight for success, the deaf child with poor communication skills and poor language will be at a disadvantage when compared with his hearing peers.

Arthur showed some interest in cognitively complex toys, and he also showed pleasure in his own accomplishments with such toys. He appeared to be at an age-appropriate level on this developmental line, and he was clearly interested in increasing his sphere of competence. His major difficulty in this area was a communicative one; he often could not understand a task or game, could not comprehend the explanations given him, and thus remained frustrated by them. He then retreated to less mature activities; but this seemed to be a response to frustration rather than an indicator either of his interests and ego ideals or of his location on this developmental line.

Correspondence Between the Lines

The fact that a particular child's positions on the various developmental lines are in or out of harmony with each other is often of greater diagnostic and therapeutic importance than the child's position on any one of the several developmental lines.

In Arthur's case, there was a good deal of correspondence between the various developmental lines listed above; most were at an age-appropriate level, with two important qualifications. First, there appeared to be a fixation at, and perhaps a characterological incorporation of some features of, the anal-sadistic phase—particularly the provocative, demanding, and torturing aspects of that period of life. Second, while Arthur appeared to be at an age-appropriate level on the developmental line of companionship, it was difficult to assess this accurately because of the restriction in his interpersonal world.

The Need for a Developmental Line of Communication

It is clear that communication plays a crucial part in many of the developmental steps expected of the growing child. I believe that the assessment of children whose disabilities interfere with communication should include some specific description of their communicative skills. Such a description implies the usefulness of a developmental line of communication—a line which has intruded itself into several developmental lines. This is a line which extends from what might be termed autistic noncommunication to shared linguistic communication. While movement along such a line is generally taken for granted in the assessment of hearing children (except in cases with severe ego defects), it cannot be overlooked in children with sensory disabilities (including both deafness and blindness), children with certain physical anomalies which deprive them of motility or of the coordinated use of their voices (e.g., cerebral palsy), and children with neurological impairments (e.g., receptive or expressive aphasias, dyslexia).

While this developmental line needs careful elaboration, it is clear that as far as progress in the development of communication is concerned, Arthur was well behind his age-mates despite his inventiveness in the use of mimicry. This deviation in development was the result of many interacting factors. Primary, of course, was Arthur's deafness. Secondary to this were his parents' fantasies of changing Arthur into a "normal" (i.e., "hearing") child and their associated resistance to Arthur's use of sign language. A further contributor to the failure of development along this line was the inner, ambivalent battle about communication and control; he did not make full use of his communicative abilities because he was not at all sure that he wanted to communicate with the people who were important to him. Here the link between object relations and linguistic development made itself felt; for a child will learn to communicate with a loved object much more easily than with an ambivalently cathected object.

COMMUNICATION AND THE DIAGNOSTICIAN

I will bring this paper to a close on a practical note. As more and more deaf children in the United States are learning to communicate at an early age via the simultaneous use of oral and manual languages (so-called Total Communication), some of the deviations in development I have described in this paper should become less frequent. At the same time more and more diagnosticians will meet deaf children whose communicative abilities rely heavily upon one or another variety of sign language. It is crucial that a psychological diagnostician faced with a deaf child be able to communicate smoothly and effectively with that child. This means that the diagnostician must be skilled in the specific sign language used by the child; lacking this, he must (as a second-best alternative) involve an interpreter in his work with the child. Without such skills or assistance, the diagnostician would be in the same position as he would be in assessing a child who speaks a language with which the diagnostician is only vaguely familiar. His diagnosis would be imprecise and uncertain;

both he and the child would leave the assessment feeling that they had not understood what had taken place between them.

BIBLIOGRAPHY

BLANK, M. (1974), Cognitive functions of language in the preschool years. *Develpm. Psychol.*, 10:229–245.

BRINICH, P. M. (1980), Some potential effects of adoption on self and object representations. *Psychoanal. Study Child*, 35:107–133.

BURLINGHAM, D. (1964), Hearing and its role in the development of the blind. *Psychoanal. Study Child*, 19:95–112.

—————— (1975), Special problems of blind infants. *Psychoanal. Study Child*, 30:3–13.

EDMONDSON, W. (1974), Preliminary experiments with a new vibrotactile speech training aid. In: *Proc. Speech Communic. Seminar*, 4:41–48. Stockholm: Speech Transmission Laboratories.

FRAIBERG, S. & FREEDMAN, D. (1964), Studies in the ego development of the congenitally blind child. *Psychoanal. Study Child*, 19:113–169.

FREUD, A. (1965), Normality and pathology in childhood. *W.*, 6.

—————— NAGERA, H., & FREUD, W. E. (1965), Metapsychological assessment of the adult personality. *Psychoanal. Study Child*, 20:9–41.

FREUD, S. (1916), Some character-types met with in psycho-analytic work. *S.E.*, 14:311–333.

FREUD, W. E. (1967), Assessment of early infancy. *Psychoanal. Study Child*, 22:216–238.

—————— (1972), The baby profile: Part II. *Psychoanal. Study Child*, 26:172–194.

FURTH, H. (1966). *Thinking Without Language*. New York: Free Press.

JACOBSON, E. (1959), The "exceptions." *Psychoanal. Study Child*, 14:135–154.

KATAN, A. (1961), Some thoughts about the role of verbalization in early childhood. *Psychoanal. Study Child*, 16:184–188.

LAUFER, M. (1965), Assessment of adolescent disturbances. *Psychoanal. Study Child*, 20:99–123.

LEVINE, E. (1960), *The Psychology of Deafness*. New York: Columbia Univ. Press.

MEADOW, K. (1975), The development of deaf children. In: *Review of Child Development Research*, ed. E. M. Hetherington. Chicago: Univ. Chicago Press, 5:441–508.

MEERS, D. (1966), A diagnostic profile of psychopathology in a latency child. *Psychoanal. Study Child*, 21:483–526.

MICHAELS, J. & STIVER, I. (1965), The impulsive psychopathic character according to the diagnostic profile. *Psychoanal. Study Child*, 20:124–141.

MOORES, D. (1978), *Educating the Deaf*. Boston: Houghton Mifflin.

RAINER, J. (1976), Observations on affect induction and ego development in the deaf. *Int. Rev. Psychoanal.*, 3:121–128.

_____ ALTSHULER, K., & KALLMANN, F., eds. (1969), *Family and Mental Health Problems in a Deaf Population*, 2nd ed. Springfield, Ill.: Charles C Thomas.

SANDLER, A.-M. (1963), Aspects of passivity and ego development in the blind infant. *Psychoanal. Study Child*, 18:343–360.

SCHLESINGER, H. & MEADOW, K. (1972), *Sound and Sign*. Berkeley: Univ. California Press.

SINCLAIR-DE-ZWART, H. (1969), Developmental psycholinguistics. In: *Studies in Cognitive Development*, ed. D. Elkind & J. Flavell. New York: Oxford Univ. Press, pp. 315–336.

THOMAS, R. (1966), Comments on some aspects of self and object representation in a group of psychotic children. *Psychoanal. Study Child*, 21:527–580.

Success Through Their Own Efforts

ALICE B. COLONNA

THE NURSERY SCHOOL FOR BLIND CHILDREN AT THE HAMPSTEAD Child-Therapy Clinic was started by Dorothy Burlingham in 1957. I worked there first as a teacher and then as therapist with some of the children and their mothers. Many of the observations made on the early development of these children were described by Dorothy Burlingham (1972, 1979) and others (Curson, 1979; Sandler, 1963; Wills, 1965, 1970).

After the children left the nursery group and went to the regional schools for the blind, contact with them was not completely lost but became quite sporadic. Several members of the staff visited the children at the new schools, held annual reunions, and made home visits. I kept in touch with some of the children by letters and occasional visits. More recently I have in addition attempted to interview several of these young people and follow them into adolescence and young adulthood.

These follow-ups have given us some information on how the blind person experiences puberty and adjusts to the problems adolescence raises for him. These problems appear essentially the same as for the sighted, but there are also differences. The blind have to cope with the same developmental tasks of adolescence that all others have to solve—choice of work which will not only provide satisfactions but economic self-sufficiency; and choice of a future marital partnership and parenthood (Anna Freud, 1958). These tasks are enormously affected and complicated by blindness, which imposes realistic restrictions.

Graduate of the Hampstead Child-Therapy Clinic, London; Research Associate, Yale University Child Study Center, New Haven, Connecticut.

I shall describe how two young people coped with these problems. The two I have chosen are among the older of the group. They are especially articulate and, with the perspective of the intervening years, were able to talk about their adolescence and provide glimpses of how they went about confronting this period in their lives.[1]

The nature of the follow-ups[2] permits only limited insights, but these nevertheless stimulate ideas, which, I hope, can be tested and expanded when the other members of the original nursery school group for the blind become willing to talk with us and share their experiences with us.

What we learn from these two young men may enable us to help other blind adolescents negotiate this period. Moreover, just as the earlier studies of the ego development of young blind children provided evidence of the role of vision in normal development, the special difficulties that are prominent in blind adolescents may provide further understanding of the ingredients of the adolescent process in human development. It is important to ascertain how far the difficulties stem specifically from blindness per se and how far these are imposed by the sighted world for reasons probably related to denial—a denial based essentially on the wish by the sighted not to face how the young blind person may feel.

NORMAN

Norman, who is now 26 years old, joined the nursery group of blind children at the Hampstead Clinic at the age of 30 months. Norman had been born without eyes, a very rare occurrence. He was the firstborn son of a young middle-class couple. Norman's mother was a very energetic and active young woman who showed a pride and determination about her son's progress which impressed the staff at once. Her many energies were directed toward providing him with opportunities to express his

1. I found that it was difficult to obtain information from those who were still in the midst of this phase.
2. In these I also draw on material by Barbara Bank, Marion Burgner, Annemarie Curson, Max Goldblatt, E. M. Mason, and Elizabeth Model. I want to express my appreciation for their permission to use these data.

own active and assertive attitude toward the world. She showed much empathy with her infant son, accompanied him on frequent hospital visits for fitting of his artificial eyes, and insisted on staying with him during these difficult procedures even when doctors and nurses urged her not to. When Norman began to attend the Hampstead nursery group, his mother was well into her second pregnancy. The arrival of a girl presented great challenges for Norman. The usual rivalry and envy reactions were intensified by his special dependency needs.

His mother found it difficult to divide her affections between two children, and her feelings about having a handicapped child changed inevitably when she gave birth to a sighted child. Her great empathy with Norman became much more conflicted. We could follow Norman through some of the difficulties he had to face as he became aware that his sister was different not only because of her sex but also because of her capacity of sight. As soon as she became mobile and could find things quickly, he became intrigued with her. He puzzled over her mysterious capacities that enabled her to do things he could not do. For a time he struggled with feelings of anger and rage and had a period of restlessness and difficulty in concentration. He was at times argumentative and negativistic and unable to settle to tasks. He seemed to be attempting to comprehend what was different about his younger sister. Despite his anger he was also fascinated by her, and they developed a close physical and emotional relationship.

Finding his way during these early years, Norman taught us a great deal. For the blind child the ordinary play activities are full of frustrations and the playroom too restrictive. Fortunately, like his mother, he had the capacity to be aware of his needs and to make these known to us. He wanted to go on excursions, walks, drives. He was curious about the world outside the playroom. I became the person who provided the opportunity for him to reach out and explore and become familiar with new people and places. This was necessary if he was to maintain his excellent capacities for learning and relating to other people. The delightful sense of humor he had shown earlier was fostered and enjoyed. Norman was very companionable in the car and would comment, his nose pressed to the window, on passersby and buildings on the street. This may have reflected his fantasy that sight was likely to come as he grew up or perhaps a joking attempt to tease and fool the adult. It probably also was related to the close empathic bond that had been a part of his early experience with his mother which made it likely that he could identify with her visual knowledge. His uninhibited curiosity and trust along with the sense of confidence and openness were unusual. For example, he would wish to touch the bottles he heard rattle and ask questions of the milkman.

The early openness was retained and evident in follow-up meetings several years later. But one of the first follow-up interviews also disclosed the great struggle involved in maintaining this attitude.[3] When Norman was 13 years old, he talked with an analyst on the Hampstead Clinic staff who was struck both by Norman's conflict and depressive feelings about his blindness and by the remarkably perceptive way Norman conceived of sight.

In my talks with Norman he recalled this first follow-up with some anger at the fact that this had been with someone he did not know, making it impersonal, while he would have preferred to talk with someone he remembered. Another criticism Norman verbalized was that he would have enjoyed being in a larger group of normal children with a greater choice of making friendships. This was interesting because in part it represented his mother's critical feelings and her attempts to have academic work introduced very early. It also represented the feeling of some of us who had worked with Norman and who had hoped that he could join the regular nursery school (for sighted children) at the Hampstead Clinic as a daily participant. Norman recalled the compromise that was arrived at, namely, regular visits were arranged during certain areas of the program, for example, music. In retrospect he felt he would have needed to be in the group all of the time in order to establish real friendships

3. This conflict had also been in evidence earlier. Dorothy Burlingham (1972, p. 14) described an incident when Norman was about 4 years old. He had thrown beads on the floor and, when told to pick them up, said in despair, "I can't walk, I can't see, I can't do nothing." Yet his ability to express his feelings and to confront them enabled him to come to terms with some of the implications of the blindness.

with the other children. Norman felt that the individual attention he received in the Hampstead nursery program for the
blind did not make it easier for him when he moved on to the
regional school. This in some degree may represent the mixed
feelings many of the parents of the children in the group had
had and which related to the different philosophy of the
Hampstead program and that of the residential institutions and
schools for the blind.

Norman wrote about his elementary school which he considered "a typically blind establishment," saying, "I won't bore you
with the details of my rather lacking education." The criticism
seemed valid. When I visited the school at this time, I gained the
impression that this curious, bright, and active child had to
spend much time in uninteresting and rote learning, quite lacking in the kind of enjoyment children of this age often feel at
school. Norman continued the account of his schooling:

> At the age of 11 I passed an exam which permitted me to go to
> what was considered to be the finest blind school in the coun-
> try, which unfortunately doesn't say much for the country. I
> spent five years at this institution and rather sadly to say I failed
> every exam put in front of me. There was a very simple reason
> for this, that being, that I disliked the staff, I disliked the sys-
> tem, and most of all I disliked the subjects in question. Well, to
> cut a long story short, at the age of 15 I was sent home for
> obtaining and consuming an unreasonable amount of alcohol.
> Actually it wasn't that I had had that much to drink. It was that
> with the liquid courage I had just obtained I started attacking a
> teacher that I rather resented.

The sad outcome of this school experience at a residential
establishment points to the estrangement which Norman felt
from the sighted adults in authority as well as to his loneliness
among fellow students. He deeply resented the fact that there
were no girls at the school and felt that all heterosexual contacts
were discouraged. He had invited the school secretary to accompany him to the local pub and felt that there had been repercussions afterward for both of them.

Norman continued:

> Anyway after failing my examinations, I was given three
> months to retake the subjects I wanted to retake and then I was

politely asked to leave. To the immense relief of both the headmaster and the rest of the staff I did.

During this time at school I had taken a great interest in music and had started to play in various rock and roll groups. So you can see that my interest in music was aroused at quite an early age. [Norman told me later that this interest had not been encouraged at school and when he asked to study more music, this was not made possible for him.] I had whilst I was at school entered and passed most of my piano examinations; consequently when I left that school, I decided to throw blind schools to the wind and go to a normal sighted Politechnic, i.e., a much less institutionalized college of education. I spent three years at this College, where I also did Judo and Karate and obtained quite high belts in both. Then I auditioned for the Royal College of Music in Kensington, which is the equivalent of your Julliard in New York. I studied guitar, composition, and singing, but I majored in the keyboard instruments, namely, piano, harpsichord, organ, and a specialized course in twentieth-century electronic music which incorporated synthesizers. To put it in a nutshell: I came out of the Royal College of Music with a diploma A.R.M.C. and an honorary degree G.R.S.M. and Graduate of the Royal Schools of Music. During this time I had been playing in clubs and hotels and by the time I left College I was pretty well known on the music circuit and especially in London.

Thus through vicissitudes and upheavels Norman has found his way to work that he enjoys and at which he excels. Despite the difficulties of the work, he seems to thrive on coping with the everyday chores and challenges of living and now gives the impression of relishing his talents, independence, and managing as well as playing in his own band.

As to the other task of the adolescent and young adult, that of finding a life partner, Norman has also shared some of his ideas and feelings. When I saw him for our first meetings, he spoke of his many experiences with girls in the context of frequent adventures and travels to several countries, but he felt that his independence and his freedom were most important. Even though several girls had been very interested in him, he was not in favor of emotional entanglements. He spoke of finding children difficult mainly in their unpredictability, noisiness, and rapid movement.

When I saw Norman a year later, he had grown a beard which lent considerable substance to his mobile and expressive face. He talked of his friendship with a fellow student at the music school. In his references to her he showed an unusual capacity to empathize with her struggles, for she had just finished a long emotional relationship and was somewhat frightened and "pressured at the thought of another relationship which could go wrong." He spoke of his increasing feeling for her and his hopes of developing the relationship, while at the same time he was able to stand back and, in deference to her feelings, avoid making her feel "closed in."

Norman's capacities to sense the feelings of another person are remarkable. He also expresses them in the way he uses his music and, indeed, in his whole style of living. This ability to relate and to "tune in" on what is going on around him has always been in evidence. For example, coming out of a crowded underground train to meet me, he spoke of the cricket matches which caused the crowd. On these trips he manages independently and is able to ask for directions and locations when necessary. Another characteristic trait that was evident in his early life has also persisted. The curiosity about the world shows in his love of travel, which he does extensively. The energy and confidence he exhibits and his active stance seem to have been present throughout his life.

RICHARD

Richard, who is now 21 years old, is working in computor programming. Although pleased with the economic independence it offers him at his age and stage of study, he is not very enthusiastic about it. Richard is most happy in his engagement to a woman 4 years older than himself. Gretchen is an accomplished folk singer whose employment as a secretary is insecure at the moment and this worries her. Although Gretchen has some light perception, she as well as Richard is essentially blind. Yet when they are together, they form a unit, supporting and guiding each other very sensitively and thoughtfully.

Richard joined the Hampstead nursery group for the blind just before his fourth birthday. As an infant he apparently had normal vision; it was at the age of 15 months that retinablastoma was diagnosed and one eye was removed. His second eye was removed 15 months later. Thus, there had been some degree of sight while he was mastering skills of motility. In the nursery group Richard showed confidence and ability in moving about and was interested in the activities offered.

We had learned from Norman and others that the blind preschool child benefits from having times alone with an adult. These times are needed in part as "auxiliary eyes" so that interpretation of the world in meaningful ways can offer some sense of order to what, without the differentiating and integrative function of vision, tends to remain a total confusion of touch, sound, and smell. Richard was frightened by confusing sounds of his environment such as a dog barking in the street, sudden shouts of the rag-and-bone man, dropping of heavy pipes in the street. Some of the confusion about the sources of these sounds seemed to have been associated with anxieties having to do with the experiences of hospitalization and loss of sight. For these reasons as well as because of his very rapid speech which was sometimes difficult to follow, individual contact with an adult was offered to Richard, whom I saw five times a week for several years (Colonna, 1968).

Like Norman, Richard wished to go out of the building on walks or in the car. He liked to move around the car, to feel the dashboard, and pretended to drive. Richard seemed to think driving was an important masculine activity which he intended to master. In part the car served to buffer the loud noises from the street, but perhaps he also attempted to find out what the world was like, as though to regain the sight he had lost so early in life and to understand what this loss of function meant.

The fact that Richard had an older brother was also important in his attempts to compete and try out physical activities, for he was very interested in sports. With his brother and father, he went to many cricket and other sport matches, trying to understand and to take part in them. Richard liked the opportunities his regional high school offered in sports, mentioning soccer, cricket, athletics, and swimming. He continues to be interested in sports, travels to foreign countries for meets, and regularly swims and skis.

In other respects, though, he was critical of his school:

I went to a single-sex school [for the blind] and I'm not really in favor of them. I can't see any harm in mixing the different sexes and it's what would happen normally if you were home and had brothers and sisters. Some sort of barrier . . . must grow up . . . especially when you get to the age of 15, 16, and upwards. Then it really does start to affect you. The staff make no effort to integrate boys with girls from outside. Strange as it seems contact was discouraged, which as you can imagine can lead to other sorts of sexual problems which are bound to occur. There being no girls but all boys, to go drinking was a form of social life. Some had far too much. Everybody on a Saturday night would go and if anyone got in a bad way the gang was supposed to help because everyone knew that there either had been or would be an evening when they needed everyone else to help them. No one really bothered about anyone else and obviously that didn't discourage the one that got drunk. The staff probably realized this. A couple of times people's drinking did get quite serious and affected others regularly. . . . Some were old enough and if they had a girlfriend, wouldn't want to go drinking as much, but with no one to think about like that, others would want to prove a point.

This letter certainly points to the longing for closeness, the sense of loneliness and emptiness which many adolescents feel. In addition, one senses the deprivation and lack of contact with supportive, sighted adults in the school.

Gretchen put forth her views more assertively and in an angrier way than Richard. She indicated that in the corresponding school for blind girls there was far more restriction and no possibility of roaming about and socializing in pubs. In her view, contact between boys and girls was encouraged only on a lip-service level. Dances were scheduled and boys invited from local schools. Girls outnumbered the boys, which made it pointedly embarrassing and humiliating for girls. She thought any pairing off that took place despite these problems was discouraged by the staff, who appeared frightened by any closeness or intimacy between boys and girls. She reported that many girls found themselves terrified by the sound of a male voice when eventually launched into employment.

Richard wrote to me of the later difficulties he experienced in finding work:

After school I went to a Polytechnic to do a course about business studies and tourism. I did a lot of geography at school and it was while doing this that I became interested in tourism. Each year of the course consisted of two terms while we were working at the Polytechnic and a third term when we were supposed to be working in the tourist industry. Unfortunately, it was this part of the course that proved my downfall. I had managed to pass my first-year exams, but nobody was particularly willing to take me on as an employee. I think this had a lot to do with the fact that there were no other blind people working in the tourist industry. This meant that we had no proof to give to possible employers to show them that blind workers could cope. Anyway this dragged on all through last summer and I still was not able to get a job. The Polytechnic said that despite this they were prepared to have me back, but I thought that would be pointless. . . . While at school I had become very keen on computer programming for a bit; so I thought that since the money was not bad and the prospects certainly much better than tourism, I'd try and get something in this field. Fortunately, by the middle of October last year a company accepted me.

Achieving this degree of success has been a hard road for Richard to traverse, and it has been as difficult a struggle for him as it was for Norman. In fact, Annemarie Curson who visited him when he was 13 felt that he was withdrawn, depressed, and embarrassed. Both he and his parents seemed reluctant to talk to her, possibly because contact with anyone from the Clinic recalled the most difficult period in Richard's early life. While there seemed to be some constraint between Richard and his parents, the father teasingly but encouragingly referred to Richard's interest in girls. He also spoke with pride about Richard's athletic and other achievements, saying that Richard had won a prize for organizing a football match and raising 450 pounds for cancer.

Thus, Richard's organizing and coping capacities were in evidence throughout his life and received strong encouragement from his family, especially his father.

It should be mentioned, though neither Norman nor Richard did so, that the active stance both young men were able to establish and maintain was possible only with the continued support and active attitude shown throughout their past and present life by their families.

CONCLUSION

Since the role of vision in extending the world of the young child is well known, it is obvious that familiarity with the environment and a sense of separateness from it come more slowly and in different ways for the blind. Lack of knowledge of danger in the surroundings enforces great restriction upon motility during development which, as Dorothy Burlingham (1972) has pointed out, results in important developmental deficits in this area. The development of perception of inner and outer sensations must proceed at a more ideosyncratic pace and individualistic fashion. How this affects drive development and the role of object relationships has been described elsewhere (Nagera and Colonna, 1965). We do not know how it affects the developments of puberty and the longings and desires that flood the ego in adolescence. How sexual attraction is affected by the lack of visual experience is not known very fully. We can guess, but it is not very clear how the blind adolescent experiences the rather conflicting messages of the sighted adult world in regard to his emergent sexuality. This kind of information as well as much else that we would like to know could be supplied only by much more intensive contacts and especially by analytic exploration.

It is clear that it is during these years that the blind have to try to understand what their future love and work life will be like and what they can legitimately expect of themselves and others. The path each boy took, while leading to a successful resolution, was a stormy one. One senses that at each step in their development, the implications of blindness had to be tested anew. One gets glimpses of the powerful wish to undo them and to join the sighted and become part of their world. Thus, Norman apparently could not use his native intelligence and talents until he went to a sighted school, and he appeared to be happy only once he functioned as an established member of a group of persons who could see. It is especially interesting that under these circumstances he can freely ask for help and accept it.

In Richard's case, the coming to terms with the fact of blindness apparently first had to take a detour—his attempts to work in tourism, which appears to be a thinly disguised wish to see the world, at least via identification. His interest and participation in active sports go in the same direction. And his choice of partner, of a partially sighted girl, permits him to have a mutually sustaining and protective relationship—one that possibly might also be based on an unconscious fantasy that together they have at least one eye. Thus one could say that in both young men the activities they chose and the active management of their lives allow them to sustain the denial of some of the limitations imposed by their blindness.

From this brief introductory look one can certainly reiterate Dorothy Burlingham's comments on hearing of Norman's struggles. She wrote:

> It certainly is a success story against difficulties and shows the problems the blind have to contend with—and how they only succeed through their own efforts. [His story indicates that] one should treat them just as one would the sighted, accepting that there are the actual limitations imposed by the lack of sight, that it takes longer to do what the sighted to, that they need someone to assist, but that they find ways of accomplishing what they wish to do.

BIBLIOGRAPHY

BURLINGHAM, D. (1972), *Psychoanalytic Studies of the Sighted and the Blind.* New York: Int. Univ. Press.
_____ (1979), To be blind in a sighted world. *Psychoanal. Study Child,* 34:5–31.
COLONNA, A. B. (1968), A blind child goes to the hospital. *Psychoanal. Study Child,* 23:391–422.
CURSON, A. (1979), The blind nursery school child. *Psychoanal. Study Child,* 34:51–85.
FREUD, A. (1958), Adolescence. *Psychoanal. Study Child,* 13:255–278.
NAGERA, H. & COLONNA, A. B. (1965), Aspects of the contribution of sight to ego and drive development. *Psychoanal. Study Child,* 20:267–278.
SANDLER, A.-M. (1963), Aspects of passivity and ego development in the blind infant. *Psychoanal. Study Child,* 18:344–360.
WILLS, D. M. (1965), Some observations on blind nursery school children's understanding of their world. *Psychoanal. Study Child,* 20:344–365.
_____ (1970), Vulnerable periods in the early development of blind children. *Psychoanal. Study Child,* 25:461–480.

Personality Development in Identical Twins

The First Decade of Life

ELEANOR D. DIBBLE, D. S. W., AND DONALD J. COHEN, M.D.

THE TWIN STUDY METHOD HAS PROVIDED PSYCHOANALYTIC INVES-
tigators with opportunities for clarifying biological and environmental influences on child development (Joseph, 1975;
Panel, 1961). Direct observation, longitudinal study, reports of
parents and other caregivers, systematic testing, and
psychoanalytic therapy have been used by analysts, following the
lead of Dorothy Burlingham (1945, 1946, 1949, 1952, 1963), to
advance psychoanalytic understanding of individuation, identification, self image, identity, and psychopathology. While
psychoanalysis places environmental factors in the foreground
of study, Burlingham demonstrated how familial and other social influences could be studied in interaction with differences in
endowment, drive, early physical characteristics, and health during the emergence of personality or character. In this way, she

Dr. Dibble is a research social worker, and Dr. Cohen is Professor of Pediatrics, Psychiatry, and Psychology, Yale University School of Medicine and the
Child Study Center, New Haven, Connecticut.

The study was initiated in 1967 in the Section on Twin and Sibling Studies,
National Institute of Mental Health, under the direction of Drs. William Pollin
and Axel Hoffer. It was directed by Dr. Martin G. Allen from 1968 to 1970, and
by the authors from 1970 to the present. We gratefully acknowledge the collaboration of Ms. Martha Werner and Ms. Gale E. Inoff.

This research was supported in part by NICHD grant HD-03008 and
MHCRC grant MH30929.

provided clinically compelling data in relation to Freud's (1916-17) "complemental series" and Hartmann's (1934-35) program for explicating the relations between Anlage and environment in development. Other analysts have extended Burlingham's methods and observations in studies in which at least one member of the twinship was psychiatrically disturbed (Demarest and Winestine, 1955; Gardner and Rexford, 1952; Glenn, 1966; Joseph and Tabor, 1961; Lidz et al., 1962; Arlow, 1960).

The study of twins with psychological difficulties has highlighted special aspects of vulnerability in twins, such as disturbances in ego boundaries, self and object representations, and narcissism (Mosher et al., 1971a, 1971b). However, psychoanalytic child psychology recognizes multiple determinants of competence and development; the twin intrapair comparison method can be used to provide insight into normal development, since socioeconomic, familial, and cultural variability are significantly reduced (Cohen, 1974; Cohen et al., 1972; Dibble and Cohen, 1980). In a twinship, each child has his own, biological and familial "control" subject. In research with twins, small differences in endowment, health, parental care, other aspects of experience are thus magnified by the availability of two individuals with identical genetic endowment and highly similar, although not identical, environmental experiences (Cohen et al., 1977a, 1977b; Dibble et al., 1978; Gifford et al., 1966; Leonard, 1961). When used over time, twin investigation offers an approach to understanding the origins of individuality at each phase of development. Yet, there have been few longitudinal studies of normal, identical twins; no previous studies have been reported on twins from gestation through latency.

BACKGROUND

This study was undertaken to assess prospectively variables and processes which had emerged, on the basis of studies of adult twins discordant for schizophrenia, as potentially important determinants of adult psychopathology (Pollin et al., 1965). These variables included biological endowment at birth, health history, physical development, and parental interaction (Pollin and

Stabenau, 1968; Pollin et al., 1966; Stabenau and Pollin, 1967, 1968). To understand these processes, families with known twin gestations were studied prospectively from the time of pregnancy through the first years of life; a broad range of observational methods was utilized. The first years of the twins' lives, from the first week through age 5 years, have been described in other reports (Allen et al., 1971, 1976; Cohen et al., 1972; Inoff et al., 1980). This presentation describes the children's physical and emotional development, parental responses, family status, similarities between the children over time, and the interaction among these various factors through the twins' first decade of life.

A child's self concept has its roots in his earliest experiences in the family (Burlingham, 1972; A. Freud, 1965; Winnicott, 1965, 1975). The sense of who he is, what he desires, and what is expected of him emerges in the interplay between his biological endowment and the myriad of encounters with important people in his life, particularly his mother and father (E. Kris, 1950). During the first years of life, the child integrates the raw materials derived from his personal history of social relations and his unique style of organizing and representing them (Erikson, 1956). Throughout these years, however, if a child is a twin, his process is complicated by the constant presence of another child, a replica of himself, with whom he spends more time than with any other. It is still unclear how this "self observation" in the external world affects the development of self representation and the phenomena of introjection, incorporation, and identification. The constant confrontation with a mirror image may retard differentiation and may prolong mutual dependence (Leonard, 1961). Later, it may blunt the full experience of disappointments, separation tensions, and oedipal frustration. During the course of development, a singleton discovers that the image in the mirror is he (Lacan, 1949); the task for the twin is to discover that he and the mirror image which lives and moves with him are, in fact, separate beings. The twins' parents, too, must learn to distinguish the individuals within the twinship. How the children and parents approach the task of individuation, and the degree to which they succeed, profoundly influence the children's self and object representations and the structure of the superego. A major emphasis of this study was to determine what influences the lines along which individuation occurs, or fails to occur, in normal identical twins. Our intention was to advance along the path described by Ernst Kris (1950):

> ... if the double approach, psychoanalytic and observational, were systematically directed toward a study of identical twins, in both similarities and differences that according to some preliminary impressions seem not unrelated to parental preferences—we would have advanced further toward what we take to be our goal: the integration of data and approaches in developmental psychology around a center rooted in the thought of Freud [p. 79].

This report brings our longitudinal study of the development of twins to the end of the latency period or the first steps into preadolescence. Among the developmental tasks of the latency period are processes which have been described in relation to ego maturation, superego formation, and management of aggressive and sexual fantasies involved with the waning of the oedipus complex. Self representations highlight competence, mastery, and industriousness. The heightened excitement, rivalry, and instinctual urges of the preceding phase of development are increasingly muted as the child's cognitive competence allows him to master school and other skills and his affective world expands to include peer groups and teachers. Latency is often described as a relatively stable or organized phase of development, a relatively more quiet period than that which precedes and immediately follows upon it. While this may be true, it is also the case that during latency one can observe the crystallization of neurotic difficulties which may become clearer as developmental tasks are more sharply defined socially. The end of latency, ages 9½ to 11½, is particularly appropriate for assessing the development of shared characteristics and individual differences in twins. During the next phase of development, personality again may be disrupted, and transient, regressive, or diffuse and shifting cathexes may lead to instability of mood and temperament (Blos, 1962; Cohen and Frank, 1975; Frank and Cohen, 1979, 1981; A. Freud, 1958).

Methodology

Families were recruited through obstetricians and Mothers of Twins Clubs. Eight families whose twins were monozygotic (identical) as tested at birth by complete blood phenotyping participated in the longitudinal studies (Cohen et al., 1973, 1975). There were six sets of boys and two sets of girls. All of the families were intact, middle class, and professional. Most of the parents were in their early 30s at the time of the twins' birth, and all of the families, except one, had one or two older children only a year or two older than the twins. Methods developed in the longitudinal study were tested and extended in clinical studies of over 50 sets of twins interviewed one to three times and epidemiological studies involving more than 300 sets of twins (Cohen et al., 1977a, 1977b; Dibble and Cohen, 1974). Data from these various studies will be integrated in presenting results from the longitudinal study.

The longitudinal study utilized a wide range of methods, beginning during gestation and changing with developmental phases through ages 10 to 11 years. Before the birth of the twins, parents were intensively interviewed about their life histories, feelings about the twin gestation, and future expectations (Allen et al., 1971, 1976). A research psychiatrist observed the deliveries, when possible, and assessed the children's condition during the first week of life. Data about the twins from observations by physicians, nurses, and others were utilized to rate each child's endowment during the first week of life on a new scale (First Week Evaluation Scale, FES) which contains six variables, rated from 1 (serious problem) to 5 (normal): general health, physiological adaptation, calmness, vigor, attention span, and neurological findings (Cohen et al., 1972). Ratings from the six areas were scored for the total FES score (maximum = 30). FES scores for six of the eight pairs showed that the firstborn (twin A) received the higher score (ranging from 15 to 30), even though twin A was not consistently the heavier newborn. Serious health problems discriminated the high FES and low FES children. Second-born children (twin B) fell in the FES range 15 to 25.

Infants and parents were observed at home every 2 to 3 months during the first year, and at 6-month intervals for the next 2 years; they were evaluated annually through age 5 years. There were periodic communications and more intensive engagement with families at times of stress or family change (moves, illness, psychological problems).

During the preschool years, the twins were assessed by a variety of measures, including formal IQ testing (table 1), psychiatric evaluation, Rorschach testing, and observation of play to determine how they coped with unfamiliar, novel experiences and their general style of interaction. Parents completed objective scales and behavior problem checklists (Cohen et al., 1977a, 1977b).

At age 5 to 6 years, a nursery school assessment of structured and unstructured play was undertaken (Inoff et al., 1980). During one half day of observation in a research setting, two raters, using validated and reliable methods, observed the children and provided scores for the following variables: exploration of the physical environment, play involvement, dependency, animation, vigor, originality, active coping, ability to delay, frenetic behavior, fearfulness of stranger or environment, tractability, types of play, and amount and maturity of speech. These obser-

Table 1

Family	Twin	Weight (lbs.	oz.)	Birth Height (inches)	Sex	First-Week Evaluation Score	Stanford Binet IQ at 3 Years
I	A	5	6	19	M	26	120
	B	4	11	19	M	15	113
II	A	6	6½	20½	F	30	127
	B	5	9	19½	F	25	106
III	A	6	8	19½	M	28	139
	B	5	8½	18¾	M	25	150
IV	A	6	13	21	F	16	128
	B	6	4	21	F	18	130
V	A	5	6½	19	M	23	88
	B	4	11¾	18	M	19	95
VI	A	7	2¼	19	M	24	113
	B	7	11	21	M	21	111
VII	A	7		20½	M	23	74
	B	6	10	20½	M	22	72
VIII	A	7	½	20	M	15	99
	B	6	13½	20½	M	24	101

vations were similar to those obtained over a far longer period by Burlingham and Barron (1963).

Neurological and pediatric examinations were performed during the first week of life and again at age 2 years by the researchers; children were followed regularly by pediatricians who provided information. A thorough neuromaturation examination was performed, at school entry, with particular emphasis on nonlocalizing or so-called soft signs and differences between the twinship (Cohen, 1976).

When the children were about 10 years old, they and their parents were interviewed and observed during a home visit. Interviews included structured and semistructured methods; the children were observed at free play and during interactions with their parents. The children's histories were retrospectively reviewed with the parents and the children. During the structured interviews, conducted individually, the family and children were asked about individual, interpersonal, intrafamilial, social, and health experiences. Each child's external and internal life was assessed, through questions about his relations in the family and outside, areas of behavioral and emotional difficulty, current interests and competence, fantasies, sexual thoughts, personal ambitions and wishes, and feelings about being a twin. In interviews with each parent, the parent was asked about each child's health, social relationships, personality, cognitive competence, and interests. Parents completed an inventory about preadolescent behavior devised by us in other studies (Cohen and Frank, 1975; Frank and Cohen, 1979). By mail, pediatricians and teachers completed a behavioral report about the child's language, physical, social, and intellectual skills, behavioral difficulties, and how he compared with other children his age.

DEVELOPMENT OF THE TWINS TO AGE 6 YEARS

In spite of genetic identity, children in each of the twinships differed, sometimes to a considerable degree, in their endowment as newborns. Within each twinship, parents responded differently to the children. This individualization of parental style usually could be traced to the interaction of two factors:

parents' perception of each child's competence, especially vigor, health, attentiveness, and ease of being calmed; and the parents' own needs, wishes, capacities, and self representation as a parent. The parental ego ideal often had been articulated by the parent before the birth of the twins; it always underwent refinement in response to the actual children and the stresses and strains experienced by the family. The way the mothers and fathers envisaged their roles as parents to their as yet unborn children, and the unfolding of their actual parental style, were related to their own childhood experiences with their parents and their siblings, to whom the twins were often later associated. These parental self representations were also a function of the meaning of the marriage and the decision to have a family. Finally, parenting reflected aspects of each individual's character, especially the manner in which aggressive and dependent strivings were modulated.

By age 3 to 4 years, children with the better newborn endowment tended to be more mature socially, more actively coping, and more advanced linguistically than the less well-endowed children. There was good agreement between nonfamily observers (such as the raters in the nursery school) and parents; those children rated as more attentive by parents were more competent copers (succeeding in reaching goals and carrying through intentions) and better talkers in the research nursery school. Children seen by parents as enjoying play were less dependent in nursery school, and those viewed as more negative showed less involvement during play in nursery school.

Similar to the observations of Hartmann (1934–35), all parents reported some behavioral problems at 5 years—except one family in which one boy had already been removed from daycare because of hyperactivity. There were considerable intratwin similarities in behavioral problems at age 5 to 6 years. For example, in family II, the girls, who were in some respects different at the beginning of life (FES of twin A was 30, of twin B, 25; IQ of twin A was 127, and of twin B, 106), both sucked their thumbs at 5 years and engaged in odd rhythmic activities; both were seen by their parents as excitable and distractible.

One set of twin boys was very close in their FES scores (22 and 23) and had low results in IQ testing in the preschool years (72 and 74). At age 5, their parents described both boys as overly active, destructive, lying, stealing from their parents, and fearful of being alone. These children were the result of an unwanted pregnancy which took place during an unsuccessful reconciliation in the marriage; the parents separated and divorced when the boys were about 3 years old. Parenting of the children seemed to have been left to an older brother and sister while the parents were preoccupied with their own difficulties. This type of family experience may be the negative environmental influence which, combined with identical genetic endowment, resulted in almost identical later behavior.

For another pair of boys who had quite divergent FES scores (twin A = 26, twin B = 15) but IQ scores of 120 and 113 in their preschool years, behavior at age 5 was finely differentiated. Twin A was seen as active, while twin B was seen as markedly hyperactive; twin A was sensitive and fearful of separation from his parents, while twin B was "sassy" and easily frustrated.

The remaining five pairs of twins had similar behavior problems reported by the parents, differences seen as only a matter of degree. This intrapair similarity may indicate the greater genetic programming of certain types of emotional difficulties, as observed in our epidemiological studies (Cohen et al., 1977a, 1977b). The presence of behavioral concordance may reflect genetic, physiological, or environmental influences, in varying degrees; exposed to the same environment, identical twins are most likely to emerge quite similarly. Or, as summarized by Ernst Kris (1950), to understand "*in what way* the 'sameness' of personality manifests itself . . . requires at least two different steps: first an attempt at greater precision in describing the equipment of the child, and secondly an assessment of the interaction of the child with the environment" (p. 79).

CONTINUITIES AND DISCONTINUITIES

Continuities and discontinuities in personality characteristics, relationships, and health were magnified in twins because they were constantly being compared. What may have been a transient upset for a singleton could become, for a twinship, a more enduring aspect of identity or familial role. We will trace aspects of continuity from birth through age 10 years by presenting summaries of descriptive data and more detailed information on several families.

TWINS SIMILAR AS NEWBORNS AND DURING LATENCY

Four sets of twins, two boy and two girl sets, showed similarities between the two children from birth to the end of the latency phase as well as continuities of behavioral style for each individual; in these twinships, competence or relative difficulty in infancy continued into the end of latency (families II, IV, V, VII). A basic similarity between the two children in a pair persisted at various stages, and each child in the twinship responded in essentially the same way to environmental experiences they shared. Each pair had developmental disturbances which seemed to be phase-specific.

TWINS SIMILAR AS NEWBORNS BUT DISSIMILAR DURING LATENCY

Two pairs of boys (families III, VI) also had very similar characteristics during the newborn period; they then developed marked dissimilarities in personality as they moved toward the end of the latency phase of development.

During the 10 years of the twins' lives, family VI became increasingly affluent and isolated itself as superior to even its rather well-to-do neighbors. The children went to an exclusive private school and, from an early age, spent their entire summer vacations in camps. Minimal "home" time was shared as a family unit, and there was little display of warmth and affection among family members; the clearest expectation of the parents was that the children be well behaved and neat. Both parents denied difficulties, either in their own lives or in the lives of their children; appearances did not match reality, since there was considerable stress of various types.

Because of edema and other medical problems, the mother spent the last 6 months of the twin pregnancy in bed; she was socially isolated during this period, since the twins' father was preoccupied, as he was to remain, with his business. Their only other child, a bright girl of 2, was cared for by a maid. The boys were born weighing over 7 pounds, and their good health continued during the next years. At 3 years, both were scoring at the above-average range of intelligence on formal testing. Their mother, however, had trouble caring for the children from the time of their infancy, and familial tensions mounted during the preschool years. All of the siblings were in constant conflict with each other; the parents, however, emphasized how well the older sister performed and contrasted her with the boys. Corporal punishment was inflicted upon the children by the father, who used a belt for discipline. The children were allowed neither playmates nor pets in the house.

During the twins' preschool years, the firstborn twin continued to be industrious, independent, and relatively mature in school and with friends. He developed various hobbies and interests in sports; although he was closer to his father than to his mother, he was occasionally punished with little provocation and less explanation. Concurrently, twin B began to suffer from increasingly severe developmental symptoms, including motor restlessness, hyperactivity, inattention, and lowered frustration tolerance. He was expelled from nursery school because of his hyperactivity; at 9 years he entered psychiatric treatment and was started on stimulant medication for his attention deficit disorder.

In contrast to family VI, family III, who also enjoyed an increasingly comfortable economic situation during the decade of the study, openly recognized the psychological troubles experienced by their second-born twin, and expressed concern about how best to help him. Twin B had a herniorraphy at 3 months and again at 7 years, when a testicle had to be removed. At 5 years, he was fearful, inattentive, hyperactive, and enuretic; he cried easily and often. At age 10, he was far more restless and moody than his twin brother, and he was less industrious. He had no close friends and was emotionally undemonstrative. He felt closer to his father. Twin A shared some of these difficulties at age 5—such as mild fearfulness and increased activity—but by age 10, he was attentive, industrious and, in sharp contrast with his brother, socially quite outgoing. He had loyal, best friends, and he was annoyed by his brother's dependence. The oldest child in this family was in psychotherapy for problems which he and his family related to his having been displaced by his younger twin siblings. The parents were warm and supportive with all the children; they helped twin A feel less guilty about his anger with his older brother, who was more on his own, and toward his dependent twin brother, who had only twin A as a companion. Twin A's wishes, expressed in the privacy of his interview, were for "peace and tranquillity."

TWINS DISSIMILAR IN THE NEWBORN PERIOD AND IN LATENCY

In the remaining twinships (I, VII), the children were dissimilar both in infancy and later in childhood. Each twinship also had quite different family experiences.

In family I, the mother was distressed when she learned that she was going to have twins. She felt that she could not give all of herself to two babies at the same time, and an intense, exclusive, all-giving relationship was, in her mind, the essence of parenting an infant. She also felt that one of the twins would always be the "underdog" and that this would be the child with whom she would most likely feel closest. At birth, twin B was the underdog. He weighed 4 pounds, 11 ounces, had a low endowment score (FES of 15), and needed to remain in the hospital after his mother and co-twin went home. Twin A weighed 5 pounds, 6 ounces, had a higher FES score of 26, and was perceived by his mother as "more businesslike" and "needing me less." Within 4 months, the unfortunate twin B suffered the additional trauma of surgery for pyloric stenosis.

The father in family I had fewer preconceived ideas about the twins but early in their infancy felt that twin B was, like him, "sickly." The father had suffered for many years from serious, chronic intestinal and associated kidney ailments. He was not involved with his family, sheepishly admitting to spending most of his time with work or community activities. Consequently, he seemed to feel more comfortable with a child who showed less dependence and could do more on his own, like his older daughter and the more fortunate twin A. The mother's need to be intensely—and perhaps overly—involved with her children somewhat compensated for her husband's lack of engagement, but it also allowed him to remain at a distance.

The parents' sense of appropriate social distance, of the line between intimacy and suffocation, was a function of their own childhood relations. The father felt that his own mother had been overly protective and that she had blunted his own initiative; yet, reconstruction of his childhood suggested that most of his actual care had been provided by a maid. He had had little contact with his father, who had been deeply immersed in business. When he became a father himself, he talked at length about the importance of providing freedom to children to be individuals through a supportive but not close relationship. He married someone who wanted just the opposite, perhaps in some measure because as a child he had been more deprived than he cared to admit.

The mother in family I did not have a close relationship in her early life; her mother was a self-taught artist who was preoccupied with her work. Her father was an educator whose major concern was his wife's well-being. Like her husband, the mother in family I had been sickly as a child and felt more attached to a surrogate mother—her aunt—than to her mother; she had lived with this aunt for long stretches of time. The mother said she had felt socially deprived as a child and had hoped marriage would make up for this; she searched for closeness in her family and with others. Since her husband tended to be remote, although not unloving, she turned to her children for fulfillment.

Twin B's frailness appealed to his mother's need to love and be loved. Although his physical condition initially required greater amounts of care from his parents, his extreme dependency continued past the time of actual physical need and progressively blocked the expression of autonomy and separation. At 3 years, twin B clung to his mother during testing and was more anxious, babyish, and demanding than his co-twin. At this point, twin B's IQ was in the high-average range (113) and twin A's was superior (120). At 4 years, however, twin B seemed to be catching up to his older brother; both boys were bright and imaginative during formal testing and informal observation. Twin A was more aggressive and domineering, while twin B was quiet and cautious in approaching new situations, a continuity which could easily be related to their endowment and experiences during the first years of life. By age 5, the parents clearly differentiated the children's behavior; little doubt existed about which twin represented the poles of dominance-submission, assertiveness-timidity, and equanimity-anxiety. The firstborn twin was seen as quite active and yet, strangely, somewhat fearful of separation from his parents. The second-born twin was whiney, easily frustrated, and less focused in his activity; he was fearful of doing things on his own, a trait which his mother recognized in herself. Twin A was described by his family as "devoted" to his father and eager to "be a man just like him."

The similarity of one twin to each parent might be explained, following Burlingham (1952, p. 87), as each twin taking possession of one parent in order to avoid the intense rivalry of the twinship. Lawrence Kolb (Panel, 1961) referred to this as "everted identification" in which a sense of personal identity develops in twins by each linking himself to a different parent. This may evolve because of definitive physical characteristics which enable one twin to receive added parental attention. The other must seek substitutive support or face a severe failure of personal development and identity consolidation. However, the relationships between the twins in family I and their parents reflected the needs of the parents as well as those of the children. The mutuality of needs between twin B and his mother led to a relationship in which the adult's affective longings perpetuated the close ties beyond the time of the child's intensive actual needs; he remained dependent, fearful, and less competent, with lack of clarity about his separate identity and about which needs were his and which were his mother's. Twin A's lesser need for dependence was not threatening to his father, who preferred remoteness, in large part as a defense against his own felt deprivation. In turn, the father was free to respond to twin A more positively, with mutual acceptance of their separateness.

In family I, identification of each twin as an individual had been emphasized from the time their mother learned she would have twins. She always talked of the differences in their characteristics and dressed them differently. Through this, the boys received reinforcement of their individual roles and experienced a dilution of identification as a unit, "the twins." Although the mother overidentified with the less well-endowed twin B from the time of his infancy, she was able to satisfy both boys' emotional needs for a warm, responsive, holding environment

(Winnicott, 1965). Twin A developed into an autonomous, creative youngster, similar in many ways to his father.

The developmental continuities in family I observed through the first years of life were disrupted as the children approached middle childhood. In his eighth year, twin A fell ill with a disorder which was finally diagnosed as Crohn's disease, a serious gastrointestinal disease similar to the chronic illness which plagued his father. After the onset of this disease, twin A became more irritable and easily frustrated, although he continued to be attentive and to make strides toward independence. At age 10, twin A had close boyfriends, but no interest in girls. In the family, he related best to his mother, who he felt understood him; she, in turn, shifted her close affection and protective concerns to him. He was enuretic; and his teacher regarded him as slow in language skills, physical, social, and emotional maturity, and as being anxious and failing to complete tasks. In contrast, twin B excelled and surpassed his brother in various areas of development, in spite of having a diagnosed perceptual reading disability. At 10 years, the children's parents saw twin B as an industrious and independent youngster, able to follow routines and well-related to both his parents. He was most closely engaged with his father, whom he resembled in many ways. He was interested in girls, although still immature in assessing others' reactions to his behavior. He remained fearful of the dark and of monsters, but, like his co-twin, he was interested in science fiction. Although he was slightly anxious, twin B did not have problems in school; his teacher thought he, in contrast to his brother, was well adjusted.

Thus, accidents of health clearly influenced the development of these twin boys, starting from the first months of their lives. Twin B overcame his difficult newborn period, in large part because of the facilitative environment provided by his mother; her capacity for caring and protecting may prove equally curative for twin A. Of great importance is the fact that both parents had experienced and, in their own ways, coped with difficulties in their lives; both had deep, empathic understanding of serious physical illness. The affective richness of the household allowed the twins to individuate and establish their own identities in the face of other forces, such as the mother's overattachment, that might have led to a retardation of individuation and separation.

Family VIII had a threat parallel to that experienced by family I. Twin A cried at birth, but did not cry again for 10 minutes, and his breathing remained sporadic. His Apgar score was 6 at 2 minutes, and 9 at 5 minutes. In the newborn period, he was pale, cyanotic, floppy, and irritable; however, no specific neurological findings were present during this time or later. During the days in the hospital, medical personnel observed that the mother played with her twin children but did not seem to know how to care for them as a parent. The first-week endowment scores for the children were a low of 15 for twin A and a middle score of 24 for twin B.

During the first year of the twins' lives, the infants' social contacts were completely with their mother or a babysitter; the father offered no help with the children even when he was free from work or study. The mother was so upset by her responsibilities and her husband's distance that the parents sought marital counseling. The mother was particularly anxious about twin A's poor health at birth. Although he did not seem to suffer any direct, physical consequences of his poor newborn condition, as early as 18 months he was described as less secure and more dependent than twin B. He always screamed more and was fed first. He did not eat as well, spit up more, and did not sleep through the night. Twin B was seen as much more easygoing.

At 2 years, twin A's IQ was 99, and twin B's was 101. The twins' physical development during the first 3 years of life was similar, but they were psychologically distinctive. Twin B was seen by his parents as aggressive and as a fighter; he was a severe biter, especially of his co-twin. He could be interested in activities by himself. Twin A was a whiney, clinging child who held onto his mother's lap. Both boys continued to suck their thumbs at 3 years, but twin A also needed the security of a blanket and a toy. Both boys were active and curious, and their mother felt they laughed at her when she tried to discipline them.

In a testing situation at age 3, the psychiatrist found twin B to be more independent, assertive, fluent in speech, and coping better. In contrast, twin A, who had experienced neonatal trauma, was more dependent and fussed about details; he looked to an adult to help him do things. The same differences in behavior were present when the children were 5 years old; at this time, the parents described twin A as afraid to be alone, crying easily, awakening at night, having temper outbursts, being bossed by other children, not having friends, being anxious, and soiling. Twin B continued to be a bubbly, affectionate, and expressive child; he was stubborn and easily frustrated, and showed his temper through fighting. He rarely soiled.

In family VIII, the parents were young, attractive, somewhat self-centered individuals for whom having twins seemed to serve as a narcissistic gratification. Both parents were disappointed in having identical boys because they already had a son and wanted at least one girl. Assuming the total responsibility for the twins was an extreme hardship for the mother, a young woman who had grown up in a family in which she had been very much favored. Although she lived far away from her parents, she continued a close, embroiled relationship with her mother and remained her father's "favorite" child. Her volatile temper was often in evidence, as during a research session when she became upset and hit twin A across the mouth.

The early life of the father in family VIII was similar to that of his wife. He was the second child and only son of an overly solicitous mother whose ambition for him was a central motivation in her life. To help him realize her ambitions, she centered the life of the family around him. His father worked away from their home city and spent little time with the family.

The twins in family VIII developed identifications with a family style in which family members related to each other as sources of gratification. Within this general similarity among family members, twin A was more demanding and dependent than his co-twin. From birth, he was the center of anxiety and stress. Yet, he was the child who carried on an important family tradition— the name of his paternal grandfather—and he received, more from anxiety than pleasure, a greater amount of concern from his parents.

At 10 years, the less well-endowed twin A worried a great deal. He lacked confidence, was reluctant to try new things, was intimidated by his co-twin, was depressed and mean. Yet, he was beginning to relate more to his parents and to friends, and he expressed curiosity about girls and liked to play with them. His teacher commented on his difficulties in conceptualization, his lack of self-control, his tendency to play rather than work, and his need for reassurance. In short, he had not mastered the important tasks of latency: he was not industrious, attentive, or autonomous. Twin A had been plagued by physical problems—especially allergies and recurrent rashes—throughout his childhood and was engaged in speech therapy. In his individual interview at age 10, he saw his major problem at school as "Others pick on me." His ambition was to be either a creative writer or doctor to "cure allergies." He wanted to be a "perfect person, never fighting," and hoped for a "better world."

Twin B, at age 10, was not only outgoing but restless, argumentative, and resentful of help. His teacher thought that his attention span was good, that he was able to follow routines; he was competitive with other students in a nonadaptive manner. In his individual interview, twin B said that he felt closest to his mother but unhappy that she "yelled too much." His most admired person was his young uncle, who had "lots of girlfriends."

In this family, the firstborn twin's unfortunate biological beginnings elicited negative interactional patterns with his parents, and this mosaic of biological difficulties and negative interaction became crystallized and fostered the emergence of reduced social and emotional competence. Familial factors also had a negative impact upon twin B's development, although he was clearly more competent from the newborn period through the early school years. Tension was reduced when the family moved to the community of the mother's parents, when the children were 4 years old. In her home community, the mother was able to find help with the responsibilities of child care. However, the twins' negative behavior and physical problems persisted until age 10. Their mother had not grown up with them but seemed more like their older, adolescent sister who joined in their activities when she felt inclined to do so. The combination of the mother's negative interaction with her children, inability to set limits for them, and the absence of a father with whom the boys could identify left the children at the mercy of their own strong impulses; they were unable to mute the aggression and oedipal tensions which are developmentally normative, but which are modulated, when things go well, with the facilitative, structure-creating assistance of parents.

DISCUSSION

Psychoanalytic theory has long held that, as Hartmann (1934–35) stated it, character phenomena will be determined by the vicissitudes of drive development as influenced by maturation, adaptation, and environmental aspects. An interactional model of child development is now broadly accepted in developmental psychology as the most useful approach for understanding the complexity and continuities of development (Cohen, 1975; Denenberg, 1981; Sameroff and Chandler, 1975; Thoman, 1981). In this multivariate perspective, biological factors, family provision, and genetics operate in the emergence of personality and individuality; persistent early adaptations gradually coalesce in a child's sense of self. His character is shaped by a myriad of interpersonal engagements and the relations between endowment and experience (Young and Cohen, 1979). This developmental point of view takes into account how the child actively shapes parental behavior and how the complex of child and parent behaviors forms an interacting system; new internal structures are seen as resting upon the basis of previous levels of organization. Competence at any point in time is viewed, not as the result of some distant factor or set of factors, but as the psychobiological composite or resultant of various internal and external processes which have influenced the child, and have been influenced by him, over the course of his lifetime.

The study of identical twins is ideally suited for confirming or questioning this model of development; to our knowledge, this cohort is the most intensively studied, longitudinal investigation of the interaction of constitutional endowment with psychosocial forces in monozygotic twins from gestation to the beginning of adolescence. Our results richly illustrate the psychoanalytic, developmental model. For example, in family VIII, twin A's life-threatening birth difficulties affected how he was cared for as an infant, and this child-parent complex led to the emergence of twin A as a clingy, whiney preschooler; in turn, these childhood personality characteristics—his constant neediness and failure to be satisfied—aroused anger, guilt, and exasperation in his mother. The child's demanding behavior reinforced maternal rejection, and this, in turn, increased the child's negative behavior. At every point, the child's and the parent's patterns of activity were mutually interactive and reinforcing.

Family I presented sharp contrasts with family VIII. In family I, the less well-endowed twin B represented the kind of child for whom his mother needed to care. Thus, her more positive responses to the child who required her special attention may have helped to overcome his earlier difficulties. Family I, again in contrast with family VIII, also had a father who related to a vigorous, more autonomous child and took pleasure in being involved actively with him; from the time of the children's birth and throughout latency, the parents in this family alternated the nature of their involvement with the children according to each child's competence, special needs, and gifts during each particular phase of development.

The observation of twins, rather than of singletons, can clarify early differentiations in the child-caretaker interaction because of the increased magnification that twins provide of the discriminations in behavior of both child and caregiver. In our cohort, the availability of detailed, psychodynamic, and historical information about each parent and his or her attitudes about the approaching twinship provided a special vantage point for understanding and analyzing psychosocial influences on child-caregiver interaction. The parental influences on the children's emerging personality were evident and could be studied before the children were born; understanding the parents' fantasies, expectations, and competencies was essential to understanding the psychosocial world into which the children were born. Even before their birth, the children in the twinship were seen as having or lacking individuality, and as having the capacity to provide pleasure or deprive their parents of it. The twins, perhaps more than singletons, were the object of fantasy and were members of the family long before they entered the world. Some parents were more interested in the rarity of being the parents of twins and were excited by the attention the twins brought; others were concerned about how to individualize the children and yet treat them equally. Some worried about whether they would have enough love for both children; others, about the competitiveness that the children would experience with each other; still other parents believed that the children would be lifelong companions for one another, helping each other through crises and always being available for support. These shadings of attitudes sometimes could be traced to the parents' own childhood experiences and disappointments (Burlingham, 1955) and were particularly vivid in relation to "negative" or unpleasant traits in the children. Parents would associate a very young child's behavior with the moodiness or hyperactivity of an uncle or aunt long before the child's behavior was sufficiently crystallized to justify such an attribution. Once these comparisons became accepted as part of the family "myth," they endured and contributed to shaping a child's sense of himself.

In four of the families in our cohort, the children were treated as a pair—"the twins"—rather than as individuals. These four— families II, IV, V, VII—were the twinships who showed the greatest continuity of competence, with children who were both either high or low in competence, from birth through the end of latency. They showed the greatest similarities of behavior and of interests; yet, they were able to express, in subtle ways, the emergence of a sense of individuality. Parental attitudes reinforced a strong intertwin identification and dependency (Leonard, 1961).

This longitudinal study demonstrates, as did our large, epidemiological study of twins (Cohen et al., 1977a, 1977b), that genetic identify offers only a partial explanation of the nature of behavioral similarity in twins. Even before their birth, the experiences of the two children in a twinship can in no way be considered to be equivalent (Dibble et al., 1978). Twins may be vastly different in birth weight and in health during the first moments and weeks of life; first-week endowment scores indicate that individual competence, psychobiologically, does not simply reflect similarity of genetics. While the intratwin comparison method offers gross control over certain aspects of the child's sociocultural world, it may be most useful in highlighting subtle differences in each child's day-to-day experience, particularly in the finely tuned interactions between the child's psychobiology and parental caregiving style.

Although all of the children in our sample experienced some "problems" in their development, some children and parents coped more adequately because of their physical, intellectual, and emotional abilities. For example, the twins in family II had good abilities at birth and lived in a supportive environment. They were very unhappy about the family's move a thousand miles from their former home, but this unhappiness did not interfere with their functioning. In family VII, in contrast, the children had only a moderate endowment from birth, and their environment was not facilitative. A move away from their older siblings and former home left them with poor coping abilities. They were a year behind in school, were emotionally insecure, and showed a great deal of vulnerability for greater problems. In understanding vulnerability or coping, no single factor can be claimed as the only, or the most important, determinant of behavior.

While the families in this longitudinal study were chosen because they were intact, middle- and upper-middle class, and interested in research, their experiences as family units during 11 years revealed the stresses and strains of our times. Of the eight families, only two were living in the same home 10 years later; several had moved more than once. While all were intact at the beginning of the study, at the end of the study, only six were still intact. The majority of the families had serious medical problems, either in one of the parents or in one of the twins; similarly, a majority had psychological problems sufficient to warrant evaluation or treatment. Perhaps the relatively gloomy picture of the first decade of these twins' lives reflects some aspect of self-selection in this population; yet, we tend to doubt this. Instead, our experience suggests the broad range and frequency of life stresses to which children are exposed, the normative nature of change and difficulty, and the multivariate nature of the determinants of competence and emotional disorder.

When one analyzes retrospective information on adult twins discordant for psychopathology, it is important to take into consideration the nonlinear nature of determinants of competence and vulnerability and the tremendous impact of accidents, such as illness, on the emergence of what may then remain stable, individual differences. Similarly, this interactional viewpoint can be useful in clinical psychoanalysis; by heightening the analyst's awareness of types of trauma and developmental discontinuities, the developmental model and the results of longitudinal studies can help guide the formation of reconstructive hypotheses to be tested by further analytic inquiry (Neubauer, 1967; Solnit and M. Kris, 1967).

Thus, as demonstrated by Anna Freud and Dorothy Burlingham (1939–45), child observation and analytic reconstruction can be complementary forms of investigation (see also A. Freud, 1951a). Each contributes to the psychoanalytic understanding of normal and pathological development as the result of the multiple forces delineated by Anna Freud (1981):

- biological endowment and the maturation of instinctual organization and cognitive capacities
- the evolution of the agencies of the mind (id, ego, superego)
- the conflicts which are inherent in life and which lead to developmental achievements, as well as neurotic disturbance
- the child's ways of resolving conflict and achieving compromises between the forces in his inner life and between himself and his world
- the nature and timing of intervention
- the accidents of health and experience which leave their enduring imprint on mental development and which may move a child from a previously established path

In explicating the relations between these forces, the study of identical twins will continue to provide psychoanalysts with fruitful experiments of nature.

BIBLIOGRAPHY

ALLEN, M. G., GREENSPAN, S. I., & POLLIN, W. (1976), The effect of parental perceptions on early development in twins. *Psychiatry, 39:65–71.*
———POLLIN, W., & HOFFER, A. (1971), Parental, birth and infancy factors in infant twin development. *Amer. J. Psychiat.,* 127:1597–1604.
ARLOW, J. A. (1960), Fantasy systems in twins. *Psychoanal. Quart.,* 29:175–199.

BLOS, P. (1962), *On Adolescence.* New York: Free Press.
BURLINGHAM, D. (1945), The fantasy of having a twin. *Psychoanal. Study Child,* 1:205–210.
—— (1946), Twins. *Psychoanal. Study Child,* 2:61–73.
—— (1949), The relationship of twins to each other. *Psychoanal. Study Child,* 3/4:57–72.
—— (1952), *Twins.* New York: Int. Univ. Press.
—— (1972), *Psychoanalytic Studies of the Sighted and the Blind.* New York: Int. Univ. Press.
—— & BARRON, A. T. (1963), A study of identical twins. *Psychoanal. Study Child,* 18:367–423.
—— GOLDBERGER, A., & LUSSIER, A. (1955), Simultaneous analysis of mother and child. *Psychoanal. Study Child,* 10:165–186.
COHEN, D. J. (1974), Competence and biology. In: *The Child in His Family,* ed. E. J. Anthony & C. Koupernik. New York: Wiley, 3:361–394.
—— (1975), Psychosomatic models of development. In: *Explorations in Child Psychiatry,* ed. E. J. Anthony. New York: Plenum, pp. 197–212.
—— (1976), The diagnostic process in child psychiatry. *Psychiat. Ann.,* 6:404–416.
—— ALLEN, M. G., POLLIN, W., INOFF, G. E., WERNER, M., & DIBBLE, E. D. (1972), Personality development in twins. *J. Amer. Acad. Child Psychiat.,* 11:624–644.
—— DIBBLE, E., & GRAWE, J. M. (1977a), Fathers' and mothers' perceptions of children's personality. *Arch. Gen. Psychiat.,* 34:480–487.
—— —— —— (1977b), Parental style. *Arch. Gen. Psychiat.,* 34:445–451.
—— —— —— & POLLIN, W. (1973), Separating identical from fraternal twins. *Arch. Gen. Psychiat.,* 29:465–469.
—— —— —— —— (1975), Reliably separating identical from fraternal twins. *Arch. Gen. Psychiat.,* 32:1371–1375.
—— & FRANK, R. A. (1975), Preadolescence. In: *Mental Health in Children,* ed. D. V. S. Sankar. Westbury, N.Y.: PJD Publications, pp. 129–165.
DEMAREST, E. W. & WINESTINE, M. C. (1955), The initial phase of concomitant treatment of twins. *Psychoanal. Study Child,* 10:336–352.
DENENBERG, V. H. (1981), Early experience, interactive systems, and brain laterality in rodents. In: *Facilitating Infant and Early Childhood Development,* ed. L. A. Bond & J. M. Joffe. Hanover, N.H.: Univ. Press New England (in press).
DIBBLE, E. D. & COHEN, D. J. (1974), Companion instruments for measuring children's competence and parental style. *Arch. Gen. Psychiat.,* 30:805–815.
—— —— (1980), The interplay of biological endowment, early experience, and psychological influence during the first year of life. In: *The Child in His Family,* ed. E. J. Anthony & C. Chiland. New York: Wiley-Interscience, pp. 85–103.
—— —— & GRAWE, J. M. (1978), Methodological issues in twin research. In: *Twin Research,* ed. G. Serban. New York: Alan R. Liss, pp. 245–251.

ERIKSON, E. H. (1956), The problem of ego identity. *J. Amer. Psychoanal. Assn.*, 4:56–121.

FRANK, R. A. & COHEN, D. J. (1979), Psychosocial concomitants of biological maturation in preadolescence. *Amer. J. Psychiat.*, 136:1518–1524.

—— —— (1981), Preadolescent development. *Yale J. Biol. & Med.* (in press).

FREUD, A. (1951a), Observations on child development. *W.*, 4:143–162.

—— (1951b), The contribution of psychoanalysis to genetic psychology. *W.*, 4:107–142.

—— (1958), Adolescence. *Psychoanal. Study Child*, 13:255–278.

—— (1965), Normality and pathology in childhood. *W.*, 6.

—— (1981), Child analysis as the study of mental growth, normal and abnormal. *W.*, 8:119–136.

—— & BURLINGHAM, D. (1939–45), Infants without families. *W.*, 3.

FREUD, S. (1916–17), Introductory lectures on psycho-analysis. *S.E.*, 16:347.

GARDNER, G. E. & REXFORD, E. N. (1952), Retardation of ego development in a pair of identical twins. *Quart. J. Child Behav.*, 4:367–381.

GIFFORD, S., MURAWSKI, B. J., BRAZELTON, T. B., & YOUNG, G. C. (1966), Differences in individual developmental within a pair of identical twins. *Int. J. Psychoanal.*, 47:261–268.

GLENN, J. (1966), Opposite-sex twins. *J. Amer. Psychoanal. Assn.*, 14:736–759.

HARTMANN, H. (1934–35), Psychiatric studies of twins. In: *Essays on Ego Psychology*. New York: Int. Univ. Press, 1964, pp. 419–445.

INOFF, G. E., HALVERSON, C. F., JR., ALLEN, M. G., & COHEN, D. J. (1980), Pathways between constitution and competence during the 1st 5 years of life. *Develpm. Psychobiol.*, 13:191–204.

JOSEPH, E. D. (1975), Psychoanalysis—science and research. J. Amer. Psychoanal. Assn., 23:3–31.

—— & TABOR, J. (1961), The simultaneous analysis of a pair of identical twins and the twinning reaction. *Psychoanal. Study Child*, 16:257–299.

KRIS, E. (1950), Notes on the development and some current problems of psychoanalytic child psychology. In: *Selected Papers of Ernst Kris*. New Haven & London: Yale Univ. Press, 1975, pp. 54–79.

LACAN, J. (1949), Le stade du miroir comme formateur de la fonction du Je, telle qu'elle nous est révélée dans l'expérience psychanalytique. *Rev. Franç. Psychanal.*, 13:449–455.

LEONARD, M. R. (1961), Problems in identification and ego development in twins. *Psychoanal. Study Child*, 16:300–320.

LIDZ, T., SCHAFER, S., FLECK, S., CORNELISON, A., & TERRY, D. (1962), Ego differentiation and schizophrenic symptom formation in identical twins. *J. Amer. Psychoanal. Assn.*, 10:74–90.

MOSHER, L. R., POLLIN, W., & STABENAU, J. R. (1971), Identical twins discordant for schizophrenia. *Arch. Gen. Psychiat.*, 24:422–430.

—— —— —— (1971), Families with identical twins discordant for schizophrenia. *Brit. J. Psychiat.*, 118:29–42.

NEUBAUER, P. B. (1967), Trauma and psychopathology. In: *Psychic Trauma*, ed. S. S. Furst. New York: Basic Books, pp. 85–107.

PANEL (1961), The psychology of twins. E. D. Joseph, reporter. *J. Amer. Psychoanal. Assn.,* 9:158–166.

POLLIN, W. & STABENAU, J. R. (1968), Biological, psychological, and historical differences in a series of monozygotic twins discordant for schizophrenia. In: *Transmission of Schizophrenia,* ed. S. Kety & D. Rosenthal. London: Pergamon Press, pp. 317–332.

———— ———— MOSHER, L., & TUPIN, J. (1966), Life history differences in identical twins discordant for schizophrenia. *Amer. J. Orthopsychiat.,* 36:492–509.

————————& TUPIN, J. (1965), Family studies with identical twins discordant for schizophrenia. *Psychiatry,* 28:60–78.

SAMEROFF, A. J. & CHANDLER, M. J. (1975), Reproductive risk and the continuum of caretaking casualty. In: *Review of Child Development Research,* ed. F. D. Horowitz, E. M. Hetherington, S. Scarr-Salapatek, & G. Siegel. Chicago: Univ. Chicago Press, 4:187–244.

SOLNIT, A. J. & KRIS, M. (1967), Trauma and infantile experiences. In: *Psychic Trauma,* ed. S. S. Furst. New York: Basic Books, pp. 175–220.

STABENAU, J. R. & POLLIN, W. (1967), Early characteristics of monozygotic twins discordant for schizophrenia. *Arch. Gen. Psychiat.,* 17:723–734.

———— ———— (1968), Comparative life history differences of families of schizophrenics, delinquents, and "normals." *Amer. J. Psychiat.,* 124:1526–1534.

THOMAN, E. B. (1981), A biological perspective and a behavioral model for assessment of premature infants. In: *Facilitating Infant and Early Childhood Development,* ed. L. A. Bond & J. M. Joffe. Hanover, N.H.: Univ. Press New England (in press).

WINNICOTT, D. W. (1965), *The Maturational Processes and the Facilitating Environment.* New York: Int. Univ. Press.

———— (1975), *Through Paediatrics to Psychoanalysis.* New York: Basic Books.

YOUNG, J. G. & COHEN, D. J. (1979), The molecular biology of development. In: *Basic Handbook of Child Psychiatry,* ed. J. Noshpitz. New York: Basic Books, 1:22–62.

Toward a Developmental Line for the Acquisition of Language

ROSE M. EDGCUMBE, B.A., M.S.

IN RECENT YEARS THERE HAS BEEN AN UPSURGE OF INTEREST IN THE
way children acquire language and the role language plays in
development. Our own attention at the Hampstead Clinic was
drawn to these questions not only by experiences with disturbance
of language in some of our patients, but also by our observations in the nursery school which showed the enormous variation in the uses to which young children put language. These
uses ranged from relatively sophisticated intellectual discussion
in children from verbal, intellectual families, to almost wordless
noise designed to gain attention or vocalize demands in children
of deprived, nonverbal families with depressed or absent parents (Edgcumbe, 1975). We also became interested in the way
very young children acquired a second or third language, and

This paper is based on some of the work of a study group on language
development at the Hampstead Clinic, whose members were: Pauline Cohen,
Carla Elliott, Rose Edgcumbe, Barbara Grant, Jill Hodges, Elizabeth Model,
George Moran, Doris Wills, Irene Wineman. Observational material was
drawn from reports of an infant observation group run by Elizabeth Model,
and a toddler observation group run by Barbara Grant and Pauline Cohen.
Material was also contributed by Anne Page and Julie Campbell, members of
an observation group run by Dr. Emmanuel Lewis at the West London Hospital.

The Hampstead Child-Therapy Course and Clinic is at present supported by
the Herman A. and Amelia S. Ehrmann Foundation, New York; the Field
Foundation, Inc., New York; the Freud Centenary Fund, London; the Anna
Freud Foundation, New York; the New-Land Foundation, Inc., New York;
and a number of private supporters.

71

how they managed to communicate nonverbally during the time they were learning English (Hodges, 1980; Moran, 1980).

In attempting to study the development of language, we, in common with many other workers, became aware of the immense importance of the prestages to verbal communication in the nonverbal interactions between infant and mother. The appearance of words conforming to adult language conventions may be viewed as a relatively late stage in the development of communication, and disturbance in the prelinguistic stages can lay the foundations for subsequent distortion and pathology in language development.

The upsurge of interest in early language development occurs in the context of a reevaluation of psychoanalytic views of early infantile development in the light of recent studies. (See, e.g., reviews by Broucek, 1979; Peterfreund, 1978; and Panel, 1980.) One important question to emerge from such reevaluation is whether the infant's learning from his environment is as passive as traditional psychoanalytic views have suggested. Even more important, perhaps, are questions concerning the quality of the early infant-mother relationship, self-object differentiation, the building up of an inner world of self and object representations; i.e., between what kind of self and object does communication take place?

Observational Evidence and Theoretical Views on Early Psychic Development

There are by now many studies by pediatricians and psychologists as well as by psychoanalysts on early infant-mother interaction. Klaus and Kennel (1976), for example, summarize studies showing that the newborn sees, hears, and moves in rhythm to his mother's voice, and that these abilities coupled with his appearance evoke responses in the mother; these synchronized interactions are essential for attachment. There is a brief "sensitive period" immediately after birth in which complex interactions help to lock infant and mother together. This locking together on a biological level is to be distinguished from the period lasting up to 6 months during which the infant develops a stable, affectionate relationship with his mother, which is the beginning of a relationship on a psychological level. E. Furman (1976) comments that this period allows the mother to transfer her self-love from the infant "inside" to the infant "outside," and his unique behaviors and interactions with her facilitate the beginning of her relationship to the infant as a separate individual.

Such studies show that the infant is contributing actively to the developing relationship even in the earliest days of life. Trevarthen and Grant (1979) present evidence to emphasize this active contribution from the child, and castigate anthropologists, education policy-makers, and sociologists for playing down the role of self-motivation in the development of infants and children. They point out that "babies act *as if* they have intentions [and] are highly successful in influencing the feelings and reactions of others" (p. 566; my italics).

Such evidence of the active contribution of the infant to the development of relationships and communication with objects enlarges the evidence on infant activity patterns and responses already presented by analysts such as Spitz (1957), Greenacre (1960), and Escalona (1963) and is a welcome corrective to the view which regards the infant as the passive recipient of mother's influence. As we have stressed elsewhere (Edgcumbe and Burgner, 1972), however, it is important to distinguish clearly between biological and psychological levels of mutual influence and interaction. This distinction is, I think, ignored by critics such as Peterfreund (1978) who considers that research on the activity and capacities of the infant provides evidence for the existence of differentiation, ego functioning, and responsiveness to objects from birth. The position is clarified by distinguishing, as Meissner (1979) does, between "object relatedness"—the real, observable interaction between mother and infant, which, however, gives us no inkling of the child's experience of the interaction—and "object relations"—the intrapsychic dimension of the subject's experience with objects, including psychic self-object differentiation. Meissner points out that the shift from object-relatedness to object-relations is made through the process of gradual internalization. Within such a frame of reference I shall trace the development of psychologically intentional communication out of the matrix of biological communication.

Theories of Language Acquisition

As psychoanalysts we have long been aware of the vital importance of language in our work. As Steiner (1976) puts it: "The
raw material *and* instrumentality of Freudian analysis are
semantic" (p. 253). Sometimes psychoanalysts are accused of
continuing to use nineteenth-century theories of language and
failing to make use of more recent development in linguistics
(e.g., Litowitz and Litowitz, 1977). If this has been so, it is,
perhaps, because at first sight much modern work appears
mainly concerned with formal characteristics of language and
the sequence in which grammatical structures are mastered by
the child: aspects which at best interest analysts only insofar as
they bear on ego development. Closer inspection soon reveals,
however, that linguistic studies have much to contribute to our
understanding of other areas of psychic development, in particular object relationships and related structural development.
For example, Clark's (1978) paper on deixis traces stages in the
development of pointing gestures whose communicative function is the precursor to the use of "pointing" words which pick
out things in relation to the participants in the speech situation:
I/you, here/there, come/go, etc. Not only is gestural and verbal
pointing an indicator of the development of object relationships
and of ego development, but the different strategies children
use in mastering such distinctions may throw light on more subtle variations: for example, in mastering the shifting frame of
reference between self and object in the use of deictic terms,
children use different strategies according to whether their approach is self- or object-centered, and this may reflect the balance between narcissistic and object libido.

There is still much work to be done in coordinating the
theories and observations of linguistics and psychoanalysis, but a
start has been made.

Lock (1980) gives a succinct summary of the history of recent
interest in language development, which he divides into three
periods according to the focus of interest on syntactics, seman-
tics, and pragmatics. In the first period Chomsky (1965) chal-

lenged the behaviorist theory of language acquisition through learning and reinforcement. Chomsky postulated that a language can be learned by uncovering its syntactic rules, without understanding the meaning of words, and that some innate knowledge of sentence structure exists which is realized through experience. This theory proved unable to account for sentences whose structure cannot be uncovered without recourse to the meaning of the words: one-word sentences in particular, but also some longer sentences.

In the second period Fillmore (1968) put forward the theory of case grammer, a rule system based on the meaning relationship between words. This also assumes universal, innate concepts having to do with identifying events such as who did what to whom and what changed. This approach permits the study of the order in which children acquire different cases; and a semantic account of stages in language development is more parsimonious than a syntactic one. Neither view solves the problem of where the ability to speak in sentences comes from, since language is seen as qualitatively different from other forms of communication, having no precursor.

The third period, therefore, turned attention to the infant's communicative abilities before the acquisition of speech, but there remained the problem that language is propositional, prelanguage communication is not, and how is the gap bridged between the two? Vygotsky (1966) answered this question by proposing that all human skills appear twice in their development: first they are constituted in interactions that take place between people (the intermental level); later they become the internal cognitive possession of one or both of these individuals (the intramental level). E.g., an infant cries in reaction to a state of discomfort, not with the intention of communicating to his mother. But she perceives him as if he were communicating; thus his ability to communicate exists through interaction with another. Feedback from others allows him to gain knowledge of his unintended ability, and it is transferred to the intramental level, becoming an ability over which he has control.

Thus, the mother plays an important role in facilitating the infant's shift from unintentional to intentional communication. There is by now a considerable literature on the mother's role in promoting language development as well as on the infant's contribution.

Bruner (1978) points out that mothers teach their children to speak, but the child's willingness to be taught is part of the innate preparation for language. He thinks that the child may have an innate ability to "crack the linguistic code," but there may also be something innate about the mother's ability to help him do so. Researchers such as Snow (1972) have shown that adults modify their speech to suit the needs and comprehension level of the child, making it simpler and more repetitive, using "turn passing" devices with young children, but not the "turn grabbing or keeping" devices frequent in adult conversation. Experienced mothers are only slightly better at doing this than other adults, and it is from this speech environment tailored to their needs that children learn, not from random sampling of all adult utterances. Bruner describes how the shared attention of mother and child at first focuses on the child's needs, subsequently extending to sensorially vivid things, or to surprising or rare occurrences. Gestures such as reaching and pointing emerge which indicate the focus of attention. Bruner places at the end of the first year the distinct step of the child's recognition "that how one vocalises affects how another's attention can be altered, that sounds and sound patterns have semanticity" (p. 66). Bruner's view is representative of those who stress the child's active participation in the language learning process, and contrasts with the more traditional psychoanalytic view exemplified by Sarnoff (1976) which stresses the passive aspect of the child's learning. Sarnoff states, e.g., that at the end of the first year verbal signifiers are acquired; the child can point to people and parts of the body when they are named; passive use of the words of others leads on to the use of words for speech and representation of thought content.

There is general agreement on the importance of the capacity to symbolize, with words becoming the most important symbols. Buxbaum (1964), for example, believes that language derives from a symbol-forming tendency, speech is genetically determined, and there exists a point in development where the need to communicate is the organizing principle which joins the symbol-forming tendency with speech to create language. Perhaps this is the point Bruner refers to at about one year; that how one vocalizes affects how another's attention is altered. Buxbaum refers to studies showing mother's role in promoting social interaction, and how mother's response may promote or delay vocalization. Preverbal communication between mother and child is intricate and complicated. She considers "partial symbiosis" to be the etiological basis for functional deficiencies, including poor speech. Mothers make speech unnecessary by understanding gestures and fulfilling wishes. Baby talk serves as a secret language which excludes others from the mother-child relationship. Anny Katan (1961) points out that verbalization of perceptions of the outer world precedes verbalization of feelings, and that verbalization facilitates the ego's control over affects and drives. She stresses the important role of the parents in helping the child to name objects, wishes, and feelings.

Perhaps the most comprehensive contribution so far to a psychoanalytic theory of prelinguistic development is Justin Call's (1980) paper which traces the emergence of language from a broader matrix of systems of communication between infant and mother, and places the development of gestural and verbal pointing within the context of the separation-individuation process (Mahler et al., 1975).

Our own attempt, which overlaps with Call's work, has been to formulate stages in language development with emphasis on its role: (1) in communication between child and object and its contribution to object relationships; (2) in discharge and expression of affects, impulses, and other inner experiences; (3) in facilitating communication within the individual's own mind, between structures of the personality and between object representations. To this end we have to consider the interaction between development in language, thinking, object relations, and psychic structure.

Our observations on infants and young children together with our perusal of the literature have enabled us to formulate five early stages in the development of language.

THE STAGES

The first three stages of the developmental line are concerned with the foundations and prestages of communicative language. They trace the development toward the intentional use of specific vocal sounds. There is a wide variation in the speed with which individual babies progress through these stages, and behavior of earlier stages continues alongside subsequent ones. In some cases progress is so rapid that these first three stages are simultaneously present for many months. It is our impression that the overlapping of stages may be greater than that found in other developmental lines, with earlier modes of communication normally used alongside later ones.

Stage 1 starts at birth. The baby is born with a number of built-in ways of attracting mother's attention to his needs and interests, and the mother responds as if he were doing it deliberately. Her responses serve to reinforce and differentiate for the infant his own noises, gestures, and expressions. The baby listens and watches, and mother's speech in turn contributes to the baby's productions. Without this response from mother, the infant's noises and gestures do not develop into communicative vocalization and words.

Once mother and child have engaged in these prestages of "conversation" the ground is prepared for the move into the next stage. The essentials of stage 2 are the differentiation in the baby's "vocabulary" of a range of sounds linked with increasingly specific inner experiences, and the value of the mother's sounds in aiding the baby to tolerate delay and frustration: indications that the first steps are occurring in the remembering and organizing of experience. These steps will permit development of the capacity to anticipate, the creation of a primitive representational world, and the beginnings of structural development.

In stage 3, the child becomes aware that vocalizing can have specific meanings and be used to influence the behavior of others. He understands the inflections of mother's voice, if not her words, before he can produce recognizable speech himself. He uses vocalization, other noises, and gestures intentionally to involve the mother during interaction, and to indicate wishes. This implies some degree of structuralization and internalization of object representation. The child has a primitive image of "mother" whose attention he wants, and enough language organization to select appropriate sounds to attract her. Vocal noises the baby makes himself help to facilitate delay, in the beginning of self-comforting.

The subsequent stages are concerned with the development of different uses of established sounds and with the development of intentional use of language. Intentionality is a difficult concept in infancy, but in our view the problem of intentionality resolves itself into the questions of when psychologically aim-directed behavior takes over from biologically determined behavior and how this transition occurs. Vigotsky's distinction between the intermental and intramental levels clarifies the way the infant's communicative ability initially exists only through interaction with his mother; without feedback from her he cannot gain knowledge of his ability. Bruner suggests that at the beginning of life the child's indications of interest are mainly related to his needs. Mothers interpret signs of desire as intentional communicative acts. Bruner places around the end of the first year the child's realization that one's own vocalization can affect another's intention, and that sounds have meaning. This would be our stage 3. This is not to say that before that babies do not have intentions in the sense of wishes and needs which they are able to convey by gesture and sound, provided the object is sufficiently attuned to interpret the infant's "requests" or "demands." But the infant remains at the mercy of the object who can assign meaning or fail to understand his communications. We may say, then, that intention in some form may have been present before stage 3, e.g., in the use of noise and gesture, to attract mother's attention, but without the realization that words are particularly effective for such a purpose; from stage 3 onward the infant develops the expectation of producing specific effects via the use of appropriate language. The intent to communicate requires sufficient structural development for the ego to have begun to take over the process of mediation between the child's id and the external world—i.e., sufficient development of the representational world (Sandler and Rosenblatt, 1962) for the child to have some form of mental representation of the object responding to the self's wish; sufficient cognitive, perceptual, and memory development to have a mental representation of the way in which the wish may be satisfied; sufficient motor and vocal development to express that wish externally in gesture and word. Language provides one mode of keeping contact with the mother as separation-individuation proceeds. Consistently produced noises associatively linked with wishes, experiences, etc., become available to the infant very early, so that separation occurs from an object with whom there is already shared language.

Once the child has recognized the value of vocalization in influencing his objects and in understanding their wishes to and feelings about him, he can move on beyond using his own idiosyncratic sounds for communicating his experiences, feelings, and wishes to learning the conventions of language used by the adults around him. In stage 4, words are used to express wishes as well as for release of impulses and affect; all this implies increasing linkage of words and inner experience, with words helping the process of differentiation among feelings and experiences as well as among objects. The child's understanding of language is ahead of his own use of it; words begin to serve as explanation and reassurance when used by the mother. The adult's words begin to convey commands and prohibitions with which the child can comply as ego development proceeds, and the object's words begin to be internalized in superego formation. The child may be able to comply with complex instructions, though his own use of words is still minimal.

In stage 5, the child's own vocabulary rapidly increases. The essential changes in this stage are that the child becomes able on the one hand to communicate verbally as well as gesturally to the object a wide range of experiences, questions, and ideas, beginning sometimes to use words as a substitute for action; and on the other hand he can use familiar phrases of his mother as part of taking over some of her caring and controlling functions. Internalized concepts now help to sustain the relationship during separation, and words may help the child to recall the image of the absent object. The child begins to use words learned from the object not only as a means of reassuring and explaining to himself, but also as a means of reinforcing demands and prohibitions taken over from the object in the beginning of superego formation.

There follow several stages in which language increasingly substitutes for action, becoming grammatically increasingly complex and associated with increasingly sophisticated thinking, understanding of inner and outer experience, and the development of reality testing. These stages will, we think, prove to be

linked with developments in structuralization and object relationships. The shift from the anal-sadistic to the phallic-oedipal
phase may well be the point at which language development
normally becomes autonomous from the mother-child relationship. In this paper, however, I will concentrate on the first five
stages, going on now to discuss and illustrate each stage in more
detail.

STAGE 1

It is difficult to know precisely what the very young infant intends or means, since we cannot examine his inner experience.
We do not even know what is the proportion of mental to
physiological experience in the infant at any given age. What we
do know is the importance for development of the mother's
treating her infant's communications as intentional. Vigotsky
refers to this stage as the intermental level. Call stresses the importance of the many nonverbal interactions between infant and
mother as the matrix out of which language communication may
eventually emerge. Klaus and Kennel survey the evidence for
the importance of early interactions in the development of the
mother-child relationship. Villiers and Villiers (1978) show that
neonates are sensitive to sound in the frequency range of normal
speech and by 3 days find the sound of speech rewarding; they
perceive breaks in speech and synchronize their movements with
these. Bruner surveys the evidence more specifically concerned
with language development, noting the importance of Snow's
observation that mothers talk about their children's needs,
wishes, and intentions as if the mothers' task were to find out
something the babies already know. A number of authors demonstrate that mothers can discriminate better than chance between different cries. Ainsworth and Bell (1974) show that by
responding to these cries the mother recruits the child's vocalizations from demand and request into more subtle communicative
patterns later in the first year of life. Their study demonstrates
that children whose mothers respond to their vocalizations during the first half year cry less and vocalize and gesture in a more
communicative way by the end of the first year.

   Thus, the newborn has the potential for developing a "conversational" interaction, and it is the mother's role to facilitate this development. Sheridan's (1960) norms indicate that by the age of 1 month the baby watches mother's face when she talks to him; he stops whimpering (but not crying or screaming) at the sound of a nearby voice; and he utters gutteral noises when content.

In summary, we may formulate stage 1 as follows: in the early days of life the baby's noises and gestures (including facial expressions and bodily movements) are either discharge processes or inbuilt biological mechanisms subserving infant-mother bonding. Although the baby may not, at first, intend it, they attract the mother's attention. Her responses (at first her actions, later her words) serve to reinforce them and begin to differentiate them for the child. Soon the baby listens and watches the mother's mouth, taking in sounds, especially mother's speech, which in turn contribute to his own productions. Without this response from the object the baby's noises do not develop into communicative vocalization and words.

A few illustrative observations will exemplify this formulation.

Joanna was first observed when her mother was trying to interpret the different meanings of her cries: the grizzle, the cry of tiredness, and the change from crying to screaming when hungry. The mother's attention had been attracted by the baby's cries, and we see her attempting to differentiate them, thus beginning to reinforce the baby's use of sound as communication. She and Joanna soon established pleasurable communication; e.g., at 8 weeks Joanna responded to her mother's smiling and talking with a smile, but as soon as mother was distracted by Joanna's older brother, Joanne stopped smiling. It was difficult to evaluate how great a role talking had in this interchange because when mother was distracted, Joanna not only lost the auditory input but also the eye-to-eye contact.

At 12 days Mary was observed gazing around during bathing and dressing, but mostly fixing her gaze on mother. She fed calmly at the breast, looking at her mother's face. The mother talked to the observer but looked at Mary during the feeding. At 2 weeks she would gurgle and chortle on waking and half-smile at her mother. By 3 weeks on waking she would smile broadly and focus on her mother. They would "chat" to each other when mother held Mary face to face. If Mary cried, she was soothed by mother's picking her up. A good example of mother treating Mary's communications as intentional occurred at 4 weeks during a breast-feeding when Mary spat out the nipple. Mother took it as a communication that Mary had had enough of the first breast, and changed her over. Mary sucked only briefly before stopping again. Mother winded Mary, holding her in a sitting position facing mother. Mother talked and Mary watched, making mouth movements as if imitating mother. Mother wondered if Mary was still hungry and said, "You're the only one who can tell me." Mary made sucking movements, and mother offered her the breast. She smiled a little, then rested again.

During the early days, still in the maternity hospital, Jane's eyes already seemed to focus on her mother's face during breast-feeding; she would cry when put down, stop when mother came back. But her mother felt herself to be clumsy, not good enough at feeding her baby. Jane was jaundiced, and mother believed she had been told not to hold her too much. However, on the sixth day she ignored this and held Jane for 2 hours, which helped her to feel they had "got together." On that day Jane was observed still awake after a feeding, mother and child both looking relaxed and content. A smiling interaction during feeding was soon established. By 3 weeks (now at home) the smile Jane gave her mother was markedly broader than the faint smile for the observer. The mother remarked to the observer that she felt hurt when her daughter became interested and absorbed in the pattern on a chair to the exclusion of her mother. Jane was observed to stare at the pattern, made noises as if "talking" to it, and tried to reach it with her mouth. But in general communication between infant and mother was developing well in this first stage, with Jane especially enjoying the interaction with mother at changing, bathing, and dressing times, as they smiled and "conversed" with each other.

STAGE 2

If mother and child successfully engage each other's attention in communication, the move into stage 2 may occur quite quickly, as the baby develops a range of sounds linked with specific inner experiences, and the mother's sound helps the infant to tolerate delay and frustration. In Vygotsky's terms, the shift to the intramental level is beginning. Sheridan states that by 3 months the baby shows by smiles, coos, and excited movements that he recognizes preparations for feeds, baths, etc. He often licks his lips in response to sounds of preparation for feeding. There is a definite quietening to the sound of mother's voice before she touches him, unless he is screaming. He vocalizes when pleased, and when he is spoken to, and responds with obvious pleasure to friendly handling, especially when it is accompanied by playful tickling and vocal sounds. He cries when uncomfortable or annoyed. Call summarizes work indicating the importance of language development in the differentiation and taming of affects. Bruner notes that reaching serves to indicate the focus of the infant's attention to external things. Trevarthen and Grant observe that as early as 2 months vocal play between a mother and baby shows remarkable similarities to conversation between adults.

In stage 2, structural development is beginning. The first steps in remembering and organizing experience permit the associative linking of sounds with specific inner experiences. The infant's noises express with increasing differentiation inner feelings such as pleasure, frustration, and anger. Noises made by the infant increasingly accompany his actions. The beginnings of mental organization allow the capacity for anticipation to start developing, and this, together with the primitive beginnings of the inner representational world, means that noises made by the mother can begin to facilitate the baby's tolerance of frustration, e.g., at feeding time or during nappy-changing. Tension discharge probably continues to be an important function of some, but by no means all, noises and gestures. The baby responds with babbling to mother's initiation of "conversation." Noises and gestures are also used to indicate external object and events which have attracted the baby's attention.

A good example of the infant's linking of vocal noises with inner experiences is provided by Richard, a child whose family valued verbal communication highly. From early on there was much vocalization by others in Richard's environment, and his mother spoke directly to him with eye contact regularly included in her communication. In addition, his older sister laughed and chattered incessantly to everyone in sight, and she would at times lean close to Richard's face to speak to him. He was in turn fascinated by his sister, watching her movements and listening to her vast range of sounds. Though a placid boy, Richard was very responsive to people in his world and demonstrated a wide range of sounds. He was moving into stage 2 by 9 weeks with vocalizations which seemed related to pleasure and contentment. At 16 weeks he laughed in response to his own somatic action—spitting up—and at this time was also gurgling, babbling, and smiling when his mother spoke to him. At 19 weeks he cried in apparent annoyance when his nappy was changed. By 27 weeks pleasurable motility (bouncing on mother's lap) was accompanied with gurgles of pleasure. At 30 weeks he showed persistent interest in a musical toy, made grunts of dissatisfaction when the music ended, and gave a broad smile when it began once more. His mother sat behind him and whispered in his ear; Richard would grin with delight, leaning far back in her lap to gaze at her.

Mary illustrates both the infant's use of noises to accompany actions and the capacity to use mother's talking to facilitate tolerance of delay. By about 14 weeks she had developed many different noises and intonations with which she accompanied her play, and which the observer thought sounded like a commentary. While waiting for a feeding, she would watch her mother with interest and smile in response to mother's talking to her.

An early example of the capacity to delay is seen in Jane at 12 weeks when she was hungry at bath-time. She cried and made rooting and mouthing movements. Mother smiled and talked to her while undressing her, and Jane relaxed, smiled and laughed at mother, and enjoyed bodily movement in her bath. In this way she was able to wait some time for her food, though mouth movements continued. Finally, during dressing, her frustration tolerance ran out and she began crying insistently.

The babbling response to mother's conversation is well-illustrated by John who was not a cuddly baby, and seemed to prefer visual and vocal to tactile contact. He preferred to face his mother rather than be held close. At 12 weeks after a feeding there were a couple of smiles from John and some contented noises. His mother and he held a charming conversation in noises and smiles, gazing into each other's eyes. To be sure, most of the input was hers, but John's ability to respond in this way gave her much pleasure. At the same age John would also smile and vocalize in response to the observer.

At 15 weeks when mother lay John on her thighs, feet toward her and his head supported in her hands, he gazed at her face, smiled, and produced a wonderful range of sounds, from coos through glutinous gurgles to what his mother described as a growl; she clearly found it intensely pleasurable when he responded like this.

STAGE 3

This is the stage in which the child discovers that vocalizing can have specific meanings and be used to influence the behavior of others. Sheridan states that at 6 months the baby shows evidence of response to different emotional tones of mother's voice. Bruner speaks of the emergence at the end of the first year of the child's recognition that vocalizing affects the attention of another, and that sounds have meaning. It is also the period during which reaching and pointing emerge as ways of indicating the focus of attention (Bruner, Sheridan). Call gives the example of a 14-month-old girl who effectively directed a group of observers by pointing, i.e., indicating her wishes. Babbling reaches a peak between 9 and 12 months, and long babbled sentences continue after this despite the acquisition of clear words, according to Villiers and Villiers, who also state that between 10 and 14 months the child may have a vocabulary of about a dozen vocables used consistently to refer to actions, objects, or situations or to achieving pragmatic goals, and these vocables provide a link between babble and the first intelligible words. They say that at this age the child becomes aware that speech sound patterns have consistent meanings or conditions of use. Sheridan puts at 9 months the infant's vocalizing deliberately as a means of interpersonal communication. He shouts to attract attention, listens, then shouts again. He tries to imitate adult's playful vocal sounds. Several authors (e.g., Bruner, Villiers and Villiers) also describe how in this period the child is learning in games such as peek-a-boo techniques of turn-taking and role-shifting, making and breaking eye contact, and the coordination of signaling and acting, which are prerequisites for conversational exchanges. Mothers increasingly expect their babies to provide an appropriate response in vocal interchanges (Snow). The development of facial expressions and gestures is described by Trevarthen and Grant in the "drop and pick up game" involving expressions like surprise, annoyance, refusal, and gestures like showing, giving and taking, and pointing.

All these achievements imply that structuralization is well advanced, permitting increasing development, organization, and control of ego functioning, while the representational world of the child is becoming complex enough to provide inner images of varied and specific interactions between self and object. By now the child is well advanced into the separation-individuation process (Mahler et al., 1975), and Shopper (1978) has emphasized the importance of audition in allowing the infant to maintain contact with mother despite being round the corner, in the dark, or having his back to her. Hearing is thus superior to visual contact when the infant enters the practicing phase.

Stage 3 can be summarized thus: the baby is beginning to "understand" the inflections of mother's voice, if not her words, even though he cannot yet produce recognizable speech himself (he may reproduce the inflection without the words). Understanding of speech is facilitated by the learning of facial expressions, as infant and mother watch and mimic each other. He tries to imitate the vocal sounds made by the mother and enjoys her repetitious naming of things, pictures, parts of the body, etc. The baby uses vocalization, other noises, and gestures intentionally to involve the mother during interaction and to indicate wishes. This implies some degree of structuralization and internalization of object representation. The child has a primitive image of "mother" whose attention he wants, and enough language organization to select appropriate sounds to attract her. Babbling as well as crying or screaming is used to call mother when the baby is alone, e.g., when waking up in his cot. Vocal noises the baby makes himself begin to facilitate delay, and this contributes to the beginning of self-comforting.

The development of inflection in interchanges between infant and mother is well illustrated by Jane. At 7½ months, instead of crying or shouting, she began to use a range of "conversational" noises to regain her mother's attention when mother took her eyes off Jane. At 8½ months she seemed to be using "Mum-mum-mum" more specifically for her mother. At 9½ months she used noises in response to questions from mother. E.g., mother said, "Are you hungry?" and Jane said, "Wah," which the observer thought sounded like an answer.

A fairly typical stage-3 interplay occurred at 10½ months: Jane was on the floor absorbed in eating a biscuit when her mother spoke to her. Jane looked up, smiled, and began to go over her range of noises. With mother's help she pulled herself up to standing, and they played for a while. Then mother and the observer began talking, not attending closely to Jane, who continued playing for a short time, then began making noises at her mother, mainly ba-ba-ba and a growling noise she had copied from father. Mother responded by talking to her and they both laughed. By 11½ months Jane enjoyed looking at books with mother, and waited expectantly for mother to name the objects pictured. Jane was attempting words herself like Mummy, doggy. Her mother was delighted with such efforts and liked to show them off to the observer; e.g., at 12 months mother told the observer to watch, then said softly to Jane, "Who's my lovely little girl, then?" Jane made a noise very like "lovely girl," and both were delighted.

Mary provides another example. As early as 19 weeks when left alone with the observer, she became quiet and looked puzzled at first, then smiled and began to "chatter" with pauses as if waiting for a response, i.e., reproducing "conversation" with mother.

By 6 months, Mary seemed to be firmly in stage 3, able to amuse herself alone in her cot, playing and babbling for long periods. Her mother's voice could reassure her at a distance at 8 months; e.g., when the observer arrived, Mary crawled to greet her and pulled herself up on the observer's knees. First she smiled, then stared unsmiling for a few seconds. Suddenly she squealed and looked back for her mother, as if worried about being with someone different. Mother spoke to her, and Mary was immediately reassured.

Richard, like Mary, could comfort and entertain himself with vocal noises when alone. At 8 months Richard was beginning to seek attention with looks and noises. He made sounds which his mother would imitate. Sometimes his own noises served to bridge the gap before the object came to him, as when he woke at 5 a.m. and "talked" to himself for an hour and a half until his father took him. Yet 3 weeks later, at 9 months, he was no longer satisfied to entertain himself in this way, but screamed until his mother came.

John shows a range of interchanges using vocal sounds. At 6 months he responded with sounds, smiles, and eye contact when his mother played and talked with him. When she put him in his baby-bouncer and continued to talk to him, he bounced and pirouetted. But when she moved away and broke off this direct contact, John became subdued even though he could still see and hear her. At 9½ months with encouragement from mother he waved good-bye in response to the observer's parting wave, and mother at this time said he was imitating actions though not sounds. At 11 months he used the sound "mamama" in demanding food or drink, crawling after mother as she prepared his food. He also said "dadada" in response to men. He understood pat-a-cake, clapping his hands when he heard the word. At 12 months he used a pleasant-sounding inflected babble about things he enjoyed, e.g., when looking at his brightly colored birthday cards. By this age he would also dance and sing to music. The dancing was a gentle, controlled, rhythmic up-and-down rocking, and the singing was clear, high-pitched sounds, a drawn-out vowel somewhere between *oo* and *a* with little tonal variation.

STAGE 4

Once the infant has discovered the value of vocalization as a way of communicating wishes and interests to the object, he moves from using his own idiosyncratic sounds to learning the language conventions of his family.

In stage 4, the child's actual vocabulary is still relatively small, but his understanding is far ahead of his ability to use words and sentences. Bloom (1974) accounts for this in terms of the child's ability to use other contextual information in addition to language. Like Call, we would stress the importance of receptive language during this period when the child is internalizing the language of others, in a process which contributes not only to his ego functioning but also to his object representations and thus to his capacity for internalized relationships.

Sheridan's norms suggest that at 12 months the infant's behavior shows that he understands familiar words in context such as family names, walk, dinner, pussy; and he comprehends and obeys simple commands accompanied with gestures. He listens with obvious pleasure to sound, and repeats adult's playful vocalizations with gleeful enthusiasm. At 15 months he is using a wide range of inflections and phonetic units, can say 2 to 6 recognizable words, but understands many more. He points to things he wishes to be given as well as in response to adult requests: "where" or "who." At 18 months he echoes prominent words; pointing at desired objects is accompanied by urgent vocalization. He tries to sing and join in nursery rhymes. By 2 years he has a vocabulary of 50 or more recognizable words and can form simple sentences.

Bruner notes that around 15 months the child can stop his own actions by saying "No, No," e.g., as he approaches a forbidden object. Our own observations suggest that at this age the child still requires the presence of the object to reinforce the "No," because the superego precursor is still very tentative at this stage. The child may also use "No" to comment on something that is gone, or something he has failed to do. Eventually he learns to say "No" to the verbal offer of things he does not want.

We summarize stage 4 thus: increasing linkage of words and inner experience allows words to help the process of differentiation among feelings and experiences as well as among objects, in addition to indicating wishes and interests to the object. The child's understanding of language is ahead of his own use of it, but he enjoys imitating the adults' words and vocalizations. He asks names of things. The separation-individuation process is facilitated by the use of language to help internalize the caring and controlling aspects of the object. Words begin to serve as explanation and reassurance when used by the mother. The adult's words begin to convey commands and prohibitions with which the child can comply as ego development proceeds, and which are gradually internalized in superego formation. The child may be able to comply with complex instructions, though his own use of words is still minimal.

An example of the child's understanding of language being ahead of his own use of it, and of the object's words serving as explanation, was seen in John at age 2¼ years. In the toddler group John was working with concentration on a puzzle, trying to fit the pieces into the spaces. His mother complained to the observer, "You should see him at home; he never plays like this, he throws everything about." The group leader asked, "John, what goes wrong at home? Are you just angry or fed up?" She did not expect an answer and was surprised when he said, "fed-up" and repeated the word a few times. His mother smiled and said she was the one who was angry because the house was such a mess. Here the observer's words seemed to have made a meaningful link to inner experience for both John and his mother.

We have a number of examples of the beginning of compliance with the object's verbal commands.

At 11½ months mother's "No" was sometimes effective in controlling John's behavior; e.g., he would reach for the catfood, she would say "No," and he would withdraw. But the effect lasted only for a moment; when the "No" was repeated, he resumed his activity. At other times he took no notice at all of mother's "No." At 2 years and 1 month in the toddler group John's mother read him a book about toilet training. In response to the picture about a little boy who made a B.M. on the floor instead of in the pot, John said, "A naughty boy." When he saw the picture of the boy who learned to "poo" in the pot, he said, "He's a very good boy." When mother finished reading, he smiled and jumped up and down happily. He grabbed the book, wanted it read again, and wanted to take it home with him.

Richard also ignored "No" from mother, who thought he understood it at 12 months along with much that was said to him. At 13 months he was using certain sounds quite specifically: *Mu* for mother, *da* for something he was pointing at, *ca* for cat, *do* for dog. He was observed to follow a two-step direction: when mother told him to get a cup and take it to grandmother, he did so immediately.

Mary's repertoire and range of use of expressive noises increased as she moved into stage 4. She began to copy her mother's words, e.g., da-da-da, and responded to spoken requests, e.g., "clap hands" at 11½ months. Play was accompanied with appropriate noises, e.g., "bam bam bam," while patting and tearing newspapers, and at 12 months, "bloom bloom" as she approached a peg and hammer toy, preparatory to banging it. At 13 months she held a toy telephone receiver to her ear and chattered to it. At this time she was also beginning to understand prohibitions; e.g., at 12 months she crawled to a table, pulled herself to standing, and reached for a picture frame. Mother said "No." Mary stopped but kept her hand there. Mother repeated "No." Mary looked sideways at the au pair who shook her head. Mary burst into tears, sat down, and reached for mother who picked her up and cuddled her, but it took some time to calm her. One month later, when she similarly made for the picture and mother said "No," Mary moved away and found a toy to play with. A typical game helping her establish an inner image of mother was seen at 13½ months. Mother was cuddling a fluffy bunny toy, which she handed to Mary saying, "Mary do it." Mary handed it to the au pair, who cuddled it, then back to mother, who cuddled it again. Finally Mary cuddled it, saying, "Aaah."

Anna could use words combined with action to demonstrate her jealousy of her brother and possessiveness of mother; e.g., at 24 months, whenever her brother touched their mother, Anna would run to her mother's lap, saying, "Anna" in a complaining tone. At this age she would comply with simple commands from mother, e.g., "You go and pick it up" after Anna had thrown toys about in a game. She also played at driving away in a toy car, saying "bye-bye."

STAGE 5

In stage 5, the child begins to take over familiar phrases of his mother as part of the process of internalizing her caring as well as controlling functions, and occasionally he can substitute words for action, as he becomes able to communicate verbally a widening range of experiences and ideas.

Sheridan says that a 2½ years the child uses 200 or more recognizable words, but speech shows numerous infantilisms. He knows his full name. He talks intelligibly to himself at play concerning events happening here and now. Echolalia persists. He is continually asking questions beginning "what" and "where." He uses plurals and pronouns: I, we, you. He says a few nursery rhymes, and enjoys simple familiar stories read from a picture book. Stuttering in eagerness is common.

At 3 years he has a large intelligible vocabulary, but speech still shows many infantile phonetic substitutions. He still talks to himself in long monologues mostly concerned with the immediate present, including make-believe activities. He carries on simple conversations and verbalizes past experiences. He listens eagerly to stories and demands favorites over and over again. He knows several nursery rhymes. Villiers and Villiers state that as children grow older, they become less dependent on context in producing and understanding language. By age 3 they can make reference to absent persons and events.

In summary: in stage 5, gestures, words, and other vocalizations are used to communicate increasingly complex ideas and experiences and to ask questions as well as to express feeling and attract the object. Words may be used independently of action. At times verbal communication begins to substitute for other forms of interaction between child and mother. Internalized concepts help to sustain the relationship during separation, and words may help the child to recall the image of the absent object. The child begins to use words learned from the object as a means of reassuring and explaining to himself and as a means of reinforcing demands and prohibitions taken over from the object in the beginning of superego formation.

A few examples of children's communication of varied experiences and ideas:

At 2⅓ years, on a sunny but very windy day, John listened to his mother telling the observer they had spent the morning in the park. Excited and eager to join in, he added, "and the sun blowed."

At 27 months Anna used the word "mine" a great deal, and this shifted from indicating possessiveness to becoming a teasing game with other children. At the same age when mother gave her water to drink, Anna pushed it away and said, "Orange juice."

At 30 months Anna was playing happily in the toddler group, enjoying many different activities. At one point, suspecting she needed to go to the lavatory, her mother picked her up and carried her off abruptly. She protested wildly. On her return the observer commented that her mother seemed cross. Anna, in an indignant tone, said, "Anna cross." She continued attempting an explanation, succeeding in conveying to the observer that she did not like to do "kaka" in the toilet.

At 24 months John was apparently absorbed in play while his mother talked to the observer. His mother said she would like to *train* as a child therapist. John looked up and said, "Choo-choo. Nellie on the *train*." His mother understood that *train* reminded him of a train trip he had enjoyed recently with a friend called Nellie.

At 22 months in the toddler group Sara did a puzzle with the observer, and named the pieces: house, boy, girl, cat, dog, mouse. The observer, making up a story about them, said, "The boy has a dog." Sara answered, "And the girl has a cat *and* a mouse." Sara has a book called "Thomas," and was puzzled to meet a boy called Thomas in the group. She commented that her book was "real Thomas." At 23 months Sara was playing at the sink and her mother offered her a towel. Sara said, "Yes, I'd like that turquoise one."

Jane provides a good example of the taking over of mother's reassuring or helping words. At 15 months she would say "oh dear" when something went wrong, e.g., when she dropped something. She had taken this over from her mother who used to say "Oh dear" when rescuing Jane from predicaments; that is, Jane was using words to reassure herself. She also seemed to be expressing awareness of connections; e.g., when being washed and dressed, she said what sounded like "Daddy's dressing gown." By 17 months she could verbally draw attention to things she saw; e.g., she said "birdie" when through the window she saw two birds fighting, and thus drew the adult's attention to the scene with a word rather than a gesture.

At 18 months all kinds of comments were appearing, e.g., "hot" when her mother gave the observer a cup of tea.

At 19 months many uses of language were heard within one hour:

1. To convey experience: Jane said "Ruth" and something the observer could not understand. Mother explained they spent the morning with Ruth. Jane several times mentioned Ruth as if the visit was still in her mind.

2. To seek help: while climbing off a chair she got her foot stuck and said, "Uck, uck."
3. To accompany action: saying "vroom, vroom" while running a bus along the floor.
4. To comment on a predicament for which she needed help: she was trying to get the lid off a tin and it stuck; Jane said, "Oh my God."
5. To make requests: Jane, mother, and observer had sung a nursery rhyme; Jane then said, "More."

The Range of Individual Differences

It is apparent that there are very wide variations in the rate at which individual children proceed through the stages of language development. This raises the question of the relative importance of endowment and environment in determining the rate of development. At present we can neither assess the role played by each factor nor give norms for the entry to each stage. We can only stress how wide the range is.

To illustrate differences in the rate at which different infants progress through these early stages of language development, the vicissitudes of development in three individuals will be described.

1. Edward B. is the third son of a woman who was depressed during his infancy, anxious about her ambivalence to her children, often rather withdrawn. During the early feeding she did not hold the baby close, and did not attempt to maintain eye contact with him. He was a placid baby, apart from a "colicky" phase which temporarily upset his feeding and sleeping routines. He did not gaze at his mother. Mrs. B. rarely talked to him while ministering to his needs, and no "conversational" babbling developed between them. After the introduction of solids at 4½ months, feeding seemed to become smoother, a more pleasurable experience to Mrs. B., who now talked lovingly to Edward after feedings while winding him.

Edward's motor development seemed the main promoter of contact and communication. As he became able to control his head movements and prop himself up on his arms, he watched people and things more intently. He showed pleasure by moving his limbs and mouthing objects rather than by vocalizing.

Around 5 to 6 months Edward began waking and crying at night, and was often grizzly and fussy in the afternoons and evenings. His mother would go to him when he grizzled, cried, or screamed, but did not respond to other vocalizations, which in any case remained minimal. At 7 months Edward was able to sit up, and at this time he became more contented, gaining pleasure from looking around him. But vocalization remained limited to crying or grizzling. If the observer tried to attract Edward's attention, he would respond with smiles but no vocalizations. At 8 months he was able to crawl, and became much more active, including managing his first steps holding on to furniture. He took great pleasure in activity, moving, grasping objects, handling and mouthing them. His mother seemed to enjoy and play with him more as he became more active. At 9 months he imitated his mother's play with toys, but there was still no imitation of her vocalizations, and little spontaneous vocalization.

Throughout this period Edward did not consolidate his language development in stage 1 and showed no signs of moving to stage 2. It seemed that vocal communication was of no value in the relationship with his mother, who did not talk much to him or respond to and reinforce his own vocalizations, while Edward may have had a constitutional preference for action rather than talk. The first sign that he might be moving into stage 2 came at 9 months when Edward began making noises of pleasure in response to eating. Around 10 or 11 months he was weaned from the bottle, which he resisted, and concurrently his vocalizations became much richer.

He was now able to indicate his wishes with gestures. When mother put him down, Edward showed his wish to be picked up by lifting his arms, pulling on his mother's clothes, but still without sounds until he sat down and cried in frustration. At this time mother was proud that Edward could understand instructions; e.g., as he approached a toy chest and mother said, "Open the latch first," reinforcing her words with gestures. Edward opened the latch before lifting the lid. He appeared capable of phase-4 achievements of understanding his mother, but the communication remained one-sided with his own language lagging behind, barely into stage 2, and Mrs. B. still showed little wish to share spoken communication with Edward.

At 13 to 14 months Edward used the word "Mama" over and over while playing, but without any clear reference to his mother. By now he would imitate words such as "Bye-bye" on being taken to bed. He had already been imitating a farewell wave for 3 months or more. He would hit his mother or father if they limited him either physically or verbally, but did not accompany this action with vocalizations that would be appropriate to stage 4.

The observer noticed that the parents sometimes misread the verbal sign Edward did give. Once with single-minded determination Edward was trying to put a large, cumbersome broom into a box behind a chair; he accompanied his activity with a repetitive sound, "Na na na." The observer thought Edward was enjoying the challenge, but the parents thought he was tired and frustrated and put him to bed. At 15 months in the toddler group Edward enjoyed going down the slide with the help of the group leader and asked her for a repetition of the game with arm gestures and the same urgent "Na na na" sound.

At this age he would also imitate adults in the toddler group, e.g., "hello" when playing with the toy telephone with a group leader. When he wanted her to put the phone on the floor, he gestured and said "down" quite clearly.

At 17 months his mother complained of his still indiscriminate use of "mummy" to people in general. Edward did indeed address the (male) observer as "mummy" when he sought help in picking up two balls at once. But when he addressed his mother as "mummy," she gave neither verbal nor nonverbal recognition that the name referred to her, i.e., giving him no help to develop a name specific to her. Similarly, when Edward appropriately said "Bye-bye" to an older brother who was leaving for school, his mother did not reinforce his use of the word by any kind of recognition of it as a meaningful utterance. By this time Mrs. B. was talking a good deal of her worry about Edward's slow speech development, yet all observers noted that she continued to ignore his vocalizations. Mr. B. dismissed his wife's anxieties, saying, "Eddy is a doer." The observer felt Edward was ready to speak by now; e.g., during one visit Edward offered a number of long incomprehensible vocalizations accompanied by rich gestural signs. Edward responded to the observer's interest and to his remarks so that the interchange had many features of a dialogue. At 18 months the observer heard Edward correctly use: there, here, dada, mama, and ta, but still without mother's reinforcing or attempting to elicit his words.

Edward, whose first tentative move into stage 2 came at 9 months, and who was not established in stage 4 at 15 months, contrasts markedly with some of the children already described, who were moving into stage 2 as early as 2½ or 3 months, into stage 3 by 8 or 9 months, and stage 4 around their first birthday.

2. Simon, by contrast, was the child of a mother who valued speech, and attended closely to Simon's language. She claimed that he said his first word, "cat," at 7 months. Her high expectations are indicated by her reply to a compliment on Simon's speech at 19 months: "He does not yet string three words together accurately."

By 15½ months Simon was already using vocalization to express his interest and excitement in a picture he recognized when he visited the well-baby clinic. When he saw the picture, he babbled excitedly (stage 3). Three months later, at 18½ months, he used a word to indicate a wish to repeat an experience he remembered from an earlier visit: in the well-baby clinic Simon stood in the middle of the room and said "Jacques" several times. It was some time before the adults realized he was asking for the musical box which plays "Frère Jacques." This use of language to communicate complex inner experience (wish linked with memory) belongs to stage 5. Much of Simon's functioning at the time was still at stage 4; e.g., at 19½ months, enjoying teatime in the toddler group, Simon repeatedly dunked his biscuit, saying with pleasure, "Bicky, bicky." When he played with the Lego pieces, he said "naughty" each time the door broke off. The observer thought he was telling off the door rather than reproving himself.

Simon shows the importance of parental reinforcement of speech development; e.g., at 22 months he listened to his mother's verbalizations about his play and repeated part of her sentences. At 22½ months he listened as she described his strides in language development. She said he knew all the colors, and he responded to the word "colors" by saying, "Red, blue, green, yellow."

By this age he was firmly in stage 5, using words and complete sentences to issue commands to his objects, to indicate remembering, and to express wishes. At 22½ months he ordered, "Mummy take doll." At 23 months, when he was stuck in the toy car, he said, "Simon out." At 26 months after having had a plain biscuit at teatime, he asked for another, "A chocky biscuit." Mother explained he always remembered once having eaten a chocolate biscuit in the group. At 26½ months when he was without his mother for the first time at the tea table, Simon asked another adult for extra food, saying, "More drink, more biscuit."

3. Charlotte L. provides an example of regression on the developmental line of language and illustrates the close dependence of language on the mother-child relationship. She is another child whose mother highly values speech. They joined the toddler group at 19 months, and Charlotte was not a happy-looking child, so special note was made at 21 months when Charlotte and her mother looked happy and affectionate together while mother was asking for words and Charlotte replied. Charlotte was able to separate easily from mother, and used speech to maintain contact. She would say "mummy" and, once she was shown where her mother was, she could go on playing. The toddler group staff noted that Mrs. L. understood Charlotte well, even when her speech was unclear, perhaps due to speaking two languages. Language enabled them to have "a long-distance relationship," and the

staff thought this was more comfortable for them than a close one. Charlotte used gesture as well as words to communicate, pulling and pointing to show what she wanted. Mrs. L. could use words to control Charlotte; e.g., at 20 months Charlotte was screaming one day because she did not want to go home. Mother whispered something to her and she was quiet. Asked what her secret formula was, mother laughed and said she had promised Charlotte some ice cream if she left quietly.

Charlotte was thus functioning at stage 4 well before her second birthday. But Mrs. L. had another baby when Charlotte was 30 months old. By 32 months both mother and the toddler group staff were concerned about Charlotte's speech which had become unintelligible, a kind of indistinct baby babbling, perhaps in identification with the new rival for mother's attention, perhaps because Charlotte recognized that indistinct speech was a sure way of gaining mother's anxious attention. Charlotte's ambivalent reactions to the new baby were evident at 31 months. During a visit to the toddler group she would run every few minutes to the pram and press her face to Margaret's, saying, "Baby" to their mother. Her mother had to remind her to be gentle. Charlotte tried to make Margaret smile by pressing her face against the baby's and saying "Gooo." She did this repeatedly, seeing that her mother seemed to approve of it. Charlotte would play only with her mother on this day, not allowing observers to share her games. It seemed to be only the mechanics of Charlotte's speech that suffered. Her desire to communicate remained on its previous high level so that she became frustrated when she could not make herself understood.

DISCUSSION

Like all developmental lines (Anna Freud, 1965), the line for language involves the interaction of several areas of psychic development, and I have tried to trace these interactions in this paper. I have done this only for the earliest stages, so that the line is not yet complete; but I thought it worthwhile first to concentrate in some detail on the early stages about which relatively little was known until recently, and which current research shows to be vital in laying the foundations for later stages.

Our observations indicate, as do other studies, that verbal language emerges out of a range of interlinked prelinguistic modes of communication which include facial expression, eye contact, gesture and tactile contact as well as vocal expressions. We know that normal speech development can be delayed by the continued use of "baby language" or "private" mother-child language beyond the time when the child is ready to begin using conventional language; or by anticipating all the child's needs and wishes to such an extent that he is deprived of the external frustrations which normally act as motives complementary to the inner urges toward communication. We would also now stress, as Call does, that facilitation of the early modes of communication in the first months of life promotes language development. Parents who fail to respond to the nonverbal communications of their infants, or to the child's idiosyncratic verbalizations which do not conform to adult language conventions, discourage the child's active urge to communicate and hinder progression to "proper" speech. In other words, speech development can be hindered as much by parental discouragement of prelinguistic communication as by excessive infantilizing of the child.

The relative weight to be attributed to maturation and environment is an area that still requires further study of normal development as well as of pathology. We have not yet systematically studied the area of language pathology, although we have inevitably been influenced in our discussions by familiarity with one or another form of speech disorder or disturbance in the use of language which individual therapists have encountered in their clinical work with patients or in other research groups. The importance of visual contact in the early development of mother-child communication is demonstrated, for example, in the language difficulties of blind children (Fraiberg and Adelson, 1973; Wills, 1979). Closer scrutiny of studies of handicapped children would doubtless contribute further to our understanding of the role in language development of various capacities of the child, by examining the result of the absence of such capacities. It would be similarly relevant to study the effects on the child's language development of handicaps such as deafness in the parents, and of parental pathology such as depression in the mother during the infant's early months.

We have centered our interest on the interactions of structural development and developing object relationships with language development, and have not specifically placed language within the context of the developing capacity for using symbolic representation, always an area of special interest to psychoanalysts.

Ferenczi (1913) stressed that the capacity for symbolic representation is an important completion of the child's gestural language. Ferenczi's period of magical gestures probably coincides with our stage 2, and the transition from our stage 2 to stage 3 would be the point of which Ferenczi says: when the "outstretched hand must ... be drawn back empty, [when] the longed-for object does not follow the magic gesture," the child must submit further to external reality to the extent that his wishes become more complicated (p. 226). We may say that recognition of the value of speech sounds for influencing external events coincides with the child's discovery that he is not omnipotent. The formulation and expression of wishes become increasingly sophisticated as the child progresses through these early stages of language development, and language becomes an important means of achieving gratification once ego development has proceeded far enough for the child to recognize that wishing is not enough, that he must influence people around him to give him what he wants or to teach him how to do it for himself. Achieving gratification of wishes via interaction with the object is thus an important motive for language development, a motive which is lost or diminished if the object is unresponsive, or if the child's perceptual-cognitive capacities are damaged.

In this paper I have particularly stressed the role of the mother-child interaction in promoting structural development in general and language development in particular. This is not to underrate the importance of innate and maturational factors in ego development. We have elsewhere (Burgner and Edgcumbe, 1972) stressed, for example, the importance of Piaget's (1936, 1937) work on the stages of perceptual-cognitive development in the establishment of the object concept. The capacity to recall an organized perceptual representation of an object that is no longer in view makes its first tentative appearance at about 5 months and is a prerequisite for our stage 3. But it takes about another year before the capacity is firmly enough established for the child to summon up the object image for purely internal reasons, i.e., not requiring an external stimulus such as the disappearance of the object. Without this capacity the child cannot reach stage 5, in which the object's words, linked with an inner object representation, can be used by the child both to reassure himself and to reinforce the object's demands and prohibitions in the absence of the object, precursors of the internalization of caring and superego aspects of the object (see also Balkányi, 1964).

I have not discussed in any detail the role of drives in language development, and it is perhaps appropriate to remind ourselves that drive derivatives provide a large proportion of the wishes which serve to motivate language development. Most of the children we have observed progress through at least the first three stages of language development during the oral phase of drive development. Many go through phases 4 and 5 while they are in the anal phase, and we have some observations (not included in this paper) which deserve to be the object of a study on the role of anal-sadistic battling with mother in the arrest or regression of language development. Also requiring investigation is the question of when language becomes independent of the mother-child relationship, and whether this might be linked to the achievement of dominance on the phallic-oedipal level, in the same way that the equation of food and mother fades out in the oedipal period (Anna Freud).

SUMMARY

I have described five early stages of language development in the context of the early mother-child relationship, stressing the importance of prelinguistic communication for the later establishment of language. In stage 1, the infant's inborn means of attracting his mother's attention elicit her responses. These reinforce the baby's noises and gestures, which, in stage 2, develop into a range of noises and gestures linked with specific inner experiences and external perceptions as structural development proceeds and the beginnings of an inner representational world is built up. In stage 3, the child becomes aware of the value of vocalizing in influencing the behavior of people in the external world, and begins to use vocalization, gesture, and expression with intent to indicate wishes and obtain their gratification as well as to communicate inner experiences and interests in the external world. At first his understanding of language far outstrips his use of it, so that in stage 4 mother's words can serve as explanation and reassurance to the child, and can convey instructions. In stage 5, he can use words learned from the object to comfort and reassure himself as well to help himself comply with parental demands.

BIBLIOGRAPHY

Ainsworth, M. D., Bell, S. M., & Stayton, D. J. (1974), Infant-mother attachment and social development. In: *The Integration of a Child into a Social World*, ed. P. M. Richards. Cambridge: Cambridge Univ. Press, pp. 99–135.
Balkányi, C. (1964), On verbalisation. *Int. J. Psychoanal.*, 45:64–74.
Bloom, L. M. (1974), Talking, understanding and thinking. In: *Language Perspectives*, ed. R. L. Schiefelbusch & L. L. Lloyd. Baltimore: University Park Press, pp. 285–311.
Broucek, F. (1979), Efficacy in infancy. *Int. J. Psychoanal.*, 60:311–316.
Bruner, J. S. (1978), Learning how to do things with words. In: *Human Growth and Development*, ed. J. S. Bruner & A. Garton. Oxford: Clarendon Press, pp. 62–84.
Burgner, M. & Edgcumbe, R. (1972), Some problems in the conceptualization of early object relationships: Part II. *Psychoanal. Study Child*, 27:315–333.
Buxbaum, E. (1964), The parents' role in the etiology of learning disabilities. *Psychoanal. Study Child*, 19:421–447.
Call, J. D. (1980), Some prelinguistic aspects of language development. *J. Amer. Psychoanal. Assn.*, 28:259–289.
Chomsky, N. (1965), *Aspects of the Theory of Syntax*. Cambridge, Mass.: M.I.T. Press.
Clark, E. V. (1978), From gesture to word. In: *Human Growth and Development*, ed. J. S. Bruner & A. Garton. Oxford: Clarendon Press, pp. 85–120.
Edgcumbe, R. (1975), The border between therapy and education. In: *Studies in Child Psychoanalysis*. New Haven & London: Yale University Press, pp. 133–147.
———— & Burgner, M. (1972), Some problems in the conceptualization of early object relationships: Part I. *Psychoanal. Study Child*, 27:283–314.
Escalona, S. K. (1963), Patterns of infantile experience and the developmental process. *Psychoanal. Study Child*, 18:197–244.
Ferenczi, S. (1913), Stages in the development of the sense of reality. In: *Sex in Psychoanalysis*. New York: Basic Books, 1950, pp. 213–239.
Fillmore, C. J. (1968), The case for case. In: *Universals in Linguistic Theory*, ed. E. Bach & E. T. Harmes. New York: Holt, Rinehart & Winston, pp. 1–90.
Fraiberg, S. & Adelson, E. (1973), Self-representation in language and play. *Psychoanal. Quart.*, 42:539–562.
Freud, A. (1965), *Normality and Pathology in Childhood*. New York: Int. Univ. Press.

FURMAN, E. (1976), Commentary in Klaus and Kennel (1976), p. 52.

GREENACRE, P. (1960), Considerations regarding the parent-infant relationship. *Int. J. Psychoanal.,* 41:571–584.

HODGES, J. (1980), The use of observation in the Hampstead Clinic Nursery School: V. *Bull. Hampstead Clin.,* 3:42–47.

KATAN, A. (1961), Some thoughts about the role of verbalization in early childhood. *Psychoanal. Study Child,* 16:184–188.

KLAUS, M. H. & KENNELL, J. H. (1976), *Maternal-Infant Bonding.* St. Louis: Mosby.

LITOWITZ, B. E. & LITOWITZ, N. S. (1977), The influence of linguistic theory on psychoanalysis. *Int. Rev. Psychoanal.,* 4:419–448.

LOCK, A. (1980), Language development. *Bull. Brit. Psychol. Soc.,* 33:5–8.

MORAN, G. (1980), The use of observation in the Hampstead Clinic Nursery School: IV. *Bull. Hampstead Clin.,* 3:38–42.

MAHLER, M. S., PINE, F., & BERGMAN, A. (1975), *The Psychological Birth of the Human Infant.* New York: Basic Books.

MEISSNER, W. W. (1979), Internalization and object relations. *J. Amer. Psychoanal. Assn.,* 27:345–360.

PANEL (1980), New knowledge about the infant from current research. L. Sander, reporter. *J. Amer. Psychoanal. Assn.,* 28:181–198.

PETERFREUND, E. (1978), Some critical comments on psychoanalytic conceptualizations of infancy. *Int. J. Psychoanal.,* 59:427–441.

PIAGET, J. (1936), *The Origins of Intelligence in Children.* New York: Int. Univ. Press, 1952.

———— (1937), *The Construction of Reality in the Child.* New York: Basic Books, 1954.

SANDLER, J. & ROSENBLATT, B. (1962), The concept of the representational world. *Psychoanal. Study Child,* 17:128–145.

SARNOFF, C. (1976), *Latency.* New York: Jason Aronson.

SHERIDAN, M. D. (1960), *The Developmental Progress of Infants and Young Children.* London: H. M. Stationery Office.

SHOPPER, M. (1978), The role of audition in early psychic development. *J. Amer. Psychoanal. Assn.,* 26:283–310.

SNOW, C. E. (1972), Mothers' speech to children learning language. *Child Develpm.,* 43:549–565.

SPITZ, R. A. (1957), *No and Yes.* New York: Int. Univ. Press.

STEINER, G. (1976), A note on language and psychoanalysis. *Int. Rev. Psychoanal.,* 3:253–258.

TREVARTHEN, C. & GRANT, F. (1979), Not work alone. *New Scientist,* 81:566–569.

VILLIERS, J. C. DE & VILLIERS, P. A. DE (1978), *Language Acquisition.* Cambridge: Harvard Univ. Press.

VYGOTSKY, L. S. (1966), Development of the higher mental functions. In: *Psychological Research in the U.S.S.R.* Moscow: Progress Publishers.

WILLS, D. M. (1979), Early speech development in blind children. *Psychoanal. Study Child,* 34:85–117.

Speech, Language, and the Vocal-Auditory Connection

DAVID A. FREEDMAN, M.D.

A DISTINCTION BETWEEN THE THREE INTIMATELY RELATED BUT nonetheless separable phenomena—speech, language, and the vocal-auditory connection—has implications for the understanding of early human development. I intend to consider both the fact that each is unique and distinctive, and the propensity, to which as psychoanalysts we are particularly vulnerable, to assume they are inextricably interwined. That the availability of speech does not necessarily imply the ability to use language is clearly demonstrated by the prowess of the parrot and mynnah bird and, in the human, the phenomenon of echolalia. Conversely, that absence of speech does not preclude the ability to use language—i.e., to communicate through the medium of a convention of mutually accepted and understood signs and symbols—is equally convincingly proven by that segment of the deaf population who are given the opportunity to learn to sign. While an intact vocal-auditory system is a necessary condition for the development of oral speech, it is only a particularly convenient medium through which language and communication can occur. It seems to me that a further consideration of the implica-

Professor of Psychiatry at Baylor College of Medicine; Training and Supervising Analyst in the Houston-Galveston Psychoanalytic Institute, Houston, Texas.
An earlier version of this paper was read at the 11th Annual Margaret Mahler Symposium, Philadelphia, May 17, 1980.

tions of these two contrasting conditions—speech without language and language without speech—may be useful.

A review of the conceptual problems encountered by psychoanalytic writers who have studied echolalia is illustrative. As a result of the repeated observation of their coincidence, there is agreement that a relation must obtain between the persistence of echoic speech and major disturbances in the ability to enter into object relations. The general position is well represented by Griffith and Ritvo (1967) who conceive of their subject Beth's echolalia "as engaging her with the continuous interplay between self and nonself, the internal and external worlds. . . her ego is fixated at a rudimentary stage where the process of the development of object relationships obtains" (p. 189). Ekstein and Caruth (1969) in a slightly more conservative vein postulate, "Before the acceptance of the object and the emergence of the concept of self, we have an example of the original struggle between impulse and delay carried out on a primitive level" (p. 132). Ekstein (1965) also has suggested that echolalia might profitably be viewed as an auditory substitute for the transitional object.

Implicit in these hypotheses are several assumptions concerning early development which seem to me to merit closer examination. What, for example, is the matrix in which a struggle between impulse and delay can occur before the emergence of a self with motivational characteristics? How did Beth acquire the awareness of self which allowed her to differentiate between her self and a nonself—not to mention an internal and external world? What are the sources of her motivation to engage in an interplay between self and nonself? What are the origins of and the nature of the object attachment in relation to which echolalia is serving as a transitional phenomenon? Given the premise that echolalia is the expression of a primitive and distorted form of object relatedness and involves some form of communication, how can we account for the remarkable propensity of echolalic children to reproduce the sounds and forms of foreign languages under circumstances in which no possibility of communication exists? I refer to instances such as Burlingham's (1964) description of a psychotic blind child, reared in an exclusively English-speaking environment, who repeated conversation in Danish, which, it turned out, she had overheard through a wall, and my own report (1977) of the reproduction of clear unmistakable Yiddish by another autistic blind boy, the child of a monolingual English-speaking family.

It seems to me that faced with such questions, most authors have postulated the operation of significant inborn psychic abilities. One assumes already present drives and degrees of structural differentiation which allow the psychoanalytic investigator to get a foothold, so to speak, a starting point from which he can begin to make use of a dynamic developmental theory. I wish to propose an alternative possibility. Rather than attempt, as I believe the tendency has been, to explain such phenomena as echolalia and the psychological development of the congenitally deaf on the basis of established hypotheses, I shall take the position that they are best regarded as natural experiments which can serve as the basis for testing the validity of a number of generally held postulates concerning early maturation and development. In this approach, I shall be following the precedent of William Harvey (1651) who wrote:

> Nature is nowhere accustomed more openly to display her secret mysteries than in cases where she shows traces of her workings apart from the beaten path; nor is there any better way to advance the proper practice of medicine than to give our minds to the discovery of the usual law of nature by careful investigation of rarer forms of disease. For it has been found, in almost all things that what they contain of useful or applicable nature is hardly perceived unless we are deprived of them or they become deranged in some way.

I shall also make use of some data which may seem remote from the ordinary sphere of psychoanalytic discourse. It is my opinion that the observer of infants and small children must take into account the tissue changes which are going on in the central nervous system during the early postpartum years. More specifically, he must attempt, when assessing the psychological implications of infantile behavior, to consider *what is possible* for the baby at any given point in development. I shall limit my remarks in this regard to some comments on the timetable for myelin deposition.

Figure 1 summarizes the findings of Yakovlev and Lecours (1967) concerning that process. Obviously the presence of

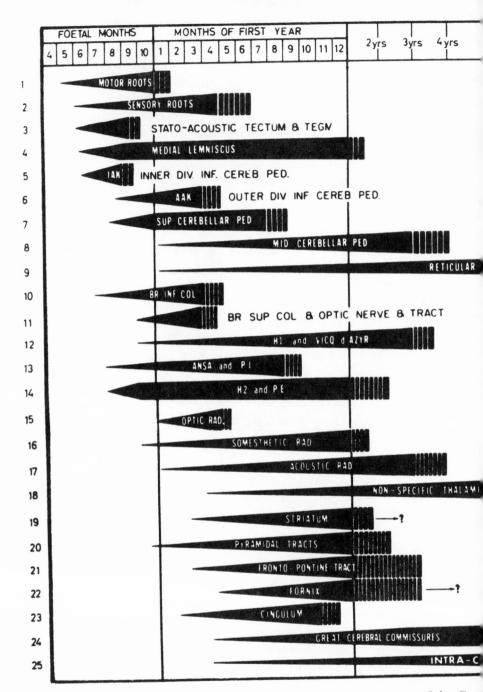

Figure 1. Timetable for Myelin Deposition in Indicated Tracts of the Cere

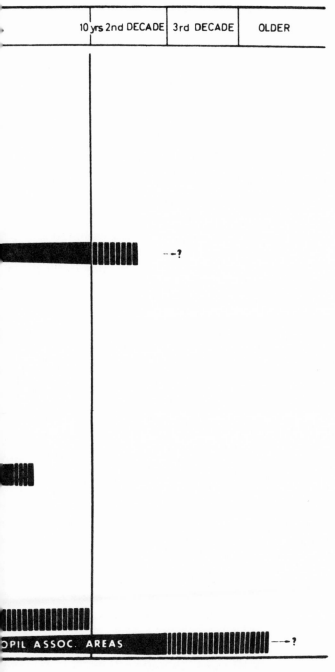

	10 yrs 2nd DECADE	3rd DECADE	OLDER

From Yakovlev and Lecours (1967)
Reprinted with permission of Blackwell Scientific
Publications, Oxford, England.

myelin in a system does not provide a sufficient basis for its ability to function. The evidence of the demyelinating diseases, however, makes it clear that adequate myelinization is a necessary precondition if a given neural pathway is to have the potentiality to function. From this perspective the pattern of deposition illustrated by this figure seems to me to have enormous implications. It can, for example, be regarded as consistent with Glover's (1932) assumption of the beginnings of psychic structure formation in a series of ego nuclei which do not become functional all at once. Of more immediate interest is the time sequence according to which the elements of the visual and auditory systems become available. These are represented in the figure by bars 3, 11, 15, and 17, with 11 and 15 representing the brainstem and cerebral (optic radiations) projection of the visual system. By the time the infant is 5 months old, the visual system is fully myelinated and therefore potentially fully functional. Reinecke (1979), an ophthalmologist, has asserted that visual function in the human achieves approximately adult capacity by 6 months of age.

This can be compared with bars 3 and 17. Bar 3 represents the timing of myelin deposition in the statoacoustical system, i.e., the brainstem system to which may be assigned, among other functions, the mediating of acoustically initiated reflexive behavior. Obviously it is highly improbable that this system can subserve such representational functions as are implied by the capacity for cognition and the establishment of object ties. It is fully myelinated before birth. By contrast, bar 17, which represents myelin deposition in the acoustic radiations, indicates that the process does not have its inception until birth and that it continues gradually enough so that it is not complete until the beginning of the fourth year. Is it, one wonders, entirely happenstance that the completion of these two maturational sequences coincide so closely with the completion of the symbiotic and separation-individuation phases? Obviously, I suspect not. Herewith the evidence I have to offer.

The vulnerability of congenitally blind children to autistic psychoses has been noted by a number of authors (Norris et al., 1957; Blank, 1958; Keeler, 1958; Parmelee et al., 1958; Fraiberg and Freedman, 1964). A very conservative estimate would place the incidence at 25 percent, with a correspondingly high incidence of less severe forms of deviance along the same lines and some instances of unremarkable psychological development. The very high incidence of deviance coupled with the close to normal development of some children with the same sensory problem makes it clear that congenital blindness per se cannot account for the autistic outcome. Rather, as Fraiberg (1974) in particular has shown, this must be the result of the effect of the child's incapacity on the mother-infant relation. It is clear from her work, as it is from a number of other studies (e.g., Bennett, 1971; Stern, 1971; Massie, 1978), that the infant's visual behavior is critical for the establishment of a symbiotic tie. The blind infant does not provide his mother with the potent inducer of bonding, which is a product of normal infantile eye behavior. There is, therefore, simply no basis for maternal joy and gratification to complement the nurturance the infant receives. Rather than a relationship such as "symbiosis" implies, the typical relation of the blind infant to his mother is more accurately characterized as parasitic. The blind infant survives on the basis of what he drains from the mother; he provides nothing to support her illusion that a mutual relation exists between them.

Clearly, no such problem with early bonding occurs among the congenitally deaf. From the standpoint of neuronal maturational considerations there is nothing about the state of deafness per se which should interfere with early bonding. The symbiotic phase should, in this group, proceed as it does in the normally endowed. I can best clarify the issue by contrasting those instances in which the deafness is totally unanticipated with the experience following the pandemic of retrolental fibrous dysplasia. In both situations the sensory deprivation is not accompanied by any external clues which might serve to indicate to the parent that something is awry. Yet the parent of the congenitally blind child regularly sought help by the time her youngster was 6 months old, while the parent of the deaf child became concerned only much later, often not until the second or even in the third year. The situation with respect to the deaf is eloquently described by Edith Levine (1956):

> The initial recognition is usually in the hands of the parents, and unless they have been alerted to the possibility of impaired hearing, the idea seldom occurs to them. Detection is further

complicated by the fact that the alert deaf infant appears to behave no differently during the first few months from his hearing peer. He, too, gurgles, coos, and vocalizes. He may even respond to certain sounds either through hearing or feeling as vibrations.

As the deaf babe grows older, however, sound fails to evoke the responses and provide the motivations it does for the hearing infant. Vocalization becomes briefer and vocal play and practice may gradually cease altogether. This often passes unnoticed if the child is an alert and active one. It is usually not until the time for beginning speech has come and gone that the parent suspects something is wrong. Even then, deafness is frequently overlooked as a likely cause for this child's silence [p. 47].

Clearly, whatever was awry with the children she observed did not interfere with their establishing a mutually beneficial symbiotic tie or their ability to undertake and complete the processes of separation and individuation. This is not, I wish to emphasize, to say that the state of deafness has no effect on development. Obviously it does. The effect, however, is neither as pervasive nor as uniform from individual to individual as is congenital blindness. Levine also writes:

This heterogeneous state makes psychological work with the deaf a highly individualized enterprise. Each case must be studied on the basis of its own particular combination of background variables. Without a clear understanding of the influences of these variables upon development, it is not possible to grasp the closeness of the relationship between them and the deaf individual's present abilities, potentials, and problems, nor is it possible to perceive the clinical clues through which a deaf person's psychological status may be disclosed and his therapeutic needs met [p. 52].

Because it does not become manifest as early in the course of development (a corollary of the fact that auditory function does not assume its preeminent role until later), congenital deafness modifies the forms of early internalizations but does not pose as massive an interference to the internalizing process as blindness does. The conditions of the practicing subphase are certainly different from those of the normally endowed, but, again in contrast to the congenitally blind child, the youngster without hearing enters into the activities of this period and those that follow with an elan and enthusiasm which, if anything, exceeds that of his hearing peer. The effects of congenital deafness will therefore be idiosyncratic and reflect more closely the details of the specific mother-infant relation rather than the fact of the sensory deprivation per se.

Early Development of Congenitally Deaf Children

I shall review my observations of a cohort of seven severely impaired little girls. Six, the victims of congenital rubella, were followed for roughly 2½ years. Observations began when they were between 29 and 36 months and continued until they were past 5 years. Their lack of hearing was the only significant congenital deficit from which they suffered. In each instance, however, the deafness was profound, ranging up to 95 decibels without a hearing aid and only correctable to from 50 to 70 decibels.

Circumstances have made it possible for me to follow the seventh girl from early infancy into adulthood. Frances F. is now in her mid-20s. Her hearing loss, the etiology of which has not been established, is somewhat milder than those of the rubella victims. Without a hearing aid she is down by roughly 60 to 80 db in the range up to 1000 cycles. Beyond 1000 cycles she experiences pain but hears no sound. Her hearing is, however, correctable to −40 db and she can function effectively with a hearing aid. Equipped with one she has been able to negotiate the developmental process into adulthood. She did well in school, albeit with some specific areas of difficulty, graduated from a prestigious college, and at present is functioning effectively as both a graduate student and junior faculty person at a major university. She had been happily married for about 3 years. All this is true despite the fact (or perhaps because of the fact) that her parents did not recognize that she was deaf until she was 2½ years old. Because the circumstances of their enlightenment seem to me to be fraught with implications, I shall describe them here. It happened at a cocktail party. In the course of a discussion with other parents of small children, the F.'s described how unusually self-reliant, outgoing, enterprising, and frenetic Frances, their third child, was. An otolaryngologist who heard their vivid account said, "She sounds deaf to me." Only then did they put together the behavior they were describing with the fact that she used no oral language. Until then they had been inclined to dismiss her failure to talk as a consequence of how interested and busy she was in other aspects of living. I shall not dwell on the power of the mechanism of denial, but emphasize that this is by no means an unusual story.

Severe hearing impairment when it occurs adventitiously— i.e., in the absence of established reasons to suspect the possibility—is rarely diagnosed before the youngster is well into the second year (Luterman and Chasin, 1970; Wright and Bradshaw, 1973; Bergstrom, 1980). Milton Levine (1980) has described a case in which the diagnosis was not made until the child was 4.[1] This is in striking contrast to the situation with the congenitally blind. The parents of babies afflicted with retrolental fibrous dysplasia—also a sensory deficit with no external evidence of the present of pathology—regularly sought help by the time their children were 6 months old.

The conclusion that the fact of major congenital hearing impairment did not significantly compromise the processes of separation and individuation in this case seems to me to be inescapable. This is not to say that her affliction has not affected this young woman's psychological development. Obviously it has in very significant ways. The effects seem, however, to be best characterized in terms of the nature of her object relations and the qualities of her perception of her self rather than in terms of the completeness of the process of differentiation or her ability to establish object ties. From my brief description it also is clear that she succeeded both in making attachments to external objects and in making age-appropriate internalizations. As she completed the processes of separation and individuation, she was able to advance on life equipped with a series of premises

---

1. The boy was hyperactive and considered by his parents and physician to be retarded until Levine established the diagnosis of deafness. That even this long delay in identification need not have the devastating effects we associate with congenital blindness is indicated by the fact that he went on to become an accountant in adult life.

about herself and what *should* be her relation to others which were not unlike those of the normally endowed child. This is not the place to consider the vicissitudes to which her deficit exposed her later in life. Suffice it to say, that as they arose, she attempted to deal with them as would a normally endowed person— according to those introjects which were consolidated intra-psychically as she established her unique and differentiated self.

This outcome is, I believe, consistent with the trend of the development of the other six girls who were described elsewhere (Freedman et al., 1971). They were selected from a much larger cohort with a view to reducing the number of sociocultural and medical variables other than deafness which might affect the developmental process. In each case, the hearing loss was the only significant residuum of maternal rubella during pregnancy.

The similarities in these childrens' backgrounds served as an adequate control for the role of cultural influences in their development. That is, one is justified in assuming that the characteristics they had in common can be attributed either (1) to the influence of the lack of hearing; (2) to the cultural stereotypes which characterized the environments of all 6; or (3) to some admixture of the two. At the same time, because of the similarities in their backgrounds as well as in the degree of their hearing loss, individual differences within the group can be ascribed either to hereditary factors or to the operation of idiosyncratic familial influences. Finally, traits they hold in common and which are not shared by youngsters with similar backgrounds may safely be ascribed to the influence of their lack of hearing.

Assessment of their functioning in the areas of motor, adaptive, and personal-social behavior with the Gesell (1940) scale failed to distinguish these children *as a group* from those with normal hearing.

Because the youngsters were already well into the final subphase of the separation-individuation process, we only have indirect information concerning their earlier development. Although prenatal rubella was known to have occurred in all cases and hearing deficits were anticipated, in no case was a definitive diagnosis of deafness made until the child was at least a year old. They are said to have been more restless and irritable in very early infancy than the usual baby, and some seemed not to want to be held and cuddled. This aside, there was even for the experienced mothers little about these infants to distinguish them from normal babies of the same age. Restlessness and irritability are characteristic of congenital rubella victims rather than of congenital deafness per se (Desmond et al., 1968).

By the time we met them, all six girls were clearly able to enter into relations with others—including myself and my associates—which reflected the presence of a well-delineated sense of self. They differentiated visiting strangers from members of their family, were appropriately shy to begin with, and ultimately "warmed up" and engaged in play. Because they were being taught by the oral method it was, moreover, possible to establish that five of the seven possessed the ability to use the first-person pronoun—an indicator of self-object differentiation which the congenitally blind child does not achieve, even under optimal conditions, until he is about 5 (Fraiberg, 1968).

Bowel and bladder control was delayed in all members of the group. This was the result of instructions given to the mothers by one of the children's teachers; they were advised to delay training until the children had passed their third birthdays. The issue of bowel training in this way became one of those shared problems which helped to throw into relief the role of individual differences among the mothers in shaping the children's development. Thus, Debbie D., her mother's third child, was trained very promptly when Mrs. D. grew tired of cleaning Debbie and expressed her displeasure with look, gesture, and a "swat" on the behind. In contrast, Cecile C., the firstborn of a very obsessive mother and the object of very intense ambivalent feelings, was the central character in a 2-year-long drama. Mrs. C. used a variety of exhortatory, coercive, and wheedling techniques, ranging from playing with Cecile while she sat on the commode to angry punishments, in her efforts to induce Cecile to "want" to use the toilet. For the other children, the problem was approached in some manner intermediate between these extremes.

At least five of the six established solid senses of their own identities as well as the capacity to enter into mutual and reciprocating relations with other human objects. Variation within the group in the development of self-object differentiation and age-appropriate object relations did not appear to be a function of the level of hearing ability. Indeed, the most serious difficulty observed in this regard occurred in Alice A., the child with the best hearing (−50db). Despite her youthfulness, we considered this to be a regressive phenomenon rather than the result of developmental arrest. Alice's overall development and her use of language deteriorated after her father was hospitalized when she was 38 months old. An only child, she was left with her grandparents while Mrs. A. was preoccupied with her husband's care. Mrs. A. made no effort to prepare the child for her departure, left the home secretly, and was gone for several days. Alice was extremely disturbed at the time. Thereafter, she showed a marked regression in her use of language. Although her hearing loss was relatively mild, she spoke little. She was also the least assertive and aggressive in the group.

It was characteristic of all of these little girls that they tended to translate their wishes into action more readily than might be anticipated from the observation of children of similar age with normal hearing. This is an observation which has been made in other groups of deaf youngsters. That is, the characteristic detour through an appeal for assistance to an older, more competent individual is less likely to occur in the hard-of-hearing or deaf child. One 30-month-old without any verbal language, for example, was found by her mother standing on a stool in front of the kitchen stove. She had the ingredients for making jello laid out on the counter and was happily boiling a pan of water!

Imitation of the actual activities of the parental figure with the maintenance of an autonomously defined external goal as the objective (as in the episode cited above) is more characteristic of the preoedipal deaf child than of the hearing child of the same age. It would appear that whatever the contribution is that oral language may be making during the practicing and rapprochement subphases, it is secondary and readily replaced by the imitative skeletomuscular activities of the otherwise healthy deaf child. There was nothing to indicate that the processes of introjection and identification were significantly affected by these girls' lack of hearing. They were distinctly feminine in their behavior and interests. Like similarly aged girls with hearing, they enjoyed playing with dolls and household equipment. Age-appropriate internalized regulation of behavior was demonstrable in all seven.

There was within the group considerable variation in the organization and channeling of assertive behavior. There appeared to be a direct relation between each child's style of handling her impulses and the nature of her relation to her mother. This can best be clarified by clinical examples.

When she was barely 2, Beryl's very youthful mother would allow her to take her 7-week-old sister from her crib and carry her around like a rag doll. Mrs. B. had concluded that it was safer to leave the side of the infant's crib down and allow Beryl to pick up the baby rather than run the risk of having Beryl climb up on the crib and drop the baby on the floor! Because efforts to limit her were haphazard and short-lived, Beryl very early learned to ignore her mother. At 5, she continued to act, in effect, with little evidence of inner restraint. In formal testing situations it was difficult to attract and maintain her interest. As a consequence, her performance was spotty. Compared to the other girls, she had a short attention span and was generally regarded as a disruptive influence both at home and at school. Her relations with her younger sister were marked by recurrent strife and a degree of violence which left observers concerned for the younger child's physical safety.

Just as Mrs. B.'s failure to impose any restraints on her 2-year-old was typical of her relation to the child, so was Mrs. D.'s management of Debbie (the youngest of a sibship of three) epitomized by her management of Debbie's bowel problems. Very clear and well-defined expectations and limits were set for this child at least from the beginning of her involvement in independent activity. They were age-appropriate in the sense that they were within Debbie's capacity to comprehend and to fulfill. It is also important that they were imposed as elements in a generally warm and loving relation. Because the consistent and predictable nature of the restraints was well established and maintained, Debbie's management of impulse posed little problem. Within the broad limits left to her for autonomous action, she was able to function with competence, confidence, and little evidence of self-doubt. Despite having one of the most severe impairments in the group, she was far in advance of the others in all developmental areas, with the possible exception of the use of oral language.

Cecile was the consistent victim of a doubting, highly ambivalent mother who oscillated between excesses of pride and expressions of hostility and rejection of the child. I have already alluded to the 2-year-long dialogue concerning bowel training in which this mother engaged her daughter. At one point Mrs. C. also decided that Cecile should not be too "rigid." To guard against this eventuality, she refused to allow her to wear a favorite dress. Only after an hour-long standoff in the course of which she explained in great detail to this very deaf 3-year-old why she must not be rigid, did Mrs. C. finally yield to the child's tears. When Cecile was not yet 3, Mrs. C. drew a map of the grounds of her apartment project and attempted to instruct Cecile from the map about where she was permitted to go. On the one hand, she encouraged Cecile in a variety of vigorous physical activities, on the other hand she agonized over her daughter's tomboy qualities. Despite good progress in development, Cecile was described by her teachers as not functioning at a level commensurate with their expectations of her. She was shy and hesitant in the classroom and in the presence of strangers.

Such observations as these indicate that these girls' deafness served as a barrier to the nuances of communication and as the focus of a variety of affective reactions on the part of the parents. Thus, it is safe to say that under any circumstances, Cecile's mother would have had difficulty in handling her hostility toward a firstborn daughter. The fact of the child's deafness compounded her problem and served as a focus for her conflictual and ambivalent feelings. When we first met, for example, she expressed concern that Cecile, "like all deaf children," might be too aggressive and hostile.

At the same time, I wish to emphasize that Cecile, like the other members of this cohort, established a well-delineated differentiation of self and object and did so according to a timetable not significantly different from that followed by the typical hearing child. In this regard these youngsters offer a striking contrast to the congenitally blind child as well as to the victim of very early environmental deprivation.

Discussion

The dramatic sequelae of congenital and perinatal sensory deprivation should not lead us to ignore the fact that these tragic conditions afflict a miniscule proportion of the population. Vital as it is to attempt to alleviate their victims' lots, it may be even more important (in keeping with Harvey's precept) to understand the implications of how the specific modality of deprivation affects the developmental process. In the case of congenital hearing loss, it would appear that a crucial consideration is the relatively late age at which auditory function assumes a critical developmental role. It is, I think, accurate to say that this maturational and developmental fact has not received general recognition. The propensity to confuse the ability to use oral speech with the development of language, therefore, continues to be prevalent. Edelheit (1969), for example, has written: "The maturation of the physiological speech apparatus, the coordination of vocal-auditory experience, and the organization of that experience in specific linguistic patterns . . . are concomitant with and correlated to the ontogenesis of the ego . . . *the ego may, in fact, be regarded as a vocal-auditory organization—a language-determined and language-determining structure—which functions as the characteristically human organ of adaptation*" (p. 410; my italics).

In rejecting this hypothesis, I am not glossing over the seriousness of the liability of lack of hearing. Rather, I am proposing that one must consider the impact of this affliction in relation to the patterns of emergence of the vocal-auditory system on the one hand and the ability to use any form of language on the other. Because of the contiguity in time of these two emergences, there is a propensity to take it for granted that they are inherently interdependent. The evidence I have presented says they are not. The fact of deafness per se does not prevent its victim from establishing a separate self and internalizing stable, predictable, well-delineated intrapsychic representations of others. It is, I believe, a corollary of this principle that the deaf child can be shown to be as capable of developing cognitive skills as his hearing peer. Thus Eberhardt (1940) wrote:

The experiments show that the world of the young deaf child is already organized beyond the perceptual level and that this organization closely follows that of speaking people. They show clearly that language [i.e., oral language] is not essential for organized conceptual thought, at least during its first stages... much of the first language development of the young deaf child in school consists of the learning of words for ideas that he already knows and uses in his everyday life, not as one might believe *a priori*, in the development of conceptual thinking by means of language symbols in a child whose world up to that point has been a more or less unorganized one [p. 4f.].

In more recent studies, in which adequate care has been taken to control for the influence of speech, the congenitally deaf also have shown no intellectual deficit as compared to the hearing (Vernon, 1967). Furth (1966), for example, has shown that the deaf readily learn to manipulate the symbols of symbolic logic. VanderWoude (1970) found that congenitally deaf and hearing children show no characteristic differences of approach to problem solving.

A recent report (Groce, 1980) is even more impressive in its documentation of the validity of the premises (1) that congenital deafness does not pose a significant interference to those early processes of attachment and internalization out of which the differentiation of self and the establishment of object relations emerge; and (2) that given access to an appropriate communications system, the congenitally deaf person (in contrast to the congenitally blind) is able to make adaptations to life which closely follow the patterns of the normally hearing. Groce studied the indigenous population of Martha's Vineyard. For roughly 250 years after they settled there in the 1640s, the descendants of the approximately 30 original families made up the vast majority of the inhabitants. Under these conditions a recessive gene for congenital deafness, which apparently was brought with them from England, became manifest in an extraordinarily high percentage of the islanders. By the latter part of the nineteenth century the incidence of this affliction on the island was 1 in 155, and in one remote village it was 1 in 25. At the same time it was estimated that for the nation as a whole the rate was 1 in 2730. The Vineyarders saw nothing unusual about this state of affairs and apparently assumed that all communities had similarly large deaf populations. Groce learned about the prevalence of deafness almost incidentally from a passing reference by an elderly islander from whom she was obtaining an oral history. She was able to obtain genealogical charts which were prepared in the 1880's by Alexander Graham Bell, but never published. These confirmed what she was hearing from her informants. She also learned that the state of being deaf had not been regarded as a significant handicap by the islanders. To the question, "How were the deaf able to communicate with you when they could not speak?" one informant replied, "Oh, there was no problem at all. You see, everyone spoke sign language." The deaf, Groce found, were fully participant in all work and play situations. Even at town meetings, "a hearing person would stand at the side of the hall and cue the deaf in sign to let them know what vote was coming up next."

That major constraints and liabilities are imposed on the deaf individual by virtue of his defect is too well established to require belaboring. It has not been my intention either to belabor or to minimize this fact. Rather, I wish to define—to the extent possible—how this mode of sensory deprivation impinges on the process of psychic differentiation and the establishment of internalized representations of external objects. I believe the data I presented make it clear that to be deaf does not impose the same barrier to these processes that being blind imposes. At least through the separation-individuation phase, lack of hearing is a relatively minor impediment and much more a function of the environment's reaction to the child's handicap than to the handicap per se. I shall present further evidence in support of this proposition.

A hallmark of effective adaptation would, I propose, be the ability to bypass an ostensible disadvantage and thus to achieve a desirable goal despite the obstacle it poses. To do so would be consistent with the generally held position that the adaptive advantage of the human species lies not in the specialization of a particular function, but in the ability to use the psychic function, intelligence, to compensate for the lack of highly specialized end organs. Can evidence of such an adaptative flexibility *based on the operation of the mental apparatus* be demonstrated in the case of the congenitally deaf? I offer the two following pieces of evidence.

1. Frances F. is a speed reader. During her early school years, when her peers were being drilled in phonetics, she was described as markedly delayed in the development of reading skills and comprehension. Approximately in the fourth grade she was able to overcome the barrier to her understanding of the written symbol which was posed by the imposition of a sound value. Thereafter, not being impeded by the necessity to sound out letters and words, she quickly acquired the ability to read very rapidly.

2. Groce reports that both hearing and deaf inhabitants of Martha's Vineyard found sign language to be of great utility in the pursuit of their occupation as fishermen. It enabled them to communicate over much greater distances than would have been possible had they been limited to oral-aural communication. At least in this area of their lives the deaf were at no disadvantage and the entire community benefited from the ubiquitous understanding of sign language.

Finally, the two following clinical vignettes are reported to underscore that (1) the thinking process of the congenitally deaf and the hearing—in this instance, the use of metaphor to communicate an affective attitude toward an object—may not be significantly different; and (2) the deaf youngster may be as vulnerable to the parental assumption that he understands a particular metaphor—i.e., has inherently the same affective attitude as the parent—as the hearing child.

Wulff (1951) described an 18-month-old girl with phobic and compulsive symptoms. When playing the patient always tidied the room and cleaned the floor. As soon as she noticed a scrap of paper, a crumb, or a thread on the floor, she had to pick it up and throw it into the wastebasket. These behaviors had begun in association with toilet training, when her parents would exhort her "to be clean." When, on Wulff's advice, they relaxed all rules and demands concerning bowel training, the child's symptoms cleared up completely. One would have little difficulty in relating this child's problem to the challenges of the rapprochement phase. At the same time one must not lose sight of the fact that it was derived directly from her parents' assumption that she could

follow their metaphorical use of the word "clean." It was therefore particularly impressive to me to find the following vignette
in a paper by Galenson et al. (1980). In this instance, both mother
and 14-month-old daughter were deaf and communication was
via signing.

> In regard to the developing capacity for symbolic functioning,
> Nora had no definitive speech or speech sign vocabulary at 11
> months. Between 11 and 14 months, she developed the inci-
> pient signs for "daddy" and "look," but not for "momma." She
> gestured by pointing at something she wanted at this time. By
> 17 months, she clearly gestured for things she wanted which
> were out of sight, but was vocalizing very little. It was most
> interesting that her first communicative sign appeared at 14
> months with the onset of toilet training. It was at this time that
> she learned the sign of holding her nose which her mother had
> taught her to symbolize having a bowel movement. It is particu-
> larly striking that this sign appeared before the sign for
> "momma."
>
> Initially Nora imitated her mother's use of the nose-holding
> sign to indicate that she had already soiled her diaper. When
> the mother saw that Nora was now making the connection
> between sign and event, she began to place Nora on the potty
> after each meal for several hours, and her mother would pa-
> tiently sit next to her, reading her a book. This practice con-
> tinued from 14 to 18 months, when Nora finally produced a
> bowel movement in the potty for the first time. She cried at this
> moment and seemed afraid to approach the potty again.
>
> *We then learned that mother held her nose as a sign not only for both*
> *bowel movement and urination, but also referring to anything that*
> *mother considered dirty. For example, this sign was used when Nora*
> *licked soap from a bubble straw, played with play dough, attempted to*
> *put a crayon in her mouth, or was messy with food* [my italics].

Evidently the likelihood that the mother who communicates in
sign will anticipate her responsive child will follow her metaphor
is as great as it is for the user of oral language.

Summary and Conclusions

The phenomenon of echolalia is cited as an instance of articulate
speech in the absence of the ability and/or the motivation to

communicate. Conversely, sign language as used by the deaf provides an example of a communicative process which does not depend on the presence of a functioning vocal-auditory system. Contrasting aspects of the early development of congenitally blind children, who tend to be autistic and echolalic, and congenitally deaf children, who show no such propensities, are then considered. The fact of blindness appears to interfere with the establishment of early mother-infant bonding. The child, therefore, does not establish either self-object differentiation or internalized self and object representations. Although his vocal-auditory system matures and he can make articulate speech sounds, he is likely to remain echolalic and incapable of using speech for communicative (i.e., language) purposes. No analogous interference with differentiation and internalization characterizes the development of the congenitally deaf youngster. Because he establishes a well-differentiated sense of self and is capable of entering into relations with external objects and internalized object representations he is motivated to communicate and will do so effectively if he is provided with an appropriate medium—e.g., sign language—for the purpose.

BIBLIOGRAPHY

Bennet, S. (1971), Infant-caretaker interactions. *J. Amer. Acad. Child Psychiat.*, 10:321–335.

Bergstrom, L. V. (1980), Causes of severe hearing loss in early childhood. *Pediat. Ann.*, 9:13–17.

Blank, H. R. (1958), Psychoanalysis and blindness. *Psychoanal. Quart.*, 26:1–24.

Burlingham, D. (1964), Hearing in the development of the blind. *Psychoanal. Study Child*, 19:95–112.

Desmond, M., Wilson, G. S., Verniaud, W. M., Melnick, J. L., & Rawls, W. E. (1969), The early growth and development of infants with congenital rubella. In: *Advances in Teratology*, ed. J. S. Mordere. London: Logos Press, 4:39–63.

Eberhardt, M. (1940), A summary of some preliminary investigations of the deaf. *Psychol. Monogr.*, 52(232):1–5.

Edelheit, H. (1969), Speech and psychic structure. *J. Amer. Psychoanal. Assn.*, 17:381–412.

Ekstein, R. (1965), Historical notes concerning psychoanalysis and early language development. *J. Amer. Psychoanal. Assn.*, 13:707–731.

_____ & CARUTH, E. (1969), Levels of verbal communication in the schizophrenic child's struggle against, for, and with the world of objects. *Psychoanal. Study Child,* 24:115–137.

FRAIBERG, S. (1951), Enlightenment and confusion. *Psychoanal. Study Child,* 6:325–335.

_____ (1968), Parallel and divergent patterns in blind and sighted infants. *Psychoanal. Study Child,* 23:264–300.

_____ (1974), Blind infants and their mothers. In: *The Effect of the Infant on Its Caregiver,* ed. M. Lewis & L. Rosenblum. New York: Wiley, pp. 215–232.

_____ & FREEDMAN, D. A. (1964), Studies in the ego development of the congenitally blind child. *Psychoanal. Study Child* 19:113–169.

FREEDMAN, D. A. (1977), The influences of various modalities of sensory deprivation on the evolution of psychic and communicative structures. In: *Communicative and Psychic Structures,* ed. N. Freedman & S. Grand. New York: Plenum, pp. 57–74.

_____ CANNADAY, C., & ROBINSON, J. S. (1971), Speech and psychic structure. *J. Amer. Psychoanal. Assn.,* 19:765–779.

FURTH, H. G. (1966), *Thinking Without language.* Glencoe, Ill.: Free Press.

GALENSON, E., KAPLAN, E. H., & SHERKOW, S. (1981), The mother-child relationship and preverbal communication in the deaf child. In: *Frontiers of Infant Psychiatry.* New York: Basic Books (in press).

GESELL, A. & ARMATRUDA, C. S. (1941), *Developmental Diagnosis.* New York: Paul B. Hoeber.

GLOVER, E. (1932), A psycho-analytical approach to the classification of mental disorders. In: *On the Early Development of Mind.* New York: Int. Univ. Press, 1956, pp. 161–186.

GRIFFITH, R. J. & RITVO, E. R. (1967), Echolalia. *J. Amer. Acad. Child Psychiat.,* 6:184–193.

GROCE, N. (1980), Everyone here spoke sign language. *Natural History,* 89(6):10–19.

HARVEY, W. (1651), *Excercitationes de generatione animalium.* London: Octavian, Pulley. Cited in: *New Engl. J. Med.,* 300(1979):733.

KEELER, W. R. (1958), Autistic patterns and defective communication in blind children with retrolental fibroplasia. In: *Psychopathology of Communication,* ed. P. H. Hoch & J. Zubin. New York: Grune & Stratton, 1958, pp. 64–83.

LEVINE, E. (1956), *Youth in a Soundless World.* New York: Int. Univ. Press.

LEVINE, M. I. (1980), A pediatrician's view. *Pediat. Ann.,* 9:3–5.

LUTERMAN, D. M. & CHASIN, J. (1970), The pediatrician and the parent of the deaf child. *Pediatrics,* 45:115–116.

MASSIE, H. N. (1978), Blind ratings of mother-infant interactions in home movies of pre-psychotic and normal infants. *Amer. J. Psychiat.,* 135:1371–1374.

NORRIS, M., SPAULDING, P., & BRODIE, F. H. (1957), *Blindness in Children.* Chicago: Univ. Chicago Press.

PARMELEE, A. H., FISHER, C., & WRIGHT, R. (1958), The development of ten children with blindness as a result of retrolental fibrous dysplasia. *A.M.A. J. Child. Dis.*, 96:198-220.

REINECKE, R. D. (1979), Current concepts in opthamology. *New Engl. J. Med.*, 300:1139-1141.

STERN, D. N. (1971), A microanalysis of the mother-infant interaction. *J. Amer. Acad. Child. Psychiat.*, 10:501-517.

VANDERWOUDE, K. W. (1970), Problem solving and language. *Arch. Gen. Psychiat.*, 23:337-342.

VERNON, M. (1967), Relationship of language to the thinking process. *Arch. Gen. Psychiat.*, 16:325-333.

WRIGHT, J. L. & BRADSHAW, R. B. (1973), Assessment of deaf children. *J. Laryng. Otol.*, 87:547-554.

WULFF, M. (1951), The problem of neurotic manifestations in children of preoedipal age. *Psychoanal. Study Child*, 6:169-179.

YAKOVLEV, P. I. & LECOURS, A. (1967), The myelogenetic cycles of regional maturation of the brain. In: *Regional Development of the Brain in Early Life*, ed. A. Minkowski. Oxford: Blackwell, pp. 3-70.

The Concept of Developmental Lines

Their Diagnostic Significance

ANNA FREUD

TO THINK ANALYTICALLY AUTOMATICALLY IMPLIES A DISSECTION of psychic material into its constituent elements, to treat each of these elements as a factor in its own right, and to trace it back to its first appearance within the psychic processes. In the technique of psychoanalytic treatment, it is the analyst's main endeavor to spotlight such items in the patient's unconscious mind, to expose them to consciousness, and then to leave it to the individual concerned to integrate what has been discovered with the rest of his personality. The analyst's task ends where synthesis begins, the latter being one of the most important functions of the ego—a function, moreover, which, according to analytic experience, proceeds best without interference from external influence.

Such limitations are set for and accepted by the analyst who works with adults in the psychoanalytic situation. On the other hand, they do not apply to developmental explorations and, above all, not to the analyst of children. To investigate development, it does not suffice to explore the past. It is equally imperative to follow each psychic element in its forward course until the

Director, Hampstead Child-Therapy Clinic, which is at present supported by the Herman A. and Amelia S. Ehrmann Foundation, New York; The Field Foundation, Inc., New York; the Freud Centenary Fund, London; the Anna Freud Foundation, New York; the New-Land Foundation, Inc., New York; and a number of private supporters.

time when it qualifies for becoming part of the mature, adult personality; to watch and describe the interaction of the various elements with each other; to study how far they help or hinder each other's advance; how they combine with each other and how they finally produce the qualities, attitudes, and abilities expected from the adult. It is precisely here that the study of the synthetic function comes into its own, and that observation of its successes and failures leads us to understand many of the characteristics, qualities, shortcomings, and defects of the average adult personality.

To have reached the stage of genital sexuality, on the one hand, and to be able to work effectively, on the other hand, used to be quoted as the hallmark of adult normality in the early era of psychoanalysis. Since then, many other demands have been added to these requirements. Normal adults also are expected to hold their own with regard to self-esteem and emotional balance, i.e., not to be wholly dependent on the affective interchange with their love objects and other fellow beings; to be in rational control of their own body and its functions and to safeguard its well-being; to discharge emotion through mental pathways, i.e., thought and speech, rather than via physical action or involvement; to reduce panic in the face of dangers to mere signal anxiety, which initiates effective defense; to have outgrown a purely egocentric view of the world, according to which all happenings are understood in reference to their own person; to see themselves on a par with others and to react to their peers on a basis of equality; to be able to enjoy pleasure but to behave and function according to the reality principle, taking full cognizance of the importance of cause and effect.

For the detailed examination of these latter, additional achievements, we can do no better than emulate the prototype constructed by psychoanalysis for its earliest "developmental line," i.e., that toward an *adult sex and love life*. According to this, the mature function depends on the step-by-step interaction and integration of four totally different factors: drive maturation, which determines the location of erotogenic zone (oral, anal, phallic, genital) and supplies the energetic (aggressive) impulse toward seeking satisfaction; ripening of ego functions, which enable recognition of and attachment to the object of the drive;

superego action, which provides checks and drive control; environmental influence, which offers stimulation and response. Normal development of the adult's sex life depends, on the one hand, on the intactness of all the influences concerned and, on the other hand, on temporal considerations, i.e., their simultaneous advance. Flaws in quality in one or more, retardation or precocity in any of them, alter the final outcome. Synthesis between them will take place in any case and inevitably, but it will result in trends toward the pathological and/or conflictual.

A similar combination of influences and sequence of developmental steps can be established for the individual's arriving at the *ability to work*. However, since this achievement is farther removed from the early analyst's central interest in the unconscious, and less obviously determined by drive activity, the attempt to break it up into specific steps has waited until more recent times.

Play has been hailed as the precursor of work by many psychologists, although pinpointing the stages on the road which lead from one to the other remains the prerogative of psychoanalysis. There is no difficulty in following the child's activities through their various stages: play on his own and his mother's body; play with soft toys; filling and emptying containers; construction toys; role play; games; hobbies; finally, work. It is a more subtle task to disclose the underlying factors which determine and shape these occupations and to recognize their diverse sources.

Behind the scene, pressure for drive-related satisfaction plays an important role: skin erotism for the play on the body; transition from autoerotism to object love for the attachment to soft toys; fascination with bodily functions for sand and water play; constructive and destructive (aggressive) tendencies for the favorite use of building blocks; phallic urges for the often overwhelming interests in cars, trains, engines, and any kind of moving construction; oedipal preoccupations for the family games, etc. These are combined with the more obvious contributions from the ego side, i.e., its step-by-step emerging functions, qualities, and interests such as orientation in the environment, curiosity, investigative spirit, adventurousness, manual skill, and fantasy. Moreover, important as the synthesis between drive and ego factors may be, an outcome into healthy play will not be reached without the proper contributions from the environment, whether by the mere provision of age-adequate toys or the even more important stimulation via parental patterns for imitation and identification. The all-important step from play to work is determined by influences from three sides: on the id side, by the age-adequate lessening of drive pressure; on the ego side, by functioning being no longer under the exclusive domination of the search for pleasure and the abandonment of this search as soon as pleasure gain ceases; on the environmental side, by the provision of the concerns, demands, and necessities which lead to the establishment of a new governing principle, i.e., the reality principle superseding the previous reign of the pleasure principle.

Examples can be adduced from other developmental lines which, following the same synthetic pattern, lead to some of the other above-named characteristics of the mature personality.

Peer relationship, for instance, can be traced from its negative beginnings in infancy to its positive achievement some time before the latency period, each stage on the way revealing itself as the combined result of id-ego-superego-environmental influence.

At the start, while from the id and environmental sides the infant-mother union reigns supreme, there is no room for peers who for id as well as for ego purposes are as if nonexistent. They come into the picture with a next step, when the perceptual function of the ego and libidinal interest of the id gradually abandon their sole concentration on the maternal object and extend to some other features in the environment. Nevertheless, at this level, the existence of other children is experienced by the infant as no different from the existence of other animate or inanimate threats to the fulfillment of his wishes and arouses the same angry-aggressive response. It needs next, on the drive side, the awakening of some need for mates which, combined with interest in play material on the ego side, makes peers acceptable temporarily, i.e., for the duration and successful completion of a play activity. However, this relationship to the mere playmate still lacks any of the connotations of friendship such as empathy, consideration, reciprocity. These latter attitudes enter into the combination only on the strength of the next, final advances: on the id side, due to a more generous and indiscriminate output of object libido; on the ego side, due to a lessening of egocentricity and selfishness; from the superego, due to newly acquired ideals of fairness and justice; and, last but not least, due to the environment adding to the mixture its demands for fair play, for taking turns, for equality of status.

Another example of a developmental line is the hazardous way in which the individual child gains *possession of his own body,* i.e., emerges from his physical union with the mother as a separate person, with the right and ability to use, explore, endanger, and safeguard his own physical equipment according to his personal wishes.

Here, a whole host of factors works together, or against each other, in turn promoting, delaying, or even preventing the desired end result. The child's body matures, develops muscular control, gross and fine motor skills. His ego develops, besides increasing orientation in the outside world, its own tendencies toward independent action, adventures, trials of strength. Drive activity urges in the direction of pleasure gain from all these available sources, disregarding possible injuries and dangers. At the same time, libidinal ties to maternal care and love steer in the opposite direction toward submission to and dependence on external control of vital physical processes. The combined results can be followed step by step.

Food intake, after the stage of suckling and weaning, remains burdened by the child's equating food with mother. This brings with it all the developmental complications of the child-mother relationship, loving and hating, craving and refusing. Following this, the impact on feeding by anal and phallic-oedipal fantasies needs to be outgrown, until eating can emerge on a rational basis regulated by the individual's appetite and the needs of his body.

Interaction between external and internal factors is, of course, well known with regard to elimination, the final control of which depends on the synthesis of four disparate influences: maturation of the sphincters; urge for urethral and anal pleasure; wish for love and approval; the mother's strict or lenient, timely or untimely method of toilet training.

With regard to independent motility, besides maturation, the environmental factor, more than any other, seems to decide the issue. Maternal possessiveness of the child's body needs to be reduced gradually, its withdrawal timed to coincide with the growth of the child's desire and ability for self-determination. If one of these factors either precedes or lags behind the other, the normal developmental outcome is seriously endangered.

The four developmental lines described above have been selected from a larger number of others to illustrate the nature, the complexity, and also the hazards implied in a child's developmental progress.

Psychoanalysis of the neuroses has familiarized us with the idea that their symptoms are compromise formations, shaped by the synthetic function and devised to satisfy at one and the same time the very different claims which bear down on the ego from the side of the drives, the superego, and the external world, the demands of neither being either wholly fulfilled or altogether rejected.

Perhaps we can do no better than to transfer this idea of psychic compromise from the area of psychopathology to that of normal developmental growth. Here, too, the individual child's ego has to cope on every step of the upward ladder toward any of his achievements with the influences which bear down on it from all sides, internal as well as external. None of the child's advances is determined from one direction only; all of them can be understood as synthetic products, compromises with and combinations of various influences. Nevertheless, the child's advance from immaturity to maturity in all vital respects will proceed smoothly and straightforwardly under favorable conditions. Innate endowment (drives and sensory equipment), personality structuralization (division into id, ego, superego, perfection of ego functioning), environmental circumstances (parental love, constancy, stimulation, control) need to be within an expectable norm without too many aberrant features. And maturation, growth, and change in all three areas need to take place at an even pace, timed to coincide with each other. If these two prerequisites, essential for normal growth, are fulfilled, the child's developmental compromises will be adaptive ones.

However, the very multiplicity of factors which determines

growth also is responsible for the extreme vulnerability of the whole developmental process. Normality of all the factors involved is an ideal, rather than the common occurrence. Endowment can be too heavily or too little weighted in one or the other instinctual direction; sensory defects may create serious handicaps; unfolding of ego functioning may be delayed or precocious, or altogether below par; the superego may be too lenient or too harsh, or inconsistent; parental care may be lacking in some essential quality. Any of these defects, if major enough, have the power to influence, halt, deflect, or distort development. The synthetic function which works relentlessly incorporates the influence from these detrimental sources as automatically as from the beneficial ones, and this results in developmental compromises which are deviant and maladaptive.

What remains to be discussed is the diagnostic significance of thinking in terms of developmental lines and our justification for using them as adjuncts to the Profile within the diagnostic process.

To me, it seems important that their study reveals the existence of a second source of pathology which is active throughout the individual's formative years, a pathogenic factor no less potent and no less ubiquitous than the conflictual one with which we are familiar. Long before a personality is sufficiently aware of environmental demands, or sufficiently divided within itself to suffer from internal strife, normal progress can already be threatened and harmed by any of the developmental disharmonies arising from any of the qualitative, quantitative, or temporal reasons mentioned above. We know a great deal about the way in which conflicts with the external and within the internal world produce the inhibitions, symptoms, anxieties, and other crippling accompaniments and forerunners of the infantile neuroses. There is no reason why we should not learn as much about the manner in which disharmonies, arrests, and deviations on developmental lines are responsible for many of the oddities, infantilisms, and borderline features of our problem children.

There is also no reason to think that the idea of two different psychopathologies dominating the picture of childhood simultaneously is difficult to maintain. Far from being incompatible with each other, the conflictual and the purely developmental sources of disturbance join forces with each other. Developmental deficiencies are a fertile breeding ground for conflict of all types: with the environment, since parents are dismayed and disapproving when faced with age-inadequate, puzzling, uneven advances in their child's progress; within the inner world where, for example, a different rate of progress of the various id, ego, and superego elements produces unacceptable, ego-dystonic phenomena.

Nevertheless, difficult as the clinical distinction between the two types of disturbance may be, to confuse them with each other constitutes a diagnostic error. It is also a grave disservice to the task of matching the child's disorder with the treatment most appropriate for it. Developmentally and conflictually caused pathologies are too different from each other in origin, nature, and structure to respond to the same therapeutic method.

What We Can Learn from Pathology about Normal Development

E. C. M. FRIJLING-SCHREUDER, M.D.

NEITHER PATHOLOGY NOR NORMALITY LENDS ITSELF TO A CLEAR definition, and I will not try to give one. Some would even question whether Freud, when he occupied himself with the study of neurosis, was dealing with pathology. They might say that he treated as individual pathology what in reality was an outcome of social circumstances. Freud (1930) himself viewed neurosis as the price we pay for civilization. It is a pity that the social changes of our time have changed this price more and more into the ubiquity of severe character disturbances. Freud sought and found general principles for the normal and the pathological processes of the mind. In this paper I want to focus on the area where pathological functioning gave us insight into the normal, directed the observations of normality, or gave us views about prevention, however narrow its scope may be.

When Freud made his great discoveries, he soon realized that they concerned a far wider field than the understanding of neurosis he was looking for. In a period of doubt (1897) when he asked himself whether his insight into neurosis was correct, he did not doubt his psychology of unconscious psychic processes and of the dream. The pathology of hysteria was at that moment unclear to him. Until then he had attributed the etiology of hysteria to early trauma, to seduction by the father. Now he

---

Read at the meeting of the Association for Child Psychoanalysis, Amsterdam, July 1980.

wrote to Fliess that such an ubiquity of perverse actions with children was improbable. From then on he sought the etiology of the neurosis in the pathogenic fantasies linked to the development of the drives (Freud, 1905). The general applicability of these insights extrapolated from pathology to normal development has been confirmed ever since. It is as in astronomy: if the calculations are right, the star is discovered.

Extrapolations from pathology to normality apply not only to the drives but to defense as well. I am thinking about *The Ego and the Mechanisms of Defense* and especially about a form of altruism which provides insight into one of the normal ways of mastering sibling rivalry. Anna Freud (1936) writes: "The mechanism of projection disturbs our human relations when we project our own jealousy and attribute to other people our own aggressive acts. But it may work in another way as well, enabling us to form valuable positive attachments and so to consolidate our relations with one another. This normal and less conspicuous form of projection might be described as 'altruistic surrender' of our own instinctual impulses in favor of other people" (p. 123). Jeanne Lampl (1957) asks: "Can we speak of 'normal' defense, or does every defensive process belong in the realm of pathology?" (p. 114). And she answers: "What I want to suggest . . . is that we view the neurotic defense mechanisms as pathologically exaggerated or distorted regulation and adaptation mechanisms, which in themselves belong to normal development" (p. 117).

The point I wish to make is the following. In the literature we can find a wealth of observations about normal children, but more often than not it was pathology that determined what we observe. If we did not know about the pathological use of defense, we would not study normal character development from the viewpoint of normal development of defense.

To give a very simple example: I could more than once alleviate the anxiety of a young mother about an eating disturbance of her 2-year-old by asking her how far the child was on his way to cleanliness. The abhorrence of "dirty" food, seen as a beginning reaction formation against dirt, gives us a clue in helping mothers with these passing unevennesses of development. But we would not have seen the link—always so difficult, but so rewarding to explain to pediatricians—if we had not known about the anal character traits which Freud described as early as 1908.

I turn now to another example where child analysis has shown us the way in the study of development: I refer to the concept of phase dominance. Describing the infantile neurosis of the Wolf Man, Freud (1918) said, "characteristic of his later life ... was this further trait: no position of the libido which had once been established was ever completely replaced by a later one. It was rather left in existence side by side with all the others, and this allowed him to maintain an incessant vacillation which proved to be incompatible with the acquisition of a stable character" (p. 26f.). Stable character formation thus depends on a rather clear sequence of phases.

The concept of phase dominance was further developed by Anna Freud (1965) who stressed the interaction between phase development of the drives and the development of the object relations. To assess the severity of pathology and the necessity for psychoanalytic treatment, the level of drive development and of ego development according to age is important, as is the secondary interference of defense with ego functions. Here criteria for normal development are taken partly from pathology and partly from direct observation of normal children. In the assessment of the necessity for treatment and of suitability for psychoanalysis, the assessment of normality and pathology play equal roles. It is to this point that much of the psychoanalytic interest has turned in the last two decades. While it is apparent in many themes, I mention only the adaptive use of regression and reaction formation. Both could be described clearly only after Hartmann, Kris, and Loewenstein's studies (1949) of the vicissitudes of the drives and the introduction of the concept of neutralization. Still more important to the core of our science was the reevaluation of the oedipus complex, the changing place given to this constellation in total development. The oedipus complex was no longer seen only as the core complex of the neurosis, but its clear formation was increasingly viewed in terms of normal development. Although the oedipus complex did not lose its significance as a fixation point in adult neurosis, more and more emphasis was put on its role as an "organizer"—to borrow a concept from Spitz (1965)—a point after which development is better integrated. Infantile neurosis became a developmental milestone.

In the symposium on the reevaluation of the role of the oedipus complex (17th International Congress, 1951), the importance of the pregenital stages for the shaping and intensity of castration anxiety was stressed. Gitelson (1952) observed that at least one third of the cases in the United States were borderline cases and he said, "I am inclined to believe that they have never integrated the phallic position" (p. 354). This marks the transition I described above, but the aim then still remained a better description of the preoedipal stages. (As early as 1931, Freud had stated that the preoedipal phase in women is more important than we had hitherto supposed.) While I shall not detail the many careful descriptions of the first stages of infantile development, I want to stress that even data gathered from child analysis are reconstructions insofar as they concern these very early developmental phases. They needed and received confirmation from direct and longitudinal child observation.

The increased knowledge widened the scope of psychoanalysis, and the changing pathology gave rise to increased interest in the study of normal development of early object relations and the hatching of the ego. Some of these insights clearly stemmed from direct concern with pathology and could immediately be applied clinically; e.g., Winnicott's (1953) concept of the transitional object and Mahler's (1968, 1975) delineation of the stages of separation-individuation led to direct improvement of technique. To recognize the wish for merging, the clinging behavior of the rapprochement phase, and to link it up with the regressions and fixations in oral and anal drive development was in certain cases of great help. It was only in the last two decades, however, that the significance of all these observations for the understanding of normal progressive development gradually became clearer to me.

Working with borderline and psychotic children, I was impressed most by the intensely disturbed mother-child relationship and the systematic disturbance of reality testing. I saw the developmental arrests and deviations, the lack of structure and of clear phase development. Later on the study of childhood psychosis highlighted the contrast with the classic neuroses and opened my eyes, in a quite different way than the study of neurotic children had done, to the progressive and organizing forces to which each developmental step gives rise. Anna Freud (1945) describes how every progression gives rise to some regression; for example, the development of perception of outer reality gives rise to denial of unpleasant reality and thereby also to a partial undoing of the development of the sense of reality. This regression may mark the beginning of reality testing, in the sense that it is followed by a gradual unfolding of the possibility to accept unpleasant reality, but it can also mark an unevenness in development. In adult analysis, we may then see, for instance, that the difference between the sexes is still denied even when reality testing on the whole is well developed. If we deal with such problems in early childhood, they may well be solved. In child analysis, we often see that entering a new developmental phase brings with it great overall progression (a point to which I shall return). In borderline and psychotic states, however, the regressive processes predominate.

In such conditions, the balance between aggression and libido may be a very unfortunate one. Speech, for example, may be so highly invested with aggression that the development of secondary process thinking is interfered with. While aggression may be partially discharged in biting, scratching, attacking, and cursing, the accompanying fantasies provoke such extreme anxiety that they generate further regressive processes. Such malignant regression, so prominent in these very disturbed children, easily leads to discouragement in those who endeavor to help the child. While our therapeutic efforts may help the child to achieve some secondary process functioning, usually large areas of primary process functioning will remain. Moreover, the patient may develop a certain adroitness in hiding these beneath a façade of reality-adapted behavior.

We should realize, however, that primary process functioning continues to play a large role even in normality. The most obvious example is, of course, dreaming. In early latency much communication between children may still be on the basis of the primary process. In adulthood, too, there is far more primary process functioning than we realize—not only in dreams and daydreams but, in a more dangerous form, in stereotyped thinking, prejudice, and rumor. With the increasing inscrutability of bureaucratic society and science, we easily fall prey to projections or wish-fulfilling credulity.

When we are called upon to assess the role of regression in normal development, it is helpful to have seen children in whom the regressive moves tend to predominate. This sharpens our eyes for detecting signs of progressive moves in children even when they react with intense regression to events such as the birth of a sibling, when their regressive moves appear to be of longer duration, or when their difficulties belong essentially to normal oedipal development.

The normal tendency to achieve progression in development proceeds via regression and frequently actually requires it. This is especially true in the area of the toddler's fantasies about pregnancy and confinement. The only abdominal product which the child is capable of producing, feces, becomes cathected anew in his efforts to emulate mother. It needs a lot of talking about babies and about his own body before the toddler is able to swallow the hurt that it is impossible for him to make a baby himself. I put such stress on talking because during this period in childhood holding and comforting no longer suffice, and intellectual understanding begins to be important. At that time speech is still a recently acquired achievement, and the management of aggression by inner speech and by fantasying and by playacting is at its height. This normal management of aggression is activated during child analysis in latency, especially in the analysis of learning disturbances.

The reconstruction of normal development from pathology becomes far more difficult in adolescence. We know about the developmental tasks that need to be achieved, but I could not say in what ways our views on pathology are influenced by what we think is normal adolescence. For instance, adjustment to the peer group may be taken as a sign of normal adolescence. The studious and romantic adolescent who prefers the company of one older friend or a few friends to that of the peer group may seem very pathological, whereas in another historical period he may be the adolescent ideal. The bashful girl who shrinks back from all contacts outside the family was the adolescent ideal in the Victorian period.

The point I wish to make is the following: the nearer we come to adulthood, the less we gain from our investigation of pathology for our understanding of normality. Many of our adult patients have solved the dual task of working with some pleasure and choosing an object, even of founding a family; yet they suffer from severe pathology. We acknowledge that there are vast areas about which we know far too little. For example, are analysts really the best judges of men? If this were so, why would all institutes complain about the difficulty of selecting candidates, whatever the method of selection may be? Adult normality seems to span a much wider field than pathology. Pathology is only the maiming of normality, the inhibition or underdevelopment of traits.

The other factor which is important in this context is that we study processes and not so much static situations. We do know something about processes in adulthood from the study of pathology. I mention the processes of pregnancy, parenthood, climacteric changes, mourning. Here certainly lies a field for further study. While the processes of mourning and the reactions to loss have attracted special attention in the last decades, we know far less about normal growth in adulthood. We are aware of the fact that in normal adults, there is a ripening of friendship, of social sureness, of parental attitudes to children or others, but a systematic extrapolation from the growth we see in a successful analysis has not come to my knowledge. Yet, from my own work I know about the great richness and variety of ways of gaining pleasure from achievements and friendships and loves at the end of a successful analysis in adolescence. Adolescents very often are sadder and more inhibited than we should wish, but it may be true that what we see at the end of a good analysis is nearer to the ideal of normality than what we see in our contacts with "normal" people.

I now turn to what should be the most promising area of the application of our knowledge outside of the treatment room—the prevention of psychic illness in childhood. Yet, in this respect, it seems to me very little has been done. Though we have all profited from the careful study of normal children and though some of the psychoanalytic insights have changed some aspects of child rearing, the fact remains that far too few child analysts are actively interested in prevention. Moreover, even for those few who are, it has been very difficult to obtain access to appropriate places where they can exert some influence by preventive interventions. In Holland the best place proved to be the well-baby clinics which serve a large part of the population. Some pediatric hospitals also provide preventive aid. But on the whole, prevention remains a difficult field. We know so much about possibly pathogenic influences, but feel so very weak and helpless when it comes to applying measures to avoid them. As far as I can see, the situation may well be worse than ten years ago. As long as psychoanalytic institutes had long waiting lists, we could stress the importance of giving preference for treatment to young people who had not yet made definite choices, for young parents, and for people who had professional contact with parents or children. More and more, however, psychoanalysis tends to become the ultimate refuge for very disturbed persons, whereas neurotic people seeking help do not get psychoanalysis. With their neurotic conflicts remaining unresolved, many foster a neurotic development in their children. But leaving this somber perspective, we can say that our knowledge from pathology has been helpful in guiding parents of under-fives and that such parent counseling has become very much better in the last decades.

On the other hand, there are many situations which we are powerless to prevent. In his study of the Dutch war orphans, Keilson (1979) describes three sequelae of cumulative traumatization: the separation from the parents; the period of constant danger to life, often spent in several foster families; and the return to normal civilization. The children's experiences in this last period were correlated directly with their later adjustment. I do not, of course, want in any way to compare these horrible cumulative traumas with things we see during normal development, but there is one lesson we can learn from Keilson's study—that the aftermath of a catastrophe in a child's life is as important as the catastrophe itself. This lesson can be applied to what unfortunately has become an everyday occurrence— parental divorce. Its effect on the child will not be limited to the period of the actual divorce, but be determined by the subsequent provisions made—the availability of both parents, their openness for the feelings of the child, etc. Or, as another example, we have generally regarded hospitalization as a pathogenic influence in a child's life. Its aftermath, the return home, the way in which the parents can be helped to deal with the anger of the young child, may be as important.

I believe that in these and related fields a great deal of work remains to be done. Thinking about prevention one would like to be able to say that child analysis is the best prevention of later neurosis. We know that this is not the case. But perhaps in the future we might find that child analysis is the method of choice to help people to "integrate the phallic phase" (Gitelson, 1952) and to form a mild classic neurosis instead of the more severe character disturbances and borderline states that too often we have to deal with.

BIBLIOGRAPHY

FREUD, A. (1936), The ego and the mechanisms of defense. *W.*, 2.
———— (1945), Indications for child analysis. *W.*, 4:3–39.
———— (1965), Normality and pathology in childhood. *W.*, 6.
FREUD, S. (1897), Letter 69. In: *The Origins of Psychoanalysis*. New York: Basic Books, 1954, pp. 215–218.
———— (1905), Three essays on the theory of sexuality. *S.E.*, 7:125–243.
———— (1908), Character and anal erotism. *S.E.*, 9:167–175.
———— (1918), From the history of an infantile neurosis. *S.E.*, 17:3–123.
———— (1931), Female sexuality. *S.E.*, 21:223–243.
GITELSON, M. (1952), Re-evaluation of the rôle of the oedipus complex. *Int. J. Psychoanal.*, 32:351–354.
HARTMANN, H., KRIS, E., & LOEWENSTEIN, R. M. (1949), Notes on the theory of aggression. *Psychoanal. Study Child*, 3/4:9–36.
KEILSON, H. (1979), *Sequentielle Traumatisierung bei Kindern*. Stuttgart: Enke.
LAMPL-DE GROOT, J. (1957), On defense and development. *Psychoanal. Study Child*, 12:114–126.
MAHLER, M. S. (1968), *On Human Symbiosis and the Vicissitudes of Individuation*. New York: Int. Univ. Press.
———— PINE, F., & BERMAN, A. (1975), *The Psychological Birth of the Human Infant*. New York: Basic Books.
SPITZ, R. A. (1965), *The First Year of Life*. New York: Int. Univ. Press.
WINNICOTT, D. W. (1953), The transitional object and transitional phenomena. *Int. J. Psychoanal.*, 34:89–98.

A Review of
Twins: A Study of Three Pairs of Identical Twins
by Dorothy Burlingham

HEINZ HARTMANN, M.D.

IN THIS BOOK DOROTHY BURLINGHAM DOES NOT FOLLOW THE beaten path of twin research. She has an approach of her own and in pursuing it presents the reader with a wealth of data and conclusions, of the greatest value also for different aspects of twin psychology.

The data were collected in the Hampstead Nurseries, observations being recorded daily, and by several observers. The setup of the Nurseries allowed of receiving mothers with their children. The object of the study was to examine "in detail the lives of a small number of twin children and their environmental and innate conditions which account for the differences between their development and that of ordinary children" (p. ixf.).

As an introduction to her investigations, Dorothy Burlingham discusses the latency fantasies of having a twin, which turn out to be reactions to the disappointments of the oedipal phase. They show characteristics of two well-known types of daydream: the family romance and the animal fantasies. The fantasy of having a twin is rather common. Those who had it may, by this fact, as

The Editors thank Dr. Ernest Hartmann and Dr. Lawrence Hartmann for permission to include this previously unpublished review, which was written in 1952, shortly after the book was published (London: Imago Publishing Co.; New York: International Universities Press).

adults be influenced in their attitudes toward real twins. In their expectations as to what constitutes the psychology of twins and especially the interrelatedness of twins, Dorothy Burlingham sees an environmental factor affecting the development of twin children reared by such adults.

Generally speaking, the author rightly emphasizes that it is of paramount importance to study which way the relationship of the mother to twins differs from her relationship to her other children. For example, having twins represents for many mothers a special kind of narcissistic gratification. Especially if twins look very much alike, as is the case with identical twins, the mothers often tend to make them even more similar looking (though they may, at the same time, be proud that they can tell them apart). This consideration is obviously relevant for the evaluation of the relative roles heredity and environment play in the concordant behavior of identical twins.

The observations recorded on the three pairs of identical twins are full of fascinating data that cannot, of course, be reported in detail here. An appendix of minute sleep charts and developmental charts adds to the value of the material. The most essential contribution is toward an understanding of the responses of one twin to the other and to the mother. The author describes examples of activity and passivity toward each other, and also reversal of roles in this respect. Instances of competition, copying, contagion of feelings are reported (the question is raised how much the constitutional identity of the twins influences them to imitate each other). There is a tendency in identical twins to form a "working team"; if disturbed by the environment, they combine forces against it. This team relationship may at least temporarily prevent them from normal contacts with other children. The reaction of one twin to separation from the other one also is very revealing; the mirror image is occasionally taken for the other twin and may be a source of comfort. The absent twin may become overestimated ("She is much bigger than me"). In order to overcome the suffering of separation, efforts at sublimation in the form of games are made. Sole possession of the mother, as would happen in the case of illness, is not so thoroughly enjoyed as one might have expected: "It appeared that the children felt the wish for sole possession of the mother too much and were too aware of the absent rival. They feared the time when the mother would leave them to visit their twin and became upset as the time for reunion drew near" (p. 51).

Twinship and mother relationship develop simultaneously and influence each other. Various attempts are made to conquer rivalry for the mother's love, for the sake of the twin relationship. Jealousy of each other is overcome by identification and by fairness (as a reaction formation against competition).

The closeness of the twin relationship is very much apparent in the material presented. One twin may substitute the other for the mother or another love object in case of frustration. They understand each other in a way that goes beyond the realm of consciousness. Twins may also complement each other, using the characteristics of the other they find missing in themselves. This close relationship, however, is often threatened by aggressive competition; it also is often responded to by a wish for privacy, individualization, and independence.

In all three pairs of twins there were differences from birth on. The earliest divisions of roles are probably determined by bodily strength. Some of the later differences can be traced to the division into one active and one passive partner. Individual characteristics may change when the twins exchange roles. Acquired differences are, in identical twins, often gradually overlaid by identifications. From this it follows that it is unwarranted to attribute the greater similarity of identical twins (as compared with nonidentical ones) only to hereditary factors, as has often been done.

Dorothy Burlingham, obviously very familiar with these implications of twinship, concludes her book with some very pertinent advice for the upbringing of identical twins.

The setup in which the author conducted her investigations was obviously particularly well suited for elucidating the problems that were in the center of her interest. The outstanding merits of this work lie in the loving care for the individual observation, in the keenness and at the same time cautiousness of the conclusions, and in the clarity of presentation. While studying the specific features of twinship, the author also succeeded in shedding some light on problems of developmental psychology in general. And, above all, the data she collected and their interpretation are essential for the answer to the heredity-environment problems, the *via regia* to which is the study of identical twins.

On Giving Advice to Parents in Analysis

ANTON O. KRIS, M.D.

THE ANALYTIC TREATMENT OF ADULT PATIENTS WHO ARE PARENTS
often comes upon problems in regard to their children. In some
of these instances the evidence of difficulty or the signs of impending trouble run well ahead of the current analytic focus or
of the patient's own ability to recognize the significance of the
matter in question. The analyst, however, may be keenly aware
of potentially adverse effects on the development of a child or of
the family as a whole. While such concerns may be far from the
patient's attention or interest as an analysand, they are vital to
the patient's interest as a parent. Interventions closer to child
guidance than to psychoanalysis may be called for in the context
of analysis. I shall try to describe and illustrate the technical
problem that confronts the analyst in these situations.

Ordinarily the analyst does not give advice to his patients in
analysis. Although he regularly makes use of his knowledge of
child development, he does not generally function as an "expert"
or as an "educator" in the analytic situation. As a participant in
the analytic method his aim is to help the patient express in
words, without reservation, all thoughts, feelings, wishes, sensations, images, and memories, i.e., to facilitate free association
(Kris, 1981). The analyst's responsibilities include not only the
function of interpretation and the willingness to experience the

Training and supervising analyst, The Boston Psychoanalytic Institute.

This paper is dedicated to the memory of Dorothy Burlingham. Its topic lies
at the intersection of her special interest in parents and my interest in the
technique of adult analysis.

drama of the transference. The analyst also is responsible for his own neutrality in regard to the patient's conflicting wishes and attitudes and for his personal anonymity (not out of slavish devotion to secrecy, but because the analysis is intended to focus on the patient). The analyst, in my view, has no right to exert authority in the treatment and holds no brief to give advice or make decisions. He must harness every impulse and action to serve his primary aim: to help the patient pursue and expand the free associations. While analysts vary in their conception of the analytic stance, there is wide agreement that the analyst should not ordinarily give his patients advice. Before I proceed to a consideration of the circumstances in regard to patients' children in which I believe the analyst is not only justified but obligated to intervene in such a way on the basis of his expert knowledge, I want to draw two distinctions.

What I shall describe cannot, I believe, be tucked away under the rubric of dealing with the patient's "acting out," even in a broad sense of that term. When the analyst recognizes acting out (the patient's expression of thought, feeling, wish, and, especially, memory in actions rather than in words), he does so principally on the basis of his position in the joint venture of analysis. The analyst's capacity to observe and to maintain perspective is, naturally, much less subject to regression and so much less influenced by inner pressures than is the patient's. Confrontation of acting out does not require an alteration in the analyst's aim and ordinary functions, nor does the analyst do so as an external authority. The analyst draws the patient's attention to the occurrence of acting out in order to facilitate expression of *current* associations in words. When the analyst addresses problems in regard to patients' children, at a time when those problems are not the present focus of free association, however, the analyst operates authoritatively as an "expert," as an educator rather than as a participant in the analytic method. His immediate aim is not to facilitate free association but to promote action outside the analysis.

Similarly, I do not regard the child guidance kind of intervention as a modification of ordinary psychoanalytic technique adapted to patients' psychological weaknesses or developmental deficiencies. These interventions are not made because the analytic process would fail to advance without such unusual assistance. They are made because of the analyst's sense of urgent need for action outside the analysis. They depend upon the analyst's relatively greater knowledge and his freedom to assess correctly situations that concern the development of patients' children.

Naturally, in all these instances I regard it as preferable to approach the problem by way of the ordinary analytic focus on free association and the interpretation of the patient's unconscious conflicts. The extraordinary measures I shall illustrate are required when the analyst expects the time course for that approach to take too long vis-à-vis the risks for the patient's child or when the parent's failure to recognize the child's problem cannot be expected to yield to such an approach. I shall leave aside, for the moment, the way these considerations relate to the analytic process and to the nature of trust in the analytic situation. The question of values, it seems to me, can best be approached after the clinical problem has been defined. It is most important, however, to emphasize that when I refer to the analyst's concern for risks to the child's development, I do not claim certainty in prediction. Far from it. The state of the art is based on insufficient knowledge of outcome, which remains the focus of much-needed clinical research. The clinician, accordingly, tempers his concern with restraint, but he needs no claim to certainty in order to respond to present circumstances.

CLINICAL ILLUSTRATIONS

CASE 1

I want to begin with a simple instance—simple in the sense that it caused barely a ripple in the analysis. A woman returned to analysis after delivering her first baby and proposed a new schedule to fit with her job. I had told her that I would do my best to meet her requests. The hours she chose, however, would have added an analytic session after eight hours away from home on two days. I suggested that this would be unwise from the viewpoint of her relationship with the baby and the baby's development. The patient rejected my suggestion, saying that she wanted to try her own way, which would give her two full week-days at home on which she would not have to feel guilty for leaving the baby. In some ways, she said, she wanted only to stay at home, though she liked her work. The associations in the remainder of the session dealt with guilt for her good fortune in contrast to other members of her family. At the end of the hour I told her that I found the schedule she proposed unreasonable. I gave her a schedule that would not extend the time away from the baby on the two days she was to go to work for a full day, though it would require her to sacrifice her wish to have the two full days at home without any interruption. "That's so unlike you," she said, amused. She returned to the theme of guilt, and I suggested that guilt over wanting to stay with the baby and guilt over leaving the baby might be interfering with her maternal "instincts" in the matter of making a schedule. Subsequent references to this exchange were exclusively positive and grateful.

I do not believe that the patient on her own would soon enough have recognized the strain that her plan might have introduced in her relationship with a baby in the first months of life. The schedule she proposed, after all, represented a reasonable compromise, from her own viewpoint, for she had not yet begun to think for two. My insistence on avoiding the risk of serious difficulty could not, however, claim to have been directly in the service of the patient's analysis. On the contrary, it might have closed off an avenue for analysis, for I could not be certain what factors entered into her proposed schedule, though guilt appeared to have been an influence along with insufficient knowledge of a baby's needs and capacities. Had the schedule problem been outside the analysis, I would, of course, have been limited to giving advice rather than insisting on the specific hours. I did, in fact, recommend that she reduce the two eight-hour days, but considerations beyond her control dictated their length. My action and advice, which did not become the subject of analysis at any later time, were accepted and appreciated by the patient as they were intended. It did not prevent successful completion of the analysis, and, in particular, the patient proved to be an excellent mother, readily capable of thinking for two. In retrospect, it appears that acute but transient interference with healthy capacities resulted from the influence of chronic conflicts in a new developmental stage and required only the temporary assistance of my intervention. The chronic conflicts, themselves, did require significant analytic resolution, though we did not happen to delineate their operation in the events described.

CASE 2

In the first months of analysis the depressed and inhibited father of a 3-year-old girl, Ruthie, mentioned his daughter's watching him dress in the mornings before he came for his analysis. Leaving home so early, he would arrange his clothes in the living room the night before, so as not to disturb his wife. His daughter, hearing him get up, would regularly join him. After one such occasion his associations included concerns about Ruthie watching television too much, but I found little evidence to support an intervention suggesting that he was concerned about her looking at him. Unsure of my ground I remained silent on this matter, though I thought that it would be better for the little girl not to be exposed to her father's nakedness under these conditions. An opportunity presented itself one day, in the fourth month of analysis, when he began speaking of his past and present difficulties in making relationships. "My wife feels she could have done a lot for me. I didn't have much human contact," he said. Then he recalled with pleasure his plans to build a fence on his property on the coming weekend. Soon he was speaking of throwing roadblocks in his own way in projects he undertakes. I pointed out the sequence of thoughts, raising fences and roadblocks, excluding people, especially his wife. I suggested that similar fences in analysis were the result of inner resistances to free association. His wife irritated him like his mother in some ways, he observed. He wondered whether his feelings for his wife were related to old sexual feelings for his mother but recognized on his own that he was theorizing. "It's clear to me that Ruthie has great sexual interest in me. She talks about having babies, with me as the father. Her attachment to Alice [his wife] has shifted to me. A little boy came to the house, and Ruthie asked whether Tommy has a penis. She's interested in all males. Tommy's father would laugh. What if we tell Ruthie in 15 years?

I hope we can tell her gently not to say such things in public. I hope we can." I noted that he made references to generalization, his own from mother to wife and Ruthie's from himself to all males and suggested that he was concerned that excessive harshness would lead to general inhibition. I added that the result depends not only on what the parents say but on how the child hears it. He wondered what he himself may have "*over*-heard" as a child. Then he described getting Ruthie up at night to urinate, as he was gotten up. He remembered walking to the bathroom. How bright it was. "Perhaps it's better to walk," he said, "but I carry Ruthie. She's conscious but might make more effort to be dry if it were less pleasant." At this point I said that I thought he was raising the question of whether his relationship with Ruthie was too stimulating for her, watching him dress and liking to be carried to the toilet. I wondered if too much excitement interfered with her developing control. He confirmed that she had mastered waking bladder control at age 2. Borrowing from the poet, I reminded him that just as good fences make good neighbors, children need controls to negotiate with the outer world. He said that he would suffer if he made love to every woman in the street and, then, quickly recognized, "You were trying to tell me something more than I was hearing." I said that he seemed to hold a theory that his mother had not been gratifying enough to him and seemed to be acting on that with Ruthie, gratifying her in ways not helpful to her. I added that without adequate controls in growing up, inner conflicts could be expected to result in inhibition. He did not know whether to tell Ruthie that he would not be the father of her babies, he said. I suggested that children need compassion for accepting reality. He now quoted a similar view from a child guidance book he was reading. I added that he could see he had been thinking about these matters and connecting Ruthie with himself. He agreed.

The following hour brought further associations to exhibitionism between generations, heterosexual and homosexual. He was taking care to diminish his own exhibitionism with Ruthie, though he seemed to feel slightly put upon by me and not altogether certain I was right. One of the sources of these feelings, I suggested, might be my departure from neutrality. The day after that he mentioned Ruthie's great pride in having been dry at night. We heard no more of that problem, in regard to Ruthie, though the theme of exhibitionism and problems of control and inhibition remained central to the analysis.

In this instance I believe that my concerns for the welfare of the little girl and for the relationship of father and child justified an emphasis and directiveness that would not otherwise have been warranted. So early in the analysis it would have been preferable to go slower, I believe, and, especially, not to say anything that might interfere with expressions of love. True, the patient was himself concerned about his relationship with Ruthie to some extent, as evidenced by his reading. I had waited long enough for that. Nonetheless, the "expert" position that implied that his actions might be harming his child could only be expected to encourage further inhibition. Or, at least, the fear of criticism and the sense of analytic interference could not be dismissed.

While I would do the same again, I cannot claim to know that this intervention of mine did not retard or interfere with the analytic process. Some analysts may well disagree with my decision. They might have confined themselves to less didactic comments despite concern for the child's development, waiting for the analytic process to develop so far that an interpretation of the patient's conflict over his relationship to Ruthie would suffice to bring about a resolution. Others, on the contrary, might regard my worries for Ruthie as excessive. The romance, they might contend, was far from dangerous, and the family might have found a solution on their own had I stayed my guiding hand. Still others might view my doubts about my intervention as surprising. The analytic method is not so delicate as all that: whatever damage might be done could not be of sufficient concern to warrant a risk for the child's development; the patient felt free enough to express at least some resentment subsequently; and I had acknowledged my unusual shift of aim in this instance.

There is room, here, it seems to me, for difference of opinion, but I believe the problem posed by such interferences with the free association method are ignored at the patient's peril. Once again I think it important to recognize that we were not engaged in the analysis of acting out. The patient's actions with Ruthie were influenced by a fantasy, I believe, in which he would provide her the gratification that he felt deprived of in his relationship with his mother and with his wife. There was no evidence, however, that this was the result of thoughts and wishes stimulated in the analytic process that were expressed in action in the relationship to Ruthie rather than in words in the transference. Furthermore, my intervention did not aim at promoting verbalization in analysis but was aimed at increasing his awareness of his relationship with Ruthie so he could modify it.

CASE 3

In the long treatment of a young man I had the opportunity to observe his engagement and marriage after much hesitation that fueled the early years of his analysis. The birth of a daughter, Nancy, brought him unambivalent joy, without parallel in his adult life. The little girl was the rare beneficiary of devoted attention from both parents, with an especially good mother. Both parents were at their own best with her.

The exciting and loving relationship between father and daughter grew splendidly. Strong bonds between them were strengthened, from the father's side, on their shared experience as first children. There was the additional transference of his love for the second of his younger sisters, who had been his childhood love, the object of his displaced erotic love for his mother and of his identification with mother in caretaking. He participated actively and willingly in taking care of his daughter. He reveled in Nancy's love for him, the more as she could furnish it with words.

The birth of a much-wanted second child, Peter, when Nancy was just under 2½, found this patient curiously unable to respond to him. The analysis showed that Peter was for him, unconsciously, the intruder, the first of his younger sisters. After several months, perhaps in part as a result of analysis, surely in part as a result of the little boy's bewitching activity, the father's interest and pride were awakened. Peter was now the only boy in the family, like himself, dark-haired, with wonderful brown eyes, in the tallest percentiles, and well coordinated. The baby's mother was likewise entranced.

It would be quite incorrect to suppose that either parent deserted the little girl, except from Nancy's point of view. Where she had at first been content to tolerate some loss of her mother, she had retained her father's relatively unaltered devotion. His rising interest in Peter, however, coincided with Nancy's increasing erotic interest in him. More and more often familiar games with her father would end unhappily with Nancy trying to run her hands over his genitals, which he would do his best to stop. Memories of his own childhood were stirred, which was helpful for the analysis, but Nancy began to lose her father, too, in a sense. That is, the attempt to solve her envy of her brother's close relationship with their mother's body by shifting from mother to father burdened the growing oedipal desires with excessive conflict. Increasingly there were bitter quarrels with her mother, who, for her own reasons, was not at her best with a daughter in this phase of development. Nancy began to sound frustrated and unhappy. She kept getting into trouble with both parents. My own concern was triggered when I heard the patient's increasingly negative comments about her, which seemed to go beyond the bounds of his unfriendly sister transference to her and to exceed his aversion to her sexual advances. I thought he was responding to an increasingly provocative self-critical child, who was inviting rejection and punishment. This, for reasons we knew well, would be a specially difficult problem for him to respond to with love and tolerance. His relationship with his father had been seriously marred by provocation and punishment throughout his childhood.

In the analysis, as I have indicated, the engagement, marriage, and life with the children brought us a very helpful, complex source of transference revival of the patient's own troubled childhood. The problem with Nancy did not seem to me to reflect current neurotic problems of her father. They did, however, need his help for solution, for it seemed to both of us that his wife could not do more. I suggested to him that if he could not overcome the antipathy to Nancy, he and his wife should consider a consultation with a child analyst, who might be able to help Nancy over this difficult period of her development. I outlined for him the sequence I have just sketched of the development of Nancy's problem.

Whether I overestimated the degree of difficulty and underestimated the natural evolution of the problem and its resolution or whether my intervention was sufficient to serve as a stimulus for the patient to manage better, I do not know. The outcome, in any case, was very soon the desired restitution of ordinary family life.

Unlike the other two examples I have given, this instance raises no doubt in my mind. My intervention promoted the patient's identification with my attitude as an analyst, helping him to be a good and understanding father and husband. The educational function of my "child guidance" intervention was closely interwoven with his own analytic interests.

DISCUSSION

I have tried to delineate a kind of situation in analysis in which the analyst finds it necessary to abandon his ordinary position of neutrality and anonymity and to replace his usual aim of promoting free association in the analytic situation with advice for action outside analysis. That is, when faced with a developmental crisis or emergency in the life of a patient's child, the analyst may *side* with his patient's parental interests and act as an *expert advisor* providing child guidance. He relinquishes the fundamental analytic interest of the patient in favor of essential aims of greater urgency which temporarily claim higher priority.

I want to emphasize that I am not focusing on some element of personal style. It is not, here, a question of many words or few, of affect freely shared or relatively emotionless interventions, or of a light touch rather than a heavy one on the analyst's part. The technical alterations I have presented are substantively opposite to ordinary analytic technique. Yet many analysts would regard them as far from unusual; some might even find them commonplace. It is consistent with the aims of analysis to seek an intervention as closely aligned as possible with the analytic process to prevent irreversible damage to a child's development. The nature and extent of such an intervention, as all other aspects of technique, derive partly from the analyst's personal style and temperament, where variety is apt to be the rule rather than the exception. Failure to intervene, however, would be a breach of trust.

Several frames of reference impinge upon the conception of trust in the analytic situation, in that portion of the bond between patient and analyst which Freud (1926) described as "no more than a certain amount of respect, trust, gratitude and human sympathy" (p. 225). The analyst, whether he is conceived of by the patient as some sort of doctor, teacher, minister, or parent figure, is seen as a person concerned with the patient's general welfare. The patient is entitled to assume that the analyst concentrates on the realization of "health values," guided by his "professional code," as Hartmann (1960) called it, following the "therapeutic imperative" (p. 55f.). How is the patient in retrospect to understand the analyst's failure to act in regard to the patient's child, when the process of analysis, perhaps too late, has caught up with events within the family? How is the analyst to understand it? Suppose that such insight into the analyst's failure to act develops midway in the analytic process; the moral question has now become a technical one: such a failure on the analyst's part could interfere with analysis prospectively, too.

There are related situations in which action is regularly taken by the analyst to secure the patient from harm or humiliation. In acting out, for example, where analytic process and external action occur in phase with each other, the analyst has no hesitation in warning the patient of danger as a step toward interpretation. Such situations are generally characterized by their reference to the patient himself and by the immediacy of their effect on rapport or alliance, as well as by their closeness to the current analytic focus. The relationship of parent and a child at risk warrants similar management, I believe.

My emphasis, however, aims to highlight for the analyst who gives child guidance within analysis that to act in this manner, no matter how skillfully, runs counter to ordinary analytic technique and may compromise the analytic process. To regard such interventions either as the analysis of acting out or as a matter of style, alone, would increase the risk of disturbing the analytic process. Recognition of the suspension of the analyst's usual aims and acknowledgment of this unusual procedure to the patient tend to diminish the disruptive impact.

BIBLIOGRAPHY

Freud, S. (1926), The question of lay analysis. *S.E.*, 20:183–258.
Hartmann, H. (1960), *Psychoanalysis and Moral Values.* New York: Int. Univ. Press.
Kris, A. O. (1981), *Free Association: Method and Process.* New Haven & London: Yale Univ. Press (in press).

The Adolescent's Use of the Body in Object Relationships and in the Transference

A Comparison of Borderline and Narcissistic Modes of Functioning

M. EGLÉ LAUFER, B.Sc.

THE PHYSICAL CHANGES OCCURRING AT PUBERTY NEED TO BE IN-cluded in the adolescent's body image. One of the factors that may prevent these changes from being made successfully is related to the superego, insofar as the superego acts as a source of the narcissistic cathexis of the self image.

The postoedipal child enters latency with a more or less stable means of maintaining the narcissistic cathexis of his self image. He knows the sort of behavior, thoughts, and emotions which ensure a sense of feeling loved and approved of internally, and how to avoid disapproval and feelings of shame. The basis for this approval or criticism is derived from the identifications with the original objects which have become structured within the child's superego during the oedipal period. Some authors such as Lampl-de Groot (1962) and Jacobson (1964) have gone further and emphasized this aspect of the function of the superego by conceptualizing the ego ideal as a separate structure, and then extending the concept of this ego ideal by deriving it from much earlier identifications with the original objects.

I would include, as part of the earliest identifications, those

Centre for Research into Adolescent Breakdown/Brent Consultation Centre, London.

made by the infant of his or her own rudimentary body image with the mother's body. I would therefore see the source of the narcissistic cathexis of the body ego in the identifications of the body image with what is experienced as the mother's relationship to the child's body. In later life the fantasy of union of one's own body with the mother's body is contained in an idealized form within the ego ideal and acts as a means of maintaining the experience of libidinal cathexis of the body image. Actual physical experiences, both of an object-related and autoerotic nature, continue to be integrated throughout childhood within the context of their relation to the maintenance of the fantasy of this narcissistic union with the gratifying mother.

The arrival of puberty is thus unconsciously experienced as a loss, represented by the loss of the child's sexually undifferentiated body. The adolescent experiences himself as if alone for the first time with his body, and rightly holds the changes in his body responsible for what he is experiencing. Masturbatory experiences, which formerly provided the most important means for the child to feel in control of actively creating the experience of the fantasy of union with the gratifying mother, now take on a new and potentially conflictual meaning. What we can then observe is the effort which the adolescent is *compelled* to make, either autoerotically or in relation to real objects, to restore that which he or she has lost. The adolescent is driven to find ways of experiencing his new body as gratified, loved, and approved in reality or in fantasy in order to avoid the anxiety which threatens to overwhelm him when he feels unable to achieve this. The anxiety becomes augmented by the experience of the loss of control of the active/aggressive components of the libidinal strivings, which in the clinical situation may appear as representing the main area of conflict for the adolescent.

Some of the technical difficulties which we regard as typical in the analysis of adolescents can thus be understood as resulting from the adolescent's feeling compelled, by the anxiety he experiences, to use his body as part of an object relationship. The demand the adolescent makes on the analyst is to be given the experience of his body being loved and wanted. Being understood by the analyst is not enough. In the transference, this demand for direct gratification can be understood as the repetition of the incestuous sexual wishes; with the less disturbed adolescent, the understanding of the meaning of what he is seeking in making these demands of the analyst can enable him to control the intensity of these demands and the accompanying aggression.

The two patients I will describe constantly presented the analyst with their need to involve their bodies in the analytic relationship. The actual manner in which each patient did so was, however, totally different. One patient, a girl aged 18, would, by her impulsive behavior and the manner in which she functioned emotionally, come under the classification of "borderline functioning." The other patient, a girl also aged 18, responded to all attempts to come close to her either physically or emotionally as intrusive attacks, and behaved as if she wished to remain totally isolated from any physical contact and from the analyst. Behind her isolation lay paranoid fears and fantasies. Her level of functioning could be seen as representing a "narcissistic personality disorder." Although I am using these diagnostic classifications purely descriptively to define a certain level of functioning, I believe that the differing use each of these patients made of her body in her object relationships can tell us something about the meaning of borderline and narcissistic personality disorders in adults.

CASE PRESENTATIONS

CASE 1

Miss B, the "borderline" patient, was potentially an attractive young woman. She was intelligent and artistically very creative. When I first saw her, she was tastefully but not strikingly dressed and gave no particular outward indications of being emotionally disturbed. She appeared to relate appropriately to me, although she seemed unable to say why she felt she needed treatment. She was living alone in a room in London. Her parents had separated two years previously. Her mother had recently set up home with another man. Miss B had been referred for psychological treatment by a gynecologist whom she had consulted because of irregular menstruation. Later I learned that her mother had also become worried because, when Miss B stayed with her, she refused to eat any meals but then would secretly stuff herself with anything that was available in the pantry.

In my interview with Miss B I also felt concerned about the very vague manner in which she talked about her immediate future plans. Despite having no clear idea of what she felt was wrong with her, she agreed rapidly with my suggestion that she might get a part-time job so that she would be able to come at the times I could see her. These details showed how eagerly and hungrily she responded to my offer of treatment; as if she felt it was an offer from me to fill her empty life. During the first few months of treatment it became clear that her feeling of emptiness could be understood as being related to the loss of the old relationship to her mother—as if because her mother no longer needed her, she was left feeling lost herself.

Miss B was the youngest child in a large family, and felt that she had always had a very special and close relationship to her mother, different from that of the other siblings. She saw this as related in some way to her mother's own need because of the unsatisfactory relationship which existed between her mother and father. More specifically she was very aware that the unsatisfactoriness related to the sexual life of her parents. Although Miss B consciously felt pleased for her mother now being happy, she also felt terribly jealous of the new man in her mother's life; she no longer was necessary for her mother. As these feelings were acknowledged, Miss B talked of what had been her greatest fear when she first left home at 16: sitting alone in her room and feeling totally unable to move or do anything. She had told me that she now masturbated when alone, and I could make the link how she needed to masturbate in order to reassure herself that she needed her body for her own needs and not only as something with which to satisfy her mother. She now used masturbation to identify both her own needs and with the mother that she longed for, as if through feeling her body being stimulated she could create the fantasy of not being alone or helpless.

As the analysis progressed, Miss B began to show her attachment to me more openly, but this was expressed only in her behavior. She found it increasingly difficult to leave after her sessions. She implied that she felt helpless and unable to control herself and get home; on a few occasions I had to call a taxi for her. At that time, although it was worrying, it still seemed part of the ongoing analytic material that was being acted out in the transference. Looking back, however, I can see that it was part of another process that was going on simultaneously and independently of the analytic work. At times I reacted to this by feeling worried, and at other times I simply felt uneasy since it seemed more as if I was being repeatedly put on the spot to maintain an analytic distance from the patient. For instance, Miss B would come into the room and go casually over to the bookcase and pick up a book and comment on it, wanting me to reply. Or she would ask to borrow a book, or just walk around the room looking at other things and picking them up. She might suddenly sit up and face me during the session; or after a long silence she got up and walked out. It was all done with an air of casual innocence which appeared to deny completely the implication of her actions, dismissing any attempts at understanding her behavior. At the time, I felt as if I was constantly being tested out, and I knew that this behavior contained all her aggression against me. Now I can see it as Miss B's actual inability to keep to the analytic framework during those times when she felt unable to contain her anxiety.

Yet, throughout this period, she brought material in the form of dreams and associations, and analytic work appeared to be proceeding. Her behavior seemed to be motivated by the need to involve me more directly with herself and with her actual body. Later, when she became more manifestly disturbed, her behavior became increasingly unpredictable. Once, instead of leaving my home (where my consulting room is) after a session, she wandered off and found a piano and started playing it. Another time I came home late at night and found her lying in the road outside my home, apparently in a semidrugged state, and I had to get her to a hospital. Looking back again, I now understand these events as a gradual intrusion of her actual body into the analytic relationship, as a constant demand that I should accept her wish for physical care and stimulation of her body, and as her experiencing my efforts to keep an analytic distance via interpretations as a rejection of her body and an implied disapproval of her wishes.

Her relationships outside the analytic situation were characterized by the same apparent vagueness and denial of any conscious motivation. She talked of the ideal relationship she had
had with a man the year before she started treatment. This was
probably her first really important relationship to a man. Although she mentioned the fact that this man had now left London and the relationship had ended, she was clearly denying
how distressed she was. The only way she could communicate
her distress to me was by cutting off her hair. Her hair had
played an important role in the relationship as something he
admired in her. She described it as an ideal relationship because
they never made any fixed arrangements to meet; whenever she
wanted to be with him, they would just happen to bump into each
other in the street. During her analysis she lived alone in a part of
London where many other lonely young people drifted around.
She said she had many friends, but she described these relationships in such a vague and idealized way that I had no real picture
of the ever-changing persons. What did emerge was that Miss B
seemed to participate in whatever sexual or drug-taking activity
was suggested to her; she lacked the ability to feel critical of or
discriminatory about the actual activity or the person involved.
The wish to have her body accepted and not to be alone with it
seemed to overcome any other feelings she might have.

At the point when we began to get closer to her feelings and
anxieties about sexual relationships, she acted out dramatically.
She spoke of having been unable to allow herself to be pene-
trated by the man she had been fond of, but that they had practiced fellatio together. The day after she had been able to tell me
this, I was contacted by a psychiatric unit where she had been
taken because her employer had become frightened by her odd
behavior at work. All she could tell the hospital staff was my telephone number. She stayed in the hospital for a short period,
keeping contact with me by phone. She was diagnosed at that
time as being schizophrenic. When I saw her again, she told me
she had in fact swallowed a great deal of hash that day and had
become quite unable to function or communicate, but that she
had still known exactly what was happening to her. On the
phone with me she could only repeatedly say "Yes." This very
worrying episode raised the question of the degree to which she

was functioning on a psychotic level, even though it could be understood as the acting out of her sexual experience and of how crazy and out of control it had made her feel.

She now began to have normal intercourse, but this did not stop her participation in perverse sexual activities. The need for the latter was specifically related to the compulsive repetition of earlier childhood experiences. As a child she had been very close to her slightly older brother with whom she had been continuously involved in mutual masturbatory games and activities. She blamed her mother for never having made any attempts to stop them, even though it had all been done quite openly. The only thing her mother could not tolerate, she said, was any anger directed at her. Miss B's father also appeared to have acted in a very seductive way. He walked around naked in front of the children; when Miss B woke early in the morning, he would encourage her to come into his bed and hold her close to his body, telling her that she must not wake her mother. Miss B now repeated these experiences with a girl and her boyfriend whom she had met at the hospital. She masturbated with the girl in front of the boyfriend and watched the girl and her boyfriend having intercourse. She identified with the girl's sexual demands on her, and derived pleasure from feeling needed in the same passive uncritical way as she had previously felt with her male acquaintances. My role as analyst was constantly to try to mobilize her awareness of her own feelings, and thus of her own body, and to help her not to feel as if she was completely helpless and without wishes and needs of her own. What she was now acting out was her wish to offer herself to me in whatever way I would want.

I do not know whether analysis would have succeeded in allowing Miss B to feel more in touch with her own body, and thus aware of her own feelings, had we been able to continue uninterruptedly. But two years after her analysis had started, Miss B's mother suddenly died. By this time we had been able to reconstruct Miss B's intense longing for physical closeness to her mother, and to relate her present hatred of her mother and of herself to her feeling excluded in favor of a man, thus implying that her body could not offer equal satisfaction. After the mother's death my main effort was to help Miss B to mourn for her. At the time it seemed as if analysis did help her work through some of the depression and anger with her mother for now leaving her completely; she even began to experience some relief about feeling freer from her tie to her mother.

Yet, once more another process was going on simultaneously. This could first be seen by Miss B's wish to hold my hand in the session. Unconsciously her wish was that I should need to hold her hand. She told me how, when she was little, she used to sit under the table and secretly hold and fondle her mother's hand while her mother went on talking to other grownups. Her fantasy was that her mother really needed her rather than the people she was talking to. Miss B was now haunted by the thought that her mother's body had been cremated, her hand was no longer available, and her mother did not need her. In all her dreams she now was in the sea, with or without her mother, floating and being engulfed; they contained all her longing for her mother and the wish for physical union and closeness with her. In the transference, she demanded that I replace the loss of her mother in reality. She became increasingly uncontrolled and had aggressive outbursts when she felt forced by me to leave at the end of the session. A crisis was reached in a session when she sat up and began to rock in a masturbatory way, and then banged her head against the wall so violently that I had to intervene for fear that she would damage herself. (Her mother had died of a cerebral clot.) She talked of wanting to masturbate, and when I suggested that she try not to, but talk of her feelings about it, she became violent and smashed an ashtray and was so out of control that I had to hold her and have her taken to a hospital.

This crisis, which temporarily brought analysis to an end, appeared to result from her inability to use masturbation to experience in fantasy the union with her mother's body, with a resulting loss of control of her violence against me in the transference where I represented the depriving mother who no longer needed her. It was clear to me at the time that the real danger lay in her directing the violence against her own body because she experienced it as useless. She had not been able to prevent her mother from dying, and now only death could reunite her with her mother's body.

While Miss B was in the hospital, she remained in daily contact with me by phone. At the same time I continued to visit her weekly in order, as I saw it, to help her maintain a sense of reality about what was happening to her. I was aware that the telephone calls enabled her to feel that through "creating" my voice for herself by dialing my telephone number, she was also able to maintain the fantasy that she had made me into her real mother and could deny any sense of loss as the result of her actions. I was concerned, therefore, about how she would react to the next holiday break when I would not be available. Despite my awareness and the hospital's cooperation, interpretations were not enough to deal with the violence and despair that were precipitated by the announcement of the forthcoming holiday: Miss B made a serious suicide attempt with every intention of dying. Luckily, she was found by a member of the hospital staff.

CASE 2

Miss N, like Miss B, made a suicide attempt and had had an eating disturbance. Miss N was referred for analysis while she was an inpatient in a psychiatric unit following the suicide attempt. During the period that she was in the unit, she had remained completely withdrawn and isolated from the other patients and staff. She was a slightly built, timid girl who looked much younger than her age and spoke so quietly that I could barely hear her. When I first saw her, she kept herself completely hidden in her coat, which she seldom removed. When she talked of what had made her want to die, one of the things she mentioned was the feeling that her body was disgusting and that she was terribly ashamed of it. Before her suicide attempt she had been unable to control a compulsive need secretly to stuff herself with food at night, and this had made her feel fat and repulsive. Later I learned that during the initial period in the hospital after her suicide attempt, Miss N had refused to eat and had become so thin that there had been concern about her being anorexic. She herself told me that she had felt compelled to make herself thin in order to be able to go on living. Thus, unconsciously she had used her ability to refuse food as a way of reassuring herself that she could maintain control of her body and its demands in order to be able to feel she could like it. Any outward indication that she no longer was in control of her body made her feel that she was unacceptable and disgusting, bringing with it the threat of her violence being directed against herself or against the object whom she saw as responsible for the loss of control. In the transference I was identified with an intrusive object that could make her lose control, while she desperately sought to remain in control of her feelings and thoughts.

My only value to her at that time was that I represented a defense against her regressive wish to have her body controlled by her mother, the intruder against whom her violence was directed. She enlisted my help in not having to return to her home after she left the hospital, but she insisted that I not tell her mother that it was her own wish. She used the fantasy that she had been able to make her mother feel useless by showing her that she now had me to care for her. She talked of having felt as a child that her mother did not take sufficient care of her body— she had not washed her hair often enough or put cream on her skin. She remembered that when she was 15, she had felt that she could now care for her own body, and that she had been conscious of feeling that she could do this better than her mother had. At that time she also decided to leave home in order to become independent of her mother, but had felt despairingly that she would just starve if she did so. In her behavior toward me she alternated between creating omnipotent fantasies to make her feel big and powerful when she no longer needed me, and being consumed with rage when these were challenged by her reality. At the same time she felt she was totally helpless and dependent on an all-powerful but intrusive mother whom she needed to give in to in order to fulfill her own needs. She defended against the awareness of her needs through making her body "dead" in many different ways. She expressed her dependence on her mother only through her need for approval from her; it was as if she could control her body but not her fear of rejection.

The first time she had gone out with a boy she had refused to see him again because she felt that her mother had not approved of her choice. But she also felt afraid of her wish to be kissed.

Miss N had always been an exceptionally good and obedient child and had fulfilled her mother's high academic expectations of her. She was an only child, and her mother had devoted her life to making her daughter into the perfect child. At first Miss N was able to come to her sessions only accompanied by her mother; she was dressed in clothes to make her look like a little girl. In the hospital setting she tried to identify with the other young patients in order to feel more normal. Being a patient in a hospital meant no longer being mother's perfect child, a thought that gave her hope. Feeling that she must have a boyfriend, she attached herself quite unrealistically to a male patient and made plans to go and live with him. She tried to copy other patients to feel like them. She threw and broke things when they did, went stealing from a supermarket together with them, and finally allowed one of the patients into her bed. But I did not understand the meaning of this behavior until much later. The only times that her involvement with other people appeared real was when it contained the demand to be protected against fantasied or real frightening intrusive attacks. When she went home for a visit and was alone with her mother, she became overwhelmed by a fear that her mother was trying to poison her. She saw her mother as jealous of her and of her relationship to her father. But the only relationship to men, including her father, she could permit herself was intense long "talks" which were meant to make both her mother and me feel jealous and excluded. Her body played no part in any relationship to men.

Miss N appeared to be engaged in a constant battle, both with her mother and with me in the transference, to take over control of her own body, rather than having to feel dependent on the object. After a year of analysis Miss N said she had had a totally new experience. She could now feel what it was like to be hungry and then choose to eat because of the hunger, rather than eat because it was the time her mother had taught her that one should eat. Making her body feel dead and without needs appeared to be her only defense against experiencing her wish to be intruded on by her mother or me. And, with regard to her suicide attempt, she said that there had been no particular reason for her to do it at that time; she had already felt dead for the last two years, so it made no difference to kill herself.

Suicide, for Miss N, was the only means by which she could express her wish to feel that her body belonged to her, to do with it what she wanted. It thus represented the *only* way of removing herself from her mother, and at the same time controlling the wish to give in to her. (This was different for Miss B, who saw suicide as the only means of reuniting her body with that of her mother and remaining a part of her.)

Later Miss N told me that she could talk only if she had previously decided that the matter was something I could help her with; otherwise there was no point in talking of it. This attitude unconsciously represented her wish to control me, so that she could continue to experience me as protecting her. Only in this way could she feel safe and in control of her violence against me. When she became more conscious of how compelled she felt to keep certain thoughts secret from me, she wrote me a letter to explain what her thoughts were. They were related to fantasies of being given an enema by a man or by herself. She said the fantasies were due to her being obsessed by a memory of her mother giving her an enema when she was 4 years old. She added that, having told me this, it must now be clear to me why she hated her body so much, and that I must burn the letter. She responded to all attempts I made to discuss the letter in the sessions with cold silence. Eventually she exclaimed in an angry voice that I should by now realize that she had no wish to talk about this matter and that she could not do so. This feeling was so intense and real for her that months later, when she told me of a dream in which there was a pile of manure, she remarked that it had been a tremendous effort to bring herself even to say such a word as "manure" to me. I saw this as her fear of losing control over her physical excitement in the session; by not talking of potentially exciting thoughts, she could continue to keep her body dead and separate from me. Her conscious fantasy of a man or herself giving her the enema contained the defense against her wish to give her body to her mother or a woman.

She actually controlled her body as completely as her thoughts and feelings in the session. Most of the time she was quite rigid, still, and silent. When she was very tense, she might begin the session by being restless and clearly showing that she was under some physical tension to speak, but she would soon restrain herself and become totally still again, as if dead. It was quite uncanny at times to hear her running eagerly up the steps of my house, arriving early for her session as if she could not wait to tell me something, and then to see her come in and after a few restless movements turn still and silent for the whole session. Her need to be in control was expressed not only in her silence and body rigidity within the session, but also at times by staying away.

When she first left the hospital, she became involved with a boy in the hostel where she was living. She stayed up late at night talking to him, but she could tell me only the number of hours she had spent with him and not what had been said or done. She became manifestly more and more disturbed and unable to function at her work or at the hostel, while she continued to maintain a stubborn secrecy about what was going on. It was clear that the more she clung to her secret, the more frightened she became of me. Because of her continued defiance and her fantasy of me as the raping woman, she eventually became so frightened of me that she was unable to come to the sessions, having to stay at the hostel all day clinging to the warden. She could not be left alone at night. I had to arrange for her to go back to the hospital, where she stayed for some months.

During the next period of analysis, as Miss N gained some sense of independence from me, she acted out her fantasy that she could now dominate and control me completely. She stayed away from sessions without informing me before or after why she had done so. No amount of interpretation could interfere with the obvious gratification obtained from feeling that now she could make me be available whenever she wanted me, rather than having to feel as if I was in control of her. She ignored all references I made to her behavior and acted as if she was totally unaware that I had any feelings. Previously in the analysis she used to say hopelessly, "But you must have feelings about what I tell you. That's why I can't risk telling you things." Now she acted out her wish that my feelings did not affect her behavior in any way—what she wanted to show me and herself was that she no longer needed my approval. Clearly, she had now reversed the old situation with her mother. Now she could experience the satisfaction she felt her mother had obtained from being in control of her. Her demands on me, although less obvious than Miss

B's, were no less intense. I was paid to have no feelings or opinions of my own, and I had to sit and be bored if she had nothing to say or if she did not come. When she did come, her silences in the session also took on a new quality. She would come, but then go off to sleep for most of the hour. I had to remain still and silent. If I tried to talk about it, she dismissed all interpretations and said she was just tired. At the time it seemed to me that this behavior was her way of controlling me, but gradually it became clearer that she was beginning to enjoy the feeling of complete union with me while she lay asleep in a foetal position. I was there for her if she wanted to talk to me; and all the feelings aroused by outside stimuli, either in her life or in mine, which she experienced as threatening her wish for complete union with me, were now under her control via sleep. Neither she nor I were to have any feelings through talking, but she could now feel safe in being joined to me via both our "dead" bodies.

She responded to holiday breaks very differently from the way Miss B did—not with uncontrolled violence and anger and a wish for physical closeness, but with depression and by becoming ill. When I interpreted her illness as her wish for me to take physical care of her, she said that she hated being fussed over when she was ill and just wanted to be left alone. She did, in fact, regard illness as a failure to control her body and as something that made her body potentially unacceptable and disgusting to the object. As a child she had had repeated nightmares of having her body covered with boils and, in associating to this, referred to herself as an "untouchable leper."

Her relationships outside the analysis at first were very unreal. She would let herself have intense feelings only for a boy whom she saw in the train and whom she could keep as a fantasy-object, while the boys she went out with had no emotional significance to her. In real relationships she was terrified of being touched, which she experienced as an intrusion into her body and which could make her lose control over her aggression. She was afraid that she would attack and kick a boy who entered her room without warning her. She was afraid that if someone in a crowded Underground train pushed against her, she might lose control and kick that person. She had dreams of breaking off men's genitals. Yet, she accepted these feelings without any real anxiety, explaining that she had been told that already as a baby she could not bear to be touched by strangers; this seemed to have reinforced the fantasy she shared with her mother of their exclusive relationship.

Miss N felt depressed and anxious when she was without a boyfriend. She said it was not because she minded being alone, but she minded going out alone and being seen alone. But then she felt anxious at the thought that people might look at the boy rather than at her. Thus, she could obtain gratification of her body only from being looked at rather than from being touched. She expressed the same feeling when she talked of never wanting babies since they were too demanding and never gave anything in return. But then she added, "Except if it is a pretty baby."

Her need to keep the relationship to a boy nonsexual was consciously related to her fear of losing her virginity. She felt that being a virgin was the only good thing she would have to offer a man; she had to keep it in order to find a man who would deserve to have her. However, she continued to feel she must try to have relationships with men for fear of being regarded abnormal. She invited a man she met casually into her room at night; and when he tried to approach her, she fought him off. She came to the session in a manic state, triumphant that she had now proved that she could withstand a man's attempt to rape her.

Thus, as Miss N began to feel her body as alive, she was compelled, like Miss B, to use it in her relationship to the object, but she used it to reassure herself that she still was in total control of her own and the other person's bodies. In the transference she could allow herself to feel that she needed me only after a long period of defiant staying away, and then ringing me to tell me that she had decided to finish her analysis. She said that she had had to experience the feeling of actually having lost the analysis before she could have any feelings about how much she needed it. Apparently, she felt safe to experience feelings only when she was alone, and therefore did not risk being rejected. Miss B, on the other hand, was panic-stricken when she was left alone with her body and her feelings related to it. When Miss B once developed a stomachache, she could not allow me to leave her and held on to me when I tried to go. Miss B, unlike Miss N, experienced her body as a means of feeling united with the object, whereas Miss N could see it only as a potential threat to being rejected and could risk bringing it into a relationship only if it was "dead" and thus totally controlled.

DISCUSSION

On a libidinal level, both Miss B and Miss N had regressed to an oral mode of functioning in their object relationships, but there was a very important difference. Miss B, with all her uncontrolled, impulsive acting out, seemed to express not only an oral demandingness and greed, but also the wish to repeat an earlier form of intense satisfaction. Even her first sexual experience was an unconscious attempt to regain the mother's breast. Similarly, her anger was always related to feeling frustrated of some gratification (libidinal or narcissistic) in her immediate life, inducing her to find means of re-creating the earlier satisfaction for herself on an autoerotic level, i.e., without the dependence on the object. Thus, although her suicide attempt contained the attack on me for leaving her, it was also an attempt to deny the reality and to feel that she could achieve the intensely satisfying relationship she wanted with me through her own activity.

In contrast, Miss N consistently starved herself of all pleasurable experiences in her life as if to avoid reexperiencing an earlier painful sense of frustration. Thus, for instance, her compulsive overeating expressed her hatred of herself for losing control of her needs, at the same time confirming her hopelessness about ever finding satisfaction in the future. Unconsciously her expectation could only be that of more painful frustration and disappointment. Miss N had secretly stuffed herself with food before her suicide attempt, which she related to her feeling that she had already given up ("became dead") at the age of 16. This was also the time from which she dated her depression, when she had changed from feeling that she was attractive and could care for herself to feeling unable to take any interest in pleasure from her body or in going out. From then on she had stayed at home.

Miss N constantly felt threatened by her overwhelming aggression and hatred, which she could control only by silence and immobility. The aggression also represented the wish to starve and frustrate me in retaliation for her own frustration. It was as if she felt that the only satisfaction she could achieve would be through turning her passive experience into an active one. As a result of my attempt to show her how she in fact was starving herself of the relief that analytic work could give her, Miss N could allow herself to begin to have some hope in the future. This suggests that Miss N had in her early infancy actually experienced more painful frustration of her bodily needs than satisfying experiences of physical warmth from her mother's body; then, as an adolescent, she was unable to endure the hatred she experienced when she saw what others had and she had no hope of achieving with her sexual body. She could only repeat the fantasy of her mother getting all the satisfaction while she had none; her suicide was the only way of depriving her mother.

While the overt behavior of these two patients showed many similarities, the differences in its underlying meaning point to differences in their development. From these I would conclude that the adolescent who functions on a "borderline" level reacts to the sense of loss engendered by the change of body image with a compulsive attempt to repeat an earlier, intensely satisfying, physical relationship to the original object. This brings with it a constant vulnerability to loss of control over the aggression against the new object, when the new actual experience does not fulfill the fantasy experience. In comparison, in the adolescent functioning on the level of "narcissistic personality disorder," I think we see an ego whose whole mode of functioning is related to the need to defend against the frustration and disappointment resulting from the pubertal changes. Their aggression which they fear they cannot control unconsciously represents the wish to retaliate for the lack of gratification and the pain of their feeling of emptiness. Having no hope of obtaining libidinal satisfaction from a new object after the pubertal changes, they need to create a feeling of narcissistic self-sufficiency. The only source of narcissistic cathexis is through complete submission to the demands of the superego.

These considerations may also be used to speculate about the genesis of another characteristic feature of borderline pathology, that is, the patient's inability to maintain any sublimatory activity. In line with the view just presented, this could be seen as a rejection of any activity that does not have the unconsciously searched-for intensity of pleasurable bodily experience. To summarize this view in structural terms, it seems that in the "borderline" patient we are seeing the result of a particularly intense libidinal investment of the body image and a corresponding sense of loss at puberty; while in the patient with a "narcissistic personality disorder" we see the result of a failure or lack of a satisfactory libidinal investment of the body image, with a subsequent defensive attempt to compensate for this lack by the premature use of the superego as a substitute source of satisfaction and an intense wish to take over the role of the depriving object.

BIBLIOGRAPHY

Jacobson, E. (1964), *The Self and the Object World*. New York: Int. Univ. Press.
Lampl-de Groot, J. (1962), Ego ideal and superego. *Psychoanal. Study Child*, 17:94–106.

The Psychoanalyst and the Adolescent's Sexual Development

MOSES LAUFER, Ph.D.

IN RECENT YEARS THERE HAS BEEN A GREAT DEAL OF QUESTIONING OF the assumption that certain forms of sexual activity or behavior should be considered as being signs of abnormality. This doubt about such categorization is based partly on the changes in attitudes and laws which have taken place and are taking place in various Western countries, but more critical for purposes of this paper is the fact that such doubt also rests on the questioning by professional colleagues of the criteria or the explanations which have been applied to certain activity or behavior and which have resulted in the classification "abnormal."

Another impetus for this doubting and questioning has come from the growing awareness by both professional and lay people that the categorization of certain activity and behavior as either normal (and therefore acceptable) or abnormal (and therefore unacceptable) has enabled part of the adult community to judge, attack, and humiliate another part of the community without much need to examine some of their own motives. "Abnormality," especially "sexual abnormality," has been used for centuries as a description of the ultimate in debasement or denigration, and it is only recently that there has begun to be some freedom in doubting this, and ultimately in rejecting this.

My own view is that, in our work with the adolescent, it is critical to separate our own views about normality and abnormality within the context of society, and our views about "sexual abnor-

---

Director, Centre for Research into Adolescent Breakdown/Brent Consultation Centre, London. Part-time member, Hampstead Child-Therapy Clinic.

mality" within the context of assessment and treatment. When
the psychoanalyst is assessing or treating, he is constantly having
to make judgments about a person's psychological development,
and it is not sufficient in the assessment and the treatment of the
adolescent to be "neutral." *Neutrality, when applied to the adolescent
patient's present and future psychosexual life, is untenable and is, I believe, contrary to the purpose of therapeutic intervention during this
period of life.* This view is based on my assumption that certain
forms of sexual activity or behavior in adolescence *always* represent, at the least, a breakdown in the developmental process of
adolescence; professional "neutrality" is therefore equivalent to
an acceptance of that developmental breakdown and its consequences in later life.

THE ISSUES

The issues which I will examine in this paper can be defined as
follows: (1) whether certain forms of sexual activity and behavior
during adolescence invariably represent a disruption in
psychological development; (2) whether such disruption, if it
exists, enables us, in assessment and treatment, to view such
activity and behavior as "abnormal"; (3) whether the psychoanalyst, in assessment and treatment, should or should not make
a judgment about such activity and behavior.

My own experience in assessment and treatment of adolescents, and the knowledge we have about the meaning that certain forms of sexual activity have to the adolescent, enable me to
answer in the affirmative to the issues defined above. More emphatically, I believe that the psychoanalyst *must* have a view
about this, and also must convey this view to the adolescent at the
beginning of or early in his contact with the adolescent patient or
prospective patient. To do otherwise is contrary to the responsibility which the psychoanalyst accepts when he agrees to undertake to try to help the adolescent.

The forms of sexual activity which need to be considered abnormal in terms of psychological development, and about which
the psychoanalyst needs to make clear his view to the adolescent
patient, are those which exclude heterosexual intercourse as the
primary sexual activity between two people. Although I will de-

fine this in greater detail later in the paper, the sexual activity and behavior which I have in mind are homosexuality, fetishism, transvestitism, and perversions.

Developmental breakdown in adolescence can manifest itself in a whole range of ways, and at times this may not be too obvious. But I am implying that certains forms of sexual activity always signify that a developmental breakdown has taken place. The way in which I define my function in my work with the adolescent, and the judgments I make about the normality or abnormality about certain forms of sexual activity or behavior, are linked directly to the view I have about the developmental function of adolescence and about the meaning of developmental breakdown during adolescence.

THE DEVELOPMENTAL FUNCTION OF ADOLESCENCE AND THE MEANING OF DEVELOPMENTAL BREAKDOWN: THEIR RELATION TO THE ISSUES

Until recently (1978, 1981) I defined the function of adolescence as the establishment of a "final sexual organization," that is, an organization which, from the point of view of the body representation, must now include the physically mature genitals. It is during adolescence that the person becomes the guardian of his sexually mature body. He establishes a sexual identity by the end of adolescence, a consolidated picture of himself as a sexual being, which is irreversible—irreversible, that is, without therapeutic intervention. Consequently, adolescent pathology can be defined as a breakdown in the process of integrating the physically mature body image as part of the representation of oneself. Whatever may be the contributory ingredients to this breakdown (preoedipal, oedipal, or preadolescent), *the essential component of adolescent pathology can be understood as being a breakdown in the developmental process whose primary or perhaps specific function is that of establishing the person's sexual identity.* The primary interference in the developmental process is in the adolescent's distorted view and relationship to his body, something which is expressed via the hatred or shame of, the fury with, the sexual body.

But I would now extend my earlier definition of the developmental function of adolescence and of the meaning of developmental breakdown. I would now include as a central task of adolescence what I would define as *the restoration of the oedipal parents,* that is, the ability by the end of adolescence to begin to forgive the internalized parents for not having protected the original childhood state of narcissistic perfection, that is, a time when the child could maintain the fantasy of having acquired the oedipal parent. Viewed in terms of the oedipal relationship to one's adolescence, it means that by the end of adolescence there should be the ability unconsciously to test the oedipal disappointments and the jealousy and envy of *both* parents in ways which remove the blaming of the oedipal parents for the earlier failures. Expressed in terms of genitality, it means that by the end of adolescence there is the internal freedom to acknowledge unconsciously that the original oedipal wish and demand contained an unfulfillable fantasy of the perpetuation of perfection and of ultimately acquiring the oedipal parent. Instead, during adolescence and especially by the end of adolescence, the person can, in normal development, be free to use oedipal identifications to enable him or her to include the functioning genitals into the body image. The adolescent can now replace and kill the parent of the same sex, without actually having to do so. It means that the oedipal guilt no longer has the same authority and power because the aggression contained in the original oedipal hatred has not destroyed the parent in reality, nor has the adolescent needed to use his or her own body as the vehicle for the destruction of the oedipal parent. In other words, the adolescent is ultimately able to feel that genitality is his right given to him by the oedipal parents, and this right removes any need or wish to destroy that genitality. This is what is meant by "ownership of the body," a process which is normally completed by the end of adolescence.

But there are certain forms of sexual activity and behavior which, I believe, represent at the least an obvious breakdown in the developmental process of adolescence, and which carry unconsciously a statement about the person's relationship to his own sexual body and to his internalized parents. These adolescents have not been able to use the period of adolescence as a time when they can begin to make amends in their relationship with the oedipal parents; that is, they have not been able, through their genitality, to identify with the parents' sexuality. Instead, these adolescents are compelled to go on using their own bodies as a means of having to try to destroy the oedipal parent. They use their bodies to live out the fantasy of the destruction of the oedipal mother—the one who remains blamed for having robbed the child, and now the adolescent, of the perfect union and of the original narcissistic perfection. In adolescence, these people must destroy their own genitality, and must continue to portray the destruction of their physically mature genitals. It is in this way that they continue to live out the fantasy of offering the mother that body which they believe the mother always wanted them to have, that is, a body without adult genitals. The unconscious hatred and blaming of the oedipal parent is, in this way, never doubted and is therefore perpetuated. For these adolescents, the end of adolescence and the move into adulthood unconsciously also signify the giving in, in a hopeless way, to the mother who they believe has destroyed their genitality or has robbed them of it. It seems that this is so for those adolescents who, by the end of adolescence, no longer have the choice but to accept certain kinds of sexual activity and relationships as their main expression of their sexuality, as is the case in homosexuality, fetishism, transvestitism, and perversions.

The additional danger for these adolescents is that the "giving in," also means that the fantasies produced during adolescence—instead of being used actively in the attempt to alter the central masturbation fantasy, which was originally established as part of the resolution of the oedipus complex (Laufer, 1976)—become integrated into the adolescent's pathological sexual organization (Freud, 1906) and strengthen the quality and the extent of the developmental breakdown. The unconscious hatred and blaming of the oedipal parent and the giving in to the mother may be the outcome in the lives of many adolescents, whether or not their sexual activity and relationships include people of the opposite sex. For those who have the internal ability to establish heterosexual relationships, and who can rely on physical genitality as the main means of sexual gratification, however, there may still be the possibility of doubting their previous internal solutions and there may still be some possibility of reversing the breakdown.

The choices of sexual object during adolescence, and especially by the end of adolescence, represents the manner in which genital sexuality has or has not been integrated into the final sexual organization. In other words, one's relations to the oedipal objects, to one's own sexual body, and to the external world also represent one's relation to reality. Although reality testing begins to function well before the oedipal period, it may also be that it is only with the need ultimately to give up the original oedipal wishes that reality testing is finally established. This oedipal solution in relation to reality should again be questioned in adolescence and be re-resolved by the end of adolescence. Those adolescents who have rejected or denied their genitality, and who unconsciously have to continue to use their sexual bodies and the sexual object to confirm their self-hatred and the hatred of the oedipal parent, however, do not in any way question their original relation to reality during adolescence. Instead, their self-hatred and their need to destroy their genitality strengthen the distortions and ultimately force them to give in forever. In other words, unless they are able *during adolescence* to question their original solutions, and to be helped to add meaning to their oedipal hatred and the rejection of the identification with the oedipal parent of the same sex, then these adolescents will have lost their chance ever to doubt the direction of their lives.

The rejection during adolescence of one's body being either masculine or feminine means that the person has irreversibly rejected the oedipal identifications with the parent of the same sex. It means that the person's relationship to his or her own body, if the object choice is a homosexual one or one in which the genitals are not the primary vehicle for sexual gratification and for the love of the sexual object, also contains the hopelessness with which they have lived since childhood. In such relationships, the function of procreation is denied or seems irrelevant. But the possibility of choice of procreation during adolescence is central to one's efforts to establish one's sexual identity. The ability to choose to be a father or a mother is a necessary part of one's relationship to oneself as a male or a female, and is fundamental in ultimately establishing one's relation to one's past.

Those relationships which, through their sexual activity, exclude the possibility of procreation strengthen the distortion of the sexual body image and must at the same time strengthen the hatred of oneself and of the oedipal object. Such relationships break a link with the past. In terms of one's present life, they may also strengthen the feeling that one's past has nothing to do with oneself, that one is simply the product of parents who hated one and who withheld the right to genital sexuality (Lampl-de Groot, 1962).

THE PSYCHOANALYST AND THE ADOLESCENT'S SEXUAL DEVELOPMENT

When the psychoanalyst undertakes to try to help the adolescent, he implicitly accepts that the adolescent will be offered the chance to examine those areas of his present and past life which have brought about the existing problems, and which are now part of the adolescent's internal life. He also undertakes to help the adolescent to get more in touch with those factors or experiences in his life which have determined the choice he has made or wishes to make about his present and future life.

The adolescent may be in agreement with the analyst's undertaking, or he may feel that he has the right to make any choice he likes without there being any need for the analyst to question that choice. But this view cannot be accepted by the analyst from the start, because there is an important difference between the person's conscious intent or choice and the unconscious factors which determine "choice." The great difficulty that the adolescent has in acknowledging and accepting the presence of factors in his life other than the conscious ones, together with the extreme power of pathology, may force the vulnerable or potentially ill adolescent to reject any definition or understanding of his behavior other than that which is conscious. He may also have to deny the authority of the past, and he may feel that any choice other than the one he has made consciously is a submission to the past, that is, a submission to the oedipal parent who he feels was responsible initially for his present mental state.

The analyst may make the error of confusing his moral and ethical views about people's "rights" and his responsibility when choosing to work with people whose future psychological lives are still in the process of being determined and finalized. If we accept that certain forms of sexual activity or behavior during adolescence are, at the least, a sign of developmental breakdown, then our primary responsibility is to help this adolescent, that is, to try to keep open the psychological options which may still exist for this adolescent. If we apply our views about people's "rights" to our function in assessment and treatment of the adolescent, we take the risk of confirming for the adolescent his unconscious belief that there is no hope, that he is worthless, and that the oedipal parents have given up any wish for the adolescent to be a sexual being and the owner of his sexual body. The adolescent who seeks help may wish for this kind of confirmation, but at the same time he may also wish for the analyst to doubt the choices made until now and to offer the adolescent the possibility of a different solution. As the result of treatment, the adolescent may feel that he can now choose actively to live his social and psychological life in one way or another; he may, in fact, choose to continue to live a life which is, for example, homosexual in terms of his object choices. Or he may understand that the only relationships which he can value, and perhaps which he can have in the first place, exclude genital sexuality. This may be an out-come of treatment, but it is based on his readiness to question and to doubt his earlier solutions.

Developmental breakdown in adolescence, as expressed by the choice of "sexual abnormality," means that the adolescent has given up hope of ever restoring the relationship to the oedi-pal parent. But by choosing "sexual abnormality" and by giving up this hope of restoring the relationship to the oedipal parent, he, at the same time, defies his conscience and thereby breaks the relationship to his own past; that is, he gives up feeling that his past and his present life are in any way his responsibility. But if the adolescent has agreed to undertake treatment, he has chosen to give the psychoanalyst the right to question his earlier so-lutions. In this sense, the psychoanalyst's "neutrality" is untena-ble, inasmuch as it is contrary to the undertaking of the analyst, and it is also contrary to the unconscious expectation and hope of the adolescent. Neutrality is, in this context, equivalent to con-firming the adolescent's hopelessness. It may also be experienced by the adolescent as yet another confirmation that "sexual abnormality" is the only right he has.

But the ability not to be neutral, especially in the face of much social opposition, means that the psychoanalyst would need to be aware of the meaning of his own adolescence in relation to his present life. It may mean the giving up of many of the idealizations of the past that we live with. It may also force us to consider the extent of our own envy of the adolescent's sexuality, and it may be necessary to risk losing some of the narcissistic gains which so many ill adolescents want to or have to offer, especially if their pathological solutions are not questioned, or perhaps more seriously, if their pathological solutions are felt by them to be idealized or overvalued.

CLINICAL IMPLICATIONS

There are a number of clinical implications which follow from what I have said. It is not my intention to discuss here the day-to-day clinical work with the adolescent in detail. Instead, I will discuss only those areas which are related specifically to the "issues" which I defined at the beginning of the paper, that is, to the psychoanalyst's attitude to the adolescent who seeks help and whose developmental breakdown has manifested itself by "sexual abnormality."

When I see such an adolescent for assessment or for the possibility of treatment, I explain to him (either at the beginning or early on in treatment) what my view is about "sexual abnormality." I explain in detail to him (and if necessary I see the adolescent a number of times for this) why I consider his present choice of sexuality as being a sign of the presence of serious trouble in himself, and that I will try to help him understand what its meaning is for him, and how it may have come about. The adolescent knows, at the same time, that it is not my wish or my intention to try remorselessly to take away his choice, but that treatment does mean questioning the choice, understanding its meaning, and possibly changing.

If, after this, the adolescent insists that his sexual life and object choices must at no time be discussed or questioned, but that we must concentrate only on one or another area of his problems, I choose not to accept to treat him. I am aware of the view held by some colleagues that treatment might ultimately lead to this examination and understanding, and that there is no need at the start or early on in treatment to take such a definite view. My past experience has shown that many adolescents who come for treatment expect either to be fooled or forced to submit, and who then may continue in treatment because of the transference relationship which has been established but without any lasting therapeutic work going on. Those adolescents whose sexual lives include "sexual abnormality" very often secretly feel that they have been fooled or cheated, and are convinced that the oedipal object, represented now by the psychoanalyst, wants them to remain as they are. Although this view can be understood during treatment, it is important from the start to separate oneself from this expectation, and to enable the adolescent to choose to accept treatment or not.

But when I say that the adolescent can choose treatment or not, it is not simply that I allow the adolescent to decide totally on his own. I discuss with the adolescent my views about his present life, and I tell him why there is reason to be worried and why he should consider having treatment. I also make it clear from the start that I do judge, and that this judgment has to do with his present and future life. Adolescents may find it extremely difficult to separate my judgment about normality or abnormality from the judgment of right or wrong, good or bad. Within the transference, however, the meaning of right or wrong, good or bad becomes a central factor and is something which has existed in the adolescent's life for years past, especially from puberty onward. But to imply that I do not judge is equivalent to avoiding the issue of normality or abnormality, breakdown or not. Beyond this, however, the adolescent is certainly aware of the fact that a judgment is being made, and for this not to be acknowledged from the start of treatment represents for the adolescent both a collusion and an opting out by the analyst.

From the start of treatment, I acknowledge the extent of the adolescent's suffering, even though the adolescent may insist that his life is proceeding well. Often, the adolescent will feel that to admit to any suffering is to risk losing the only things or people who offer any pleasure or who make him feel worthwhile. This anxiety has to be acknowledged from the start, but at the same time it is also critical to acknowledge the extent of the adolescent's aloneness and inner emptiness. The adolescent is aware, from the start, that I view his present life and his choices as signs of the presence of severe trouble within himself, and he knows that for me to be neutral cannot be true.

BIBLIOGRAPHY

FREUD, S. (1905), Three essays on the theory of sexuality. *S.E.*, 7:125–243.

———— (1906), My views on the part played by sexuality in the aetiology of the neuroses. *S.E.*, 7:271–279.

———— (1931), Female sexuality. *S.E.*, 21:223–243.

LAMPL-DE GROOT, J. (1962), Ego ideal and superego. In: *The Development of the Mind.* London: Hogarth Press, 1966, pp. 317–328.

LAUFER, M. (1976), The central masturbation fantasy, the final sexual organization, and adolescence. *Psychoanal. Study Child,* 31:297–328.

———— (1978), The nature of adolescent pathology and the psychoanalytic process. *Psychoanal. Study Child,* 33:307–322.

———— (1981), Adolescent breakdown and the transference neurosis. *Int. J. Psychoanal.,* 62:51–59.

LOEWALD, H. W. (1979), The waning of the oedipus complex. *J. Amer. Psychoanal. Assn.,* 27:751–775.

The Significance of Pets for Children

Illustrated by a Latency-Age Girl's Use of Pets in Her Analysis

IVAN SHERICK, Ph.D.

INTEREST IN ANIMALS IS UBIQUITOUS IN CHILDHOOD. CHILDREN are drawn to or frightened by animals. Almost all children, at one time or another, wish to have a pet of some kind, with variability in the choice being quite remarkable. It is surprising, then, that there is so little psychoanalytic literature that has had as its focus the significance of pets. Undoubtedly, valuable insights exist and are probably embedded in the clinical case literature (e.g., Kupfermann, 1977). The symbolic significance of animals in the development of phobic and obsessional psychopathology is illuminated convincingly in Freud's classic case studies of Little Hans (1909a), the Rat Man (1909b), and the Wolf Man (1918). In none of these cases, however, was the significant animal a pet. I have had the opportunity in child analytic work with a latency-age girl to observe directly the many psychological meanings that pets had for this child.

In most child patients, animals are drawn into their psychopathology as the object of a phobia. In contrast, Laura's use of pets took on a philic direction. I do not mean to designate

Clinical Assistant Professor of Psychology in Psychiatry, University of Michigan, Ann Arbor, Michigan; Lecturer, Michigan Psychoanalytic Institute; Arbor Clinic, Ann Arbor, Michigan.

I am grateful for the helpful suggestions in understanding Laura made by Ms. Agi Bene and Dr. Salo Tischler.

it as a zoophilia (Rappaport, 1968) insofar as this is suggestive of a perversion; Laura had not yet reached puberty, so that the final direction of her libidinal wishes was unclear (A. Freud, 1965, p. 212). What I observed might have developed in a pathological direction if Laura had not had the benefits of analysis. Why Laura's use of pets took on a philic rather than a phobic quality was an interesting question, which could be partially answered as her analysis deepened.

In "Analysis of a Phobia in a Five-Year-Old Boy" (1909a), Freud remarks, "Animals owe a good deal of their importance in myths and fairy tales to the openness with which they display their genitals and their sexual functions to the inquisitive little human child" (p. 9). Several years later, Freud (1913) said, "There is a great deal of resemblance between the relations of children and of primitive men towards animals. Children show no trace of the arrogance which urges adult civilized men to draw a hard-and-fast line between their own nature and that of all other animals. Children have no scruples over allowing animals to rank as their full equals. Uninhibited as they are in the avowal of their bodily needs, they no doubt feel themselves more akin to animals than to their elders, who may well be a puzzle to them" (p. 126f.).

Such observations which are now commonplace, but perhaps too much so for us to stop and take notice, cause us not to be very surprised that Laura found a certain kinship with animals and could utilize them as objects for identification, externalization displacement, etc., via which she expressed her conflicts and sought to resolve them in an adaptive fashion. What makes Laura relatively unique as a child analytic patient is the emphasis that she placed on her pets as well as her use of them in the actual analytic hour. Through such means, she established distance which enabled her to bring her conflicts and wishes to the fore and to accept my interventions. When I made an attempt to bridge the gap between her pets and herself, she often yelled me down, as if I had violated the distance which she had established and which she needed if any therapeutic exchange between us was to take place. I often had to speak about her to the pets—this distance was sufficient.

Woods (1965) writes: "Because the human-pet relationship is one step removed from the highly charged conflictual relationships with persons, many patients are thereby able to see themselves and others with greater clarity, with less denial and repression, and with greater insight. . . . To ignore the patient's pet may be to ignore an essential dimension of the essence and meaning of the patient's life" (p. 119). Going further, Levinson (1964, 1965, 1969, 1970) has developed a special technique in child psychotherapy which advocates the deliberate introduction of a pet as an adjunct to therapy. Searles (1960, e.g., p. 16) also places great emphasis on the "nonhuman environment" and its significance to man's life. He stresses that a pet (specifically dogs), in addition to taking on important symbolic meanings, has value in and of itself as an object to man.

CASE PRESENTATION

BACKGROUND

Laura L. began analysis at the age of 9 and was in treatment for 3 years. She was the youngest child in a middle-class family. A brother, 3 years her senior, had been in analysis with a colleague for 2½ years because of fears and anxiety. He had shown much improvement, and it was because of his favorable experience that Laura sought analysis. Laura's mother was an attractive woman who once had acted and modeled clothes; she was very vain and very concerned about appearances. Although she catered to Laura's wish for pets, this satisfied many of her own needs; by providing animals as substitutes for her own maternal care, she could maintain a superficial emotional relatedness to her daughter. She had been married once before but divorced early upon discovering that her first husband was a homosexual. Laura's father was an athletic-looking businessman. He was very much a sportsman, enjoying fishing, hunting, and the horse races. He worked long hours and was often absent from the home.

Laura's relationship with her brother was mutually helpful on the surface—she rubbed his back when he was having asthmatic breathing difficulties, and he encouraged her to seek analysis and supported her use of treatment to help her with her anxieties. She was, however, very envious of him, often complaining of all the attention his asthma brought him. They shared a bedroom until she was 9 years old. An earlier attempt to separate them was aborted when Laura became fearful of sleeping alone. A latent reason for the timing of the referral was probably Laura's recognition that her brother would be leaving the primary school that they both attended and his supportive influence would be abridged considerably.

Laura had few friends, although she did have an enduring relationship with one girl who was a classmate. She often said that she preferred animals to people, and her conversations at home always involved animals. These sentiments were similar to her mother's feelings as a young girl. Laura's ambition was to be a veterinarian. In part, this choice of career was based on a reaction formation which was guarding against sadistic impulses, but, nevertheless, it showed indications of becoming a sublimation. Laura actually nursed ill animals back to health; e.g., she cared for a bird with a broken wing that she had found on her balcony. Heiman (1956) and Menninger (1951) both point out how the care of animals aids in the sublimation of instincts.

Her personal history was uneventful. At the age of 3 years there had been a week-long separation when her parents left on vacation; at around 6 years she had a tonsillectomy. At the hospital, she reported to have loved the attention she received from the nurses, and to have cried when she had to go home, although she also spoke about wishing to go home.

Both of Laura's parents were very concerned with tidiness. As an infant, Laura was described by her mother as a "dirty, messy" eater, and her father was always objecting to Laura's table manners. Mrs. L. believed that Laura's toilet training was completed by the time Laura was 17 months old, but Mrs. L. continued to supervise Laura and even wiped her bottom clean until latency. Laura's relationship with her mother seemed to involve control, e.g., struggles about getting ready for school and choosing clothes. My speculation was that the antecedents of this type of relationship could be found in both feeding and toilet-training experiences.

The parents' main presenting complaint had to do with Laura's reluctance to separate from her mother. Because of this, there was some hesitancy in Laura's participation in afterschool activities. She was very shy and very suspicious of strangers, to the point of being fearful of being kidnapped. There was an obstinate, clinging silence when she was angry with her mother. As a toddler, Laura had been kept in a harness which had restrained her locomotion. This restraint highlights Mrs. L.'s efforts at control and vividly portrays the paradoxical complaint/wish about Laura's inability to separate. In addition to separation difficulties, Laura was preoccupied with animals, and neglected other activities, such as ballet, which Laura liked. Stomachaches also were a frequent complaint of Laura's. Lastly, she was unable to learn mathematics.

Laura was a very attractive, dark-haired, fair-skinned, latency-age girl. At times, she appeared very feminine, with the movements and the grace of a ballet dancer, whereas on other occasions she appeared more like a "tomboy," arriving with one knee sock down to her ankle, bruises on her shins, her hair tousled, and her shirttails out of her skirt. At first, she was very timid, soft spoken, and excessively polite, but as the analysis progressed, she became excessively seductive, controlling, denigrating, and demanding. In many respects, her behavior and manner of relating were more typical of a prelatency child.

THE EMERGING CLINICAL MATERIAL

During the first week of treatment, she shyly portrayed herself in a whisper as loving animals, caring for them, and wishing to be a veterinarian. When her pets were sick, she nursed them. To care for them and to study them, however, required controlling them, which she experienced as cruel (sadistic, at a deeper level). Fears of abandonment appeared to be connected with the caring-noncaring conflict. During a brief illness, Laura herself felt like a "stray kitten" with no one to care for her.

Laura quickly became more coquettish, teasing, and sexualizing. She wanted me to chase her out of the building and into the garden. She claimed that she wanted to do "naughty things." She told me about Fanny, a bitch, the litter mate of her pet male dog, Chip. Fanny (who belonged to her aunt) was in heat. Laura wished to have Chip give Fanny puppies, but said disappointedly that her mother objected to this.

Toward the end of the second month of treatment, Laura actually brought her dog into the session. She claimed that she brought it in so that I would not tease her. Chip was really meant to function as a watchdog against her heightening excited feelings—a part of her liked the excitement, but another part of her was frightened by it to the point of her leaving the room. She spoke about how "frisky" her pet was, how he could not sit still, and how he was more excitable than other dogs. By telling me about Chip's excitement, she also told me about her own in the treatment situation with me.

About one month later, after Laura had been ill for a week, she again brought Chip with her. The first 10 minutes were spent with Laura giving Chip commands, e.g., "sit." By showing me how she commanded Chip, she showed me how important it was that she be in control of things. Laura whispered a "seize" command to Chip. She asked me to stand up, gave me a pillow, and wanted me to have a pillow fight with her. Her intention was that Chip would get excited and "seize me." In an interview with her mother (whom I met with every 12 weeks), I had learned about Laura's apprehensiveness about being left alone and her anxiety that a stranger might knock on the door. Mrs. L. had reported that Laura closed her bedroom door and insisted that Chip be with her. Laura volunteered that Chip went "crazy" if someone knocked on the door; Chip barked and scared people away. She had brought Chip to protect her from me in the same way that he protected her from strangers.

With about 10 minutes of the hour remaining, Laura wanted to leave the room. She had tied Chip to the couch and now spoke to him in reassuring terms, as if she expected him to object to her leaving the room. She went out, but came back immediately after he cried. This was repeated. By these means, she showed me the difficulty that she and her mother had about separating. It was as if she was her mother and Chip was Laura. She continued to walk out of the room and return immediately upon hearing Chip cry or bark. Once Laura gave Chip her cape, almost as if it was a transitional object. As she spoke to Chip, her tone became more irritable. It looked as if it was as difficult for Laura to leave Chip as it was for him to be left. My thinking here was that much of Laura's anxiety about strangers was really an identification with her mother's anxiety in this regard. Mrs. L. was phobic about sexual assault and seemed to inculcate such anxiety into her daughter. (Mrs. L. had in fact said that she used excessive words of caution in this regard with her daughter.) Thus, Laura's anxiety about strange males appeared to be fueled by sexual excitement.

It seemed that Laura found her positive oedipal wishes frustrated and was afraid of mother's anger because of the sexual rivalry. A session from the 22nd week of treatment is illustrative. Laura wanted to look out of the window and watch her mother entering the clinic. She expressed displeasure that her mother did not return at the time she had promised. Laura also noted that the clinic receptionist was not at her post. Laura drew a cat and said that "something" was missing, the tail, and asked me to complete the cat. She then said that her mother once forgot to pick her up at school. Then she wondered how old I was and followed this up with the expression of a wish to give me some baby guppies. My conjecture was that Laura was pleased about the absence of both mother and mother substitute (receptionist), and defensively expressed this as displeasure. In the same way, she dealt with her wish to get rid of mother by projecting it onto mother: mother once had not picked her up at school. Furthermore, there was anger at mother for not having given her a penis, and the disappointed wish that this could in some way be made good by father and, in the transference, by the analyst. The following day, she wrote: "I love Mommy, Daddy, and my brother very much. I am worried about things. I don't want to tell you what they are yet."

Positive oedipal feelings intensified along with guilt. Fears of being abandoned reappeared, stemming from projection of death wishes toward her mother. Laura began to allude to bedtime rituals that seemed to be precautionary measures against masturbating. In this context, she told me a dream whose characters were animals. She claimed that she had had this dream over a year ago when she wished for a pet dog. She dreamed that she heard music downstairs in the garden. In the garden were animals dancing. She went and danced with an elephant. There were no associations to this dream. In the context of the emerging material, the dream could be understood as a fulfillment of her wish to receive a penis/baby from her father, the pet dog being a substitute.

Laura regressively attempted to gain favor by adopting masculine aims, while retaining father as the love object. She seemed to be comparing herself in an unfavorable way to her brother. When this was pointed out to her, she became very defensive and threatened to break off the table leg. A few weeks later, however, she pretended to be a veterinarian and wanted me to say that my dog had hurt its penis.

The next week Laura introduced a new game, "Show Dog," which was to occupy us intermittently. In this game, we used a soft toy dog. It appeared that by means of this game she hoped to obtain reassurance that she could still be admired and approved by me despite having injured herself "permanently" by masturbating.

After the first summer vacation, there was a reintensification of separation anxiety. She seemed fearful of being abducted in the streets, but would not talk about this. Instead, Laura spoke about her aunt's dog, Fanny, who was mistreated at obedience training and who consequently became fearful of strangers. Feelings of loss were experienced in an earlier form as fear of abandonment and in a later form as castration. For example, she announced that she had attended to a stray kitten earlier in the day. A little later in the hour, she told me that she had "lost" a finger at school—a dog bit it off. She then poked her finger in some holes in the wall of the office. I wondered if her "naughty" finger would be bitten off for poking—for doing something exciting and forbidden. She said she wanted to poke a hole through the wall in order to see into the adjoining room. Later, I could comment on her curiosity about what went on in her parents' bedroom and her feelings of exclusion. In a subsequent session she wanted to play "eye doctor," and I could connect her wish to see exciting and forbidden things with her fear that her eyes would be punished.

At around the time of her 10th birthday, Laura became angry with her brother, but suppressed such feelings. He had taken some of the attention away from her by having an asthmatic attack. I tried to get Laura to see that she was angry with her brother, but she was unable to accept this. Instead, she noticed her mother with Chip, her pet dog, and said that she hated Chip because he woke her up at 4:00 A.M. (sometimes she was awakened in the middle of the night by her brother's wheezing). Such displacement onto her pets was a typical defense of Laura's. The following day, she had many nice things to say about Chip.

Laura had always portrayed her home as an idyllic setting, but the next week she spoke about the various activities in which her mother was involved and which demanded lots of her mother's time. Feeling lonely, she turned to her pets as playmates. She had worried once that her mother would forget to pick her up at the clinic. When I tried to connect her separation anxiety to her repressed anger at her mother, Laura responded by saying that she only wanted to speak about Biafran children because their mothers had been killed.

Laura decided that she wanted a rabbit as a pet. This wish was to occupy us for many months. She said that her mother had promised her one, and they were waiting for the proper moment to ask her father's permission. She spent several sessions trying to reassure herself that her father would not refuse her request. The many requests for things she directed to me pointed to the displacement of this wish. She also spent a great deal of time deciding what color rabbit she wanted, what breed it should be, and what name to give it. In the ensuing months Laura indicated the degree to which her wish to have a rabbit was overdetermined.

Laura would pretend that the rabbit, Flopsy, was with us and pretend to care for it as if it were her baby. She would pretend to bathe it, to brush its fur, and to feed it. Laura's comments that the rabbit should be "tough" were understood as fears that this idealized, wished-for substitute might not be able to withstand her ambivalence. She said that I should not be squeamish when she spoke about the rabbit defecating. She seemed to attribute to me her realization that even this idealized object might be disappointing. This comment also pointed to the anal component of her caring for her pets: in it, she expressed her own anal interests and reenacted her mother's earlier overconcern with Laura's bowel movements.

The time, she felt, was getting close to when her father would be asked about the rabbit. She believed that it would be best to wait until just after he had granted her brother's request for tropical fish; she explained that she had obtained her dog in similar circumstances, because her father could not refuse her then. (Apparently, in the past, her father had acted impulsively and granted her wishes immediately. I wondered if Laura experienced the impulsive granting of her wishes by her father as a successful seduction on her part. I was reminded of Mrs. L.'s comments to me, in passing, that her husband had once urinated in front of Laura in order to satisfy her inquisitiveness.) Laura began to speak in endless detail about the type of collar she would buy for the rabbit. A collar was indeed purchased, and she brought it in with a lead and pretended to walk the imaginary rabbit about the room.

Around the time of her brother's Bar Mitzvah, Laura was feeling particularly envious and hoped that the rabbit would be a compensation. She began one session by pointing out that she was wearing high-heel shoes. She had brought in a box filled with her parakeet's molted feathers to show me the brilliant colors. It was as if she brought them to show me that she had lost something prized which she wanted me to replace. Laura told me why the rabbit had to be well trained and obedient, namely, so that it could accompany her into a store. The next day, Laura told me that Chip, always being chastised for being "naughty," had had an operation. She claimed his "anal gland" had been removed and some fur shaven off. During this time, her narcissistic injury was combated in a futile fashion by her repeated attempts to draw horses, which, however, never quite reached her standard of perfection.

In her games with the imaginary rabbit Laura portrayed her mother as being an interfering person who restricted instinctual pleasure at all levels. Laura often accused her of entering the clinic early, thereby conveying her belief that her mother wanted to interfere in her relationship with me. Ambivalence toward mother was fueled by envy of her brother and her feeling that he had gotten the better deal. As was usually the case, Laura brought this material in a displaced manner in the context of speaking of animals. She told me that Fanny might be given away. Laura said her aunt neglected Fanny; she never walked her, yet she was angry with her for urinating on the rug. Laura would "murder" her aunt if she gave Fanny away. Most of the time her aunt's 1-year-old daughter pulled Fanny's tail, but the latter was blamed for growling. Laura chastised her aunt for having no time for Fanny ever since the child was born. If she were a dog, Laura reported, she would bite people, except for babies. A little later, Laura said that she probably caught her cold from her brother. Displacing anger presumably from her brother, she said that she hated Chip. Later, as we walked down the stairs, Laura cautioned me not to "walk on" her "tail."

After the spring vacation, Laura spoke nonstop, in a mildly excited way, about the wished-for rabbit, Flopsy. Earlier in the day she had been to a very fashionable department store and had visited its pet shop. She and her mother had been impressed with the "show" rabbits on sale there and had arranged to be contacted the next time the shop received a new litter of baby rabbits. She emphasized that they were "first-class show rabbits," and seemed to compare them to inferior rabbits she had seen in an outdoor market. Laura squealed with delight as she spoke of how cuddly the baby rabbits were.

Laura claimed that, as a child, her mother used to bring stray kittens home. Hence, Laura felt that her mother was sympathetic to her wishes to have a rabbit and other pets. I began to point out systematically that Laura felt she and her mother were similar. Later on in the week, during a "pet-shop game," Laura enacted how she would select a baby rabbit by choosing one whose mother was a first-class *show* rabbit (her mother had been a model). Laura referred to herself and her mother as "the girls" and to her father and brother as "the boys." Although Laura felt closely tied to her mother, she was extremely envious of her.

In play, Laura portrayed Flopsy as cheeky, a trait she claimed she sought in her rabbit. Laura acted like an overly restraining

mother, but at the same time suggested a concealed encouragement of the rabbit's "naughtiness." I commented about the two
messages given by the mother (enacted by Laura) so that what
was meant was different from what was said. It was like a mother
who tells a child it is all right to venture around the corner alone,
but her voice gives away a feeling and wish that the child not
separate. After this, Laura had Flopsy straining at the lead while
she scolded it for being naughty. She said that Flopsy would
"wear herself out," which was "good" because it would make it
less active. This "double-bind" situation was conveyed vividly by
Laura bringing in a harness and making the imaginary rabbit
wear it, thus limiting its "mobility" while subtly encouraging it to
be naughty. It was at this point in the analysis that I learned of
Laura's harness as a toddler; interestingly, it had a picture of a
rabbit on it.

Two weeks later, she announced that she and her mother were
going on a holiday for a week. A little later, she told me that if
Flopsy became scared, it would mean that her rabbit was brought
up badly. Next, she wanted me to pick up the imaginary Flopsy
to see if it was scared. In this way Laura was telling me that her
mother's being scared made her scared, and vice versa. The next
day as Laura entered a cross-walk, she was struck by a car (driven
by a male), but not hurt. The day after the incident she brought
in a knife ostensibly to cut up the carrot that she had brought in
to feed the pretend Flopsy. She put her bowl and spoon away,
but left the knife on the table near where I sat, and she stood up
and went to the window. I interpreted that she had brought the
knife to tell me that she shared her mother's worries about
dangerous men; and her leaving the knife near me indicated
that I might be the dangerous man. The car incident was really a
defensive attempt to consolidate the close, clinging relationship
to mother.

Laura enacted positive oedipal fantasies in a safer, displaced
way via her dog Chip. She brought him in and announced that
he would soon be 4 years old, which, for a dog, was like being 28
years old. She referred to Chip as her "young man." Later, she
cuddled Chip, lay on the couch with him in a seductive manner,
and teased him verbally.

During many sessions, Laura spent some time reading aloud
from her book on the care of household pets. She went into

detail about the intended rabbit's diet, its hutch, and the harness that it would wear. Many times she told me the hutch would arrive on such and such a day, but when that day came there was the invariable excuse to account for the delay. Dissatisfaction with her father repeatedly was expressed via our relationship in the form of complaints about the things I provided for her.

She began one week by reporting that her father said she was too young to have a foal. The family had bought a cottage with adjacent land on which Laura hoped to ride a horse. Sensing her disappointment, I commented that it looked as if she would have to postpone caring for a baby until she was old enough to have her own baby. Laura remarked that the rabbit would be like a baby. A little later, she said that to buy a rabbit one should look at the mother rabbit to get an idea of the size and shape that the baby would be when it grew up. In a pet shop Laura had seen a beautiful mother rabbit which was "gentle and good-natured," but which became angry with her babies when they jumped on her. This seemed to be her paradox, namely, how a beautiful, gentle, good-natured mother could also be angry with her child, and it was something she could not accept becase of her intolerance of her own ambivalence. Occasionally, she would have me "hold" the pretend rabbit, scold it for its naughtiness, or be "nice" to it, an enactment of the mother transference.

At the first meeting after the vacation, beginning the third year of analysis, Laura brought in Sooty, her new male, 10-week-old rabbit obtained during the summer. The beginning of our session was concentrated on Sooty; Laura told me about the hutch, how Sooty was allowed into the apartment, how she fed him, brushed him, and washed his paws. She referred to him, not in a disapproving way, as "stupid," "naughty," and "piggish eater." Sitting quietly, and holding Sooty on her lap, Laura told me about her summer vacation and concentrated on her pony riding. Her father intended to buy her a pony in a year's time and keep it at their summer cottage. The following week, Laura began by telling me that in 6 months' time her father might buy her a foal and keep it at the cottage. She continued to speak about her father's interest in doing this and how she looked forward to it. She went on to tell me about the new riding trousers she was getting, the new bird cage, and so on. The emphasis was on obtaining new things. I sensed a certain dissatisfaction, despite the fact that she had obtained her idealized rabbit during the summer.

Laura continued with the theme of being excited. She externalized this feeling onto Chip whom she had brought in. He was said to be a "lunatic" (excitable). Her own excitement had to do with the wish that father now buy her a pony. This move from the rabbit to the pony was a progressive move into preadolescence. She wanted a pony from a stud that was on a farm near the cottage, but then the pony would be high-strung. In her sessions she spoke about how she must be allergic to "fur"—she claimed that she would get a rash on her cheek when she rubbed up against Chip or Sooty. She complained that she and Chip were "bored," and followed this with material having to do with masturbation. Eventually, her masturbatory excitement and pleasure having to do with positive oedipal wishes, her guilt feelings afterward, her worry that she had injured herself, and her suspicion that the analyst/mother knew all this and condemned her could be interpreted.

Laura spoke about a contest in which she wanted to enter her rabbit. The pet shop where she had purchased Sooty had replied to her query and told her that Sooty was a "pure-breed," which made him eligible for the contest. Because she sometimes felt ordinary and not special, it was important for Sooty to be pure-bred. Chip, on the other hand, bit Fanny. It would seem that Chip and Sooty, in this instance, reflected an externalization of her "bad" and "ideal" self representations (Sanford, 1966). Chip was "sly," a "Hitler," because he bit people and growled. Lady, a puppy that Laura had had when she was younger, on the other hand, was not vicious, but nervous, and could not be housebroken, and had to be given away. Other material suggested that Laura may have experienced her tonsillectomy at 6 years of age as a punishment (castration) for anal messiness (Lady) and oral greed and biting impulses (Chip). Fanny's faulty bladder control revived fears of abandonment that Laura had experienced when Lady was given away.

Anger at mother was displaced onto the female receptionist at the clinic and toward her aunt. The receptionist was intensely hated because she advised Laura not to bring her rabbit every day (there was a boy who attended the clinic at the same time who was phobic of animals). After one such incident Laura had a rare outburst of temper at home. She also complained the following week of her aunt's yelling at her uncle, of whom Laura was fond, and at Fanny, the dog, and Laura wished the aunt would jump in the lake. Laura's increased tolerance for anger toward her mother, albeit displaced, permitted Laura to resist reinstating the close attachment to her mother when the latter entered the hospital for minor gynecological surgery. Several weeks later analysis was temporarily interrupted by me because of the death of a relative. Laura speculated that my wife had died. Analysis at this time focused on her oedipal rivalrous feelings. From this point onward, Laura no longer complained of stomachaches.

In the spring after learning of her acceptance to an academically challenging secondary school, Laura wished to end treatment after the third summer vacation because of her busy school schedule, and we entered the termination phase of the analysis. Laura's wish to terminate her analysis was acceptable to me, especially because progressive development had been reinstituted.

Laura now talked again about obtaining a pony. In part, the pony represented a wished-for substitute for the anticipated loss of the analyst/father. I had all along suspected that Laura was defending against depressive affects associated with low self-esteem and feeling unloved, stemming from the internalization of her parents' excessively high expectations. The material began to suggest a tentative move in the direction of her experiencing some of this depressive affect (prognostically favorable), the impetus being termination of her analysis.

Laura was able to use her pets to master her feelings of loss during the ending phase of her analysis; by keeping them on a lead and always "close at hand," she was able to protect against the possible loss of her cherished objects. The death of pets in the past and feared death of her cherished pets in the future were means by which she could begin to cope with feelings of loss (Heiman, 1956; Levinson, 1967; Mahon and Simpson, 1977). Marie Bonaparte (1940) beautifully writes how her pet dog became a talisman for her that conjured away death. The dog became a substitute for a cherished childhood nurse who took care of her when she was a child and ill.

Laura was sad for a classmate whose rabbit had died. She accused me of not feeling sorry. She was sad for her girlfriend, too, who was supposed to have one of the rabbit's babies. She drew a picture of a girl, erased the face, then spoke about breeding horses when she was older, and then drew a horse. She then drew Chip, who was with us in the session, and became very controlling of him. I said she felt that she had no control over people coming and going, whereas she could control her pets. I added that she felt my departure as a disappointment and loss to her, and wondered if I was saddened too. Laura said that Chip was cold and uncomfortable, and she covered him up with her coat and pillows. The next day, she was critical of me for saying "hello." "Why do you say 'hello'? You see me every day!" I said that she was sad that we would soon say "Good-bye," and that was why she was angry with me. Laura brought Sooty to a session several days later and reenacted her purchase of him. As a "boy" rabbit, Sooty was more costly than a "girl" one—because the boy rabbit had nicer markings and was more in demand. Soon thereafter, in another session, Laura told me that Sooty was good-looking, but there were nicer-looking rabbits, although he was the "best." What color rabbit would I have? In this way, she disclosed her imagined shortcomings, but wondered if I, like father, could still love her, and there was additional working through of this painful fantasy.

In the early part of the summer, Laura actually obtained a mare and a foal (a female) and brought in the bridles belonging to them. Laura gave me riding lessons, e.g., how to hold the reins, the difference between trotting and galloping. This type of session was repeated many times. She would pretend that the table was a horse. There was an element of control involved in teaching me and testing me about horseback riding, but there was also an element of sharing her interest with me as she did with her father with whom she went riding. It is interesting that for the first time one of her pets was a female and not a male.

In a final interview, Laura's mother reported that Laura was much more mature emotionally, coped better, and did not "panic" as she had in the past. Separation difficulties had diminished, and Laura could even express anger directly toward mother. Hence, the gripping identification with her mother had loosened. Once Laura was able to extricate herself from her mother, Laura's self-esteem became more solid. Mrs. L. implied, however, that Laura's ambitions to be a veterinarian were beyond Laura's capacity. Mrs. L. reported that when she had been young, she, too, had wanted to be a veterinarian, but relinquished the idea because she lacked ability. Later, Mrs. L. was critical of feminists, thinking that these women wanted the best of two worlds, which was impossible. In part, the feeling that came across was Mrs. L.'s underlying self-depreciation as a woman and her identification of Laura with herself. I believe that in her adolescence Laura might once more be faced with regressive moves toward greater dependency and identification with mother, but that analysis, by loosening the tenacious preoedipal tie to mother and reinstituting progressive development, has provided her with independent resources to resist.

In her last session, Laura was able, albeit indirectly, to express sadness, anger, and gratitude. Six months later, I received a card from Laura: "I am fine and love my new school. All my pets are fine except dear old Sooty, who became ill; he was put to sleep by the vet. He got a kind of cancer. I now have another rabbit whom I love, too, just as much called Sandy. He is all gray, and white on his tummy. Merry Christmas."

DISCUSSION

Laura's intense involvement with animals was present long before the analysis began. It was, of course, highly overdetermined and received contributions from various sources. Here I shall concentrate primarily on her use of pets in the analysis and touch upon some of the reasons why her use of pets was philic. Many factors contributed to and reinforced this preoccupation with pets.

This family, particularly Mrs. L., encouraged Laura's interest in pets. Although they lived in a relatively small apartment, the family accepted various encroachments on their space from the many different pets belonging to Laura and her brother. In part,

Mrs. L.'s encouragement was due to her own interest in pets; as a young girl she had wanted to be a veterinarian. It is likely that she obtained vicarious pleasure through Laura's involvement with pets. Mrs. L. also may have encouraged the pets in order to displace anger from herself because she might have felt that she was not a "good enough" mother. Because of the nature of her own narcissistic needs, Mrs. L. may have been burdened by the natural demands of her child for physical and emotional closeness. Feeling this way, she may have directed the expression of such needs by Laura toward pets as substitutes for herself. Laura, in many respects, was mother's pet. She was an object to be restrained by means of a harness. She was an object whose needs were conscientiously taken care of. She was an object to be related to emotionally in a manner more narcissistic than object-directed, that is, to be stroked but then dismissed, and whose loyalty and affection were to be taken for granted.

In reality, Laura cared and nurtured her pets with a high degree of competence. She was very knowledgeable about animals, their habits and needs, and how to provide for them. She spent a great deal of time reading about them both in and outside of her analysis. Laura's involvement with her pets appeared to be an arena in which both aggressive and libidinal wishes could move in the direction of being sublimated.

In her analysis, Laura's use of pets served both communication and resistance. Very early in her analysis, by telling her dog to "seize" me, she portrayed her wish and fear regarding her sexual aims toward me. By vividly showing me her inability to separate from her pet, she illustrated the mutual identification between herself and her mother and the separation difficulties they encountered. Resistance to uncovering her internalized conflicts was manifested by having Chip serve as a watchdog to protect her from me as a dangerous man. Through this means, she externalized the conflict between her conscience and her sexual wishes. Laura's rabbit fantasy served as a resistance insofar as her communication about it permitted her to avoid dealing with a painful reality and, instead, to deal only with her pleasurable fantasies and to create a ray of hope.

Via her pets, Laura was able to reenact and master her relationship and identification with her mother, aspects of which she felt to be ego-dystonic. Heiman (1956) writes, "The preponderance of . . . feminine attitudes in the establishment of . . . relationships with dogs perhaps derives much of its significance from mother-child relationships" (p. 578). Searles (1960) points out that many children grow up with mothers unable to show affection toward them, because of their own pathology, but who can show much tenderness and care for nonhuman elements of the family environment such as plants or pets. "The child then grows up with reason to think that if only he were a plant or an animal, he might gain access to his mother's love" (p. 267).

Anna Freud[1] pointed out that Laura used her pets to demonstrate that one should care for animals. In her enactment Laura was the "good parent," but it soon became evident in watching Laura's play that the love she showed her pets could not be trusted. Hence, Laura often treated Chip in a cruel fashion. Anna Freud felt that Laura played out love and hate simultaneously with the dog. This ambivalence of feeling was also evident in Laura's relationship with me and was understood predominantly as an aspect of the mother transference. Pets served Laura well as recipients of her love and hate, and they remained loyal. She did not project hostile wishes onto pets, so she did not fear attack from them and therefore was not phobic of them. Moreover, she also strove to protect pets from harsh owners, thus indicating her reaction formations. This was suggested in her protective feelings about her aunt's dog Fanny, who was a displacement figure for Laura's envied brother, just as the aunt stood for Laura's mother. In part, because of identifications with controlled but neglected pets, Laura felt angry and consequently feared object loss. Separation anxiety was exacerbated when Laura experienced rage in response to Mrs. L.'s limitations on her autonomy in many areas of functioning, e.g., restraining her locomotion; controlling her feeding, toileting, and dressing. Displacing instinctual expressions from herself, Mrs. L. seemed to have provided Laura with pets as substitutes. Because of this tendency on Mrs. L.'s part, I suspect that one major determinant

---

1. In a discussion of a paper in which I presented different issues arising in the analysis of this patient, at the Hampstead Child-Therapy Clinic, London, on June 23, 1971.

originally leading Laura in the direction of a philic use of pets was her intense object hunger.

The painful reality that Laura avoided uppermost by creating her rabbit fantasy was the frustration connected with her oedipal wishes. Her father knew of her interest in rabbits but never volunteered to purchase one for her. He seemed unresponsive to Laura's oedipal overtures, relating instead to her anal messiness. In the analytic relationship this was enacted by Laura's refusal to clean up at the end of sessions. When Laura decided, however, that the proper time had arrived to ask her father to buy her a rabbit, he did respond favorably. For practical purposes her wish was granted because she was on vacation from school and had plenty of spare time to tend to the rabbit. Additionally, Laura chose this as the "proper time" to ask father because she knew he would be busy fishing with her brother. Hence, Laura anticipated that her father would feel guilty about neglecting her and would not refuse her request for a rabbit. The fantasy in which she was mother to the rabbit (baby) also enabled her to avoid conscious rivalry with mother for father. In fact, Mrs. L. repeatedly reinforced Laura's wish for a rabbit by accompanying her on visits to pet shops, thereby collaborating in her daughter's fantasy and displacing the rivalry directly from herself. In reality, mother "could be," so to speak, and Laura could interact with her as a younger child, i.e., passive and in need of care. (There were many somatic complaints during this stage of the analysis which prompted her mother to be a "good," caring mother.) Heiman (1956) writes, "By displacement, projection, and identification, a dog may serve as a factor in the maintenance of psychological equilibrium" (p. 584). For Laura, her imaginary rabbit permitted the unfolding of the oedipal drama in a displaced form.

The pathogenic coloring of Laura's oedipal complex with preoedipal fears of object loss was clearly illustrated. Fears of object loss exaggerated castration feelings (and penis envy), and vice versa. Hence both object loss and castration as dangers often appeared together. Intense preoedipal rage directed at mother made it extremely difficult for her to deal with additional anger normally felt in oedipal competition. Laura's position in relationship to her mother seemed predominantly to be an anal controlling one, manifesting itself in a hostile clingingness and sadomasochism. Thus, the aggressive and libidinal aspects of Laura's early psychic development, particularly that experienced during the rapprochement subphase of separation-individuation, which overlaps with the anal stage of drive development, influenced the genesis of her infantile neurosis (Settlage, 1971, 1979).

Laura was creatively adaptive in her defensive use of pets, primarily using externalization, displacement, and identification. But nowhere was her ego strength and creativeness better displayed than in her rabbit fantasy. Flopsy, the imaginary rabbit, which Laura pretended was often in the room with us, was very much akin to an imaginary companion. In fact, the rabbit seemed to hold less value for Laura when it became real (Sooty). Like an imaginary companion, her imaginary rabbit was in many ways a narcissistically chosen object. As Nagera (1969) and others have suggested, an imaginary companion is similar to a daydream and is an attempt at wish fulfillment. Furthermore, the imaginary companion, among other things, becomes an outlet for the externalization of aspects of the self that cause conflict and also embodies superego aspects. Nagera (1969) points out that the imaginary companion "fills the emptiness, neglect, loneliness, or rejection which the child seems to be experiencing" (p. 194). Since the imaginary rabbit served all these functions for Laura, one can say that it was similar to an imaginary companion.

Dorothy Burlingham (1952) described another group of daydreams, "animal fantasies," which are typical of the latency period:

> The child takes an imaginary animal as his intimate and beloved companion; subsequently he is never separated from his animal friend, and in this way he overcomes loneliness. This daydream is constructed in much the same way as the family romance, with this difference: the child does not here choose a new family, does not repeat a similar experience under improved conditions, but chooses a new companion who can understand him in his loneliness, unhappiness, and need to be comforted. This animal offers the child what he is searching for: faithful love and unswerving devotion. There is nothing that this dumb animal cannot understand; speech is quite un-

necessary, for understanding comes without words. These animal fantasies are thus an attempt to substitute for the discarded and unloving family an uncritical but understanding, dumb, and always loving creature. . . . They [e.g., animal fantasies] are . . . a reaction to the disappointment in love that is experienced during the oedipal phase [p. 2f.].

These insights by Dorothy Burlingham certainly were confirmed by Laura's use of her imaginary rabbit. It served Laura as her devoted, loyal, available companion, and also as her fantasied oedipal baby.

Laura's pets, both fantasied and real, became symbolic substitutes for her ideal self. Before she started analysis the sick pets that she cared for and nursed back to health represented the cared-for, protected, and loved child that she longed to be. Through the confirmation of her pets as to their having met pedigree standards (enacted in her Show Dog game), the experienced phallic narcissistic imperfections were disavowed and her narcissism guarded. Her beautiful "pure-bred" rabbit represented the ideal self that, free from any guilt and taint resulting from masturbation, was capable of being admired, loved, and cherished by her parents. The horse under her was symbolic of the penis that she desired. Thus Laura's use of pets elevated her self-esteem. Pets were objects through which she regulated her narcissism.

Unlike the adult patient, Laura was permitted actually to bring her pets into the analytic situation. With adults we adhere more closely to abstinence because of their greater frustration tolerance; we expect them to tell us about pets rather than to show us (enactment) along with telling us (verbalization). The analyst of adults can learn much from genetic accounts of childhood pets. I also suggest that much can be discovered about adulthood pets. Pets are important in symbolic, object-directed, and narcissistic ways.

BIBLIOGRAPHY

BONAPARTE, M. (1940), *Topsy*. London: Pushkin Press.
BURLINGHAM, D. (1952), *Twins*. New York: Int. Univ. Press.

FREUD, A. (1965), *Normality and Pathology in Childhood.* New York: Int. Univ. Press.

FREUD, S. (1909a), Analysis of a phobia in a five-year-old boy. *S.E.,* 10:3–149.

―――― (1909b), Notes upon a case of obsessional neurosis. *S.E.,* 10:153–320.

―――― (1913), Totem and taboo. *S.E.,* 13:1–161.

―――― (1918), From the history of an infantile neurosis. *S.E.,* 17:3–123.

HEIMAN, M. (1956), The relationship between man and dog. *Psychoanal. Quart.,* 25:568–585.

KUPFERMANN, K. (1977), A latency boy's identity as a cat. *Psychoanal. Study Child,* 32:363–387.

LEVINSON, B. M. (1964), Pets. *Ment. Hyg.,* 48:243–248.

―――― (1965), The veterinarian and mental hygiene. *Ment. Hyg.,* 49:320–323.

―――― (1967), The pet and the child's bereavement. *Ment. Hyg.,* 51:197–200.

―――― (1969), *Pet Oriented Child Psychotherapy.* Springfield, Ill.: Charles C. Thomas.

―――― (1970), Pets, child development, and mental illness. *J. Amer. Veterinary Med. Assn.,* 157:1759–1766.

MAHON, E. & SIMPSON, D. (1977), The painted guinea pig. *Psychoanal. Study Child,* 32:283–307.

MENNINGER, K. A. (1951), Totemic aspects of contemporary attitudes toward animals. In: *Psychoanalysis and Culture,* ed. G. B. Wilbur & W. Muensterberger. New York: Int. Univ. Press, pp. 42–74.

NAGERA, H. (1969), The imaginary companion. *Psychoanal. Study Child,* 24:165–196.

RAPPAPORT, E. A. (1968), Zoophily and zoerasty. *Psychoanal. Quart.,* 37:565–587.

SANFORD, B. (1966), A patient and her cats. *Psychoanal. Forum,* 1:170–176.

SEARLES, H. F. (1960), *The Nonhuman Environment,* New York: Int. Univ. Press.

SETTLAGE, C. F. (1971), On the libidinal aspect of early psychic development and the genesis of infantile neurosis. In: *Separation-Individuation,* ed. J. B. McDevitt & C. F. Settlage. New York: Int. Univ. Press, pp. 131–154.

―――― (1979), On the aggressive aspect of early psychic development and the genesis of infantile neurosis. Read before the Michigan Psychoanalytic Society.

WOODS, S. M. (1965), Psychotherapy and the patient's pet. *Current Psychiat. Ther.,* 5:119–121.

Some Notes on the Application of the Diagnostic Profile to Young Blind Children

DORIS M. WILLS

ATTEMPTS TO MAKE A PROFILE FOR THE YOUNG BLIND CHILD IM-
mediately raise the general question of how we would define
satisfactory development in such a child. It is our hope that blind
children will *eventually* develop in such a way that they can adapt
to the sighted world and bring their own special contribution to
it—their great sensitivity to sound and their ability to widen our
observation of the world by the freshness of their approach,
based as it is on the use of less usual sensory modalities. But,
particularly in the early years, the blind child has a difficult and
circuitous path before him; he needs time if he is to organize his
outer experience in his own fashion and if he is to come to terms
with his inner needs. Therefore at nursery school age even relative adaptation to sighted norms cannot be our main criterion; it
could be said that the child who makes such an adaptation too
effectively does some violence to his inner needs. The Profile for
the blind child also alerts the observer to specific questions, but,

The work with blind children is part of the Educational Unit of the
Hampstead Child-Therapy Course and Clinic and as such was maintained by
the Grant Foundation Inc., New York. The research work with the blind was
assisted further by the National Institute of Mental Health, Bethesda, Mary-
land.

The research was directed since its inception by Dorothy Burlingham. I am
deeply indebted to her for help with the work on which this paper is based, and
my thanks are also due for many helpful comments on the paper itself to A.
Curson and A.-M. Sandler.

217

since we are still in the process of learning about the early development of blind children, the answers we can supply often
lead to further questions and delineate areas of uncertainty.
This was Nagera and Colonna's experience in 1965 when they
wrote "Aspects of the Contribution of Sight to Ego Drive Development," a paper which made extensive use of Profiles. In my
paper I draw on their formulations and reexamine them in the
light of more recent observations and ongoing work with blind
infants and children.

By way of introduction, I want to point to some general considerations that have to be borne in mind in assessing blind children against the Profile. Nagera and Colonna and Dorothy
Burlingham repeatedly emphasize that *much of a blind child's
behavior, his fantasies and symptoms, cannot be understood in the same
way as can those of a sighted child.* Blind children lack the sensory
modality which plays the major role in the perception and
understanding of the world around. Because of this they suffer
many setbacks and evolve some unusual strategies. They mostly
show little facial expression; without this and the interchange of
glances to help us, we can repeatedly misinterpret their behavior. Indeed we are, to a very large degree, in a similar position to the children's parents, since we too are wedded to our
lifelong experience of understanding the world through vision.

This is well exemplified by the frequent confusion of two
common types of behavior in blind children. The first is regression proper, the blind child's tendency to slip back from object
cathexis to cathexis of the self and autoerotic behavior. The
second type of behavior, which often *looks* like some kind of
withdrawal of object cathexis, may well cover the child's attempt
to recall the past in order to make sense of a current situation and
collate it with a past experience. The two types of behavior can of
course be superimposed. We need to be aware of this kind of
distinction in evaluating the overt behavior of such children.

Their difficulty in becoming fully aware of reality lays the
ground for disturbances in this area. The blind child's perception of the world is much more easily disturbed by adverse early
experiences. He has much more difficulty in building up, first,
the idea of "me" and "not-me" and then a firm image of a solid,
reasonably safe world around which obeys certain rules and

which slowly becomes more predictable. He makes general assumptions too easily on the basis of an isolated experience.

For example, when I was driving 7-year-old Sam[1] home on a bumpy road, he asked me, "Was that a baby you ran over just now?" When Sam was under 3 he was in a major car accident in which relatives were killed. While this would traumatize a sighted child, he would have been reassured by observing hundreds of vehicles driven safely as he grew older. This enables the sighted child to put the early experience in some kind of proportion. Insofar as aggression motivates such a question, the sighted child would express it in a much more displaced way. *He could not misunderstand the happening to this frightening degree.* Such a mistaken assumption, in Sam's case about the behavior of his objects, lays the ground for further misunderstanding. We have other examples of the blind child showing surprising misapprehension of the world around, which must interfere with his full comprehension of later experiences.

A further result of the blind child's vague awareness of the world around leads to a blurring of the border between the ego and reality. Work on artificially induced perceptual deprivation indicates that adults in such states tend to hallucinate.[2] And these are after all people with structuralized personalities, who have developed egos which can (usually) differentiate between fantasy and reality. Our young blind children have the advantage in that they are not deprived in all sensory modalities, only in a major one, vision, but their egos are in the process of developing and of learning to understand reality. Since this remains vague for some time, it acts, like a Rorschach ink blot, as a screen for fantasies. If the child does not differentiate between the fantasies and reality, which is quite often the case, he is in difficulties. Even when the child does make the differentiation unaided by sight, fantasies are experienced as comparatively real, whether they are agreeable or disagreeable. And if they are dis-

---

1. All children cited in this paper are within the normal range of intelligence or above. All are educationally blind, that is, they have had to learn Braille.

2. Heron (1961) reported that adult subjects in a state of temporary perceptual deprivation tended to hallucinate in the sense of "perception without object," though the majority did not imagine what they "perceived" to be "real."

agreeable, the blind child cannot turn for relief to the solid visual world (which comforts *us* so much, for example, on waking from bad dreams).

There is another point of which all workers with the blind are aware, namely, the degree to which such a sensory deficit interferes with the balance of cathexis between inner and outer reality. Without sight, which seems to butter the world with cathexis—it appears to give far more continuous pleasure and meaning to the world around than any other sense—the child's own preoccupations tend to exercise too much pull.

In their 1965 paper Nagera and Colonna summarize the developmental problems of their blind group thus:

> Even when the blind child grows up under the most favorable circumstances (which are rarely encountered) in terms of ego endowment, good early mothering, reasonable environmental conditions, favorable object relations, etc., there is a point at which the development of one or another ego function clearly requires a contribution from the side of vision. When that contribution is not available, a disruption in the development of a specific function ensues. In turn, the insufficiency of these functions or of other aspects of the ego leads to further developmental interferences in all areas in which such functions are a necessary prerequisite [p. 269].

In general, the view Nagera and Colonna put forward, that there are two very different possibilities of development for blind children, one fairly normal and one atypical, is in line with our more recent experience, and an attempt will be made below to stress the significance of those moves which may be essential if the blind child is to progress comparatively normally and which, if not negotiated, lead to grave and perhaps irreversible distortions of development.

It has to be admitted, however, that we are far from knowing just how best, in the absence of sight, to facilitate these essential moves in development. As mentioned above, adverse or traumatic external happenings have an exaggerated impact on the blind child. Again, one is forced to conclude that the blind child's enormous dependence on the mother as auxiliary ego, in almost all areas, during his early years, means that any cue she misses will alter the ultimate picture quite disproportionately. We cannot rely to the same extent on the child's drive to normality and independence which might enable him to surmount a number of adverse experiences at the hands of the mother, and indeed of the environment, as it does for the sighted child.

In particular, however, Nagera and Colonna's point that certain children do not seem to lag much behind the development of sighted children may be questioned. The children give this impression, but on close acquaintance often prove to be using great energy to fit into the sighted world and to be masking considerable developmental lags in other areas. Here we should distinguish between the congenitally, totally blind on the one hand and those with some early visual experience, however brief, or with a residue of vision, however slight, on the other. We should watch when and how the children in each group manage to make an optimal adaptation in the light of our knowledge of the difficulties that beset their path.

THE DRIVE DEVELOPMENT OF THE BLIND

LIBIDINAL DEVELOPMENT

In 1963, A.-M. Sandler spelled out one of the main early sources of imbalance of cathexis between the inner and outer world in blind children. She made an assumption about the early drive development of the blind infant which in principle has stood the test of time—that infants blind from birth will show a greater or lesser degree of fixation to the very earliest phase of development in the first 3 months of life, the predominantly passive oral phase, in which the passive experience of bodily gratification is dominant, and that a basic pull toward self-centeredness will always be present.

Oral behavior in blind children appears to be very varied. When Nagera and Colonna wrote their paper in 1965, we had followed very few infants, and those we had observed sucked not only the bottle but fingers as well. Since then we have followed children who had to be helped to take the particular small step from bottle to finger or other substances:

Boris as an infant sucked his bottle well, but tended to keep his hands in a neonatal position. Although he touched nearby objects fleetingly, he had to be encouraged to suck his fingers. It was hoped that this would help with hand cathexis and get his hands into midline, which is an achievement apparently motivated to a large extent by sight (Fraiberg, 1977b). He never noticeably mouthed objects in his early years.

When Cynthia was referred at 9 months, she held her hands fisted most of the time. She loved her bottle and could often be observed sucking her tongue, but never her fingers. The mother was encouraged to play with Cynthia's hands; this soon became mutual hand-play and led to a more normal use of them. At the same time this child refused all attempts at the introduction of spoon-feeding, much preferring her bottle. While Cynthia had been weaned to the bottle successfully at 4 months, it seemed that the small step to sucking anything other than a bottle (or her tongue) was not undertaken because of a strong preference for the known experience.

Some preschool blind children do use their lips and tongue for investigation, but no mother known to us reported the insatiable mouthing of everything in which sighted children so often indulge. The whole expression of the oral drive in the blind child appears to suffer special vicissitudes in its development. It merits further study. If Hoffer (1949) is right when he says that the sighted infant's hands are libidinized by sucking, perhaps we should regularly encourage this in blind infants.

The battles over moving to solids, and over self-feeding, often reported by mothers of young blind children, appear to stem from the fact that, without sight, *any* change in feeding is felt as a change in the mother. Toilet training is often late, but is not experienced by mothers as an area of such intense conflict. The tormenting behavior that accompanies the anal phase, however, can be seen in some blind children, while in others, often the totally blind, it appears to be suppressed in favor of the child's use of the mother as an auxiliary ego in coping with the external world.

Nagera and Colonna comment that in blind children there is a marked overlap of phases and that the children seem "incapable of leaving behind the previous phases when a new developmental move occurs" (p. 271). This failure to abandon a previous phase may be motivated to some extent by their strong tie to the known routine, their clinging to the past, to the familiar, which must give a feeling of safety. All the stimulus to development provided by seeing the behavior of older siblings and adults is missing.

Nagera and Colonna's comment that "all earlier forms of gratification remain ego syntonic" (p. 272) is exemplified in the following illustration of a regressive move to the body for self-comfort:

> Cynthia (9 years), who was very intelligent, and very successful in school, had reached the phallic-oedipal phase. But she indulged in genital and anal masturbation in my presence without any obvious guilt. She often used such behavior to ward off painful affects.

We must beware of assuming, however, that "autoerotic behavior" always has the same significance that it has for the sighted child. Dorothy Burlingham (1965) remarks:

> Blind children are often called "withdrawn" . . . overinvolved with their own bodies, apparently more given to autoerotic indulgence. I believe it is more correct to say that the blind child makes use of his own body and its experiences to compensate for his lack of experiences in the external world [p. 204].

Such behavior *may* in some situations represent a recall of being touched by the mother, an attempt to repeat sensations received at her hands, and so be mainly object-related. It nevertheless carries its own dangers.

CATHEXIS OF SELF

One can readily observe the behavior described by Nagera and Colonna as an "extreme dependence upon the object world . . . shown in an inability to maintain their own self-esteem and cathexis of the self when the object world withdraws cathexis from them" (p. 272). Their example of a child who easily withdrew to manneristic gestures in the nursery school, but was active in the one-to-one situation of treatment, carries conviction. But sometimes behavior which appears stereotyped has content which we do not catch, and this must be borne in mind. (Fantasy content will be further discussed in the section on the ego.)

CATHEXIS OF OBJECT

Blind children do of course achieve object permanence and object constancy[3] but the developmental stages prior to the moves are more at risk than those of the sighted child. Without sight to attract him, the blind child has the task of extending his interest in his own body to interest in the mother's body. Without the help of sight to organize the discrete sensory impressions (such as voice, touch, smell) he receives from her, he has to become aware that she is a separate creature, and that she has a similar body with a continuing existence. Indeed Fraiberg (1977a) found that none of the blind children in her study was able to sustain a search for the mother, implying the belief that she "must be someplace," until they reached the late age of 25 months.

While blind children do reach a degree of object permanence, it is doubtful whether the object has the same quality and is as vivid for the blind child in these early years as it is for the sighted:

> Sam (5 years) was seen by Mrs. Sandler while I was away. When he recalled her one day on my return, he said, "Pretend you're Mrs. Sandler." This was not a game; he wanted her back again, and compensated for her lack in this way. On another occasion I was to buy him something after he had left me, and he said with surprise, "When you're in the shop, I'll be in the nursery," as if my continuing existence when absent from him was unexpected, or as if the thought of it had lacked the vividness it would have for the sighted child.

This different quality and slower development of object permanence in the young blind child must in turn affect the development of object constancy. He has to build on this somewhat shaky foundation and learn to recognize that the angry mother is

---

3. By "object permanence" is meant that stage when objects are perceived as continuing to exist even though absent. By "object constancy" is meant a later stage, when the child not only perceives objects as continuing to exist, but manages to maintain an inner image of them, which is mainly *positively* cathected, irrespective either of satisfaction or dissatisfaction (A. Freud, 1965).

still the loving mother (without being able to see that she still *looks* much the same) or he may withdraw from her. He has to learn to fuse his positive and negative feelings for her so that the positive predominate. Object constancy is a difficult achievement for a blind child and is of even greater importance to him than to the sighted child because, particularly in his early life, his mother acts as his auxiliary ego and mediates much of his experience.

We have noticed that some blind children make a stronger relationship to their therapist than sighted children of the same age. This can be based in part on splitting: the blind child feels it is too dangerous to be dependent on anyone not wholly reliable and kind.

During a film session I accidentally knocked the lights over with a great crash. I explained at once, "Silly Miss Wills broke the lights," to which Sam (6 years) replied, "*Bear* did it" (he was very frightened of the teddy bear). Later he again said, "Bear broke lamp." When I said he seemed afraid to say *I* did it, he replied. "Then I wouldn't like you."

Dorothy Burlingham (1940, p. 258) describes Sylvia, who disliked the prospect of a new teacher, but turned to her completely when she was to have her first lesson, and warded off her anxious and hostile feelings by defensively identifying with their object, the teacher. This is, of course, basically a problem of mastering ambivalent feelings. Blind children who are immature or disturbed may show oscillation of love and hate (Wills, 1970).

We have made further observations confirming Nagera and Colonna's statement that blind children tend to cling to anyone present because of their vulnerability when familiar objects are not available. We also have noted a switch to someone present who temporarily could be a better auxiliary ego, even though the familiar object was available:

When I took Sam (10 years) to the Natural History Museum, he was excited and a little apprehensive. However, he readily transferred his hand to that of an attendant who was talking about a stuffed elephant to him, leaving me to wait.

Dorothy Burlingham (1940) makes the point that the blind need a great deal of psychic attention to maintain their contact with another person.

We cannot count on young blind children cathecting the *inanimate* world with the same speed and certainty as do sighted children. For blind children, people are far more attractive than inanimate objects since they make a much more varied sensory impression. We have noticed how quickly children arriving in weekly boarding school know all the teachers and other workers by voice. An additional heading, such as "Cathexis of Inanimate Objects," would be useful to elicit the stage the child has reached in extending his interest to the inanimate world.

AGGRESSION

While it is true that aggression is often not obvious in the fully blind child, we have the impression that different forms of its discharge sometimes go unnoticed and may stimulate rocking and other motor activity.

Simon (2 years), who moved well, showed this openly; he ran up and down the garden when mother would not do as he wished.

Dorothy Burlingham (1961) describes a 7-year-old who used swaying movements as a substitute for aggression. Again, the expression of aggression may be delayed and go unrecognized.

Examination of our analytic records suggests that some congenitally blind children, and those who lost their sight during the first year, may have considerable difficulties in fusing libidinal and aggressive feelings to the object and that the (unfused) aggression is often defended against to the child's detriment.

In 1961, Dorothy Burlingham described the children's fear of their own aggression. More recently we have observed further examples:

Sam (7 years) explored this with me when I drove him home from weekly boarding school. His queries would begin with: "What would you do if I . . . smacked you hard, knocked your head off?" (He added that mother did this to someone once.) "What would you do if I broke the brake?"

Many children control the expression of aggression in order to preserve a positive contact with the holding object. This control, coupled with the marked lack of facial expression, makes it easy for us to be misled and to assume that the child is warding off anger in some way instead of merely avoiding its expression.

Cynthia (9 years) showed no obvious reaction, and made no reference whatever to me, when I started to see another child in her boarding school during my weekly visits. When I suggested to her that she must have found this hard, she did not deny it and said with unusual tartness, "Then why did you do it?"

When one interpreted what appeared to be a defense, Cynthia repeatedly did not respond with relief or guilt but immediately acquiesced in a matter-of-fact way, showing she was well aware of many of her wishes, but had learned not to show or express them.

Indeed, one's task with blind children often seems to be an attempt to discover the essential child with his or her normal drives and affects. These become "iced over" in an attempt to keep the very necessary support of the available adults, and probably to avoid painful clashes in which the blind child will nearly always be defeated. But the resulting behavior frequently deceives us all.

The Ego of the Blind

In this section Nagera and Colonna comment that many of the children they studied showed marked fears of animals. They query how much of this is defensive activity against the drives and how much adaptive. While one would, of course, have to know the child well in order to decide this issue, it is a common observation in boarding schools for the blind that the more inhibited children are the more fearful, suggesting some projection of the aggressive drive representation. We have made some recent observations on individual children:

Cynthia was placed in weekly boarding school at 5 years. She slowly overcame her fear of the school swimming pool, but her fear of the Hoover at 9 years was on a phobic level. She expected it to trip her up so that she would fall in the dust and, among other things, to get on top of her when she was in bed at night.

In the case of Sam, his fear of the Zoo, whatever phobic mechanisms were otherwise involved, probably also was linked with earlier traumatic experiences when his parents had taken him through fun fairs. At 10 years, Sam always chose the Zoo for a holiday outing, although he was apprehensive about the animals. He would not go into any of the bird or animal houses, and particularly avoided the tiger house, although he wished me to go in alone and report back to him.

These fearful reactions, stemming from an association to an earlier overwhelming or disagreeable experience, are sometimes hard to understand because, to a sighted person, the association is not obvious.

We tend to take for granted in sighted children a relatively undistorted awareness of reality. This is more tenuous, and certainly more vulnerable, for blind children. The level they have reached in understanding their world at any one time will further modify their ongoing ego development. Where they have acquired gross misconceptions, these may even determine the course of their total personality development. The heading "Awareness of Reality" could be used, for example, to cover age-adequate awareness and understanding, age-adequate ability to use pretense, and to note gross distortions due to misunderstanding, and projection or other measures.

As regards fantasy life, Dorothy Burlingham suggests that we often do not catch blind children's fantasies. Some children may not have the language to express them; others show them in their play where we may only slowly come to understand them. For instance, the following appeared to constitute a regression to autoerotic behavior, but it contained some object-related fantasy:

Cynthia in her third year would rotate in the middle of the room, fingering her own hands and talking "scribble." Later when she was 6 she used similar play in her sessions, turning her dolls round. She agreed with my suggestion that when she herself had turned around, she had pretended that other children were playing with her. She added, "I still do, I make up all their voices." She then admitted to concocting a continuous fantasy when she was not actually occupied with schoolwork (at which she was excellent). She kept these fantasies to a large extent secret. They were difficult to follow and probably often checked by adults telling her to "talk sense."

Sam (5 years) often pushed a swing door to and fro while rocking foot to foot if his nursery school teacher withdrew her attention. But during his "special hour" with me, his therapist, his opening and shutting a door were the basis of much play, which he himself initiated, around goings and comings at home.

The play of the young blind child with an adult is frequently concerned with actual events, which he wishes to repeat exactly as he experienced them—an example of his use of the adult in his attempt to master *external* experience. It is reminiscent of the earlier role play of the sighted child. Both sighted and blind introduce virtually no changes in the former event at this stage because first they have to establish a sense of reality. Since this takes longer for the blind child, this type of play persists into later years and easily suggests that he suffers from a paucity of fantasy.

The blind child's later ability to show his fantasies in what is sometimes called "fiction play" involving pretense not only is dependent on his having acquired a basic sense of reality but is greatly furthered if he can use toys as symbols for people. This ability to symbolize always seemed to be retarded, especially in fully blind children. This impression is supported by Fraiberg (1977a), who found a protracted delay in the blind child's capacity to represent himself in play. This delay must account for the fact that it is extremely difficult, if not impossible, to establish a transitional object in the blind child's very early years. Any toy or possession used for comfort is soon abandoned. The blind child remains centered for much longer on his real objects.

The result is that pretense is established later in blind children. The Maxfield-Buchholz Scale (1957) places "usually differentiates between 'pretending' and actual fact" in the sixth year, which would be late for a sighted child. Moreover, pretense easily breaks down under the pressure of anxiety, due sometimes to projections onto toys, for example, of dangerous impulses.

There is another difficulty about the blind child's play: it frequently *looks* bizarre so that the adult does not understand and further it:

During the class's play session in a boarding school for blind children, Cynthia (5 years) was sitting at a table with a box of 2-inch cubes which she appeared to be handling and banging in an aimless way. Sitting next to her, however, I was able to elicit the fantasy: two blocks were mother and father; the rest, the family who danced (here Cynthia banged the blocks hard in competition with the noise around). Subsequently they wetted their beds.

When a sighted child is playing in the presence of an adult, the adult can often easily pick up the drift, offer props to further the play, and help to relate inner and outer experience by a few suggestions. The fact that the adult understands and tolerates the displacement of libidinal and aggressive behavior increases the child's tolerance of these drives and leads to their modification and mastery. This is an important aspect of noninterpretive play which is sometimes overlooked.

Early mobility in the blind child is of great importance since he has to explore his unseen world. Late independent walking is often found in association with backwardness in other areas.

At one time we assumed that rocking, a rather prevalent habit among blind children in Western cultures, arose from some early curtailment of the child's free movement in the interests of safety. While this may play a part, rocking may sometimes be linked with a kind of ongoing hunger for symbiosis, for reunion with the mother. Physical contact will often stop it at an age when diversion would be the solution if the child were sighted. One gains the impression that blind children who are carried a good deal on the mother's body do not rock as much. Verbal reports from West and East Africa and India, where most young children are carried on the mother's body to a far greater extent, suggest that rocking is not a problem in these societies.

While rocking may originally be based on some kind of symbiotic hunger, as the child grows older, it takes on many meanings; it is then often used as a safe pathway for motor discharge.

Nagera and Colonna deal at some length with the very important area of speech development in blind children. Stressing the degree to which other ego functions are dependent on the acquisition of speech, they conclude that "whatever interferes with the child's ability to acquire such symbols may bring aspects of his ego development to a near standstill" (p. 279). This is our continuing impression. Nagera and Colonna also comment on a tendency to concreteness in the children's thinking. We also have noted that the children sometimes understand language, used figuratively, in literal fashion well into latency, much as far younger sighted children do. At times words may even be understood as *synonymous* with what they represent to an extent not found in the sighted population:

Arthur (3½ years) persistently asked his father to say that he had brought a toy home for him. His father pointed out that in fact he had no toy, but Arthur persevered, requesting that he should *say* it. Eventually the father gave way, whereupon Arthur asked, "Where is it?"

Though some blind children are very silent during their first year, it is, on the whole, after the first year that their speech development often becomes more obviously different from that of sighted children and shows some anomalies (Wills, 1979). Fraiberg (1977a, 1977b) reports a delay in the ability to use two words appropriately and to form two-word sentences, She also reports a delay in the free use of "I" because of a difficulty in the development of self representation, presumably linked with symbol formation.

In our experience, some children who eventually achieve normal, direct, speech show many delays and unusual features en route. It may be that these children, who are after all eventually successful, are demonstrating, not only their difficulties, but ways around them, and study of their progress may help us with children who become arrested—for instance, those who persist with echolalia.

Blindness makes speech development hazardous not only because it is difficult to learn language about a world the child cannot see, but because many of its prestages are missing or at risk. All the very early responses of mother and child to each other's facial expression, which lay the groundwork for vocal interchange in the sighted child, simply do not occur. Furthermore, the blind child's vocalizing interferes with his listening. In some cases mothers have to work very hard to get the child to vocalize at all, to make vocal interchange pleasurable, and then to show the child he can use it as a tool not only for affecting his objects but also his environment.

We have the impression that the ego's controls over drive activity are uneven in these children. Where libidinal and aggressive drives are object-directed, they are often strictly controlled, either consciously, or unconsciously through repression, displacement, and so forth; this is because of the child's dependence. Where they are autoerotic, however, they often appear uncontrolled and are primitive in expression.

The Superego Structure

Nagera and Colonna comment that in their group it was difficult to find signs of guilt when specific transgressions occurred. The instances they cite, however, are concerned with autoerotic activities about which, as described above, blind children show little or no guilt (see also Burlingham, 1965).

Some specific factors must be operative to allow autoerotic activities to remain ego syntonic. These children suffer because siblings and parents move away from them and they cannot easily follow, so that their own bodies remain the one readily available source of comfort. It is also possible that mothers may be more permissive of autoerotic activities in a blind child; certainly he misses surprised and disapproving glances from others. He is also handicapped because he cannot imitate or identify with the more controlled behavior of others since he cannot see it. This pull to self-centeredness is in line with A.-M. Sandler's (1963) supposition described above.

Guilt in the blind seems to be most apparent in object-related situations:

Adam (4 years) was cross because the teacher had been away, saying she was horrible and he did not like her, and he would throw her in the river. In a moment he added, "I won't really, you know."

Richard (4 years) was kicking another child under the table. He said that it was not he but Sam who was doing it. The teacher said she knew it was he, and he looked upset.

Development of the Total Personality

Nagera and Colonna state, "A marked retardation and unevenness in the development of the total personality as shown on the Lines of Development seem to be the normal picture in this group of blind children" (p. 283); we continue to have the same impression.

It can easily be overlooked, however, that a blind child is busy attempting to master experiences *different* from those which the mother may be offering, "through which he goes on his own and for which he receives neither acknowledgment nor praise" (Burlingham, 1965, p. 195).

One area of development seems particularly important for preschool blind children. Descriptively this is covered by the developmental line which progresses from "dependency to emotional self-reliance and adult object relations" (A. Freud, 1965). If the blind child has made a move from biological unity with the mother to a need-fulfilling relationship with her and others, together with a widening of cathexis from his own to his mother's body and her surroundings, there is a good basis for further development.[4] Gross irregularity in the other lines seems of less importance than would be the case if the child were sighted:

At 3¾ years, Sam arrived at the clinic nursery school in nappies and with a bottle hanging from his mouth. He was a much-loved child, quickly made a good relationship with his teacher, and soon used the opportunities the nursery school offered to make moves in many areas of development, including feeding and cleanliness training.

The behavior of otherwise well-functioning blind preschool children suggests that the child continues to fall most obviously behind on those lines which demand physical skills, movement, and orientation. In general, however, the lines developed for sighted children need modification and elaboration before they are applied to blind children—if our aim is to elicit the subtle differences in development.

REGRESSION AND FIXATION POINTS

Nagera and Colonna comment that, in this area again, behavior which would be symptomatic of levels of fixation in a sighted child may not prove to indicate this in a blind child. For example,

---

4. Unfortunately, developmental scales for young blind children tend to have few items covering the all-important early steps in the mother-child relationship, stressing, rather, steps in the cathexis of inanimate objects, which we would regard as of secondary importance.

the inhibition of touching, which young blind children often show, does not necessarily imply a fixation in the anal phase. In the past we sometimes attributed this inhibition to an over-compliance with a mother's normal and constant prohibition, "Don't touch"; but the observation of very young children suggests that it is linked with avoidance and is almost equivalent to the sighted child's turning away from, or not looking at, something strange.

Another example: young blind children often dislike getting their hands sticky. Apart from the usual reasons for this, the stickiness interferes with the child's need to be guided by accurate touch in the absence of vision.

The degree to which these children regress, sometimes only temporarily, in a new situation continues to astound us:

Boris (3 years) was very well orientated at home where he moved freely about the flat. On arriving at our nursery school accompanied by his mother, he completely lost his power of orientation. Not until his second term did he begin to move more freely in this new environment.

This regression can also be observed in children entering weekly boarding school at 5 years. The ease and degree of regression are a measure of the constant effort these children are compelled to make in order to maintain their orientation, their awareness of people, and their knowledge of things around them. Rather than sustain this effort, some abandon it and resort to their familiar inner world of memories and fantasy, achieving a feeling of safety in this way.

DYNAMIC AND STRUCTURAL ASSESSMENT (CONFLICTS)

The whole pattern of internalized conflict may be somewhat different from that of the sighted in these young blind children. Their difficulty in perceiving outer events leads to misunderstanding. Their further difficulties in differentiating inner from outer events and fantasy from reality allows of a great deal of externalization and projection. All this confuses the picture both for the child *and* the observer. Organization of internalized conflicts certainly appears to come later. But without further analytic investigation, many questions must remain unanswered.

ASSESSMENT OF SOME GENERAL CHARACTERISTICS

FRUSTRATION TOLERANCE

Nagera and Colonna comment that frustration tolerance is difficult to evaluate. While these children allow themselves much direct drive gratification, they suffer excessive frustration in their dealings with the external world. If we accept that these blind children allow themselves drive gratification mainly of an *autoerotic* kind, then we can add that they have little frustration tolerance in *this* area; for example, it can be extremely difficult to help the nursery school child who rocks to more age-adequate behavior. However, a blind child cannot avoid frustration in dealing with the *external* world and eventually resigns himself to much of it. This very resignation probably augments his intolerance of any frustration in the area of direct autoerotic drive gratification, so that these two very different reactions have a causal link.

The children show a variety of reactions to frustration in dealing with the external world. In early life some children have tantrums when they cannot manage a practical task. As they grow older, this may give way to withdrawal to fantasy. Because of the lack of expression, it is easy to miss the children's feelings of failure, they merely give up, or get a sighted person to help them.

SUBLIMATION POTENTIAL

Nagera and Colonna make the point that in blind children there occur at a given age important rearrangements in their personalities which sometimes allow satisfactory sublimations to take place. This is certainly observable, but without more analytic material it is difficult to spell out this very important change in more detail.

PROGRESSIVE DEVELOPMENTAL FORCES VERSUS REGRESSIVE TENDENCIES

We have the impression, with further experience, that it is difficult but very important to help the blind child displace interests away from the body:

Cynthia (9½ years), who had developed a very little sight in her fourth year, said she and I should think of something nice. She sat wriggling and masturbating a little, and then said that she was thinking about fires. With encouragement she told a confused story about one. This was not immediately interpreted, but subsequently she was offered a toy fire engine and some crude drawing materials which she could manage. She became completely involved with these materials and the body movements ceased. (She would at this stage never draw in school.)

Though talk, noise-making, and music all help, they do not appear to offer the same easy pathway to sublimation of drive derivatives as the many vision-dominated activities that we offer to sighted children.

Perhaps the lack of an easy pathway to sublimation lies behind the sudden jump in development that Nagera and Colonna note, and which occurs in some blind children: the confusions of earlier life are kept secret (or repressed) and the growing child exchanges passive compliance with the demands of sighted people for an active striving and competitiveness for their approval.

CONCLUSION

Bruner (1961) suggests that "one of the prime sources of anxiety is a state in which one's conception or perception of the environment with which one must deal does not 'fit' or predict that environment in a manner that makes action possible" (p. 206). Blind children are *repeatedly* confronted by such situations which, without sight, they cannot easily investigate; and to deal with them they turn to memories of the *past* to attempt to find a precedent and to regain a feeling of safety. This must play its part in their apparent egocentricity, and must account for the extraordinarily detailed memories some of them show. Their behavior frequently deceives us, and just as we have learned how to look below the surface of sighted children's behavior, we have to learn how to do the same for blind children if we are to help them fulfil their potential.

While there are fortunately few blind children in Western societies, their study throws light on certain steps in development which go relatively unnoticed in sighted children and may help us in our work with them. Again, the blind show some features common to other groups of children such as borderline cases and those who are mentally handicapped. All three groups, for example, tend to show a strong tie to routine. It would be interesting to tease out how far such behavior is the normal reaction of an ego with a damaged apparatus in an attempt to organize experience, and how far this behavior is a reaction to the specific handicap. The Profile remains an excellent method of spelling out such similarities and differences. Even though it demonstrates our lack of knowledge, it indicates the area where further study is badly needed.

BIBLIOGRAPHY

BRUNER, J. S. (1961), The cognitive consequences of early deprivation. In: *Sensory Deprivation,* ed. P. Solomon et al. Cambridge: Harvard Univ. Press, pp. 195–207.

BURLINGHAM, D. (1940), Psychoanalytic observations of blind children. In: *Psychoanalytic Studies of the Sighted and the Blind.* New York: Int. Univ. Press, 1972, pp. 227–279.

_____ (1961), Some notes on the development of the blind. *Psychoanal. Study Child,* 16:121–145.

_____ (1965), Some problems of ego development in blind children. *Psychoanal. Study Child,* 20:194–208.

FRAIBERG, S. (1977a), Congenital sensory and motor deficits and ego formation. *Annu. Psychoanal.,* 5:169–194.

_____ (1977b), *Insights from the Blind.* New York: Basic Books.

FREUD, A. (1965), Normality and pathology in childhood. *W.,* 6.

HERON, W. (1961), Cognitive and physiological effects of perceptual isolation. In: *Sensory Deprivation,* ed. P. Solomon et al. Cambridge: Harvard Univ. Press, pp. 6–33.

HOFFER, W. (1949), Hand, mouth and ego-integration. *Psychoanal. Study Child,* 3/4:49–56.

MAXFIELD, K. E. & BUCHHOLZ, S. (1957), *A Social Maturity Scale for Blind Pre-School Children.* New York: American Foundation for the Blind.

NAGERA, H. & COLONNA, A. B. (1965), Aspects of the contribution of sight to ego and drive development. *Psychoanal. Study Child,* 20:267–287.

SANDLER, A.-M. (1963), Aspects of passivity and ego development in the blind infant. *Psychoanal. Study Child,* 18:343–360.

WILLS, D. M. (1968), Problems of play and mastery in the blind child. *Brit. J. Med. Psychol.,* 41:213–222.

_____ (1970), Vulnerable periods in the early development of blind children. *Psychoanal. Study Child,* 25:467–479.

_____ (1979), Early speech development in blind children. *Psychoanal. Study Child,* 34:85–117.

PROBLEMS OF INSIGHT

The papers comprising this section were presented at the Hampstead Child-Therapy Clinic International Scientific Forum on "The Significance of Insight in Psychoanalytic Theory and Practice," London, November 9 and 10, 1979.

Insight

Its Presence and Absence as a Factor in Normal Development

ANNA FREUD

Self-Knowledge as the Communication Between Id and Ego

THE EXTENT OF AN INDIVIDUAL'S KNOWLEDGE OF HIS OWN PSYCHIC processes is one of the foremost problems which confront the psychoanalyst. Most members of the profession are concerned with this, above all, as a phenomenon within the analytic treatment situation and significantly influenced by it. I maintain here that it is of no less significance as a factor within the ongoing developmental processes and of decisive influence on their positive or negative outcome.

The word used within the psychoanalytic terminology for this specific manifestation is "insight" (i.e., the English translation of the German *Einsicht*). Freud used the term *Einsicht* almost exclusively for a patient's acknowledgment of the presence and significance of his psychological troubles (*Krankheitseinsicht*), though it occurs in his *Gesammelte Schriften* occasionally also as denoting "knowledge" in general, and in one special instance as

Director, Hampstead Child-Therapy Clinic, which is at present supported by the Herman A. and Amelia S. Ehrmann Foundation, New York; the Field Foundation, Inc., New York; the Freud Centenary Fund, London; the Anna Freud Foundation, New York; the New-Land Foundation, Inc., New York; and a number of private supporters.

This paper is simultaneously published in: *The Writings of Anna Freud*, 8:137–148. New York: International Universities Press, 1981.

denoting "revelation." The German adjective *einsichtig*, which is derived from the noun, means "reasonable," "open to argument," "not stubborn," while its English form "insightful" means "knowledgeable." In fact, whenever we find the term insight used by English authors, it is always as a synonym for self-knowledge, i.e., for the links between consciousness and the unconscious, for understanding the reasons for one's moods and feelings, the relationships between past and present, the motivations for one's actions, one's predilections or their opposites.

TWO OPINIONS CONCERNING INSIGHT

Taking this wider connotation of the term as our starting point, we find in the psychoanalytic literature two contrasting opinions concerning it. There are many authors who maintain that it is the task of analysis to return to the patient the insight he has lost due to his neurosis, i.e., due to the crippling use of defenses employed against the upsurges from the id and embedded in his symptomatic compromise formations. There are others[1] who express the point of view that psychoanalytic treatment takes the patient much further regarding the capacity for insight than is achieved by the normal person who has never undergone psychoanalytic therapy. Personally, I incline strongly toward this second opinion. I believe that the psychoanalytic technique opens up for the analysand a possibility to view his inner life to an extent never reached under the normal conditions of life, thus not merely *restoring* but *creating* insight. I also believe that this fact is responsible for a complaint frequently heard from young individuals who have undergone successful analytic treatment. To their own astonishment, they find it quite difficult to communicate with those of their contemporaries who have not undergone the same experience. The new way of looking into and at themselves which they have acquired in analysis isolates them to a certain extent. Or, to put it in other words: they are now more insightful than their peers, a fact which makes them stand out among them.

1. See in this connection Hansi Kennedy (1979) and Clifford Yorke (1965).

Two Standards of Behavior: Toward Inside and Outside

As analysts, we take it for granted that the amount of insight possessed by an unanalyzed person is minimal, and that this is due to the protective barrier between id and ego, erected to shield the latter from any excessive awareness of mental discomfort, pain, anxiety, narcissistic hurt, etc. However, this explanation, although enlightening in one respect, leaves many questions unanswered in others. It fails to answer, for example, why the mental apparatus is so selective in its avoidances; why it can blind itself to unpleasure provided this arises from within, while there is no equivalent response to unpleasure which threatens from external reality. There is, after all, no lack of evidence from mountaineers, explorers, rescuers, firemen, political dissidents, and others that they are able to brave the adverse consequences of their actions and have no inclination to shut their eyes to them, as they might do in the case of internal danger. There also are the scientists who relentlessly pursue the truth in their physical fields, but accept at the same time the most shallow rationalizations with regard to their own psychological motives.

It needs additional explanation *how* human beings can, at one and the same time, be heroic and cowardly, truth-loving and victims of self-deception;[2] *when*, at which points of development the different behavior toward inner and outer reality comes into being; *why* the defense mechanisms which ward off unpleasure work in one direction only, i.e., toward the inner hazards; *whether* the analytic techniques of free association, dream and transference interpretation are really the only means of widening the individual's awareness of the psychic processes within himself; and *where* in his progress toward maturity similar chances exist for increasing insight.

Even though it may be impossible at present to find answers to

---

2. That the difference between the two attitudes cannot be explained simply by the presence or absence of fear is borne out by the remark of a little boy who was admonished by his mother not to be so fearful of the dark. "Imagine," said the mother, "what you would do if you were a soldier," to which the child replied very wisely: "Soldiers are also afraid. They just do not mind."

all these questions, the mere posing of them might prove a profitable exercise.

INSIGHT VERSUS ORIENTATION: A QUESTION OF TIMING

The described discrepancy between insight (into the psychic processes) and orientation (in the external world) seems to start with the maturation of ego functions in the first two years of life. It is these functions which, very gradually, turn the drive-dominated, almost animallike newborn into an acceptable social being. They humanize him in the sense that they make him susceptible to influence from the environment, promote his emotional attachment to the object world, strengthen his desire to comply with the parents' wishes; in short, they serve his adaptation. However, at the same time, and especially in the second year of life when the infant becomes mobile, they also represent a danger. While the balance between the strength of id and ego forces is still a precarious one, there is the distinct possibility that whatever the ego learns may be drawn totally into the service of the id, in fact, helping it to attain the fulfillment of drive derivatives which are unacceptable to the environment, bringing with it the threat of punishment or loss of love, and, instead of serving adaptation, disturbing it. This, then, is the moment when defense sets in.

Defense activity, as understood in analytic theory, begins in the most primitive way with denial and externalization, and advances from these to introjection and projection, repression and reaction formation, sublimation, etc. With their combined aim of blotting out, keeping off, deflecting, and mitigating the id derivatives, they represent the (partial) enmity of the ego toward the id, i.e., the need to protect the ego organization itself as well as the ego's relationship to the environment from the disruptive interference of the drives and the urgency with which they strive for fulfillment.

DEFENSE MECHANISMS AS IMPAIRMENT OF EGO FUNCTION

The defense mechanisms of the ego, however, do not only oppose and modify the id wishes. They do not only borrow some of the characteristics from the primary processes, as, for example, when turning a striving into its opposite, a process which makes use of the identity between opposites which exists in the unconscious; or when externalizing a wish, a process that is very similar to the easy displacement of strivings which occurs within primary process functioning. They also have another close and potentially damaging relationship to ego functions which often escapes notice or, rather, becomes visible only during the earlier periods of development.

Attention, perception, memory, reason, reality testing, understanding of causality, secondary process thinking improve constantly during the whole course of early childhood. They help the child to orient himself and alert him to dangers, whether these arise from water, fire, heights, imprudent actions, or from evoking disapproval. The keener these functions are, the safer the older child can feel in his environment, in contrast to the less developed toddler who is in permanent need of adult protection. While threats from without are adequately dealt with in this manner, however, dangerous impulses from within do not respond to the same methods. They are more difficult for the child to combat when they are perceived, acknowledged, and remembered, and for that reason defense not only turns directly against the id derivatives themselves but tries simultaneously to put the relevant ego functions, at least partially, out of action. From then onward, perceptiveness of the external world takes precedence over perceptiveness of internal processes. Insight becomes doubly blunted, every defense against the drives damaging at the same time one or the other of the developing ego functions.

Denial (of internal unpleasure) sets in simultaneously with the child's progress toward correctly perceiving, apperceiving, and acknowledging facts in his surroundings. Thus, while his senses are sharpened in one direction, they are, by the use of this defense mechanism, at the same time blunted in another. Reality sense with regard to the outside world and denial with regard to internal processes are obviously at cross-purposes with each other. What suffers is insight.

Externalization is widely used by the young child to ascribe his own unwanted feelings, wishes, and impulses to some outside agency, whether human being or animal, and so to escape responsibility for them. *Projection* acts similarly, while *introjection* appropriates wanted items, qualities, and attitudes from other people. This merging with the affairs of others happens while, at the same time, the child's differentiation from others and sense of his own identity are built up. There is no doubt that the two moves run counter to each other, the latter dominating the relations with the outer, the former the relations with the inner world.

Isolation, a much-used defense mechanism for the purpose of splitting feelings from factual experience, works simultaneously with the development of the all-important synthetic function whose purpose it is to create a whole out of the miscellaneous experiences of life. While the synthetic function binds the various parts of the personality together, thus creating the self, isolation, for its own defensive purposes, estranges them from each other and keeps them apart.

Rationalization, which deceives the individual about his motives for action, runs counter to the important ego capacities for cognition, fact finding, and reality testing.

Denial in fantasy obscures and changes to the opposite what reason and logic try to present to the individual as unalterable facts.

Finally, and perhaps most importantly for the fate of insight, *repression* destroys the intactness of memory which, at this time, is in the process of being perfected as a function. With the withdrawal of conscious cathexis from dangerous, frightening, and upsetting items of psychic content, memory becomes incomplete, and gaps and deletions interrupt its coherent sequence. It is especially these gaps which the widening of consciousness in analytic therapy attempts to fill.[3]

In case the developmental outline sketched above is at all correct, we have to picture the child as emerging from his early

3. There are certain clinical experiences which reveal that damage to memory by repression can go beyond the blotting out of inner experience and spread to the ordinary events of life. An example of this is a boy patient who had developed such consistent "forgetting" for his wrongdoings that his memory also became unreliable for the purpose of learning, for totally permitted pursuits, etc. He had altogether turned himself into a generally "forgetful" person.

years with his ego well equipped for formal learning and doubly protected against inroads from within, on the one hand, by the defense mechanisms which have been chosen and, on the other, by their dimming the very functions which otherwise stand him in such good stead for the exploration of the world. Whether this contrasting attitude toward within and without is totally explained by his individual needs, i.e., in ontogenetic terms, is an open question. It may go back to phylogenesis, when men had to maintain themselves in surroundings which were more hostile and dangerous to them than any of their own instinctual drives.

THE CHANCES TO REGAIN INSIGHT

A MISSED CHANCE IN THE LATENCY PERIOD

Since, according to the foregoing, the individual's restriction of insight is based on the hazardous imbalance of id and ego forces in the under-5, the weakening of the id and the strengthening of the ego in the latency period should alter the situation and enable the latency child to be less defensive. However, this is not what happens. On the contrary, latency children, and especially those with a strong superego, rely all the more on their existing defenses. There is no spontaneous move toward dismantling them and taking a closer look at themselves. Even in analytic treatment, they display the most extraordinary resistances against this possibility. They get furious with the analyst's interpretations, which they consider unfair. According to their own belief, they have done the right thing to deflect or to close their eyes to their drive derivatives, and even under the reassuring guidance of the analyst, they are reluctant to believe that a clearer view of internal happenings would increase, not lessen, the chances of moral control.

ADOLESCENCE AS A SECOND CHANCE

Whoever works with adolescents, analytically or otherwise, is impressed with their extreme preoccupation with themselves. Whatever happens in them looms very much larger than any events in their everyday life. There is an unmistakable move toward and wish for insight, which, however, takes on a peculiar form. Thought, wishes, fantasies, fears, and judgments are translated into concern with cosmic, political, or philosophical matters. They are, thus, as far removed from the personal sphere as possible. Obviously, such adolescents hope to understand what happens in themselves in the less frightening terms of the world at large.

Nevertheless, this attempt to gain or regain insight also fails or, rather, remains abortive.

CHANCES FOR INSIGHT IN ADULT LIFE

We do not expect any spontaneous changes in the capacity for insight once development has ceased. Within the adult individual, the relations between id and ego are regulated by his own personal defense organization, and they remain permanent unless there are upsetting alterations in the relative strength of drive and ego forces, or unless frustration, regression, and intolerable conflicts lead to pathological, symptomatic compromise solutions. It is only in these instances that analytic therapy is called upon to widen the ego's view of what is happening in the unconscious and, with it, its area of effectiveness. Under all other circumstances, normal life can proceed however limited the amount of self-knowledge at the disposal of the individual.

There are, however, some exceptions to this common rule.

Poets are renowned for knowing almost as much of unconscious motivation as do analysts or successfully analyzed persons. Even though their insight is not always directed toward their own psychic processes, it is most impressive with regard to the figures they invent. One of the reasons for this may be that in the creative writer the unconscious and consciousness are not closed off from each other by the usual barriers. On the one hand, the phenomenon of "inspiration" gives evidence that elements from the id have no difficulty in reaching the conscious surface; on the other hand, ego functions are not prevented in the usual way from penetrating the id.

There also is the other possibility that for the creative artist, the respective importance of inner and outer events is reversed. What is of real relevance for him are the psychic events, as they happen in him, or as he fashions them in his creations, while reality is comparatively negligible. Therefore, he can direct toward the inner world the same undiminished ego capacities which ordinary people use for orientation outside.

There are, finally, some rare individuals who, driven by the wish for discovery and regard for truth, succeed in transgressing the protective borders between their internal agencies. On their own, and open-eyed, they investigate what lies beyond consciousness, in the spirit of examining strange tribal customs in a dark continent. It may be interesting to remember that Freud thought of himself as an explorer of this kind.

BIBLIOGRAPHY

Kennedy, H. (1979), The role of insight in child analysis. *J. Amer, Psychoanal. Assn. Suppl.,* 27:9–28.

Yorke, C. (1965), Some metapsychological aspects of interpretation. *Brit. J. Med. Psychol.,* 38:27–42.

Insight

The Teiresian Gift

SAMUEL ABRAMS, M.D.

WHEN HIS KINGDOM WAS BESET WITH "PLAGUE AND PYRE," OEDIPUS was advised that the curse would be lifted only if the unknown assassin of his predecessor, Laius, was revealed and punished. He summoned to his court the one man in Greece who might help him, Teiresias, "the lord clairvoyant to the lord Apollo."

After some hesitation based on consideration for the king's feelings—"Now it is my misery," he noted, "then it will be yours"—the seer told the truth. Oedipus received the revelation of his guilt with rage, counteraccusation, disavowal, confusion, cries of conspiracy, and exhortations of contempt for the prophet and his alleged wisdom. He further disputed the charge of villainy by reciting the record of his past achievements; it was he, after all, who had once heroically liberated Thebes by solving the riddle of the Sphinx. When reminded of this, Teiresias repeated his accusation; this time, however, he expressed himself in an inspired way. He proposed the truth in the form of a riddle. In the course of solving it, Oedipus found his doom and his salvation (Trilling, 1967, pp. 11–15).

What was the source of Teiresias's gift?

Robert Graves (1955) offers a highly condensed version of the myths accounting for the wise man's talent.

Clinical Professor, The Psychoanalytic Institute, New York University Medical Center.

This paper was also presented at the Baltimore-D.C. Psychoanalytic Society, November 17, 1979, and the Cleveland Psychoanalytic Society, March 1, 1980.

. . . on Mount Cyllene, Teiresias had seen two serpents in the act of coupling. When both attacked him, he struck at them with his staff, killing the female. Immediately he was turned into a woman and became a celebrated harlot; but seven years later he happened to see the same sight again at the same spot, and this time regained his manhood by killing the male serpent. . . . Some days later Hera began reproaching Zeus for his numerous infidelities. He defended them by arguing that, at any rate, when he did share her couch, she had the more enjoyable time by far. 'Women, of course, derive infinitely greater pleasure from the sexual act than men,' he blustered.

'What nonsense!' cried Hera. 'The exact contrary is the case, and well you know it.'

Teiresias, summoned to settle the dispute from his personal experiences, answered:

'If the parts of love-pleasure be counted as ten,

Thrice three go to women, one only to men.'

Hera was so exasperated by Zeus's triumphant grin that she blinded Teiresias; but Zeus compensated him with inward sight [2:11].

In this version of the Greek myths, the Teiresian gift of inward sight originates somehow from the primal scene, bisexuality, and the impelling double triangle of tabooed desire. Effort, integrity, inventiveness, and courage are necessary to grasp and transmit insight. The myths also burden the word with diverse meanings—truth, clairvoyance, revelation, wisdom (confusing "inward" sight with "outward" sight). And they add a particular ambiguity: just what is it to have insight? Did Teiresias possess all knowledge and merely tap whatever was needed for the task at hand? Was it a trait that led him to instant awareness, like divine wisdom? Or was his gift the ability to *acquire* the truth? Is insight what one owns, what one is, or what one does?

In fact, it is all of these. Insight is a noun, a "truth," in psychoanalysis, a useful discovery. This denotes something one possesses. Such insights, i.e., truths, have been frequently studied. There have been investigations into their hierarchy, recommendations about the sequence in which such insights are to be acquired in the course of treatment, and more recently even disputes about the therapeutic usefulness of self-awareness altogether. There have also been studies of the ways in which the insights of analysts are technically transmitted to their patients; often, such studies address abuses in technique (Zilboorg, 1952; M. and W. Baranger, 1966; Appelbaum, 1975); indeed, one paper on the subject is titled "The Curse of Insight" (Bird, 1957).

The root word is also a modifier in its adjectival or adverbial form, e.g., an insightful idea or insightful thinking. In this usage the word implies a valuable quality imparted to a thing or action. It is also used intransitively as a predicate adjective or predicate noun, e.g., "he is insightful" or "he shows insight." This usage suggests a trait or ability.

In English, however, the word insight is not known in its *transitive* verbal form, a form that would connote mental work. Yet there must be a specific coordinated activity, the expression of an achievement in the mental organization, which yields psychological discoveries. In the absence of a verb "to insight," it has been necessary to use inadequate substitutes, e.g., to know, to look inward, to process. As a transitive verb, "to insight" might be defined as the psychological activity of discovering and integrating truths about oneself, a complex way of knowing.[1]

The phenomenon is worth the highest priority of attention for analysis. As Bibring (1937) notes, "These active ego tendencies of integrating and assimilating are, perhaps, the most important foundations of cure" (p. 187). This transitive verbal form may well be precisely that insight which Blum (1979) refers to in his felicitous phrasing as the "condition, catalyst, and consequence" of psychoanalytic work.

This investigation concentrates upon such insight-producing mental activity, empirically and conceptually. Two "good analytic hours" (Kris, 1956), one from an adult, the other from a child, provide the data for listing descriptive features and anchoring conceptual formulations. There are many products of insight-producing activity. Analysts are particularly mindful of one of the more important of these, the evolving theme, since it plays such a crucial part in guiding interpretations. The other

---

1. For other definitions and usages in psychiatry and psychoanalysis see Brill (1929), Zilboorg (1952), Bibring (1954), Richfield (1954), Kris (1956), Ludwig (1966), Rosenbluth (1968), Pressman (1969), Blum (1979), and A. Freud (1979).

products—the typical affective concomitants, for example—
tend to be more ambiguous, far more difficult to discern. Some of
them may suggest therapeutic progress, others signal obstacles.
Hence, an empirical listing of the psychological expressions of
insight-producing activity should be clinically useful. Offering
material from both an adult and a child case demonstrates the
developmental transformations of such expressions.

CASE ILLUSTRATIONS

CASE 1

At the time his analysis began, Mr. R. was a professional man in
his early 30s. He had sought treatment because of problems with
superiors at work and with his wife and children at home. He felt
unnecessarily submissive at his job and saw himself as an incompetent father and inadequate husband. The following session
occurred after 2 years of an analysis that was to last 1,200 hours.

The initial emotional atmosphere was not especially notewor-
thy. Mr. R. began by describing an incident that had involved
him with his 4-year-old daughter. Envious and resentful of her
younger brother, she had been moved to action and struck him.
Concerned about the effects this might have on his son, Mr. R.
reprimanded his daughter and then lost control and hit her.
While describing this, the emotional atmosphere of the hour
began to thicken. With a sigh, he noted that he and his daughter
were probably alike in many ways. He moved to what seemed a
different topic and to a slightly altered mood. His boss was burdening him at work, and his wife was requiring greater responsibilities of him at home. I sensed an accusation toward me in his
remarks, a complaint of the demands of the analysis, but I said
nothing. He spontaneously returned to thoughts of his little girl.
His self-observations intensified and became more focused. The
other day he had observed his daughter in her dancing class and
had recognized his pleasure while admiring her. Prior to his
analysis, he had scoffed at the loving affection that parents held
for children, but now . . . and then a pause. He became restless,
sullen again, and his voice seemed more muffled. He described
in a tentative fashion that he had just become aware of a shift in

his mind from the image of his daughter in her ballet class to the memory of having been drawn to the muscularity of some men in a Broadway chorus line. He interrupted the narrative with an accusation. I was burdening him, requiring too much of him in his treatment. Another pause and then two or three loud disclaimers: he had no sexual interest in men! I was a bad analyst for trying to put such thoughts into his mind or of dragging them out if they happened to be there. Then he recounted a suddenly recalled dream of the night before. It was reported in incomplete sentences, rapidly, and with feeling.

> Some man in outer space. Lost or in trouble. I am picked to save the man. To be a martyr. Terrible possibilities. I might be seriously injured or killed. In a place, like a planetarium. A large dome above and behind me. Suddenly the roof opens and some water leaks in. Somehow this was miraculous like the tears of the Virgin in a painting. A sense of relief; I would accomplish my task safely. I woke frightened, in spite of this feeling.

The end of the report of the dream ushered in restlessness. When he had described the water leaking in, the childhood colloquialism "to leak" for to urinate had occurred to him. Water coming in from above and behind was like someone urinating on him. The emotional atmosphere was very heavy now, well defined as anxiety, and he was able to acknowledge the feeling. He recalled a discussion of some earlier hours concerning his childhood confusion between urine and semen. He attacked me again, briefly and with considerably reduced intensity.

The topic of his daughter returned. Recently he had found her bent over looking backward between her legs at a mirror. She shyly explained that she had been searching for her penis; she believed it was hidden somewhere in her rectum. The patient recalled it as a startling but illuminating moment for him. He had reasoned that she had been envious of her baby brother and wanted to be anatomically like him. He added in a rather benevolent and detached manner that he could understand such a problem.

I made a comment, perhaps responding to the extent of the defensive retreat I sensed in his manner. I said that he seemed more tolerant of his daughter's desire to be some other sex than he was of his own desire. The anxiousness returned. Trying to be calm, he considered the possibility that wanting to be a woman might not be so terrible. No, he argued with himself, it was all right for a girl to want to be a boy, but the other way around was "homosexual." He said this word with disgust. Then he came back to the view that it might not be so terrible and then underscored his sense of new discovery with an assertion: he wanted to be a girl, it really was *in* him. He recalled sitting on the toilet the night before thinking to himself that he felt so alive inside.

CASE 2

Alan was almost 8 years old at the time the following hour occurred. He had originally come to analysis because of fearfulness and the beginning of a phobic disposition that threatened his development. This hour occurred after 1½ years of a treatment that was to last 3 years.

For a few months, Alan had spent a part of each analytic session preparing a bottle of poison. His attention was fixed on this task and was sustained from one hour to another, although it was not his only activity. This mixture, first begun as father's aftershave lotion, was filled with items that ordinarily collect in the pockets of little boys: seashells, stones, bottle caps, toy bullets, watch gears, and so forth. Sometimes it seemed as if Alan had gone to the trouble of collecting precisely to bring objects to his hour. When I wondered aloud for whom the poison might be intended, he replied, "Shut up."

On this day he arrived after having seen the motion picture *Superman*, in which the spinning of the earth was dramatically represented. Alan appeared to have been particularly taken with this phenomenon, so much so that he put his poison aside to ponder, "If it turns around and around like that, how come we always stay on top? Why don't we fall off?" I knew he expected some answer from me, but I offered no response. I remembered that he had once asked his father how things burn and had been advised of the relationship between combustion and oxygenation. Alan amused adults with this information. "Fire uses up oxygen," he would say, as if this phrase had added something of substance to his comprehension. It would have been possible to tell him about gravity. He would have submitted to the word without comprehending anything about the phenomenon he was so curious about. He remained absorbed with his question, staring upward with a faraway puzzled look that always implies a gazing inward. I silently joined him in that look. "I got it," he said after a while, with a startle as if a light-switch had been suddenly thrown, "we are all walking in one direction and the earth is turning the other way so we keep staying on top." He laughed with delight at this "logroller" explanation that was his own. But this was merely a prelude. The perplexed look returned. He was preparing himself for a second question.

In the film, Superman's adoptive father dies when his adopted son Clark (alias Superman) is just 18. It is an almost instantaneous death. A dozen or so years later Lois Lane, Superman's girlfriend, dies in a mud slide following an earthquake. Superman arrives moments too late to rescue her. In an agonizing scene, the man of steel struggles with the memory of his biological father from the planet Krypton warning him that he is not to use his great power in any way that might change the course of the earth's history. Superman tears himself from this injunction, soars into the stratosphere, begins to circle the earth rapidly counter to its ordinary spin at such a high speed that he eventually reverses it, and reverses time itself. He promptly returns to earth at that point in time when Lois is only suffocating in the mud slide and not yet dead, and he promptly rescues her.

These widely scattered sections in the film about death and dying had been occupying Alan, and he brought them together to frame his second question: "If Superman could push time backward, how come he let his father die, but he saved his girlfriend?" The question was asked with a curious combination of anxiousness and a wry smile. I recognized that Alan was on the threshold of some important observations about himself. At the moment, however, the focus was clearly on Superman's behavior. There was no ready connection to the poison, nor did he attempt to generalize from the particular. Superman's motives were something "outside" and had no relationship to him.

Toward a Phenomenology of Insight-Producing Activity

Mr. R.'s and Alan's hours are "good" ones, alive with expressions of underlying, insight-producing mental activity. The expressions lend themselves to comparisons and contrasts.

There is a palpable atmosphere of emotion in both. The feelings are well defined in each of the illustrations, although Mr. R. has a greater repertoire of affective responses. Neither patient appears overwhelmed, despite some suggestion of strain. Both exhibit effort and attentiveness. Mr. R's attention seems diffuse at first, but it gradually becomes focused upon his own mental activities as the theme develops. Alan's attention is also concentrated on his attempts to solve what he perceives as challenging intellectual puzzles inside his head.

Both Mr. R. and Alan are able to hold together the potentially discordant components of each topic. Mr. R., for example, describes his observations of his daughter in her ballet class, the memory of his earlier detachment as parent, the warmth of the moment, generalizations about the relationships between parents and children, similarities between himself and his daughter—all in a way that suggests they comprise a coordinated whole. Similarly, Alan's reflections of the earth's spin, his speculations and concrete impressions, his puzzlement and pleasure, his effort and relief are offered in a setting of harmonious connections. There are differences. Mr. R. deals with his own internal problems more directly, while Alan approaches them through outside figures and events. Furthermore, as Mr. R. moves from one topic to another, the relevance of the seemingly disparate sections becomes increasingly recognizable to him, i.e., the harmonious organization extends. Alan is far less able to recognize the thematic or affective connections; his ability to put things together meaningfully is more limited.

Mr. R. moves freely between time periods, simultaneously mindful both of their separateness and of a psychological continuity. Alan is very much swept up in the present; his past is only faintly relevant to the experiences of the moment, and his future is unknowable space. Both adult and child, however, seem unaware of the passage of time as each moves along in the sessions.

Both exhibit startle or surprise upon arriving at their discoveries (Reik, 1933; M. and W. Baranger, 1966; Pressman, 1969), and both convey conviction. There is something very direct in this feeling of new knowledge. Mr. R. knows of his wish to be a girl by direct "acquaintance."[2] Alan's discovery of his logrolling explanation to account for the effects of gravity is also felt directly. However, the inner secret desire linking his poison and Superman's choice is not known and perhaps still unknowable either by acquaintance, by someone else's testimony, or by his inference. Alan seems not yet able sufficiently to separate and reassemble the constituent components to acquire the kind of integrated comprehension demonstrated by Mr. R.

During the hours, adult and child have a distinctive individual presence, an expression of intactness and separateness. However, there is a difference in the way the two succeed in defining the harmonious unity of their beings. Here Alan is somewhat less successful than Mr. R.

In both examples, there is empirical evidence of psychological work during the moments surrounding the discoveries, but each responds somewhat differently to the observable evidence. Both react with noticeable surprise or startle at the instant of the "Aha!" a clear affective expression. But beyond the "Aha!" lies something else—ambiguous sensations that reflect the change of condition or organization that underlies this new way of knowing. The sensations may be the psychological accompaniments of the transformational processes that occur whenever there is a new fitting together. Mr. R. seems very aware of the sensations of something else going on inside of his mind. Despite its ambiguous nature and the realization that it is different from the antecedent experiences, he feels obligated to account for it. He does so with metaphors, e.g., ideas are being "dragged out" or

2. The classification of knowing by acquaintance, by testimony, and by inference was suggested by Bertrand Russell (1929) and has attracted several psychoanalytic authors, e.g., Richfield (1954), Bychowski (1966), Rosenbluth (1968), Kennedy (1979).

"put into" him and issues are "alive" inside. The metaphors that allude to his awareness of unconscious processes at work will soon be invaded by fantasy. Alan, in contrast, seems less attentive to the ambiguous sensations.

To summarize this listing of empirical components to insight-producing activity:

1.   Attention, initially diffuse, becomes increasingly focused.

2.   In the affective realm, an emotional tone that is compelling is evident; it is kept within bounds, tends to become more discriminated, and stays appropriately coordinated with the expressed ideas.

3.   Components such as memories, dreams, observations, and experiences that initially appear unrelated to one another are increasingly recognized as linked; this is both more obvious and more far-reaching in the adult, who appears more capable of coherence within and between topics.

4.   Despite the feeling of timelessness, there is free movement within time periods, an awareness of the meaningful relationship between past and present. This is far more obvious in the adult.

5.   In the midst of all this mental activity, both adult and child seem well defined and impart a sense of inner unity.

6.   At the moment of the "discovery," the "Aha!" each recognizes that something new or different has happened. Both express startle or surprise. In addition, Mr. R. is aware of the presence of some ambiguous sensations which he attempts to account for by metaphoric allusion. The child seems either unmindful of such feelings or elects to ignore them.

TOWARD A CONCEPTUALIZATION OF INSIGHT-PRODUCING ACTIVITY

Metapsychology permits empirical phenomena to be examined from multiple points of view with the aim of enriching the theory and practice of psychoanalysis.

Structure. Insight-producing activity may be looked upon as the expression of a variety of ego functions acting conjointly. The more important are: the capacity for self-observation (Kris, 1956; Gray, 1973); the capacity to experience, tolerate, and control affects (Zetzel, 1949; and in Panel, 1960; Galinsky and Pressman, 1970), to differentiate them and orchestrate them; the capacity to tolerate and limit regression and action (Kris, 1956); the ability to represent perceptions in a stable form, differentiate outer and inner, object and self with precision and coherence (Mahler et al., 1975); the ability to balance accommodative and assimilative tendencies and to process stimuli at an optimal level of cognitive functioning (Piaget, 1936); the capacity to recognize continuities within the discontinuity of time frames; finally, and perhaps the most important of all, to integrate the components in a harmonious fashion (Freud, 1919; Nunberg, 1931; Hartmann, 1939; Kris, 1956; Murphy, 1959; Neubauer, 1979) so as to effect changes in breadth, intensity, and quality.

Economics. Changes in breadth may be accounted for, in part, by the lifting of inhibitions following relief from the constrictive defensive strategies. Changes in intensity may be accounted for by the freeing of feelings otherwise devoted to struggle. But changes in quality, the inevitable consequences of transformational processes—how can they be conceptualized?

Freud usually used an energic configuration to account for transformations (e.g., 1923, pp. 30, 54). His economic propositions have been much maligned recently, partly because they seem antiquated, partly because they are so misused. In the present state of our knowledge, however, energic configurations may still be a most satisfactory way of conceptualizing qualitative changes in the mind, provided the "as if" nature of such explanations is not mistaken for reality. Kris's account (1956) of economic shifts during the activity of insight, for example, seems quite useful for solving some of the practitioner's dilemmas.

Insight-producing activity entails taking things apart and putting them back together differently. It is the highly specialized expression of fundamental differentiating and integrating capacities, the operation of a relatively intact higher level of mental organization. The new assemblage of drive and defense, desexualized and/or restructured, is an entirely different product from what has preceded it. To demonstrate that models implying energic change are useful in accounting for such transformations, it may be profitable to move once more to concrete clinical data. The illustration is again taken from Alan struggling with scientific theorizing of quite an analogous sort. Not very long after the hour described earlier, he was confronted with transformations in his potion. How he applied his thought processes to the problem is instructive.

While Alan's work on his poison continued, I had arrived at some idea about whom he wanted to kill and why. In his play he dramatized what he could not yet articulate or comprehend. I was trying to think of ways to help Alan recognize and assemble the elements so that he might feel them directly and gain useful new knowledge. Shortly after his eighth birthday he brought a prized gift that had marked the occasion, a chemistry set. "Now," he announced, "I can make a real poison." He discarded the old mixture with an air of contempt for his past childishness. Closely adhering to the letter of the accompanying instruction book, he made a solution in one test tube, another in a second, and combined the two clear liquids to produce a colored precipitate. He repeated this several times with "surprise" and with pleasure. It struck me that here I had a way of testing the limits of Alan's capacity for explanation. How did he conceive of the differences between mixtures, solutions, and compounds? "What happened in that test tube?" I asked. "You see," he tried to explain, "I put this liquid into this one, and then this colored thing came out." This is mere description and not explanation. "How come?" I wondered. "It's what the directions said would happen," he offered, submitting and still not explaining, blurring what and how. "But how does such a thing happen?" I pressed. "It's magic," he said, now with a bit of irritation. We both expressed discontent with such a conceptual retreat. "How is it possible that this clear solution plus this one makes this colored stuff?" As I asked this, it occurred to me that I was requiring this child to attempt to conceptualize transformations. "I got it," he replied, and his answer was between metaphor and contrived humor, "the reagents react; they love each other, they get excited, it's like having a baby." He reached for a prototype of interaction and transformation that was very much in keeping with his own current developmental achievements. He was now substituting analogy for explanation.

Alan had readily understood what mixtures were. The components that went into his original poison were all concretely available to his continuing inspection. Solutions offered only a slightly greater challenge. With his entrenched object permanence and by virtue of his capacity for simple logical inferences, Alan could recognize that the powdery substance, while no longer visible, was still there some place in the water, recoverable by evaporation. A solution was simply a slightly more complex mixture. The appearance of a new compound upon mixing the two solutions proved a far more challenging cognitive task. Something different had risen from the combined components that was neither the one nor the other, not a simple mixture of the two, not one within the other—in short, a discontinuous event. The product was qualitatively different. Alan could not lean on the Niels Bohr theory of atomic structure, and even if he had some awareness of it, he would have been unable to comprehend or apply it appropriately. Alan created a model from his own experience. His theory had no heuristic virtue, at least for chemistry. But it satisfied him, in part because it clouded his confrontation with ambiguity and discontinuity. Metaphor and analogy had restored his feeling of control.

While the task of conceptualizing qualitative change in the outer world is trying enough, it is even more taxing to comprehend transformations within the mind, e.g., progressive discontinuities in ways of knowing. This is almost as much of a problem for adult scientists as it can be for neurotic children. We too must guard against confusing explanation with mere description, blurring what and how, magic and science, metaphor and analogy. Metapsychological models make a concession to ambiguity, but stimulate further investigation; in the present state of our knowledge they serve a necessary function.

In psychoanalysis, heuristic models have been devised from components of structure and energy. The energic propositions, e.g., the spectrum of instinctualization to neutralization, are helpful for conceptualizing changes in quality (see, e. g., Richfield, 1954; Kris, 1956; Murphy, 1959; Neubauer, 1979). Alternate proposals include the application of the topographic hypothesis with its propositions of difference between primary and secondary processes, or a systems-theory approach implying progressively differentiating organizational hierarchies.

Genetic and Dynamic. To what degree is insight-producing activity an ordinary expectation of maturation and to what degree is it related to conflict and its resolution?

If the myths of Teiresias properly convey the views of the ancient Greeks, they seem to have been convinced that antecedent conflict engagement and resolution were essential prerequisites for insightfulness. Analysts may hold a similar view. Typical infantile psychological struggles must be met and overcome if the capacity for insight is to be acquired. To be sure, maturational processes underlie the acquisition, and specific ego apparatuses that are primarily autonomous from conflict (such as cognitive structures) are necessary components. The achievement of insight that is usefully applicable within an analytic setting, however, requires oedipal-phase engagement and at least partial resolution through superego formation.

The antecedent conflicts may further be viewed as imparting both general and specific influences. From the perspective of the general, the ability to reason maturely requires that significant developmental landmarks be suitably traversed. Even when this occurs, however, the infantile prototypical experiences can be expected to return as models or metaphors in the midst of insight-producing activities (see also Kris, 1956). Such phrases as "you put it in me" or "you dragged it out of me," used by Mr. R., suggest that the discomforts occasioned by the awareness of ambiguities and discontinuities in the wake of transformations may customarily be relieved by reviving a personally meaningful paradigmatic experience. Ordinarily this poses no clinical problem. There are two occasions, however, that require active analytic attentiveness. In the first, the patient may peremptorily mobilize the metaphor or exaggerate its implications because he is so intolerant of the ill-defined expressions that accompany his psychological work. In this, he draws too much attention to the past precedent in an endeavor to avoid the attendant discomforts of the present ambiguities. Something like this happened with Alan when he playfully insisted that the chemical product might be understood as a consequence of reagents in love. In the second problematic occasion, the patient regressively converts the stylized metaphors into the vulnerable neurotic dispositions from which they were culled. In such a situation, the very act of understanding is swept up into the transference neurosis. This certainly happened with Mr. R.; interpretation and insight were briefly arrested by fantasies of penetration and impregnation.

From the perspective of specific genetic and dynamic influences, insight may be limited or impaired as a result of deficits in one or more of the ego functions required to set it in motion or sustain it. For example, poor affect control or impaired differentiation may disrupt or curtail the capacity for insight-producing mental activity and consequently serve as a serious obstacle to psychoanalytic work.

Developmental and Adaptive. An advantage to having placed data from an adult and child side by side is its yield for the study of developmental aspects of insight (see also Kennedy, 1979; Abrams, 1980). The achievement of mature insight-producing activity requires that a series of functions evolve, that the anticipated sequence of increasingly complex cognitive structures emerge, and that both functions and structures be effectively incorporated into new higher-phase organizations. Children's ways of knowing differ from adults'. The capacity to perceive and to organize perceptions changes in accordance with new developmental phases; consequently, states of adaptedness and relationships to reality can also be expected to change in an expected sequence. The enhanced capacity to know strengthens both.

DISCUSSION

The value of an empirical and conceptual study rests ultimately in its practical yield. This investigation may lend itself to several uses.

To begin with, it should prove helpful in child analytic work. The ability of a clinician to recognize the developmental sequence in ways of knowing may contribute to his technical skills, enhance his evaluation of the therapeutic process, and allow for a more precise assessment of progress. Truth cannot be quite the same for children as it is for adults. As a practical matter, for example, it may simply not be possible for a 4-year-old child to discover that the act of sexual love is a genuine expression of affection between two people. He can neither sufficiently exempt his poorly differentiated aggressivity nor recognize the qualitative differences of adult interactions. Nevertheless, a child in analysis is genuinely insightful if he successfully defines phenomena in accordance with his expected phase achievements. A 4-year-old's distorted view of love is also a real discovery, a developmentally accurate truth.

Second, and consistent with these considerations, the study may add to the psychoanalytic contribution to the distinction between creation and discovery.[3] Many of the descriptions of experiences during acts of creativity are strikingly similar to those that occur in the midst of psychoanalytic insightfulness or scientific discovery (Kris, 1950; Kanzer, 1955). The artist's inspired inventiveness can be highly focused, is often accompanied by intense affects, may be punctuated by regressive processes and a loss of the sense of time, frequently becomes organized around infantile prototypes, and invariably yields a product of sophisticated synthesis. Creation and discovery can be said to lie on a spectrum. There are clearly defined differences at each end, and there is a blurred middle. In general, the distinction between the two may rest on the balance achieved between the need to account for stimuli in accordance with goal-directed thinking and the psychological processing of stimuli based on primary process thinking.[4] Where psychological processing overrides the actuality of the stimuli or encompasses them too much into a preformed fantasy or regressive structure, the resultant product is closer to an artistic creation. Where processing further refines stimuli so as to insure that the actualities will be a feature of future judgment, the resultant product is closer to discovery. Naturally, the distinction is most difficult to make in the blurred middle.

Such a delineation may be helpful in clarifying the therapeutic task. Clinical analysis is often viewed as an art and a science, a

3. See Kris (1939), who wisely adds the caveat that studies of this kind are intended to focus strictly on psychological phenomena and should not be misconstrued as implying judgments.

4. This is akin to Piaget's hypotheses (1936) concerning the equilibration between accommodative and assimilative tendencies; analysts' views differ, however, since they are much more mindful of the instinctual influences on such tendencies.

potentially blurred middle. Models of functioning and entrenched perspective can influence the character of clinical work. Two well-known psychoanalytic theoreticians have clearly articulated their somewhat divergent positions. Reexamining them proves instructive and could help further concretize the implications of this study.

Toward the "discovery" end of the spectrum, Hartmann (1939) as psychoanalyst/scientist writes:

> Permit me a digression on the nature of thinking *in the psychoanalytic situation,* in which the predominant object of thought is the subject himself. . . . Thinking renders basically the same service in the psychoanalytic situation as it does when it is directed to the external world. . . . Interpretations not only help to regain the buried material, but must also establish correct causal relations. . . . We cannot assume that the ways in which children connect their experiences, and which later become conscious in the course of psychoanalysis, could satisfy the requirements of the mature ego. . . . The mere reproduction of memories in psychoanalysis can, therefore, only partly correct the lack of connection or the incorrect connection of elements. An additional process comes into play here which may justly be described as a scientific process. It discovers (and does not rediscover), according to the general rules of scientific thinking, the correct relationships of the elements to each other [p. 62ff.].

Toward the "art" end of the spectrum, Schafer (1978) as psychoanalyst/constructive historian writes:

> A psychoanalysis consists of the construction of a personal past. It is not *the* personal past but *a* personal past. However convincing it may be, it remains a construction, merely a history of a certain kind [p. 8].
>
> . . . one cannot establish either the historical sense or the current significance of a fact outside of some context of questions and methods for defining and organizing the material in question. Only by steadily thinking in terms of the infantile, body-based psychosexual and aggressive conflicts can the Freudian analyst define, as psychoanalytically relevant information, what he or she will then use in interpretations [p. 10].
>
> . . . interpretation is a particularized creative action performed within a tradition of procedure and under-

standing . . . facts are what it is psychoanalytically meaningful and useful to designate, and what it is meaningful to designate is established by the facts; one finds the sort of thing one is looking for [p. 13].

A final use of this study is in the adult clinical realm. Obstacles and resistances that arise while patients attempt to mobilize insight-producing activity surface clearly when one observes the moment-for-moment movement in the current of free association. Where ego or developmental defects blunt the growth of any of the critical components of insight-producing activity, the associative stream becomes disrupted or flows aimlessly, and analysis is usually not possible. Such obstacles deriving from defects in functions should be distinguished from the more customary resistances that can be overcome once they are recognized. For example, insight-producing activity may be inhibited by an invading unconscious fantasy. The very action of understanding becomes part of the transference neurosis; mutuality, thought, and integration are threatened. An even more insidious resistance sometimes appears in a certain kind of patient who "creates" knowledge rather than acquires discoveries. Such patients may give the impression of continuing insightfulness. Tilted too much into a narcissistically bound assimilative tendency, they invent "truths," mere artistic products, highly stylized symptoms. The movement seems swift, but it fails to effect those transformations that yield a final new consolidation.[5]

BIBLIOGRAPHY

ABRAMS, S. (1980), Therapeutic action and ways of knowing. *J. Amer. Psychoanal. Assn.*, 28:291–309.

APPLEBAUM, S. A. (1975), The idealization of insight. *Int. J. Psychoanal. Psychother.*, 4:272–302.

BARANGER, M. & BARANGER, W. (1966), Insight in the psychoanalytic situation. In: *Psychoanalysis in the Americas*, ed. R. E. Litman. New York: Int. Univ. Press, pp. 56–72.

5. Shelley Orgel suggested this kind of resistance to me while we were discussing this section of the paper together.

BIBRING, E. (1937), A theory of the therapeutic results of psycho-analysis. *Int. J. Psychoanal.*, 18:170–189.

—— (1954), Psychoanalysis and the dynamic psychotherapies. *J. Amer. Psychoanal. Assn.*, 2:745–770.

BIRD, B. (1957), The curse of insight. *Bull. Philadelphia Assn. Psychoanal.*, 7:101–104.

BLUM, H. P. (1979), The curative and creative aspects of insight. *J. Amer. Psychoanal. Assn. Suppl.*, 27:41–69.

BRILL, A. A. (1929), Unconscious insight. *Int. J. Psychoanal.*, 10:145–161.

BYCHOWSKI, G. (1966), Discussion. In: *Psychoanalysis in the Americas*, ed. R. E. Litman. New York: Int. Univ. Press, pp. 73–78.

FREUD, A. (1979), The role of insight in psychoanalysis and psychotherapy. *J. Amer. Psychoanal. Assn. Suppl.*, 27:3–7.

FREUD, S. (1919), Lines of advance in psycho-analytic therapy. *S.E.* 17:159–168.

—— (1923), The ego and the id. *S.E.*, 19:13–59.

GALINSKY, M. D. & PRESSMAN, M. D. (1970), The principle of tolerance as related to the psychoanalytic process. *Bull. Philadelphia Assn. Psychoanal.*, 20:212–222.

GRAVES, R. (1955), *The Greek Myths*. Baltimore: Penguin Books.

GRAY, P. (1973), Psychoanalytic technique and the ego's capacity for viewing intrapsychic activity. *J. Amer. Psychoanal. Assn.*, 21:474–494.

HARTMANN, H. (1939), *Ego Psychology and the Problem of Adaptation*. New York: Int. Univ. Press, 1958.

KANZER, M. (1955), Anality in inspiration and insight. *Bull. Philadelphia Assn. Psychoanal.*, 5:114–115.

KENNEDY, H. (1979), The role of insight in child analysis. *J. Amer. Psychoanal. Assn. Suppl.*, 27:9–28.

KRIS, E. (1939), On inspiration. In: *Psychoanalytic Explorations in Art*. New York: Int. Univ. Press, 1952, pp. 291–302.

—— (1950), On preconscious mental processes. In: *Psychoanalytic Explorations in Art*. New York: Int. Univ. Press, 1952, pp. 303–318.

—— (1956), On some vicissitudes of insight in psychoanalysis. In: *Selected Papers of Ernst Kris*. New Haven & London: Yale Univ. Press, 1979, pp. 252–271.

LUDWIG, A. M. (1966), The formal characteristics of therapeutic insight. *Amer. J. Psychother.*, 20:305–318.

MAHLER, M. S., PINE, F., & BERGMAN, A. (1975), *The Psychological Birth of the Human Infant*. New York: Basic Books.

MURPHY, W. F. (1959), Ego integration, trauma, and insight. *Psychoanal. Quart.*, 28:514–532.

NEUBAUER, P. B. (1979), The role of insight in psychoanalysis. *J. Amer. Psychoanal. Assn. Suppl.*, 27:29–40.

NUNBERG, H. (1931), The synthetic function of the ego. *Int. J. Psychoanal.*, 12:123–140.

PANEL (1960), Criteria for analyzability. S. Guttman, reporter. *J. Amer. Psycho-anal. Assn.,* 8:141–151.

PIAGET, J. (1936), *The Origins of Intelligence in Children.* New York: Int. Univ. Press, 1952.

PRESSMAN, M. D. (1969), The cognitive function of the ego in psycho-analysis. *Int. J. Psychoanal.* 50:187–196.

REIK, T. (1933), New ways in psycho-analytic technique. *Int. J. Psychoanal.,* 14:321–334.

RICHFIELD, J. (1954), An analysis of the concept of insight. *Psychoanal. Quart.,* 23:390–408.

ROSENBLUTH, D. (1968), "Insight" as an aim of treatment. *J. Child Psychother.,* 2:5–17.

RUSSELL, B. (1929), *Our Knowledge of the External World.* New York: Norton.

SCHAFER, R. (1978), *Language and Insight.* New Haven & London: Yale Univ. Press.

TRILLING, L. (1967), *The Experience of Literature.* Garden City, N.Y.: Doubleday.

ZETZEL, E. R. (1949), Anxiety and the capacity to bear it. In: *The Capacity for Emotional Growth.* New York: Int. Univ. Press, 1970, pp. 33–52.

ZILBOORG, G. (1952), The emotional problem and the therapeutic role of insight. *Psychoanal. Quart.,* 21:1–24.

Insight

Pleasurable Affects Associated with Insight and Their Origins in Infancy

CHARLES A. MANGHAM, M.D.

THE WORD "INSIGHT" IMPLIES "I SEE INTO MYSELF," OR "INTO MY mind." There is, of course, no "eye" which sees into the mind; there is no space which the mind occupies; there is no physical mind to be "seen into." "Insight," then, is a metaphor taken from an actual experience an individual has with his environment; specifically, the metaphor is taken from the experience a child has with his mother. In this experience the child perceives his self, his mother, and the interaction with her as "seeing into" him, and knowing and understanding what she sees. This perception by the child of the experience with mother is then internalized and experienced by the individual as self-awareness, self-understanding, or seeing into oneself, all of which can be thought of as forms of "insight."

This mother-child process also incorporates the attachment of words to feelings and behavior, and the way this "naming" sometimes results in a feeling of success, a feeling of mastery, and a reduction of tension and psychic pain. The mother's "naming"

Training and supervising child analyst, Seattle Psychoanalytic Institute; Clinical Professor, Department of Psychiatry and Behavioral Sciences, University of Washington, Seattle, Washington.

I am indebted to Dr. Theodore Dorpat and to Marga Rose-Hancock and to my colleagues at the Northwest Clinic of Psychiatry and Psychoanalysis for their invaluable constructive criticism in preparing this paper.

and the analyst's interpreting thus both create meaning—insight—but are also linked by the early affective bond.

I approach insight from a developmental point of view which owes much to Edward Hoedemaker, a colleague with whom I was associated from 1951 until his death in 1968. In particular, I draw on his discussion of the internalization by a child of the limit-setting and consistent behavior of his parents. "Thus he [the child] perceives himself, and others, *as his parents have perceived him,* and behaves towards himself and others *as his parents have* behaved towards him" (p. 35).

Since the primary source of an infant's experience is his mother, a logical extension of this thinking would be that a child's consciousness or awareness of any portion of his behavior or thought or feeling would come from having experienced a mother's awareness of this behavior, thought, or feeling either within the infant or within herself. In other words, awareness of something within the self is a function of maternal awareness and is a function of the relationship between the mother and her infant.

The literature on early infantile development and the fate of primary narcissism and omnipotence stresses the environment in which the interactive process of insight is nourished. At the beginning the infant is totally undifferentiated in his psychic state; there is no self and no object. The initially gratifying interactions occurring between mother and infant at first belong neither to the mother nor to the infant because of the lack of differentiation (Sandler and Rosenblatt, 1962; Sandler and Sandler, 1978). As time goes on, the infant gradually discovers himself and his mother as separate entities and begins to develop mental representations of himself and his mother interacting with one another. The site of these pleasurable interactions then shifts from the undifferentiated state to a metaphorical place outside himself and under the control of his mother. The infant now perceives the mother as an omnipotent extension of himself: she is the gratifier of needs, the protector against pain.

To the observer, the relationship between mother and infant appears to be a countless number of feedback interactions in which the child makes some kind of verbalization and the mother repeats and imitates in an identical way until a "congruence" (Shapiro, 1970) is achieved. When this congruence or mutuality is established along with a certain degree of object differentiation, the child can perceive in the mother a confirmation and affirmation of his own actions and experiences. To cite a typical series: the smiling of the infant produces smiling in the mother; the smiling in the mother is accompanied by an affective experience of pleasure in the mother; this affective experience combined with smiling is then communicated to the infant by the actions of the mother so that the infant also begins to associate his own smile with pleasurable experiences of an affective nature within himself. The aspect of naming becomes part of the picture as he grows older and begins to babble, and the mother babbles back in imitation. Slowly the babble gains meaning and global words begin, such as "momma," "dada." Mother begins to name not only what the child sees in the external environment but also subjective states in the infant, for example, hungry, happy, sleepy.

It is my contention that long after infancy, the naming and establishment of words in connection with subjective experiences and behavior carry with them a sense of the reestablishment of the early primitive congruence and mutuality with mother and a sense of primary narcissism and infantile omnipotence. Joseph Sandler (1960) describes this as a feeling of safety actively created by the ego through protective distortions of perceptions. The ability to maintain "ego-tone" and create a feeling of safety is an ego function, related to what has been called a transmuting internalization (Tolpin, 1971). In this, bits of the interactions between mother and infant become organized and synthesized into an integral part of the ego's regulatory structures related to self-esteem, "ego-tone," and the "background of safety."

Shapiro (1970) describes the naming process by the mother for the child as an early feature of object relations as well as a first step in language development: "During development a mother's words become an intimate functional complement to the child's visual, tactile sensory experience of things. That concepts emerge in the course of this growing body of experience is a built-in feature of the human mental apparatus. *The tendency of the central nervous system to integrate is paralleled on the level of psy-*

chology by the tendency to synthesize and categorize and to make hierarchic organizations in accord with meaning" (p. 403). This is consistent with Sandler's thoughts on the creation of meaning and organization. This process of learning to know "demands a firm synthetic link not only between what is said and what is experienced in other levels (in a transference or in life, or with genetic roots), but this linkage leads to new mental schemata which may be the scaffolding of what has been called insight" (Shapiro, p. 405).

Kennedy (1979) traces the developmental line for the capacity for insight. Using clinical material, she demonstrates that insight as such is not developmentally possible in the early years of life. Apparently, naming or interpretation is dealt with age-appropriately according to the immature state of the child's ego. Kennedy quotes Kris, who said that "Insight depends on the 'integrated sequential operations of several ego functions'" (p. 13). These integrated sequential ego functions reflect various developmental levels occurring sequentially and epigenetically, finally resulting in insight as we know it in the adult. Kennedy sums up her "attempt to construct a developmental line for the capacity for insight: from the infant's transitory awareness of pleasurable and painful feeling states to the adult's detached and objective self-observation with an intrapsychic focus which, together with the ego's integrative functions, brings insight into useful psychic context" (p. 23).

In view of what I consider to be the early roots of insight, I would suggest that insight has certain illusory qualities related to unconscious affective links to archaic structures and functions which re-create the experience of a sense of safety, reestablish psychic mutuality and congruence with the mother, and reinstate the old sense of infantile omnipotence.

Such "illusory" insight can be illustrated by an experience I had with a Navaho guide in Arizona while I was touring the Monument Valley. The guide was a 50-year-old, illiterate, but loquacious Navaho man who told fascinating, entrancing stories about his family and his children and their experiences when they smoked marijuana and used Mescaline. He gave explanations of the cold spring weather based upon his personal mythology, explaining that apparently someone had been telling "winter stories" this spring and that this had created the cold winterlike weather. In listening to him I made an intense effort to follow his thinking and reasoning, and in doing so abandoned my usual ways of judging and critically evaluating what I heard. I entered into his belief system as I would enter into a patient's system of belief through empathy, or as a patient would enter into my system of belief when I make an interpretation. With this Navaho man I experienced the feeling of accepting his value system, e.g., that it was wrong to use Mescaline or marijuana indiscriminantly for nonreligious purposes and solely for pleasure or gratification. I believed with him that it should be used only for ceremonial purposes in the presence of a priest. Similarly, I experienced a belief without criticism of his explanation of the cold weather.

Later, in thinking this over, I experienced a sense of amusement, condescension, and distancing from this old man and his stories; but I also had a sense of incredulity and amazement that I could so easily begin to believe without critically judging the things he had been telling. This experience hints at the sense of interpersonal closeness which a listener may experience in a regressed situation. In other words, I had a new "insight" created by regression and by a wish to believe and understand the old man. There was a feeling of pleasure and mastery and also a sense of closeness and comfort with him. However, this insight was only partial and did not stand the test of reason; when I left my guide, I also abandoned the new "insight."

I suggest that in analysis some of the insights gained from partial interpretations by the analyst are similar or analogous to the "insight" I had with the Navaho guide. The analyst and the patient enter into a system of shared beliefs which is part of regression in the transference. The patient experiences through the analyst's interpretations the pleasurable affects which accompany congruence and mutuality, as they did in the earlier mother-infant unity. The analysand is led by and attempts to maintain this affective pleasure associated with this congruence. He follows the analyst into a new belief system which encompasses the new understanding. However, if the interpretations prove not to "fit" the patient's inner and outer worlds, he will not regain a sense of safety and and reestablish the feeling of infantile omnipotence. It is this affect which helps to carry the "insight" provided by interpretations, especially if the latter have what Hartmann (1951) called "multiple appeal," i.e., address themselves to all structures of the personality. If the interpretation is inexact or inaccurate, it is rejected and the analyst is experienced as nongratifying.

An example of "insight" resulting from an inaccurate analytic interpretation occurred in a case reported by a colleague. A young man in the terminal phase of his analysis had just been married and had returned to the analysis after the honeymoon. His regressive symptoms and behavior were interpreted by the analyst as a "fearful stepping away from the position of adult manhood with its responsibilities." With this interpretation the patient seemed to regress further and to become more feminine and more infantile. He felt the interpretation was belittling. There was no "fit"; although the interpretation may have been accurate at some deeper or less relevant level, something else was paramount to the patient. The analyst/mother did not understand, there was a failure in empathy. There was no affirmation of this "belief system" of the analyst by the internal or external reality of the patient. The analyst was then experienced as ungratifying, and the inexact interpretation/insight was rejected by the patient.

A second interpretation was obviously accurate and allowed the same patient to proceed constructively toward termination of his analysis. The second interpretation was that he was holding on to the hope that he could get the emotional responses he had wished for all his life from his analyst/mother before the possibility of such gratification was lost forever. With this correct and more relevant interpretation the patient began to grieve for the wished-for mother (as separate from the person of the analyst) and to move again toward termination. Congruence was established: there was a "fit" which resembled the old unity of the mother-child relationship. The patient accepted and internalized this bit of interaction and in exchange was able to differentiate between the analyst as a real, empathic object and the other image of the analyst as a depriving transference object. He took in a transmuting internalization and in exchange gave up an unattainable goal of gratification by his analyst/mother in the transference.

In summary, I believe that insight is the culmination in adulthood of a long process of cognitive and affective development in which definite sequential phases can be observed. The early mother-child experiences of mimicry and naming result in a sense of congruence, mutuality, and unity, and bring about the pleasure of mastery and a re-creation of the sense of infantile omnipotence which comes from being at one with the mother. These affective experiences involving the internalization of mother's affirmative verbal feedbacks have adaptive value to both internal reality and external reality. They reinforce the critical examination of subsequently gained insights and those offered in analysis by interpretations. Understanding the developmental aspects of insight lends important refinements to analytic techniques.

BIBLIOGRAPHY

HARTMANN, H. (1951), Technical implications of ego psychology. In: *Essays on Ego Psychology.* New York: Int. Univ. Press, 1964, pp. 142–154.

HOEDEMAKER, E. D. (1960), Psycho-analytic technique and ego modifications. *Int. J. Psychoanal.*, 41:34–46.

KENNEDY, H. (1979), The role of insight in child analysis. *J. Amer. Psychoanal. Assn., Suppl.*, 27:9–28.

KRIS, E. (1956), On some vicissitudes of insight in psychoanalysis. In: *Selected Papers of Ernst Kris.* New Haven & London: Yale Univ. Press, 1975, pp. 252–271.

SANDLER, J. (1960), The background of safety. *Int. J. Psychoanal.*, 41:352–356.

———— & ROSENBLATT, B. (1962), The concept of the representational world. *Psychoanal. Study Child*, 17:128–145.

———— & SANDLER, A.-M. (1978), On the development of object relationships and affects. *Int. J. Psychoanal.*, 59:285–296.

SHAPIRO, T. (1970), Interpretation and naming. *J. Amer. Psychoanal. Assn.*, 18:399–421.

TOLPIN, M. (1971), On the beginnings of a cohesive self. *Psychoanal. Study Child*, 26:316–352.

Reminiscences and Insight

GEORGE H. POLLOCK, M.D., Ph.D.

THE TOPIC OF INSIGHT IS A WISE CHOICE FOR THE BEGINNING OF A new scientific venture in our field. Insight articulates with all facets of psychoanalysis, including the scientific and philosophical, and has been of pivotal significance from the very beginning of our discipline.

My current research on aging as part of ongoing development has specifically focused on the processes of adaptation to change. As part of my study I have had the opportunity to observe insight attainment, utilization, and concealment in individuals of different adult groups, including the elderly. In the elderly (but also in children and in some middle-aged adults), one can observe repetitive themes in the narratives, stories, and reminiscences communicated to the researcher. In the elderly, these frequently are dismissed as manifestations of senile change or unfounded fantasies. Even if these reminiscences are not of real events, they do have meaning, and this meaning is of significance to our understanding of such aged individuals.

My own experience leads me to conclude that such repetitions may be important to the individual in various ways, e.g., adaptational attempts, relational-communication attempts, self-therapeutic attempts. The recollections or fantasies of the past expressed in reminiscences help the elderly maintain a sense of continuity between past and present and between inside and

Director, Institute for Psychoanalysis of Chicago; President, Center for Psychosocial Studies, Chicago; Professor, Department of Psychiatry, Northwestern University.

Supported in part by the Anne Pollock Lederer Research Fund of the Institute for Psychoanalysis of Chicago.

outside. The events, relationships, and feelings recalled also maintain a sense of "me-ness." These recollection-reminiscences bridge time and maintain the sense of individual personality, especially when there is an inner awareness of diminishing ego intactness and competency. In some individuals, the frequently repeated tales of the past are similar to the repetition, remembering, and working-through sequences observed in the psychoanalytic treatment situation. In some, the obsessive reiteration-and-recounting is similar to mourning work where recalling-and-expressing is part of the self-healing process. In some elderly, the recounting allows the investigator to observe the consistencies of the accounts as they are restated. Even if inaccurate in all details, they are accurate in their reflections of the intrapsychic state of the individual. When the psychoanalytic researcher notes content and context in which certain accounts are given, and is aware of the transference meanings of the communications, these additional data allow insight into the present and past mental and emotional life of the person. Again, the purposes of the reminiscence may be many, varied, and complex. I have found that reminiscence is a way of returning to the past, especially to periods of life when satisfactions and mastering took place. In some, the return is to past traumatic situations where attempts to "work through" these past, but still present, intense mental and emotional disturbances seem clear. The insight of the psychoanalytic observer allows for understanding the meaning of what is otherwise considered "the ramblings of old men and women."

In my own personal experience and in my work with others who have had psychoanalytic treatment, insight or "re-insight" can come relatively quickly in rediscovering exacerbated unresolved conflicts, the return of old defensive patterns, and their repeated transference manifestations. With such insights one can understand and rework the past as it is manifested in the present. As I shall show, insight and work go hand in hand.

I now turn to clinical data to illustrate and elaborate some aspects of how the therapist gains insight. A 90-year-old man, Mr. A., quite intact physically, had to be placed in a residential nursing facility after the sudden death of his wife. She had, up to the time of her death, cared for him in all ways and had, at times, felt quite distressed by his failures of memory. He was initially bewildered at the time of his loss, but gradually reestablished a psychological equilibrium through the support of his children and grandchildren. He spent several months in his own home with a housekeeper caring for him—but this was costly and in addition quite isolating. The painful decision on the part of his children to move him to the residential home exacerbated their own mourning processes for their mother, their increasingly incapacitated father, and the "breakup" of the family home with the dispersal and disposition of many possessions, each of which had emotional meaning to them.

Mr. A.'s initial adjustment to the new "home" was uneventful. He spoke little of his wife's death (they had been married for close to 60 years), and adapted to the routine of the institution. Gradually he began to talk about Russia, his birthplace, and his family of origin, most of whom were now dead. The vividness of his descriptions and the constant repetition of certain stories, though uncomfortable to the listeners, took on a pattern.

Mr. A. wished to see his sisters, his parents, his paternal grandfather. This latter figure had been especially important to him as he was the replacement for the mother, who died when he was an adolescent. The association between myself and the bearded grandfather was clearly in evidence. In resurrecting this material figure of the past, Mr. A. seemingly attempted to replace the lost mother and the lost wife with the now reinstated grandfather who was embodied in the present. At times he would treat me as a son, tearfully talking about how it was so wonderful to have family. This compensated old man had no insight into his transference reactions, although the meaning of his repetitive reminiscence presented a pattern which allowed me to have insight into Mr. A.'s defensive and adaptational structure.

When Mr. A. was angry and upset, he talked about the inhumanity of the Czar's government which suppressed Jews. As he felt better, he would shift and talk about the greater equality that the Communist regime had instituted. Lenin was seen as the good father who wanted the best for the helpless people. Stalin, described far less glowingly, was seen as the "strong man" who saved Russia from the tyrannical Nazis. Although Mr. A. was aware of Stalin's activities, he did not see Stalin as a tyrant.

In the course of his reminiscences, spontaneously related, he slowly and in bits and pieces told his life story. Each recollection had meaning in terms of current transference reactions as well as past history. His father, as a little boy, fell from a tree. Because of inadequate medical care, the father's fractured leg was improperly set and the father became crippled. The father's mother, a strong and dominating matriarch, opened an inn for travelers in the small Russian village in which they lived. The father had two sisters. These women, who never married, identified with their domineering mother.

. Into this household came Mr. A.'s mother, a young woman who was orphaned early in life and who came from a distant village. A marriage was arranged, and the docile young woman came under the control of the matriarchal household. At least eight children were born in quick succession, and then the mother died. Her father eventually left Russia to live and die in Palestine.

Mr. A. had been the third child and first son. He described how his demanding father frequently beat him in order to "teach" him to be an upright and dutiful son. In late adolescence he finally ran away from home, came to Odessa, and then made his way to the United States, where his two older sisters and several of his younger siblings lived. He received no support from his paternal grandmother and his paternal aunts. They, like his father, were harsh, cruel, and at times also physically brutal.

Upon arriving in Chicago, Mr. A. taught himself English and through self-education and hard work became a pharmacist. He was shy, socially inept, and a "loner." His sisters helped him and arranged a marriage to a kindly, depressed young woman. This woman had previously wanted to marry another man, but her father had rejected this man. All of Mr. A.'s adult life was characterized by hard work, anal compulsiveness, identification with helpless people, and a political orientation to the left. He did not beat his children, but lectured them and tried to teach them to be upright and conforming. The identification with his father and paternal grandmother and aunts was clear but never verbally acknowledged. The course of this man's life had a tragic quality to it—he repeated patterns of his own family that he had found so painful in his own childhood. He attempted to justify and rationalize all of his behavior and values in terms of doing what was right and just, and yet he was unaware consciously of what he was actively doing to his wife, whom he tried to dominate and with whom he fought, and to his children, whom he intimidated in frightening ways.

Yet, he was always overly generous to his customers. Interestingly, his shop was located in a Slavic neighborhood where he was beloved by his customers who revered him as he had revered his saintly grandfather. This figure was described as a kind, giving man who removed himself from his family as Mr. A. had with his own family. Throughout most of his adult life in Chicago, the patient did not write to his remaining siblings in Russia and rarely, if ever, talked of his childhood. In the nursing home, however, the reminiscences that emerged went back to his life of 8 plus decades. No attempts were made actively to interpret his behavior. He seemingly wanted to tell his stories to anyone who would listen and understand. He demanded little and still attempted, even though enfeebled, to be as independent as possible, feeding himself and moving on his own without assistance.

The patterns of his life were clear; the methods of defense and coping were understandable; the relations he established were explainable. Yet he had no insight into them. His dreams of being in Russia, seeing his mother, playing in the village as a little boy, paralleled the reminiscences. Evidences of intrapsychic conflicts were present but not confronted or dealt with. He seemingly had made his adjustment with life, although the barrenness and solitude had persisted for almost 90 years. What I have addressed here is the issue of insight in the observer, not the patient. The "therapist" could understand, but had no reason to intervene.

Hollós and Ferenczi (1925), in their classic study of the psychic disorder of general paresis, have described how psychoanalysis helped to understand insightfully the meanings of the psychotic symptoms of patients with this disease, especially the delusions that were so commonly observed. Anatomical-pathological changes in the brain had been seen as causal. Hollós and Ferenczi, however, had insight into the importance of endogenous psychological factors in determining the content of the delusions and were not content to consider only the exogenous, toxic features of the disease. In analogous fashion, I am suggesting that the psychic content of the reminiscences of senile individuals also has internal psychic meaning. This does not suggest that there are no cerebral pathological factors at work, but rather implies that the psychic contents of these productions have significance in different ways, i.e., psychic meaning related to much earlier times as well as to current situations. In several other instances I have, on carefully exploring the memory deficits of the elderly, also found psychic meaning to their lapses, which seem akin to what Freud (1901) described as slips of the memory. Psychological investigations of such symptoms, usually attributed to organic changes in the elderly, can yield insights into the psychological organization of the individual. Psychic determinism may be found even in the so-called organic psychological manifestations of aging and the aged.

Hollós and Ferenczi found that paretics wish to repress their insight into their disease, even though their concealed self-insight can be ascertained from the understanding of their delusions, from their dreams, and from their poems. The idea of insight repression can be found in other types of patients who presumably have discovered their deeper patterns but cannot deal with them. This suggests that insight or discovery is not sufficient for therapeutic change. Instead, additional working through of what one has learned is required if there is to be meaningful therapeutic success. The discovery of meaning in personal phenomena is different from the determination of cause and effect or antecedent-consequent linkages. This distinction highlights the important difference between inductive understanding derived from the transference repetition in the psychoanalytic situation and deductive understanding arrived at by reconstruction. Reconstructive insight is less likely to be demonstrable than inductive insight. Both types of insight, however, have their place in psychoanalysis.

At particular times repetitive stories and reminiscences may change in emphasis and even in detail. When this occurs, I examine the discrepancies and try to understand them either from a transference point of view or from a frame of reference that includes external stresses. An example of this was observed in an 83-year-old woman, Mrs. B., whose husband had a transient cerebral ischemic attack which incapacitated him for a period of time. Where previously he cared for his wife's needs, now she had to support and assist him. She herself was anxious about the possibility that a similar illness might afflict her. Where previously she spoke in glowing terms of her father—he had been very successful in business, caring for his wife and family, taking them on trips to Europe and the Far East, etc.—after her husband's illness she began slightly to shade the stories and bring out some of her father's faults; for example, he would go on business trips, leaving the mother to care for the children; he would take her brothers but not Mrs. B. to the ballgames. I asked why she was emphasizing features of her father that she had previously not discussed. Initially she was perplexed but then, with great insight, wondered if it had anything to do with her husband's condition. As we talked further, she jokingly said, "Important men abandon me—even you are going off for a long vacation." Freud (1906) suggested that if an analysand is asked to retell a dream, additional aspects may be recalled and worked with. In a similar fashion, changes in reminiscences are significant. The discovery of their meanings may open new areas for therapeutic work.

Mrs. C., a 75-year-old widow, in talking of her reactions to the sudden death of her husband 5 years earlier, described how during the bereavement period a friend paid her a condolence call. The friend asked, "How old was Mr. C. when he died?" She looked at him and said, "Mr. C.? Mr. C.? Who is he?" After an interminably uncomfortable silence, she excaimed loudly, "Oh, my God—I must be senile!" In the course of our work, she added, after telling me of this episode, "I don't think I was senile—I think I was so shocked that I blocked everything out, including the name of my husband. Do you think I might have also had some hostility to him?" This question stimulated productive self-examination and reflection about many issues— some extending back into her early childhood.

I wish to emphasize that many may have insight into aspects of their functioning which they have had to push away for a variety of reasons. The psychoanalyst can facilitate the rediscovery of that which was removed from awareness—or perhaps the uncovering of that which was buried but which had and can still have vital importance. But discovery is not enough, just as insight is not enough for the analysand. Insight is the creative beginning of understanding at many levels for the psychoanalyst—of the communications of the analysand, of the psychological state of the analyst, of the fit between the clinical and the theoretical, of the more general scientific value, and even as a means of more carefully delineating one's own world view and value system. If insight is discovery or inspiration (Kris, 1950, 1956), then elaboration, working through, and further detailed investigation are necessary complements to consolidating the gains attainable through "opening the door" to new realms of awareness.

Rather than summarize my position, I wish to raise questions about additional aspects of the subject of our consideration for possible discussion and examination:

1.   Is insight a process that has several components, each with their own lines of development but which converge in time to yield new knowledge?

2.   Can we identify the developments of the capacity for and the utilization of insight throughout the course of life, before, as part of, or after psychoanalytic treatment?

3.   What is the relationship of insight to ways of observing and learning?

4.   Are there levels and types of insight which can be examined and differentiated over the course of a psychoanalytic treatment, and which may be similar or different for the psychoanalyst and for the analysand?

5.   What is the relationship of insight to creativity?

Doris Grumbach, a contemporary novelist, has recently written an essay on "Creativity: Flights of Fancy and Leaps of Faith" (1979). In conclusion, I wish to quote a few passages from her work. Perhaps in reading this, we might substitute "insight" for "creativity" and achieve a new level of insight into insight.

Creativity is the synapse between what is known and common and accepted, and what is unknown until now, uncommon and unexpected. It is the leap between the surmise and the conviction, the conjectural and the inevitable. It is the guess made certain.

Every solver of problems and difficulties is creative: the person who studies a question, or the cause of apparent failure, examines alternatives; considers even absurd, contradictory, and incredible solutions; and then, in a prodigy of choice, changes failure to success, doubt to certainty, ignorance to knowledge. A solver of problems, in Sigmund Freud's words, is one who disturbs the sleep of mankind. [p. 64].

Insight does this initially, but the subsequent sleep, as a result, will be more sound, more restful, more refreshing.

BIBLIOGRAPHY

Freud, S. (1901), The psychopathology of everyday life. *S.E.*, 6.
———— (1906), Psycho-analysis and the establishment of the facts in legal proceedings. *S.E.*, 9:97–114.
Grumbach, D. (1979), Creativity. *Chronicle of Higher Education,* 19:64.
Hollós, S. & Ferenczi, S. (1925), *Psychoanalysis and the Psychic Disorder of General Paresis.* New York & Washington: Nervous and Mental Disease Publishing Company.
Kris, E. (1950), On preconscious mental processes. In: *Selected Papers of Ernst Kris.* New Haven & London: Yale Univ. Press, 1975, pp. 217–236.
———— (1956), On some vicissitudes of insight in psychoanalysis. In: *Selected Papers of Ernst Kris.* New Haven & London: Yale Univ. Press, 1975, pp. 252–271.

Insight as Metaphor

LEONARD SHENGOLD, M.D.

WHEN PRESENTED WITH A TOPIC, ONE TENDS TO CONNECT IT WITH what one has already thought and written about. And then, with some presumption, these connections can be called insight. I have yielded to this temptation, here where the assigned subject is the meaning of insight in psychoanalysis; and what I have to say will illustrate this limited narcissistic kind of insight. At least I begin with what is indispensable about any definition of insight: it involves making connections.

"Only connect!"—I am quoting E. M. Forster's (1910) pre-scription for England in *Howard's End*—"only connect the prose and the passion!" (p. 187): that is to say, connect the ideas and facts and the will and ability to act with the emotions. In our psychoanalytic language, this has been applied to insight by Valenstein (1962), "mutative or dynamic insight... amounts to... extended self-knowledge, combining... affective-conative and intellectual cognitive components" (p. 323).

I am connecting insight to one of my own papers which is a minor commentary on some of the metaphors in Freud's *Interpretation of Dreams* (Shengold, 1966). I want to stand beside Arlow and champion metaphor in these days when psychoanalytic concepts and language have come under attack for using it. To paraphrase Forster, psychoanalytic prose should be full of passion and its conveyer, metaphor. Trilling (1940) has written that Freud pictured the mind as a poetry-making organ. Metaphor is inherent to human thought and, it follows, is essen-

Clinical Professor of Psychiatry at The Psychoanalytic Institute of the New York University Medical Center.

tial to psychoanalytic work.[1] We must be aware of the limitations and defensive uses of metaphor and still be able to employ and translate it. (The ability to act with an awareness of limitations is part of the power granted by insight.) The word *insight* is a metaphor; its original meaning was a seeing "with the eyes of the mind or understanding" (*Oxford English Dictionary*, 5:337). Arlow makes a statement that connects the function of metaphor with the function of insight: "In my view metaphor is an inherent quality of language in general and of how the human mind integrates the experiences of the individual. Metaphor typifies how perception and memory are integrated in terms of similarity and difference" (p. 373). Here metaphor performs, as does insight, by connecting, by integrating, by granting perspective.

Freud's use of metaphor was what stuck in my mind when I looked up Freud's use of the word *insight*. It came as no surprise to learn that Abrams (see *This Volume*, p. 251ff.) and Blum (1979) had also begun their research by combing through the *Collected Works*; it is what an analyst *should* do. Abrams had learned from Guttman (1979) that Freud had used the word *insight* 195 times, but the only use I had been able to find was the one that everyone knows from the 1931 preface to the third English edition of *The Interpretation of Dreams*: "Insight such as this comes to one's lot but once in a lifetime" (1900, p. xxxii).[2] What does this famous statement, expressive of both pride and humility, imply about insight?

In my paper on Freud's use of metaphor, I had examined some implications of a few of the images that Freud intertwined with his central metaphoric plan in the dream book, that plan being of course a journey through a landscape. I indicated what I feel is a crucial *place* in the journey of that book: a turning point at the beginning of chapter 7 where Freud (1900, p. 509) changes direction to plunge into the depths (into the "veritable

1. "The communication and interpretation of unconscious meaning is made possible largely through the use of metaphor" (Arlow, 1979, p. 363).

2. Anna Freud (see *This Volume*, p. 241f.) says that in German there are only two instances in which Freud used *insight* (*Einsicht*) in the sense of *revelation* (as in the above quotation, which Freud wrote in English); the many other uses of *Einsicht* or *Einblick* simply denote "knowledge of" or "insight into illness," i.e., awareness of being ill.

hell" (1916–17, p. 143) of the wishes from the unconscious. (Freud's, like Dante's, is a cosmic exploration involving the mind and the universe.) That turning point is marked by the Dream of the Burning Child. The speech in that dream is, "Father, don't you see I'm burning?" The dream and therefore the dream question are not Freud's own, but they can be linked with the child Freud's exhibitionistic urination in his parents' bedroom, and with his own dream after the death of his father: "You are requested to close the eyes" (1900, p. 317). Both dreams refer to sight, to the metaphor of sight as understanding; and both dreams are to be connected with the mature and measured assessment of Freud's achievement addressed to the fathers of this world to take heed of or to ignore at their peril: "Insight such as this comes to one's lot but once in a lifetime." By 1931 the child's burning had been tempered to a cool glance backward at the white heat of inspiration of the years that followed the death of his father.

The metaphors that interconnect with that of the journey include views and prospects, locomotion, ascents and descents to heights and depths, explorations, demonstrations, light and fire, darkness. They are all involved with the map of the world within and the world outside the mind—with how the world without is registered within. They are aspects of the journey that leads to—I am using Arthur Koestler's phrase—insight and outlook.

Freud's 1931 statement about insight concerned a display of dynamic knowledge that revolutionized our concepts of the inner world (involving the self, the view within and insight), but that also threatened the outer world of the authorities (outlook), as the man who linked himself with Copernicus and Darwin reminded us.

The insights in the dream book were gained from Freud's "journey" of self-analysis, from his exploration of the minds of his patients, and from contrasting the two: from a looking inside correlated with a looking outside.

Insight/outlook and inside/outside are confusing and ambiguous distinctions that lead, in psychology, to the metaphysical and the moot. What is inside? What is outside? I know that the world outside my mind is represented within my mind. I know that I can observe myself and can make discoveries about my

inner world. I know that insight and outlook are inextricably
linked in my mind as, to use Sandler and Rosenblatt's (1962)
metaphor, its representational world. I know that at some early
point in development mental representations of states of feeling
and functioning within the body are linked with representations
of things outside the body—primal mental connections basic to
metaphor and the process of insight. I know.... I know.... I
know—despite this iteration I must face the philosophic challenge of Montaigne's "What do I know?" Putting aside, as we
must, the expectation of ever successfully completing our search
for the "real" structure of the inner and outer worlds, we are left
with sharpening our metaphors; left with the shadows on the
wall in Plato's cave, which we sometimes choose to regard as two
caves—the cave of the world and the cave of the mind. Experientially we feel that we know what inside and outside mean, and
that the two are related; that the look within cannot be dissociated from the look without, and vice versa. In our analytic
work we repeat not only Freud's discoveries but also his way of
integrating them. To explore the mental world of our patients,
we empathize and we listen; what we find must be correlated
with our knowledge of our own inner world. In my usage here,
the analyst's insight into the patient's mind is really *outlook*; his
view into his own involves insight. Our work connects insight and
outlook (in the above senses); we try to remove resistances and to
interpret transference, and hope that the patient will be able to
learn to connect and to correlate for himself. When the patient
merely borrows the analyst's "outlook" (the analyst's view into his
mind), it is not insight and there is no integration (Kris, 1956a).
The patient must slowly and painfully make the mental contents
and finally the correlative power his own.

To return to the metaphor of the journey, insight involves,
first, an ability to see and, second, an ability to stop freely and go
freely through the inner world that contains both changing and
relatively stable representations of our selves and of our human
and other environmental objects. The comparative freedom of
this mental locomotion symbolizes an optimal flexible relation to
and between those structural elements of our minds that register
the inner pictures of the world inside and the world outside our
bodies—those two environments of our psychic apparatus that

Freud (1940) speaks of in the *Outline*. When Valenstein (1962) describes insight as mutative and dynamic, we can connect this with aspects that pertain to a "good" metaphoric traveler: action, locomotion, flexibility, choice. To speak less metaphorically and more experientially, we should be able to see and know what we are and were; who we are with and have been with; and where we are and where we have been. And we should know the limits of what we know and what we don't know, both as to contents and qualities of our knowing. Who we are involves how we feel. Intrapsychic travel (the flow, the stops, the reversals) requires the available interplay of the "affective-conative and intellectual": feelings, desire and will, and ideas. And implicit—implicit even in the acquisition of mental representations, for that matter—is gaining the power to coordinate, to synthesize, to put it all together so that one can say "Look!" to the parent, or "Eureka" to oneself. And this look should involve not only integration, but an integration that furnishes perspective, balance, and proportion.

A journey includes at the least a going from place A to place B (at least from here to Karlsbad, as with Freud's favorite Jewish passenger[3]). Only distance and the traversal of distance can provide perspective. But insight is not a simple linear journey; it is full of stops and forks in the road (including the one at Thebes), a journey that leads to all sorts of connections along different planes and in different dimensions, including the dimension of time. For integration and perspective, time travel as well as internal space travel is needed. The development of the ego— and this is more than metaphor—involves locomotion: an emotional separation from the mother is necessary, and this is enhanced greatly when the child can first crawl and then finally walk away. Only with the mastery of locomotion is the child able (if his correlated psychic development allows) to attain the idea of distance, to compare size and shape, and to explore and con-

---

3. Freud calls it "the 'constitution' story. An impecunious Jew had stowed himself away without a ticket in the fast train to *Karlsbad*. He was caught, and each time tickets were inspected he was taken out of the train and treated more and more severely. At one of the stations on his *via dolorosa* he met an acquaintance, who asked him where he was travelling to. 'To Karlsbad,' was his reply, 'if my constitution can stand it' " (1900, p. 195).

trast the sensory qualities of things, which makes for his own
internal sense of perspective in space.[4] With the development
and maturation of the powers of memory and language, these
journeys outward are registered and a traveling within the mind
becomes possible and may eventually give a perspective in time.
But many repetitions are required—one must go from here to
Karlsbad many times to be able to remember and to correlate the
journey with other journeys. And (to connect the passion), as
with Freud's *Schnorrer*, one's "constitution" must be able to stand
the trip. Too much feeling, the effects of too many traumas, and
the "journey" of insight can suddenly be interrupted, or continue aimlessly.

The sense of perspective that starts with the ability to go from
one place to another demands an integration of various points
with different kinds of connections, including contradictions,
contrasts, and simultaneities. To shift to our theoretical
metaphor, secondary process should be optimally enriched by
primary process (Noy, 1978). This complex development culmi-
nates in the attainment of emotional and moral perspective;
these imply the ability to distance without dissociation or denial,
and the power to modulate affect and values. To obtain this kind
of insight requires the full maturation and use of the mental
apparatus (Kennedy, 1979)—the mastery over the drives, implying the proper developmental unfolding of defense mechanisms
(A. Freud, 1979, p. 6), and the luck with external reality that
permits at least the transient coexistence of the philosophic yet
active mind ("thought is trial action") with a free range of emotions: the prose connected with the passion. If a person's "constitution," his psychic structure, does not permit him to reach
Karlsbad in his life, we can try to help him get over the *via
dolorosa* with psychoanalysis. Neubauer (1979) says, "during
analysis, insight fluctuates topographically and structurally. But
at the end of treatment we expect a new structural stability" (p.

---

4. Here is a quote from Blaise Pascal (1670) that pertains to the internalization required for perspective in and about space: "It is not in space that I must
seek my dignity, but in the ordering of my thought. . . . By space the universe
comprehends me, swallows me like a speck; by thought, I comprehend it" (p.
198).

34). Reaching, or at least approaching, Karlsbad requires structural stability and structural flexibility. One most important, currently challenged point of view about insight is implicit in what I have stated (and in the metaphor of what one encounters on the journey): insight involves the seeing and the engagement with intrapsychic conflict by the patient; this is part of the *via dolorosa* of analysis. There are many psychic healers who seek to obviate the journey and the conflict with the promise of salvation through supplying the good parenting and love they feel, and their patients feel (and they both may be right to feel) that the patients lacked. Karlsbad, like Rome, meant to Freud a place one never quite arrives at. We should not foster the goal of arriving at the unattainable by delusion.

CASE PRESENTATIONS

CASE 1: IF MY CONSTITUTION CAN BEAR IT

Mr. A., in his 20s, came for treatment mainly because he was aware that he had a pattern of starting off projects and commitments with great promise only to end up courting and achieving failure. He was able to see that he had a need to fail, and even a little of how he managed it; but, characteristically, he did not feel it. He was one of those provocative but predominantly passive and masochistic people who deserve Samuel Butler's typically twisted old saw: " 'Tis better to have loved and lost, than never to have lost at all." The passion that went into his losing was very far from the young man's responsible awareness. A compulsive need for emotional isolation and intellectualization barred the way to responsibility and a feeling of identity. Despite a surface of charm, wit, and even brilliance, Mr. A. suffered from what E. M. Forster calls "the underdeveloped heart"—functioning for the most part like a marionette (although with a kind of desperation in his search for someone to pull the strings). His emotional aridity was not complete; there was some anxiety, some ability to care about other people—and I could dimly sense the tip of an iceberg of great rage.

During his first hour he told me an obviously important early memory. "You Freudians will like this," said he (depersonalizing

me), "I'm going to tell you how my mother showed me her bush."
He had asked to see his mother's genitals when he was 5, and she
had responded by taking him into the bathroom and "providing
a display in three-dimensional depth" (a typical example of the
patient's ironic and elliptical speaking style). This short journey,
reported as prose without any passion, was often mentioned
subsequently, almost always with the original tag of metaphoric
slang: "the time she showed me her bush," the affect frozen by
the reduction to cliché. Moreover, the metaphor referred to the
sight of the blur of the mother's pubic hair and avoided the
mysterious, unfathomable, yet fully exposed genital abyss. (He
stated several times, without giving details, "She showed me *everything*."

My reaction was, if he tells me this memory the first hour, what
is he going to remember later on?—but this underestimated his
isolation. It was reassuring to find, several months later, that it
was a long torment for him to tell me that he had the habit of
picking his nose; *that* he really felt. The incestuous exhibition, in
contrast, seemed freely available and often came into his
associations—but it was not filled in emotionally, no details were
added, and he never connected it with his current sexual life or
with his feelings about his mother.

During the first session he had also said, "I'm very bright I
know, but the people I work under tell me that I sometimes act as
if I can't add one and one to make two." I noted the metaphor,
"working under," with its passive connotations; and also the
primal scene implications of the inhibition of putting one and
one together. I wondered if the first hour had not indicated the
analytic path; I could sense the defenses of isolation and of
avoiding responsibility, and I sketched out (a most premature
but not, as it turned out, inaccurate "outlook") the analytic task as
the patient's need to make meaningful connections with his unconscious fantasy life that were implicit in his metaphors: of
seeing the bush, of *being under*, of watching *one and one make two*.

After about 3 years, during which the voyeuristic memory and
the momentary image that accompanied it had appeared in his
associations many times, disconnected except for witticisms that
he refused to analyze, more resistance appeared. The patient
began to be no longer able to talk about the confrontation with

his mother with humor or without anxiety. He was remembering more about what he had seen and how he had reacted. He "associated" with characteristic movements of his hands whenever he talked about the "bush." After this had been pointed out, he said that he felt he was reproducing his mother's gestures when spreading her labia. He started to react to the memory of the sight of her pubic hairs—as if these were now detailed in a naturalistic painting, rather than the black "impressionist" smudge of the "bush." His emotions and the feelings in his body began to flow in accompaniment to the memory: the excitement, then the feelings of inferiority about his penis; next the too-muchness, the overstimulation and terrible intimations of anxiety and rage. These feelings were sampled, as it were, as he began to relive the event in his memory and in relation to the transference of both parents onto the analyst. His passive sexual strivings became part of the struggle, and so did the beginnings of very real suffering over the reawakening of castration fear. The terror of his aggressive impulses took the familiar form of erotizing the pain. The analyst was assigned the role of the conductor on the train to Karlsbad and was administering an emotional beating. In the course of the attempt to analyze all this, the patient appeared to be more responsible for understanding what his mother and father were like and even to contrast this with how he felt about them and reacted to them. The promise that was there in so many of his enterprises was beginning to appear in his analysis. Alas, this turned out to be the usual harbinger of trouble. The flow that connected the prose and the passion was too much for him. He could not bear the intensity of the excitement, rage, and anxiety, especially as his passive sexual and murderous impulses focused on the analyst and onto passionate impressions of his parents. He felt he would explode; he would harm himself; he would harm me; he would harm his parents. He hated his mother for what she had exposed him to. He was again involved with perceptible intense emotion and in a remarkable sensory way with his own body and with that of his mother. He was saying to me, in effect, "Father, don't you see I'm burning?" He was aflame with passions he felt he could not master, and he demanded a father who would, magically, keep mother's behavior in control and take all the bad feeling away.

And the old pattern won out: all the promise, now meaningfully connected with his mother's exhibition, led to the need to fail—a spiteful mixture of self-punishment, masochism, and revenge (just as the initial excitement of seeing his mother's genitals had led to overstimulation and rage). The patient manipulated his realistic situation to get an excuse to leave the analysis. It is possible that he may return to continue his journey in the future, and will discover what lies behind the screen of his mother's "bush." Or he may be one of the many whose "constitution" cannot stand the insight that psychoanalysis offers: an integration and a conviction that threaten to bring a traumatic past back to life. The child who says, "Father, don't you see I'm burning?" ultimately has to be able to stand the searing impulses, preoedipal and oedipal, that lead to overstimulation and rage, incest and parricide. And insight also means giving up the promise of the much-needed, good, magical parent. We must accept the sad truth that only those whose egos are strong or capable of being strengthened will be able to face the "hell" of the unconscious and the realization of one's place in the universe. This was a truth well known to Dostoyevsky's Grand Inquisitor who rebukes (and at first intends to *burn*) the returned Christ for having expected too much of men, for having asked them to accept truth and free choice rather than "mystery, miracle and authority":

> Thou didst choose all that is exceptional, vague and enigmatic; Thou didst choose what was utterly beyond the strength of men. . . . Didst Thou forget that man prefers peace, and even death, to freedom of choice in the knowledge of good and evil? [1880, p. 302.]

Mr. A. had approached and then run away from the threshold of freedom of choice—a place in the journey of his analysis that had been reached when metaphor, slowly stripped of its defensive function, had led to memory and the experiential.

CASE 2: INTEGRATION AND ESTABLISHING PERSPECTIVE

A successful man, married and a father, Mr. B. had for several years warded off his passivity with a rather stubborn resistance to analysis, which he seemed to regard as a wrestling match with his analyst. Whenever he allowed his feelings to appear, anger toward me predominated, sometimes rationalized by fancied slights. He did his best to maintain that he had no deep feelings for me; he felt more comfortable with anger than with love. His emotions could intensify suddenly, which frightened him, and he characteristically disowned them by a kind of dramatic projection; he would provoke people, cause them to react, and proceed to aggravate or placate them while he felt he was observing it all from an emotional distance. Although his work had nothing to do with the theater, he lived his life as if he were an actor. Only at rare moments was he responsible for his feelings. His marriage seemed based in part on mutual need for emotional isolation. Shortly before the session that I shall describe, he had begun to realize that beneath the surface of acting *as if* his analysis did not matter to him he cared intensely. I had always known this from his faithful attendance, his passionate provocativeness, and his intermittent ability to engage in free association and analytic work.

He started the session in a philosophic, transcendental mood, very unusual for him; his customary show of stormy affect was absent and he sounded calm: "You are of course not my enemy. You seem to me to be really a good, even a kind, person. You have been dependable and just, not like my father. And yet I hate you as I hated my father and I see that I expect that you will hate me as my father hated me."

The patient had convincingly presented his father as a brutal and insensitive man married to a frightened, passive, yet seductive woman who had turned to her son for comfort and rescue. It was not at all evident that the father had consistently hated his son, but he had responded violently to the son's persistent provocations. And I had heard many instances of unprovoked cruelty toward the patient.

Mr. B. continued: "I know that I hate others with the terrible kind of hate my father always showed when he was crossed. What is different today is that when I *say* you are good, and yet I *know* I still hate you, I feel alright about it."

The emotional balance is tentative and preliminary. Emotional change comes slowly, and this hour marks a beginning. The loving "good" (denoting a feeling which leaves him so vulnerable and is therefore so dangerous) is *said*, the more familiar hate is *known*. The patient went on to recollect a theme of recent sessions: fantasies about a woman he is tempted to have an affair with at his office, and his employer who reminds him of his analyst. He had, in effect, been outlining a scenario for a sexual triangle:

> All that talking I have been doing about triangles, I have not felt involved in it. It has been like a shadow play, even though I could have really put it into action. But today, somehow I feel that triangle and how it relates to my father and mother; I feel it in three dimensions. [This is said with excitement and involvement.] I feel the good feelings, and the bad feelings; the sex, and the jealousy. It's all mixed up, but it's real. It's not bad or good, it's bad-and-good. I hate my father and I love my father. You know this sounds like fancy intellectual stuff, but today it is different. It is all real and palpable; it's like a bowel movement!

I was aware of some intellectualizing defense at work, but also felt convinced that the patient's feelings did have a different and more authentic quality—convinced in part by the patient's excitement and involvement as he brought out his homely metaphor. It had marked a kind of epiphany and he had been close to tears.

With this overdetermined association to his anal erogeneity, the patient was also unconsciously bringing in the perspective of time: the "wrestling matches" over his bowel training and subsequent anal overstimulation; the more distant past when the bowel movement was me/not me and inside/outside and self/object representation. These regressive paths were for future exploration, as was the reverse direction and the road to Thebes, Laius and Jocasta, which he had touched on in his associations. But in the remainder of the session, the patient continued to show that he had temporarily made and integrated connections which established a sense of perspective, differentiation, modulated affect—while holding onto the feeling of psychic reality as "palpable" reality. Primary process was felicitously intertwined with secondary process. The "anal grasp" of the bowel movement by his anal sphincter which had emerged from the unconscious to supply an experiential component of memory was facilitating the grasp of the ego. The session ended with weeping, with expressions of gratitude for the "feeling of wholeness" it had brought him. He was for the time being not an overwhelmed child but a man who was feeling what he was like as well as what his father was like; he felt able to deal with his analysis and his life. Of course, he quickly descended from this plateau of insight to more conflict and suffering in the depths; but the heights were there to be scaled again.

It is obvious that this good hour was the result of many small accretions of insight achieved in the course of, to use our metaphor, "working through." I want to emphasize, however, that what seemed to bring and to convey conviction in this hour was the association to the bowel movement as a metaphor for the real and palpable. The patient had brought into consciousness as a nodal affective point a piece of the "pleasure-physiological body ego" (Fliess, 1961, pp. 246–254).[5] The association brought on an intense flow of affect involving erogeneity—one might almost call it "body affect." This phenomenon, which in this session seemed to break through the *as if* defensive wrapping around the patient's emotions, can itself be viewed *as if* (I am in a labyrinth of metaphor) the word-presentation "bowel movement" suddenly approached the intensity of a coming toward consciousness of a thing-presentation (another never-to-be-arrived-at Karlsbad). The sensory intensity, combining affect and body sensation, furnished an ingredient that somehow endowed full dimensionality and conviction. Although one must beware of false conviction, which can range from quasi delusion to hallucination (Kris, 1956b), attaining conviction (consistent with being able to know when conviction is not appropriate and to operate without it) is part of what should follow from insight. Conviction is necessary to test reality and makes possible the firm setting of limits, the responsible awareness of doubts: this I know, this I don't know, this I think I know. Conviction leads to a feeling of identity. In this sensation, the feeling of reality, conviction, and identity—feelings whose integration marks the full op-

---

5. I am reminded of the effect of the official announcement of President Eisenhower's "healthy bowel movement" following his myocardial infarct in communicating both the vulnerable mortality and the reassuring vitality of a public figure.

eration of insight as a process—were brought together, albeit following years of preparatory work with specific insights, by the enabling concatenation of metaphor. Metaphor had evoked the experiential.

The metaphor *insight* refers to the coming to consciousness of that power metaphor itself possesses to make psychic connections of force and meaning. Insight is a "condition, catalyst and consequence" (Blum, 1979, p. 66) of the psychoanalytic process: Blum's elaboration of what Kris (1956a) calls the "circularity" of the insight process (p. 261). Analysis can be conceived of as a concentration on the characteristic metaphors of a patient: what and how they connect; how they are coordinated; what prevents or arrests the connective flow; how metaphor can be used for defensive purposes; the need to evoke the patient's awareness and responsibility for his metaphors, and especially for the passions attached to, or contained in, them. Arlow (1979) says, "Psychoanalysis is essentially a metaphorical exercise. The patient addresses the analyst metaphorically, the analyst listens and understands in a corresponding manner" (p. 373f.).

The defensive as well as the expressive use of metaphor can be traced back to the "symbolic equation" (Fliess, 1973, p. 49) of elements of the world of objects with basic elements of earliest infantile experience that Freud conceived of (in the 1911 and 1914 additions to the dream book) as *that which is symbolized.* Fliess (1973) has called the latter "an element or function of the pleasure-physiological body ego" (p. 8). The symbolic equation is a developmental base for the ego functions of registering objects, language, and testing reality. Peto (1959) says of symbolism that "finding and evaluating external reality is to a great extent determined by refinding one's own body in the environment Thus the body image is of decisive importance in grasping the world around us" (p. 230). These primal metaphorical links of the "pleasure-physiological body ego" with representations of the external world (links so full at first of sensory perception and intense affect, combining the affective-connative and intellectual) are the first steps toward our thought, language, memory, and insight. Metaphor in this sense marks the beginning and the continuing road of the journey of our lives.

CONCLUSIONS

Metaphor leads to memory and the experiential: this is the first phase of the insight process. There is a genetic principle at work in relation to attaining the feelings of conviction and of "the real." When we use metaphor freely and creatively, we resuscitate something of that period of wonder of the second year of life when we are establishing both a sense of self and a registration of the external world by the laying down of mental representations—both equating and differentiating the inner and outer worlds. Mahler (1974) calls it the time of psychological birth. The sensory intensity stemming from the drives and body feelings matches and blends with the great excitement involved with the wish to explore and possess the universe (and especially the parents), as the universe (and the parents) are being separated from the previously inchoate and undelineated self. This wish to know has all the intensity of a drive. The child is exploring and discovering, and developing what Piaget (1937) calls evocative memory. It is a time of elation over the power to make inner and, with the attainment of locomotion, outer journeys. (The child can feel, "Father, don't you see I'm burning?" during this time of incandescence.) There will eventually be (the "rapprochement phase" of Mahler) the painful discovery of limitations and of dangers—a sort of developmental *via dolorosa*.[6] Metaphor provides a repetition of the earliest *body-affect*-laden connections and differentiations between the inner and outer world and evokes the earliest experiential feelings of inside and outside, the awareness of the existence of self and things. When these connections approach some of their primal fervid quality in our consciousness, without jeopardizing our integrative powers, we can speak of insight. Metaphor that leads to insight

6. The *via dolorosa*, the road of suffering from Pilate's court to Golgotha, has at its end an equivalent of "Father, don't you see I'm burning?": "And at the ninth hour Jesus cried with a loud voice, 'Eloi, Eloi, lama sabachthani?', which means, 'My God, My God, why hast thou forsaken me?'" (Mark, 15:34).

supplies a factor of conviction of real experience about the past. Metaphor leads to memory.

Metaphor is, in its function of supplying and evoking the earliest experiential feelings of inside and outside, "transitional" in Winnicott's (1953) sense: "It is assumed that the task of reality-acceptance is never completed, that no human being is free from the strain of relating inner and outer reality" (p. 240). Winnicott goes on to speak of the strain being relieved by "transitional phenomena": transitional objects, child's play, artistic creativity. In a sense, metaphor and language are the basic transitional phenomena, mediating and providing links in both directions between the inner and outer world.

Perhaps it is the access to the ego's responsible, conscious, integrating awareness of these early sensory and affect-charged representational connections between the pleasure-physiological body ego and the external world that stands for the approach to Karlsbad of the journey of insight. Freud (1916–17) had told us that our exploratory psychoanalytic work is directed neither toward the drives nor toward the actual causal beginnings of symptoms, but at some place above "the roots of the phenomena . . . at a point which has been made *accessible* to us by some very remarkable circumstances" (p. 436; my italics). We try to make accessible to the ego for its work of synthesis these registrable beginnings of metaphor, these early "experientially charged" connections of representational psychic structure whose actual first roots cannot ever quite be arrived at. Similarly, we can never quite recover the "actual" past or ascertain the "true" external reality. We try to get as close as possible, and perhaps the journey matters more than the attainment of the goal. We must not be deterred by the defensive powers of metaphor to distance the experiential. For insight is the seeing—the awareness of the journey we have and are embarked on—and the linking, as best we can, of the life of psychic fantasy with the memory of what was experienced. Only connect, we ask of ourselves and our patients, insight and outlook, past and present, memory and fantasy, prose and passion.

BIBLIOGRAPHY

ARLOW, J. A. (1979), Metaphor and the psychoanalytic situation. *Psychoanal. Quart.,* 48:363–385.

BLUM, H. P. (1979), The curative and creative aspects of insight. *J. Amer. Psychoanal. Assn. Suppl.,* 27:41–70.

DOSTOYEVSKY, F. (1880), *The Brothers Karamazov.* New York: Modern Library, n.d.

FLIESS, R. (1961), *Ego and Body Ego.* New York: Int. Univ. Press, 1972.

———— (1973), *Symbolism, Dream and Psychosis.* New York: Int. Univ. Press.

FORSTER, E. M. (1910), *Howard's End.* New York: Vintage Books, 1954.

FREUD, A. (1979), The role of insight in psychoanalysis and psychotherapy. *J. Amer. Psychoanal. Assn. Suppl.,* 27:3–8.

FREUD, S. (1900), The interpretation of dreams. *S.E.,* 4 & 5.

———— (1916–17), Introductory lectures on psycho-analysis. *S.E.,* 15 & 16.

———— (1940), An outline of psycho-analysis. *S.E.,* 23:141–207.

GUTTMAN, S. ET AL., eds. (1979), *The Concordance to the Standard Edition of The Complete Psychological Works of Sigmund Freud.* Boston: G. K. Hall & Co.

KENNEDY, H. (1979), The role of insight in psychoanalysis. *J. Amer. Psychoanal. Assn. Suppl.,* 27:9–28.

KOESTLER, A. (1949), *Insight and Outlook.* New York: Macmillan.

KRIS, E. (1956a), Some vicissitudes of insight. In: *Selected Papers of Ernst Kris.* New Haven & London: Yale Univ. Press, 1975, pp. 252–271.

———— (1956b), The personal myth. In: *Selected Papers of Ernst Kris.* New Haven & London: Yale Univ. Press, 1975, pp. 272–300.

MAHLER, M. S. (1974), Symbiosis and individuation. *Psychoanal. Study Child,* 29:89–106.

NEUBAUER, P. B. (1979), The role of insight in psychoanalysis. *J. Amer. Psychoanal. Assn. Suppl.,* 27:29–40.

NOY, P. (1978), Insight and creativity. *J. Amer. Psychoanal. Assn.,* 26:717–748.

PASCAL, B. (1670), Pensées. In: *Blaise Pascal,* ed. & tr. M. Bishop. New York: Dell, 1961, pp. 163–256.

PETO, A. (1959), Body image and archaic thinking. *Int. J. Psychoanal.,* 40:223–231.

PIAGET, J. (1937), *The Construction of Reality in the Child.* New York: Basic Books, 1954.

SANDLER, J. & ROSENBLATT, B. (1962), The concept of the representational world. *Psychoanal. Study Child,* 8:128–145.

SHENGOLD, L. (1966), The metaphor of the journey in *The Interpretation of Dreams. Amer. Imago,* 23:316–331.

TRILLING, L. (1940), Freud and literature. In: *The Liberal Imagination.* New York: Viking Press, 1950, pp. 34–57.

VALENSTEIN, A. F. (1962), The psychoanalytic situation. *Int. J. Psychoanal.,* 43:315–324.

WINNICOTT, D. W. (1953), Transitional object and transitional phenomena. In: *Collected Papers.* New York: Basic Books, 1958, pp. 229–242.

Insight as an Embedded Concept in the Early Historical Phase of Psychoanalysis

ARTHUR F. VALENSTEIN, M.D.

PSYCHOANALYSIS ORIGINATED DURING THE FINAL DECADE OF THE nineteenth century, a particularly productive time in recent intellectual history. We might date modern rationalism from the seventeenth century and Descartes. It was in the eighteenth and nineteenth centuries, particularly the latter, however, that rationalism took the direction of enlightenment, and in so doing a trend to humanize science gathered momentum. This imbued the cultural and educational atmosphere at a time when Freud was being educated, and as he came into maturity. The climate of nineteenth-century liberalism expected that man should solve his problems through science. Starting in those days with a classical education, one came readily to the teaching of Socrates that virtue is the thing, that everything depends upon knowing. If you know, you can really do it. Whether it would be from the Greeks, where the inscription on the Delphic temple was "Know thyself," or from the New Testament (John 8:32), "The truth shall make you free," the message was clear.

Freud's own statement (1927) was:

> We believe that it is possible for scientific work to gain some knowledge about the reality of the world, by means of which we can increase our power and in accordance with which we can

Clinical Professor of Psychiatry, Harvard Medical School; Training and Supervisory Analyst, Psychoanalytic Institute of New England, East.

arrange our lives [p. 55]. . . . We may insist as often as we like that man's intellect is powerless in comparison with his instinctual life, and we may be right in this. Nevertheless, there is something peculiar about this weakness. The voice of the intellect is a soft one, but it does not rest till it has gained a hearing. Finally, after a countless succession of rebuffs, it succeeds [p. 53].

Peter Gay, the historian, writing on Freud, emphasized his exceptional honesty, and its corollary, Freud's passion for knowledge:

> The most conspicuous trait in Freud's character, indispensable to his capacity for generating insights and his patience in developing them into a general psychology, is his uncompromising commitment to truth. It was so powerful, he found it so natural, that he rarely troubled to justify, let alone analyze it. If it is impossible to elucidate completely, its principal strands— curiosity, singlemindedness, and intellectual courage—are manifest. Freud, above all, wanted to know. That his passion for knowledge had its origins in his infancy is beyond doubt; we may apply to him the general observation he offered in the case history of Little Hans: "Thirst for knowledge and sexual curiosity seem to be inseparable" [1978, p. 72f.].

In 1925, Freud explained that "hearing Goethe's beautiful essay on Nature read aloud at a popular lecture by Carl Brühl . . . that decided me to become a medical student" (p. 8). Interestingly, in that essay Goethe represents Nature as a woman who lets her children explore her secrets.

Be that as it may, Freud's first foundation in science was in biology (an identity he never abandoned), in that as a medical student he did basic research in comparative neurohistology, very much under the "influence of two of his outstanding teachers and sponsors: Ernst Brücke, the famous physiologist and histologist, and Theodore Meynert, the equally eminent psychiatrist. Both these men belonged to the expanding group of scientists who followed with determination the shift from the preceding era of philosophy of nature to the organistic-mechanistic approach inspired by Positivism (Comte). Brücke attempted to reduce psychological functions to physiological laws which in turn were based on chemical and physical processes" (Bibring, 1976).

Thus, Freud started as a neurologist, publishing some 20 articles on neurology between 1877 and 1897; and his "Project for a Scientific Psychology" [1895] and his book *On Aphasia* (1891) represent his efforts, in the beginning, to build a bridge between neurology and psychology. Nor did he ever abandon the hope that *some day* a fuller understanding of physiological and chemical processes might supplant the metaphorical language of psychology. At the close of *Beyond the Pleasure Principle* (1920) he wrote:

> Biology is truly a land of unlimited possibilities. We may expect it to give us the most surprising information and we cannot guess what answers it will return in a few dozen years to the questions we have put to it. They may be of a kind which will blow away the whole of our artificial structure of hypotheses [p. 60].

According to Jones (1953), Freud met Breuer "at the Institute of Physiology, in the late seventies, and, sharing the same interests and outlook, they soon became friends. 'He became,' Freud says, 'my friend and helper in my difficult circumstances. We grew accustomed to share all our scientific interests with each other. In this relationship the gain was naturally mine'" (p. 223).

From December 1880 to June 1882 Breuer treated what has become the now famous case of hysteria, that of Fräulein Anna O., abruptly terminating the treatment in the midst of a transference pseudocyesis which greatly alarmed him. Breuer (guiltily) fled the scene but shortly afterward recounted the case to Freud, the details of which (including Anna O.'s self-discovery of a cathartic "chimney sweeping" while in a "hypnoid" state) had a profound effect upon Freud.

I will curtail further historical and biographical details and move ahead now to Breuer's and Freud's *Studies on Hysteria* (1893–95) and the associated papers of those years by Freud, namely "On the Psychical Mechanism of Hysterical Phenomena" (1893), and "The Neuro-Psychoses of Defence" (1894). By that time Freud had spent an interval in Paris with Charcot, had learned something about hypnosis as Charcot's method of dramatically re-creating the "exceptional state of mind" conducive to the development of "fixed ideas," which he saw as particular to hysteria and apparently susceptible to correction through countersuggestions.

However, based upon Breuer's experiences with Anna O. and her self-innovated "talking treatment" or "chimney sweeping," certain heretofore forgotten memories, connected as they were with strong emotion, were reproduced, with a disappearance of her symptoms. As Freud (1893) put it:

> For Breuer learnt from his first patient that the attempt at discovering the determining cause of a symptom was at the same time a therapeutic manoeuvre. The moment at which the physician finds out the occasion when the symptom first appeared and the reason for its appearance is also the moment at which the symptom vanishes [p. 35]. . . . Now we have found that in hysterical patients there are nothing but impressions which have not lost their affect and whose memory has remained vivid. It follows, therefore, that these memories in hysterical patients, which have become pathogenic, occupy an exceptional position as regards the wearing-away process; and observation shows that, in the case of all the events which have become determinants of hysterical phenomena, we are dealing with psychical traumas which have not been completely abreacted, or completely dealt with. Thus we may assert that *hysterical patients suffer from incompletely abreacted psychical traumas* [p. 37f.].

Significantly though, in discussing the circumstances under which memories, with their quanta of "strangulated affect," become dissociated and hysterically symptomatic, Freud not only mentioned the focal effect of a "trauma so great that the nervous system had not sufficient power to deal with it in any way, [but also] ideas to which reaction was impossible for social reasons (this applies frequently to married life); or lastly the subject may simply refuse to react, may not *want* to react to the psychical trauma. In this last case the contents of the hysterical deliria often turn out to be the very circle of ideas which the patient in his normal state has rejected, inhibited and suppressed with all his might" (p. 38).

The original traumatic hysteria associated with Charcot's and Janet's notion of an inherent weakness of will or constitutional inadequacy, or possibly even a consequence of degeneracy, conceivably syphilitic in origin, had been reformulated by Freud, first as "hypnoid hysteria," in those individuals with a tendency to dissociation, and "the emergence of abnormal states of consciousness."

But then, going beyond a further formulation of "the pure retention hysteria," in which "splitting of consciousness plays an insignificant part, or perhaps none at all," and in which "the reaction to traumatic stimuli has failed to occur," Freud wrote finally of "defence hysteria" (i.e., conflict hysteria, as it was to become known), an "'acquired' hysteria, since in [these cases] there was no question either of a grave hereditary taint or of an individual degenerative atrophy" (1894, p. 47).

> For these patients whom I analysed had enjoyed good mental health up to the moment at which *an occurrence of incompatibility took place in their ideational life*—that is to say, until their ego was faced with an experience, an idea or a feeling which aroused such a distressing affect that the subject decided to forget about it because he had no confidence in his power to resolve the contradiction between that incompatible idea and his ego by means of thought-activity [p. 47].

There, in a single brief paragraph, was the germinal concept of psychic conflict, soon to be known as conflict at an unconscious level due to repression.

I turn finally to the issue of the theory of the practice of therapy at that time, with the implicit and, in a special sense, the imminent emergence of a causational or motivational theory of neurosogenesis, and of insight itself, as the principal therapeutic agent. Even though the theory of treatment was explicitly a tension, i.e., affect, management theory, and in this sense mechanistic, and an ego psychological approach, nonetheless, implicitly, the power of explanation loomed throughout.[1]

1. Freud first used hypnosis in order to accomplish a full abreaction of the dammed-up tension. Later he employed suggestion without hypnosis as the technical maneuver, pressing his hand upon the forehead of the patient, or taking her head between his hands (see Breuer and Freud, p. 270f.).

Ostensibly the essence of the "telling," in minute compelling detail, of the heretofore forgotten memories or thoughts which were considered to be trivial, was to free the dissociated strangulated affect. Yet, in the case history of Miss Lucy R., Freud wrote:

> Occasionally, when, after three or four pressures, I had at last extracted the information the patient would reply: 'As a matter of fact I knew that the first time, but it was just what I didn't want to say', or: 'I hoped that would not be it.'
>
> This business of enlarging what was supposed to be a restricted consciousness was laborious—far more so, at least, than an investigation during somnambulism. But it nevertheless made me independent of somnambulism, and gave me INSIGHT into the motives which often determine the 'forgetting' of memories. I can affirm that this forgetting is often intentional and desired; and its success is never more than *apparent* [1893–95, p. 111].

And in his Discussion of Fräulein Elisabeth von R., Freud wrote:

> I have not always been a psychotherapist. Like other neuropathologists, I was trained to employ local diagnoses and electro-prognosis, and it still strikes me myself as strange that the case histories I write should read like short stories and that, as one might say, they lack the serious stamp of science. I must console myself with the reflection that the nature of the subject is evidently responsible for this, rather than any preference of my own. The fact is that local diagnosis and electrical reactions lead nowhere in the study of hysteria, whereas a detailed description of mental processes such as we are accustomed to find in the works of imaginative writers enables me, with the use of a few psychological formulas, to obtain at least some kind of INSIGHT into the course of that affection. Case histories of this kind are intended to be judged like psychiatric ones; they have, however, one advantage over the latter, namely an intimate connection between the story of the patient's sufferings and the symptoms of his illness—a connection for which we still search in vain in the biographies of other psychoses [p. 160f.].

The fascinating point is that as early as 1895, the term *insight* has already appeared twice; and to the effect that the patient's recapitulation of the event, under hypnosis or suggestion, would give an *insight* to the listener, to the doctor, as to the motivation behind the hysteria. But is it not also implicit that the "insight" might be available to the patient, too, now that the precipitating events or fantasies and the conflicts therein are conscious? Clearly, insight was important to Freud, devoted as he was all his life to rationality, to the search for facts, for explanations, even for the truth; all of this is consistent with the Weltanschauung which he took for himself and for psychoanalysis from science (1933).

Although the stated explanation given in the studies on hysteria was the one modeled on neurophysiological mechanistic modes of tension management, of affect recovery and reduction, the unstated or the implicit message was a purely psychological one. It was already apparent that the neurosogenetic determinant of the hysteria was conflict at an unconscious level leading to a hysterical conversion and symptom elaboration—in that sense a dissociation within the total ego. And it carried the message that if a person recognized the past origins, if he or she gained an understanding—that is to say, an insight about what in fact had transpired, and what the conflicts hidden behind the symptoms were—that would exert a "curative" effect.

Freud at this time did not use the term insight for the patient or for the process, but clearly the implication was that knowing the truth,[2] acquiring a convincing explanation with respect to the motivations behind the illness, especially about the paradigm experiences and fantasies, which Freud soon thereafter reformulated in terms of psychic reality—making them conscious should have a "curative" effect. As Freud put it so succinctly in the early papers: "Hysterics suffer from reminiscenses."

It appears, retrospectively, that the insight element was there from the beginning, but not yet given a central place in the treatment process. The aim became the recovery of memories by

2. The use of the term *truth* is bound up historically with psychoanalysis—as to whether memories recovered into consciousness are to be considered factual as such; or whether they are more or less subject to distortion by fantasy elaboration, not to mention transference effects, etc.

the lifting of repression to the point that conflict could be resolved at a conscious level through reconciling the heretofore unconscious "incompatibilities." The outcome, in consequence, could be the achieving of psychic coherence or integration through conflict resolution, as we would put it now. However, resolution of conflict, i.e., the reconciling of the "incompatibilities," is achieved by virtue of an inner integrative trend, now metapsychologically structured as ego activity.[3] In this respect we have returned to a conception which is curiously parallel to the earlier notion of reinstating a (psychic) coherence, an integration of the dissociated parts according to the "strangulated affect" theory. For it was finally this theory which rationalized the clinical effort to bring about a *complete* catharsis, the treatment approach which prevailed during 1893 to 1895.

This leads then to currently relevant questions regarding the significance of insight for the psychoanalytic therapeutic process. "Splitting of consciousness" or (mental) "dissociation" was considered "the basic phenomenon of . . . neurosis" (1893–95, p. 12). Perhaps analogously we now might ask: To what extent is neurosis ultimately attributable to a failure of integration? Rather than insight having a direct "curative" effect, it is probable that the enhancement of integration, i.e., the restoration of ego function consequent to the gaining of insight into conflict, enables one to deal consciously with problems at a secondary process level.

3. "Where id was, there ego shall be" (Freud, 1933, p. 80).

BIBLIOGRAPHY

Bibring, G. L. (1976), Freud and the understanding of human nature (unpublished).
Breuer, J. & Freud, S. (1893–95), Studies on hysteria. *S.E.*, 2.
Freud, S. (1891), *On Aphasia*. New York: Int. Univ. Press, 1953.
———— (1893), On the psychical mechanism of hysterical phenomena. *S.E.*, 3:25–39.
———— (1894), The neuro-psychoses of defence. *S.E.*, 3:43–68.
———— (1920), Beyond the pleasure principle. *S.E.*, 18:3–67.
———— (1925), An autobiographical study. *S.E.*, 20:3–74.
———— (1927), The future of an illusion. *S.E.*, 21:3–56.

_____ (1933), New introductory lectures on psycho-analysis. *S.E.*, 22:3–182.
_____ (1950 [1895]), Project for a scientific psychology. *S.E.*, 1:283–397.
GAY, P. (1978), *Freud, Jews and Other Germans*. New York: Oxford Univ. Press.
JONES, E. (1953), *The Life and Work of Sigmund Freud*, vol. 1. New York: Basic Books.

CLINICAL CONTRIBUTIONS TO PSYCHOANALYTIC THEORY

Self Theory, Conflict Theory, and the Problem of Hypochondriasis

ARNOLD D. RICHARDS, M.D.

THE WIDENING SCOPE OF PSYCHOANALYTIC TREATMENT HAS INI-
tiated a controversy in psychoanalytic theory and technique.
Central to this controversy is the issue of the place of the self in
psychoanalytic theory. Two broad and apparently antithetical
positions have been taken. The first position is that radical revi-
sion of psychoanalytic theory is necessary to account for new
data relating to the self and to explain specific forms of
psychopathology, particularly narcissistic personality disorders.
The second position, to which I subscribe, is that current
psychoanalytic theory is adequate to account for the
phenomenology and psychopathology of the self and that therefore an alternative model or an alternative theory is not necessary (Richards, 1979).

The first position is represented primarily by Kohut (1971,
1977) and his followers, whose theory appears to rest on four
basic principles: (1) the concept of narcissism as a separate and
independent line of development; (2) the centrality of a single
metapsychological point of view—the economic—and the stress
on contentless mental states; (3) the delineation of two specific
self-object transferences, which I view as manifest-content, descriptive designations rather than as having inherent diagnostic,
dynamic, and genetic significance; and (4) the overriding importance of empathic introspective modes of observation and the

Faculty, Psychoanalytic Institute at the New York University School of
Medicine, Department of Psychiatry.

downgrading of the observational, cognitive, and synthetic aspects of the analyst's functioning in the analytic situation.

This theory, I believe, severely neglects the importance of the role of unconscious conflict in mental life and views unconscious conflict and developmental deficit as polar opposites rather than interactive variables. This exemplifies a general trend and an important weakness in Kohut's theorizing—theorizing in terms of forced dichotomies.

Kohut's metapsychology starts from the proposition of two kinds of libido: narcissistic and object; two kinds of patients: narcissistic and neurotic; two kinds of transferences: idealizing and mirror; two different conceptions of the mechanism of therapeutic action of psychoanalysis: transmuting internalization and change through insight; two kinds of anxiety: disintegration anxiety and anxiety stemming from drives; two kinds of aggression: nondestructive assertiveness and destructive aggression; two kinds of objects: self-objects and oedipal objects; two kinds of dreams: self-state dreams and wish-fulfilling dreams. The theory finally resulted in two broad classifications of the human situation: guilty man versus tragic man; guilty man suffering from conflicts and tragic man suffering from developmental defects caused by parental empathic failure. For Kohut, conflict theory is applicable only to guilty man, with self theory applicable to tragic man. It is therefore hardly surprising, since Kohut sees people today as essentially tragic rather than guilty, that he considers the conflict-drive model as less relevant and less applicable to psychopathology and the clinical situation than the self model. Nor should it come as a surprise that in his later writings, particularly in the *Restoration of the Self,* Kohut moves toward discarding the classical drive-conflict model and toward adapting a unitary position in which the psychology of the self is transcendent. This new psychology contains, according to Kohut, "a whole new concept of man," one quite distinct and different from the Freudian concept.

Since self-theory psychopathology results from developmental deficit, Kohut is in effect proposing a deficit model of psychopathology. This raises the question: should we limit ourselves to the consideration of two models—a conflict model versus a deficit or self model—or would we do better with three, as

Arnold Cooper (1980) has proposed: the conflict model for neurosis, the self model for narcissistic patients, and an object relations model for borderline patients? Or why not the five models of the mind offered by Gedo and Goldberg (1973)?

In psychoanalysis, as perhaps in all sciences, questions are more easily asked than answered. But in psychoanalysis, *unlike* many other sciences, questions are particularly difficult to answer because of the special problems of access to its unique data and validation of its propositions. It is not an overstatement to assert that our methodological problems have no bounds. It is rarely possible to propose or execute the crucial experiment that will resolve a particular point of theoretical controversy. It seems to me that to make dialogue more fruitful we should focus on clinical as well as theoretical issues. In line with this idea, I shall attempt to move closer to the heart of the issues I have outlined by considering a single syndrome—hypochondriasis. I hope to be able through the clinical material to assess the relative explanatory power and therapeutic yield of the alternative psychoanalytic models: the conflict model of ego-id-superego psychology and the deficit model of self psychology. I believe that hypochondriasis is a particularly suitable focus because self psychologists view the syndrome as pathognomonic of the disorders of the self and indicative of a state of self-fragmentation and loss of self-cohesion rather than a compromise-impulse-defense constellation.

Although my focus will be on the clinical data, theoretical concerns are equally important. After all, the analyst's theoretical stance determines how he or she listens, what is heard, and how the analyst relates to the patient; all of these of course influence the data obtained.

CASE PRESENTATION

The patient was 27 years old, married, with one child, when he entered analysis because he was intensely anxious about his health. He presented bizarre somatic complaints and the conviction that he was sexually deteriorating. He was convinced that there was minimal but definite diminution in his pubic, axillary, and facial hair, that he was undergoing feminizing physiological alteration which was producing a feminine fat distribution, enlarged breasts, potbelly, and a change in the pitch of his voice. He experienced chest pains, which made him fear that he was going to have a heart attack, especially after intercourse. He was convinced that there was something wrong with the condition and configuration of his penis, a worry that could be resolved only by testing it through masturbation, often in front of a mirror. He worried that he was suffering from premature senility and that he was about to have a stroke. He linked these concerns to one another and explained them with the diagnosis that he had a generalized arteriosclerosis which was cutting off the blood supply to his heart and brain. He explained the fact that physicians had been unable to find any corroborating evidence of his diseases with the notion that the changes were subclinical: had the EEG or EKG been taken a day earlier or later, the results would have been different. He acknowledged that his thinking was illogical, and in spite of the strength of his hypochondriacal symptoms, he never ceased to function on an extraordinarily high level.

The onset of the symptoms had occurred about 4 years earlier, at a time when he was preparing to take a number of important independent steps, including going abroad (to study) and making plans to get married. During an examination occasioned by a minor illness, a physician commented that he might have a slight heart murmur; this touched off concerns about hypertension and heart disease. While he was abroad, he developed abdominal pains, which at first he attributed to bad food. A diagnostic GI series was negative for ulcer but made him worry that the X-ray had damaged his genitals. One psychiatrist he saw treated him with tranquilizers, and another saw him for psychotherapy twice a week for about a year. The latter referred him for analysis, which he agreed to start, not at all convinced that his problems were not physical, but willing to try anything to reestablish his health.

He described his childhood as "idyllic": his mother had doted on him, and his father, a passive, cautious, moderately successful businessman, had remained benignly enough in the background. It was only in the course of the analysis that more telling details emerged. The mother, whom the patient perceived as all-knowing and all-powerful, was ridden with fears and superstitions. She was afraid to handle her newborn son and worried about each new step in his development: that he would fall when he was learning to walk, would choke when learning to feed himself, would fall out of his crib during the night. Until he was an adult she advised him about his clothing, his diet, warned him about the dangers of sports, of other boys, and of encounters with girls, sexual or otherwise. And his childhood idyll was interrupted suddenly, when he was 5 years old, by the birth of a sister. So terrifying to him was his mother's pregnancy and the birth of his sister that he was totally amnestic for the year surrounding it. He was told, however, that he had responded to the loss of his mother's attention by completely refusing to eat until a doctor advised his parents to pay more attention to him. He also was told how pleased his father had been about having a daughter, and analysis revealed that the patient had felt particularly upset by his father's attention to the new baby.

The patient grew up in a one-bedroom apartment, sleeping in the same bedroom with his parents, who had twin beds. When his sister was born, she was given his crib, and he slept in one of the twin beds, his parents sharing the other. When he was 8 the family moved, and he and his sister shared a bedroom until he was 12. From then on, he slept in one bedroom with his father, his sister had a room for herself, and his mother slept in the living room. The patient described his father as quiet and passive, strong but not athletic, and not particularly bright. His mother encouraged him to think that he was intellectually superior to his father, an idea the patient absorbed as his own when he was still a boy. That he was exhibitionistic is attested to by one of his earliest memories, or it might have been a fantasy: when his grandmother was dying, he said, "Don't die, grandma, look at me in my new sailor suit."

His parents, particularly his mother, severely discouraged expressions of his sexuality when he was a child. Although he did not remember her forbidding him to masturbate, a reconstruction of that possibility was made when he observed his mother's reactions to watching his own son play with his penis. He remembered how his mother made fun of any girls that he had an interest in. When the patient was in the latency period and as a young adolescent, his mother suffered several serious illnesses and operations, many details of which were replicated in his own physical symptoms.

He continued to live at home while going to college until his fourth year there, when he moved into the apartment of his girlfriend—his first girl and the one he married a few years later. I should add that this girl, the first with whom he had intercourse, found no fault with his sexual performance and had apparently had enough experience to have been able to judge. It was when he left her to go abroad that his symptoms appeared.

I turn to a brief account of the part of the analysis that is relevant to my thesis. Although the patient for many months insisted that there was nothing I could offer because his symptoms were physical and not psychological, a specific transference configuration soon emerged. He saw me as a dangerous, omnivorous person who was robbing him of his time, his money, and his independence, and who was placing him in great physical danger by treating his symptoms as though they were psychological rather than physical. A recurrent image that appeared in fantasies and dreams was that of a leech sucking his blood. He viewed me as strong and himself as weak, fragile, and needing to be taken care of. He spent many sessions ruminating about my penis, imagining himself sucking it as though it were a nipple. The accompanying fantasy was that he would thereby gain power from me which would make him more potent in relation to the woman, but would not incur the wrath of the male rival because he would be giving him pleasure as well. Other homosexual fantasies experienced in the analytic situation and about me, particularly fantasies of anal penetration, were elaborated with the idea that my penis would extend into his penis, making it harder and stronger and making him more potent.

He felt the more he told me about himself, the more he put himself in my power and control, and that only my death would liberate him. His dreams and fantasies of me as a devouring figure could be recognized as a replication of an unconscious childhood image of his mother, whom he had experienced as robbing him of his autonomy, his physical competence, and his independence by her overprotectiveness and anxious overconcern. He gradually came to see that successful independent action on his part resulted in an increase of suffering from his symptoms and was related to his symbolic movement away from his mother. His inability to tolerate autonomy and success stemmed from his identification with his weak, passive father, and even more from his need to feel inadequate and dependent in order to conform to his mother's idea of him. He feared that he would lose her as he became an adult; after all, she had told him that she was always afraid that she would lose him if he learned to do things on his own. He saw the delicate balance with which he had had to walk the line between ambition and illness, between autonomy and infantility.

When he had occasion to criticize a man considerably older than himself, he was immediately consumed with anxiety that the attack would cause him to lose the man's love and friendship. About his superiors in his firm, he brooded, "If they don't step down, how will I get ahead? But if they die, who will take care of me?" As the aggression implicit in these questions gradually became conscious, he was able to be more critical of his superiors.

The patient's conflicted feelings about surpassing his father were elucidated in the transference when he was aware of feeling anxious because he had the thought that he was intellectually superior to me. This was followed by ruminations that he had cerebral arteriosclerosis so that, on the one hand, he felt smarter than the analyst and, on the other, felt that his brain was deteriorating: the somatic concern disavowed his intense competitive wishes. He recalled how he had acquired considerable skill in playing ping-pong when he was an adolescent, but would deliberately lose when he played with his father because he did not want to embarrass him.

At the beginning of the analysis, he had no recollection of observing or hearing anything sexual going on between his parents. He could only imagine them lying motionless next to each other all night. He reported experiencing a profound sense of disbelief when he learned about the details of sexual intercourse. His denial of the relevance of primal scene experiences was countered by the following dream, which he reported: "I am in a large empty room sitting against the wall. A couple on the other side of the room are having intercourse. I can see the man's back and not his penis, and I feel relieved. He motions to me to have intercourse with my wife. I feel relieved because he will not be able to see me, just as I couldn't see him. I wake up and have a feeling that I am in a twin bed and my wife is in the bed next to me." The connection between the dream and the sleeping arrangement as a child was clear enough, given the fact that he and his wife slept in a double bed. Clarification of primal scene memories showed that he experienced intercourse as an attack by the woman on the man. His sickness had protected him from the dangers of a sexual relationship with a frightening woman. Success in the sexual area was just as frightening as it was at work: he consulted a physician for a recurring pain in the groin following intercourse, a time when he felt in greatest danger of suffering a heart attack. He could recognize the extent to which his sexuality had been discouraged by his mother, who viewed it as an area over which she had no control. For her, he realized, his sexual maturity meant that he would inevitably leave her to seek another woman. Fantasies of invagination or a vagina appearing on his abdomen suggested he would be willing to give up his penis altogether to please her. This fantasy had both positive and negative oedipal determinants, and could also be understood in context as a relinquishment of an organ which pushed him to be independent of his mother. He recalled that the development of his potbelly and the enlarging of her abdomen were parallel processes. I asked him what came to his mind about the thought that he was like a pregnant woman, and he replied, "A woman with a penis."

Turning into a woman, as in his almost delusional preoccupation with his feminizing changes, was both a regressive solution to his positive and negative oedipal conflicts and a means of avoiding separation from the preoedipal mother by identifying with her. Being sick fit nicely into this entire conflictual nexus because sick meant feminine, weak, and castrated, but also pregnant and powerful. The constant perusal of his body for suspected tumors as well as other features of his hypochondriacal concerns could be connected with pregnancy, specifically with his mother's pregnancy when he was 5. Repressed memories of that experience returned, directly represented in his symptomatology, and served to organize his illness. For example, he connected his concern about losing his hair with an image of the smooth, hairless skin of his baby sister. The disturbing nature of this experience for him had to do with his losing not only his mother's undivided attention but also the exclusive love of his father. Hence his refusal to eat until his mother's worry over his health restored her to him.

As these conflicts were worked through, the patient offered what seemed to me a telling insight: "I split myself into two persons when I am worried about my health. One is being taken care of and one is taking care of me. I have become in effect the child and the mother. I am my mother and my body is myself as a baby. I attend to every hair on my body. I attend to my own aches. There is no one to take care of me, to watch over me, so I do it myself. I am afraid to let go. I have a fear of something terrible happening if no one is watching me."

Although this insight was followed by marked improvement in his symptoms and a more positive feeling toward me and the analysis, this transference developed as a resistance to termination. He wished the analysis would go on forever, to achieve in this way the longed-for union with his mother. Contemplating termination, "a step toward independence," exacerbated symptoms that had abated considerably during the previous years. In fact, there was a recurrence of the very symptom that had plagued him during a previous period of decompensation. He developed abdominal pains and the conviction that he had an ulcer. This time, however, he was able to undergo a GI series without the dire psychological consequences that had occurred the first time. Central to this was his newly gained ability to see that his concerns were related to the impending termination and his fears of being independent. He was able to accept the negative findings of the internist, and the pains gradually subsided.

DISCUSSION

According to the psychology of the self, hypochondriacal preoccupations indicate the lack of a cohesive self, a lack consequent to the mother's failure to respond in a properly empathic fashion to the child's bodily and emotional needs. Hypochondriacal states are pathognomonic of self psychopathology and, along with feelings of fragmentation and depersonalization, can best be understood as indicating disturbance, or impending disturbance, of the self or self representation, rather than as a consequence of unconscious conflict. Kohut (1977) regards hypochondriasis as a displacement onto the body of what he calls disintegration anxiety—an unverbalizable dread of loss of the self, "the fragmentation of and the estrangement from his body and mind in space, the breakup of the sense of his continuity in time" (p. 105). The worries about physical defects are "replicas of the anxieties of childhood and [the] need for the attention of the missing self-objects" (p. 161). Kohut's concept seems to hark back to Freud's (1914) explanation of hypochondriasis as a withdrawing of libidinal cathexis from objects and a turning of it onto the self—of transforming object libido into narcissistic libido. Freud consistently placed hypochondriasis in the same category as actual neurosis. Both were "toxic" in nature and more medical than psychological (1916–17, p. 389).

Freud's earliest reference to a case of hypochondriasis occurs in an 1893 letter to Fliess. There he writes of a man, age 42, who upon the death of his father developed hypochondriacal fears of cancer of the tongue. The man also reported that he had practiced coitus interruptus for the previous 11 years, a fact Freud considered of primary etiological significance. The death of the father, he felt, was only an immediate precipitating factor. In the discussion of masturbation, Freud (1912) said, "I see nothing that could oblige us to abandon the distinction between 'actual neuroses' and psychoneuroses, and I cannot regard the genesis of the symptoms in the case of the former as anything but toxic" (p. 248). Freud chided Stekel for "overstretching pathogenicity" and seemed concerned with maintaining his position that the symptoms of actual neurosis, whether neurasthenia or hypochondriasis, are essentially contentless and essentially unanalyzable. This is certainly evident in *Beyond the Pleasure Principle* (1920) where Freud refers to hypochondriasis as akin to traumatic neurosis, referring presumably to the view that it is caused by an unmanageable flood of sexual exertion which causes toxic changes in the hypochondriacal agents.

Although these references indicate that Freud included hypochondriasis in the category of the actual neurosis and stressed its traumatic and somatic origins, there is some evidence that at least prior to 1912 Freud struggled with choosing between a somatic and psychogenic etiology. Although his theoretical remarks clearly favor the somatic view, several clinical comments suggest the psychogenic view. In 1898, Freud was advancing the idea that hypochondriasis can be caused by self-reproach. He said, "Self-reproach (for having carried out the sexual act in childhood) can easily turn into *shame* (in case someone should find out about it), [or] into *hypochondriacal anxiety* (fear of the physical injuries resulting from the act involving the self-reproach)" (p. 171). Finally, Freud's uncertainty about the issue of a somatic versus psychogenic origin of hypochondriasis and his dissatisfaction with his classification of hypochondriasis as an actual neurosis may be indicated by the following comment in a letter to Ferenczi dated March 18, 1912. "I always felt that the obscurity in the question of hypochondria to be a disgraceful gap in our work" (see Jones, 1955, p. 453).

In the psychology of the self, the course of the analysis would focus on variations in the cohesiveness of the self, particularly as they can be related to empathic failures on the part of the analyst and manifested symptomatically in the patient by feelings of fragmentation, depersonalization, and hypochondriacal preoccupations. The analyst would help the patient see the connection between the empathic failures he experienced in the analysis and the empathic failures he had experienced as a child. This process would result in what Kohut calls transmuting internalizations, thus repairing the structural deficit in the patient.

A diagnosis would be based on the manifest content of the transference and of the patient's symptoms and pathology. Genetic explanation would be, on the one hand, very specific and, on the other hand, presented as universally operating; namely, of parental empathic failures in childhood. Issues related to drive derivatives and conflicts with regard to the patient's past or in the here and now of the analytic situation would not be stressed. I consider this view unidimensional, for it looks only at the self, a concrete and reified entity which is never really defined but whose state of being—cohesive, fragmented, overstimulated, understimulated, overburdened, or underburdened—is presented as of paramount importance. Clinical findings not relevant to this construct are discarded.

Certainly, the etiological significance of my patient's mother's

intrusiveness is clear; but what has to be worked out in the
analysis is the *specific* way in which conflicts produced by the
unpleasure of this experience and others, the vicissitudes of both
libidinal and aggressive drives, have influenced the patient's unconscious mental organization. Only by understanding how he
defended himself against the anxiety evoked by conflict can the
nature of the patient's symptoms and of his relations to his
analyst and to others in his life be modified.

Before explaining my patient's symptom in terms of conflict
theory, I had best define what I mean by conflict theory. I am in
accord with Brenner (1976) who believes that intrapsychic conflict develops when a drive derivative or self-punitive trend is
perceived as dangerous. The danger produces unpleasure—
anxiety or depression—which evokes unconscious defenses
against the unconscious wish. The resulting symptom is a compromise between the wish and the defense; anxiety is either
diminished or abolished, depending on the success of the defense. The aim is to avoid unpleasure. The conflict may be between ego and id or between ego and superego. The four
calamities producing unpleasure are object loss, loss of the object's love, castration anxiety, and superego condemnation. Conflict can thus be preoedipal as well as oedipal. I also agree that the
origin of hypochondriasis is similar to that of conversion symptoms: the symptom expresses in body language a fantasy which is
a compromise between wish and defense (Arlow and Brenner,
1964, p. 173). Clinical illustrations of this view in the literature
include a paper by Macalpine and Hunter (1953) on the
Schreber case which identifies an unconscious fantasy of intestinal pregnancy as underlying Schreber's hypochondriachal
symptoms, and a paper by Broden and Myers (1980) who relate
several hypochondriacal preoccupations in several of their patients to underlying unconscious beating fantasies.

Conflict theory is multidimensional: it stresses the principles
of multiple function, multiple determination, the importance of
the repetition compulsion, and of unconscious fantasies which
are linked with childhood memories and perceptions, with all
their distortions. Of course, this complicates both conceptualization and interpretation.

Returning to my patient, I contend that viewing his symptom

in terms of cathexis, recathexis, and hypercathexis, or in terms of developmental deficit keeps us on a descriptive, manifest-content level which seriously impairs our ability to help the patient understand *why* he feels the way he does. I believe that this understanding is necessary for successful treatment. Equally inadequate are formulations that view the symptom simply as preoedipally rather than oedipally determined, or that rely on the positing of a prestructural, preconflictual realm, for they pose false dichotomies and result in excluding from consideration a large sector of the patient's experiences.

What were the childhood experiences that were crucial in this case? I would cite the following: (1) the patient's mother's over-solicitousness and overprotectiveness when he was an infant; (2) the child's exposure to great admiration for his intellectual achievements, simultaneously with strong physical discouragement of physical activities and equally strong discouragement of all sexual behavior; (3) his father's passivity, timidity, and remoteness, and the patient's sense that he was smarter than his father; (4) the sudden expulsion from his special position when his sister was born; (5) his observations of the bodily changes that occurred in his mother during her pregnancy, observations of her genital, and observation of the anatomy of his newborn baby sister; and (6) primal scene observations.

We can point out some of the multiple determinants of the patient's hypochondriacal symptoms with regard to both their form and content. In a general way the symptoms represent a continuation of his childhood relationship with his mother; he hovers over himself as she hovered over him. The symptoms enable him to maintain the illusion of the persistence of this special relationship between himself and his mother and to defend against the twin dangers of losing her and her love.

This state of affairs is very similar to the attitudes toward health of motherless, institutional children described by Anna Freud (1952). "The child actually deprived of a mother's care adopts the mother's role in health matters, thus playing 'mother and child' with his own body" (p. 79). Anna Freud asks whether this behavior does provide a clue to the understanding of adult hypochondriacal attitudes. She states, "With children analytic study seems to make clear that in the staging of the mother-child relationship, they themselves identify with the lost mother, while the body represents the child (more exactly: the infant in the mother's care)" (p. 80). The similarity between my patient's statement, already quoted, "I am my mother and my body is myself as a baby" and Anna Freud's formulation is striking indeed.

The danger of castration is warded off through identification with his mother in which the perception of her as being injured and castrated is countered by the unconscious fantasy of her having an internal penis (the illness growing inside), the model for which is pregnancy, in which baby equals penis. The danger of castration connected with his oedipal wishes is countered by his assertion that he is "old, ill, impotent, or female." Superego condemnation is also avoided by the formula: I am not bad, just sick. Castration anxiety is defended against by displacement— the body as phallus—and by turning passive into active: "You can't do it to me; I have already done it to myself."

The prospect of termination and the impending separation from the analyst were similar to the situation he experienced when he was abroad. In both instances he developed a hypochondriacal conviction that he had an ulcer. Both situations revived the childhood situation when he was 5. The danger then was loss of the object, his mother—and to some extent his father—as well as loss of their love. He also risked moral condemnation because of his aggressive wishes toward his father, his mother, and his sister. Being in the oedipal phase, his heightened libidinal needs for his mother increased his competitive striving toward his father. His aggressive wishes as well as his libidinal needs toward his mother were exacerbated by her unavailability for him because of her attention to his sister. Finally, the aggression of sibling rivalry was ushered in for him by his sister's unwelcome appearance on the household scene. When he was 5, his compromise solution was not to eat, thereby at once infuriating his mother, forcing her attention from his sister to himself, and, as he himself put it, "punishing myself for my own greediness." Similarly, in the analysis, if his symptoms returned, I would continue to have to spoon-feed him and would not replace him with another patient.

During the termination phase of his analysis, as well as at the time of his mother's pregnancy, my patient was experiencing intense conflicts. He wanted to depend on me and hated me for this dependency. He experienced both libidinal *and* aggressive feelings toward his mother, his father, and his sister. Yet, anger toward his parents made him feel diminished as an independent person and as a man. The patient's symptom of not eating during the crucial time when his mother gave birth was short-lived, and the basic conflicts—which were both oedipal and preoedipal—were not resolved; a temporary peace was achieved at the expense of marked repression. He denied his angry feelings, remembered his childhood as idyllic, maintained the view that his parents never had intercourse with each other, became a model boy and student, looked after his sister and never teased her, and never masturbated. His envy of his sister was submerged; his envy of his father, the oedipal rival, was made nonoperative by the idea that his parents did not have a private sexual relationship which excluded him.

But the whole scenario became unstuck when he was confronted with the prospect of leaving home and getting married, and subsequently at times when independence, active mastery, sexual performance, and the surpassing of rivals were called for. The hypochondriacal symptom then appeared as a compromise formation.

Why this particular choice of symptom rather than some other? This brings up the issue of choice of neurosis, which is one that Freud struggled with and one that has never been resolved. In this instance, however, the details of the hypochondriacal symptom, its specific content, can be related almost point for point to specific details of the traumatic childhood situation, his mother's pregnancy, and to a lesser extent her illnesses during his latency period and early adolescence. The symptom is meaningful in terms of conflict, content, and genesis, rather than merely indicative of a general failure to develop a cohesive or stable self representation in response to his mother's general failure of empathy.

I have reserved one question in order to raise it only after the patient had been described as fully as is possible in a brief presentation—the question of diagnosis. Some analysts might ask whether the patient was suffering from a symptom neurosis or from a narcissistic personality disorder. I think he was suffering from both. Indeed, this brings me to my basic point—the unnecessary confusion caused by positing two separate lines of development. That my patient was narcissistic is indisputable—his intellectual grandiosity, his exhibitionistic traits, his preoccupation with his body, all attest to it. It did not occur to me at the time I treated him, nor would I find it particularly helpful today, to view these traits apart from his problems in separation from his mother, from his fiancée, or from me. The problem he had in separating from his mother profoundly affected his choice of a wife and his subsequent relationship to her, sexual and otherwise; his rivalry with his father affected his relations with other real or imagined rivals. At the same time, the difficulty he had in enjoying success when on his own made it harder for him to loosen the tie to an intrusive and engulfing mother.

The diagnostic question I asked myself was of a different order. It had to do with the severity of the illness. The high level of certain aspects of my patient's functioning and his capacity for meaningful object relations, many of the details of which I have not presented at length in this report, favor a "less sick" diagnosis. On the other hand, other features of the psychopathology, particularly the bizarre quality of some of the details of his preoccupation and the almost delusional way in which he clung to some of his beliefs suggest a "more sick" diagnosis. I would suggest that the unevenness manifest in the patient is not unusual in clinical work and points up the difficulty posed by setting up clear-cut diagnostic categories. It also calls into question theoretical approaches that rely upon clear-cut diagnostic categories to justify technical departures.

I return to the four basic principles of the psychology of the self which I enumerated at the beginning. I have already dealt with the issue of making a sharp distinction between narcissistic and object-libidinal developmental lines. It seems to me that for this patient these issues were interactive and intertwined. Secondly, the material points up the limitations of making a single metapsychological point of view, the economic, with its stress on contentless mental states the central issue. From time to time the patient said, during a session, that he felt as if his body was flying off in all different directions. Perhaps this is what is meant by disintegration anxiety. But this patient's mental states were never, as far as I could tell, devoid of specific mental content that could be expressed in everyday language—the language of current need and wish and fear, and the related language of childhood need, wish, and fear. With regard to the third principle, specificity of the two major self-object transferences, I found that I was able to understand the analysand-analyst interactions as they emerged without them. Idealizing and mirror transferences are broad, descriptive designations, useful in the early stages of treatment when we do not yet know too much about the patient. It seems to me that the self psychologists assign to these transferences more weight than they can bear and, even more to the point, thereby narrow the analyst's focus.

With regard to the final principle—the overriding importance of empathy and introspection—my position, in contradistinction to Kohut's, is that the psychoanalytic method of inquiry depends upon a wide range of affective, perceptual, and cognitive processes applied by the analyst to his own observations of, and reports from, the analysand. Empathy and introspection clearly are part of this method but are neither primary nor exclusive. In any case, it is my firm conviction that this patient's achievement of insight and the resulting change in his psychic structure and subsequent modes of adaptation would not have been possible without the calling into operation of the ego's cognitive and synthesizing functions on both my part and his.

I think there can be no question but that this patient was struggling with severe conflicts. He wanted to be rid of his sister, but he wanted to retain his parents' approval—and his own self-approval. He wanted to be close to his mother and win her approval by being like her; but if he did this, he would feel castrated because she did not have a penis. He wanted to replace his father in his mother's affections, but he also wanted to retain his father's love and approval. He wanted to be independent, but this would have meant losing his mother because to have her was to need her. And so he developed symptoms which expressed his need for his mother, his identification with her, his fear of castration, and punishment for his hostile wishes.

CONCLUSION

I do not argue against the usefulness of the concept of the self as it relates to the importance of certain broad identity themes which characterize each of us, themes by which we organize our experience. But I want to stress that these themes are inevitably the result of the outcome of the vicissitudes of the important childhood conflicts and are related to the expressions of these conflicts in adult life. And at the root of these conflicts are indeed the core calamities of childhood—loss of object, loss of love, castration anxiety, and guilt. Evidence of the importance of all four could be found in my patient.

If Freud's drive theory is not relevant to disorders of the self (see Kohut, 1977, p. 68), then perhaps we should add a fifth calamity—loss of the self—to the usual four. This, I would suggest, is the essential point raised by those advocating a psychology of the self. My own opinion is that, before we accept the fifth calamity, we should be certain that it is not reducible to the other four. I think the law of parsimony prevents us from doing otherwise. For the fifth calamity to be useful, it would have to be firmly rooted and situated in the conflict-compromise formation nexus that includes the other four dangers, the drive derivatives, and the concept of defense. This the psychology of the self has not achieved or even attempted. We must wonder why.

BIBLIOGRAPHY

ARLOW, J. A. & BRENNER, C. (1964), *Psychoanalytic Concepts and the Structural Theory*. New York: Int. Univ. Press.
BRENNER, C. (1976), *Psychoanalytic Technique and Psychic Conflict*. New York: Int. Univ. Press.
BRODEN, A. & MYERS, W. (1980), Hypochondriacal symptoms as derivatives of unconscious fantasies of being beaten or tortured (unpublished).
COOPER, A. (1980), Some current issues in psychoanalytic technique (unpublished).
FREUD, A. (1952), The role of bodily illness in the mental life of children. *Psychoanal. Study of the Child*, 7:78–80.

FREUD, S. (1893), Letter 14 [to W. Fliess]. *S.E.*, 1:4–186.

──────── (1898), Further remarks on the neuro-psychoses of defence. *S.E.*, 3:159–185.

──────── (1912), Contributions to a discussion on masturbation. *S.E.*, 12:239–254.

──────── (1914), On narcissism. *S.E.*, 14:67–102.

──────── (1916–17), Introductory lectures on psycho-analysis. *S.E.*, 16:389.

──────── (1920), Beyond the pleasure principle. *S.E.*, 18:3–64.

GEDO, J. (1979), *Beyond Interpretation.* New York: Int. Univ. Press.

──────── & GOLDBERG, A. (1973), *Models of the Mind.* Chicago: Chicago Univ. Press.

JONES, E. (1955), *The Life and Work of Sigmund Freud,* vol. 2. New York: Basic Books.

KLEIN, G. (1976), *Psychoanalytic Theory.* New York: Int. Univ. Press.

KOHUT, H. (1971), *The Analysis of the Self.* New York: Int. Univ. Press.

──────── (1977), *The Restoration of the Self.* New York: Int. Univ. Press.

MACALPINE, I. & HUNTER, R. A. (1953), The Schreber case. *Psychoanal. Quart.*, 22:328–371.

RICHARDS, A. D. (1979), The self in psychoanalytic theory, the self psychologies and the psychology of the self. *Issues in Ego Psychology*, 2:20–29.

ROTHSTEIN, A. (1980), Toward a critique of the psychology of the self. *Psychoanal. Quart.*, 49:423–455.

Anxiety, Symptom Formation, and Ego Autonomy

SAMUEL RITVO, M.D.

THE ANALYSIS OF PATIENTS WITH SEVERE, CHRONIC PSYCHONEUROT-
ic illness characterized by repeated attacks of intense anxiety
and a profusion of symptoms provides the incentive for examining anxiety and symptom formation from the standpoint of
vicissitudes in the functioning of the ego. This requires consideration of the intrasystemic relations within the ego with particular attention to the generation and perception of anxiety, to
shifts in the autonomy of functions of the ego such as judgment,
reality testing, and some aspects of cognition, and to splitting of
the ego in the defensive process. The impairment of the ego's
functioning in relation to anxiety and symptom formation has
implications for technique in these cases. These questions of
technique are relevant to basic issues concerning the analysis of
the ego.

This study is based on the analysis of a group of patients who
have in common the experience of traumatic conditions in the
first two years of life. Here I use the definition formulated by
Greenacre (1967): traumatic conditions are "*any conditions which
seem definitely unfavorable, noxious, or drastically injurious to the development of the young individual*" (p. 128).

The most readily identifiable experiential referents of
traumatic conditions in the early life of these patients are distur-

Clinical Professor of Psychiatry, Yale University Child Study Center; Faculty, Western New England Psychoanalytic Institute and New York
Psychoanalytic Institute.

Presented as the 30th Freud Anniversary Lecture to the New York Psychoanalytic Society, April 15, 1980.

bances in the parent-child relationship with their frequent concomitant somatic illnesses, and prolonged, repeated separations. The disturbances in the parent-child relationship stem in large measure from the personality disorders and neurotic illnesses of the parents, particularly their anxiety, aggression, and depression which result in qualities of parenting that aggravate rather than mitigate the traumatic condition. Other disturbances in the parent-child relationship may stem from inherent vulnerabilities in the child. The somatic illnesses that appear most frequently in the infantile history of these patients and often continue into adult life are skin, gastrointestinal, and respiratory disorders.

Apart from their severe anxiety and psychoneurotic symptoms these patients are characterized by their polymorphous-perverse sexual development. I believe they are the same type of individuals who have been the focus of a series of papers by Greenacre (1941, 1971) on the predisposition to anxiety, pregenital patterning, fetishism and the body image, and regression and fixation. Sprince (1962) reported a similar case in an adolescent girl. I believe that Anna Freud (1965) was referring to the same clinical group when she spoke of developmental disturbances in the first year or two of life where the mother and the adult environment do not meet the developmental needs of the infant. The infant may then be severely stressed as manifested in sleeping, eating, growth, and somatic disorders. As adults their extreme passivity and helplessness in the face of their anxiety and symptoms regularly contrast with impressive achievements in their lives requiring a high degree of organization and control, often calling upon those very functions which are woefully impaired in the psychic realm of the neurotic conflict and symptoms. Particularly impaired is anxiety as a signal function of the ego.

As Greenacre observed, these individuals are referred to as borderline cases by many clinicians, but I agree with her that the designation contributes nothing to our understanding of them and does not do justice to the complexities they present. I find that they are neither borderline nor psychotic. They comprise a special group in whom anxiety does not have primarily a signal function but is a readily generated affect which has become ingrained in the character and is a prominent feature of the pleasure-pain experience.

Two brief case examples will illustrate the early traumatic history, the part played by the selective impairment of autonomous functions and by the pain-pleasure sequences in the formation of symptoms. The examples also illustrate how analyzing the intrasystemic conflicts contributes to the therapeutic influence of the analysis on these patients.

A young man, Mr. A., came for analysis in late adolescence because of acute anxiety attacks, nausea, anorexia, abdominal cramps, and vomiting in connection with his fear of homosexual fantasies about a friend who was now far away and no longer part of his daily life. He had a lifelong history of intense anxiety and had suffered since childhood from many phobic and obsessional symptoms. He idealized his friend's athletic build and his prowess with women and compared his friend's physique with his own appearance, which he felt was weak and unattractive. He also compared his friend's freedom, boldness, and enjoyment with women with his own feeling that they were physically strange and repulsive, genitally mutilated, controlling, and demanding. He was angrily determined that he would not yield to their blandishments, and would not give them the sexual or other pleasures they seemed to demand. He suffered intense, conscious castration anxiety, fantasizing himself the victim of accidental or intentional castration many times a day, a fear that was aggravated by his having several times suffered intense testicular pain from a twisted spermatic cord.

His birth weight was above average, and he was described as a strong, healthy, mature infant by his family and physician. In infancy he had eczema, vomited excessivly, and was said to have cried incessantly and to have been very difficult to soothe and comfort. In A.'s first year his father was separated from the family because of his work. During this time, A. lived in a totally female household with mother, sisters, grandmother, and female helpers until the father reentered the family when he was about 2. The degree of stress in the mother-child relationship must have been severe because the mother openly and obviously suffered almost daily anxiety attacks and phobic and obsessional symptoms throughout the patient's life. Besides, her apprehen-

siveness must have been aggravated by the neonatal death of her
first child, followed by a subsequent stillbirth and several miscar-
riages before the birth of the patient. The nature of the infantile
illnesses indicates somatization as a major mode of organismic
response to the infant's experience of distress as a consequence
of the poor nurturance. The somatic illnesses abated at the age
of 1½ when a calm, level-headed nurse entered the household
and remained until A. was 7.

When the patient was in his third year, his mother, given the
choice between a family vacation and summer camp for the children, decided to send him and his older sisters to camp. From
that time on he never spent a summer with his family and left
home permanently in early adolescence. Nevertheless the ties to
his family remained close and strong. The mother was loving
and seductive as well as harsh and frightening, which his sisters
took as a license to tease and torment him. He resented his
father for not defending him against his mother and for not
showing an interest or pride in his son's achievements.

The patient was exposed to primal scene experiences
throughout his childhood. His mother insisted he use a bathroom at night that required him to go through the parents' bedroom, though there was another bathroom available. Into his
adult years his mother encouraged his presence when she was
dressing and undressing. One of the effects of his exposure to
the mother's nudity was that he developed the conviction that he
could be in her presence, look at her, and not see her body. He
utilized this long practice in denial and disavowal in his tendency
toward splitting of the ego and disruption of the autonomous
ego functions, which were such prominent features in the ease
with which he formed neurotic symptoms.

When the early somatic disturbances abated, he remained
with skin sensitivities, an easily upset gastrointestinal tract, rocking, head-banging, and vigorous head-shaking from side to side.
He was enuretic until the age of 10. The head-shaking continued
into adult life. He resorted to it in efforts to relieve tension,
anxiety, and obsessional states. With rocking and head-shaking
he could induce a state of absorption with his bodily sensations
and rhythms that ended in a calm, spent feeling which he
likened to the postorgastic state. In this manner he could bring

an end to an obsessional delirium. He had frequent anxiety attacks in connection with phobic symptoms in the phallic-oedipal period and early latency. Later in latency and in preadolescence obsessional symptoms became more prominent. Despite these severe neurotic difficulites he was able to perform academically at a very high level, and to establish and maintain close and loyal friendships with both men and women. Early in the analysis he was able to establish his potency with a woman. After that he avoided sexual contact for several years. Instead, he masturbated with fantasies of the sexual relationship his friend was having with a woman.

Throughout most of the analysis the defenses against passive-feminine strivings were prominent in the transference. Demonstration of strength and masculinity through resistance and opposition to the analyst was a point of pride. Being agreeable, attached, dependent, and trusting were shameful signs of weakness and exposed him again to the danger of abandonment. Although the analysis of current and infantile conflict was relevant and productive, the patient felt that the analysis had not greatly influenced his proneness to attacks of anxiety or his aversion to women, although he had established a close liaison with a woman he thought he would some day marry.

Contradictions and inconsistencies in the patient's ego functioning were strikingly evident. His anxious hyperalertness had contributed to his being a shrewd and sharp observer of people and the details of his surroundings. He prided himself on being able to know what people were thinking and feeling, what their motivations were, what their attitudes were toward him. I noticed how he was frequently inaccurate and incorrect in his observations about me and quite obviously in other situations as well. The convictions he developed were based on externalizations and projections of old and strongly held views of his own, while his judgment and self-monitoring were impaired by the strength of the beliefs which had their origins in his wishes and fantasies. I was also struck by how readily this highly educated and intelligent young man could delete or set aside his knowledge and replace it with old, infantile beliefs and misunderstandings, as, for example, his convictions about female anatomy or the intentions and behavior of women toward men. Also impressive was the feeling of helplessness before these myths and the power he accorded them in determining his actions or his inability to act. His passivity and helplessness before them were also in the service of his seeming determination to defeat me, even if it meant the sacrifice of his own goals in the analysis and in his life.

Close observation of the process of symptom formation revealed that a critical point in forming a symptom was the distortion, deletion, or illogical, irrational evaluation of elements of the external reality. During one examination period he became severely anxious and agitated, convinced that he had failed several examinations. He focused on one with special concern, feeling not only that he had failed, but that he would be accused of plagiarism for his use of an idea which he had first learned about from another student. Some meanings of the symptom could be understood. These examinations were the first test after he had made a career choice and had had some difficulty gaining admission to the school. He chose this examination for forming the symptom because the course dealt with an area of his father's interest and expertise, an area in which he had a total inhibition and inability to function even in an everyday practical fashion. It was a function he had completely abdicated and left to his father and sisters, who were experts. The accusation of plagiarism derived from his feelings of inadequacy and inferiority and his hostile desire to overcome them by stealing from someone who possessed what he desired and needed. I also focused on how he had put aside his judgment about the knowledge he had acquired in preparation for the examination and the content of what he had actually written on the examination. We also scrutinized the specific details of how he had used the plagiarized idea. It became clear that rather than plagiarizing, he had used the idea legitimately as part of his discussion of the question and that he was well aware of the distinction between these two uses. In fashioning a danger situation out of one which he knew was not actually dangerous, he was able to generate an anxiety state and control the intensification of it while the eventual relief was quite assured. Whenever the opportunity presented itself, I brought his attention to the way he managed these cognitive, judgmental, reality-testing functions, stressing the ways in which he substituted himself as the passive subject of the conditions he created rather than as the active deviser and initiator of the symptom. Eventually the patient referred to this as "working with a net." He also observed that "at certain points I send up a pinch hitter."

Another illustration is from the analysis of a woman, Ms. B., who came to analysis because of her long-standing severe anxiety attacks, phobic symptoms, and lifelong enuresis. She easily incurred the criticism and dislike of her mother but was the favorite of her father whom she resembled more than her siblings did in body build, appearance, and temperament. B. was the one selected by her father to be like a son to him, and she relished this special relationship. Along with this she bore the heavy burden of identification with the father's numerous severe neurotic symptoms (Ritvo and Solnit, 1958, 1960). In infancy and early childhood she had suffered repeated attacks of croup with upper respiratory infections. She remained sensitive to respiratory irritants and as an adult suffered from angioneurotic edema and eczema, usually in conjuction with anxiety attacks and increased aggression. Poor medical care had contributed to frightening experiences in the hospital in connection with an appendectomy in childhood, a tonsillectomy as an adult, and a Caesarean section necessitated by the failure of the cervix to dilate in a difficult labor. The childhood illnesses had been all the more frightening because of her mother's helplessness and panic in the face of illness or injury.

The patient's anxiety states and phobic symptoms were of two types and both implied a threat to life. One was concerned with fear of heart disease, cancer, or long-term complications of her abdominal surgery. The other was a fear of poisoning from injurious substances in her food, air, or water. The anxiety attacks and symptom formation continued even after many of their genetic roots in the past had been brought into consciousness or reconstructed, as well as their origins in the transference and in current conflicts with her husband and mother which aroused intense hostility and death wishes. I then began to focus on the anxiety and symptoms as current active creations rather than passive experiences visited on the patient, and to examine the changes in ego functioning which made it possible for the patient to create the symptom. The anxiety was intense as long as the dangerous environmental conditions contained unknown elements which she could exaggerate to frightening proportions. Because of her long history of sensitivity reactions in her respiratory tract, the patient was particularly alert to respiratory irritants and became aware of them more readily than the people around her. She also reacted excessively with anxiety, especially at a time when current conflicts in her life linked up with old conflicts of the same nature. At such points the generation of anxiety and the formation of symptoms had the advantage of avoiding recognition of her feelings toward husband and mother, which brought with them feelings of guilt and self-reproach as well as the danger of the loss and alienation of a needed object. The generation of the anxiety was also contingent upon the exact nature and extent of the danger being unknown to her, though it was possible for her to determine and eliminate it. In this way the patient was able to feel herself the threatened victim of an uncontrollable external danger which she could exaggerate to frightening proportions and had to avoid. However, she could generate anxiety and create the symptom only by temporarily putting aside the reality-testing, judgment, and problem-solving capacities of the ego selectively in those areas which impinged on the neurotic conflict and the formation of the symptom. This ensured that the patient potentially had control over the reduction of the anxiety and the attendant relief because of the knowledge that the danger could be determined and controlled. When this mode of anxiety generation and symptom formation was made conscious and worked through in its subtle variations, the patient was able to abate and control the anxiety attacks to a much greater degree than before.

In those persons with early intense anxiety who go on to become severely psychoneurotic, anxiety becomes part of their character, pervades nearly every aspect of their psychic life, and takes on intricate special functions in the psychic economy. The early experience of anxiety in connection with somatic illness results in a lasting disturbance of the body ego, i.e., of the psychic representation of the surface of the body and of the image of the body. These continue to be unusually intensely cathected into adult life. The ideational contents associated with them retain peculiarities related dynamically, usually defensively, to the experience of their infancy and early childhood. The image of the body is distorted, disfigured, mutilated, or defective. They are acutely alert to body functions, and their functional disturbances are many, suggesting sensitivity of the autonomic nervous system and highly practiced feedback mechanisms. The bodily habitus, configuration, and posture are all utilized to give form and expression to the image of the body and to the conflict- and anxiety-laden image of the self. Mr. A. maintained what he referred to as his "low profile," carrying himself in a stooped posture since childhood in order to avoid stimulating attack and danger of all sorts. As a child the strategy was fraught with both anxious and gratifying side effects because his mother took him from doctor to doctor, forced all manner of straightening appliances on him, and exhorted him constantly to stand up straight. Ms. B. used her combination of short stature, rotund habitus, and quick, agile motility to express bodily her jolly, bouncy, rubberball defense against the anxiety related to her castration fears and penis envy as well as her deeper fears of bodily disintegration and depression. This was only one of many uses of her body configuration and organ functions to give representation to her anxiety and neurotic conflicts.

These individuals have a deeply rooted narcissistic interest in and concern about their bodies. The body and its image may at one and the same time be a cause for anxiety and play a central role in the defense against the anxiety and the efforts to control it. Concern about the body plays an important role in the types of neurotic symptoms formed by them. They readily generate the conviction that they have heart disease or cancer, or have caused internal damage from swallowing foreign bodies or breathing noxious substances. Frequently the forbidden incestuous sexual and aggressive fantasies make their contribution to the symptom apparent by the patients' attributing the disease or bodily damage to contagion or to transmission through bodily contact in the manner of a venereal disease. All manifestations of castration anxiety assume an unusual intensity. This extends to the fear of the woman's body, which is reacted to with a strong aversion on two basic counts—because it arouses castration anxiety and because of the need to defend against the sadomasochistic fantasies.

The buildup of sexual excitement may be experienced as a threat to the integrity of the body and its boundaries, with images of falling apart, explosion, rupture of the skin, and running out of the body contents (a persistence of the passive outflow fantasies accompanying the earlier enuresis). These images, arousing intense anxiety, may accompany the first ejaculation or nocturnal emission and be a factor in suppressing masturbation in adolescence.

The body and its mode of representation in thought and fantasy can also have a role in the defense against the danger of being overwhelmed by intense anxiety. Mr. A. viewed his body as a strongbox. While he contained his thoughts and fears, he felt in control of them. In verbalizing them, he gained some mastery but at the same time lost some control of them. A similar aim of gaining mastery and allaying anxiety motivated his masturbation with homosexual fantasies. The decision to masturbate was made with the knowledge that it would bring a pleasurable relief of anxiety. His fantasies were about the attractive male physique, which was comforting and soothing. Someone so manly as to have that attractive physique must be able to master his fears. He fantasied that he himself would eventually acquire that attractive male body. Interestingly, these fantasies paralleled his experience with his parents. His mother was so nervous and fretful, she was unable to provide the assurance to calm his fears, whereas his father, whose body approached the ideal male physique, was calm, even, and steady.

These individuals live in an almost constant state of excitement and heightened tension in which the affect of anxiety is prominent. These states have an addictive and erotized quality. The patients pursue them and even feel strangely uncomfortable without them. These states are erotized in the sense that they are closely associated with sexual and aggressive fantasies and their abatement is sought and achieved through masturbation or bodily activities which have acquired a special relation to the regulation and discharge of tension. They are intimately connected with sexuality in a more general and subtle fashion via the manipulation of the pain-pleasure gradient and sequence inherent in the buildup and relief of anxiety. The activities tend to be rhythmic and repetitive, like head-banging and rocking. Mr. A. used head-banging and rocking from infancy as a way of regulating organismic states of arousal, tension, and anxious affect. Through the latency period an autoaggressive, masochistic quality was prominent in the banging. He banged his head against the wall or the bed until he bruised himself. It could also be soothing, gentle, and solacing. He resorted to it anytime he was anxious or worried about his parents' safety, his own health, schoolwork—anything that produced an unpleasant or painful affect. Rocking his head and body transported him into a different reality. It gave him a power to dispel unpleasant states like waving a magic wand.

The profuse anxiety manifestations have complex defensive relations to the external and internal world of the individual. The constant anticipation of danger contributes to the establishment and elaboration of hyperalertness to dangers emanating from the environment. This vigilant stance functions largely in the service of externalizing or projecting dangers arising from the internal world in the attempt to master the internal dangers by mastering or defending against the external ones which represent them. This feature plays a large role in symptom formation because it is always an external danger which is the apparent motivation for the symptom. The hyperalertness may also have adaptive value. Through a change of function it becomes part of a distant early warning system and is sometimes instrumental in the protection of life and limb, operating in a direction opposite to accident proneness. The anxious, hyperalert Mr. A. who anticipated a castrating attack every time he went out on the street once averted serious injury to himself and his companions by anticipating that a car coming toward them might jump the curb and come directly at them. The anxious, phobic Ms. B. with the childhood history of croup and angioneurotic edema became expert at detecting all manner of noxious fumes in her environment when nobody else was aware of them. She was the only one in her family who found pieces of wood, glass, and metal in a well-known national brand of ice cream, though they all ate it together.

The affect of anxiety, generated and perceived by the ego, also has specialized functions in the constant effort to regulate and defend against the threats and dangers arising from the internal environment in connection with sexual and aggressive fantasies. The so-called free-floating anxiety which is characteristic of individuals with high levels of anxiety is actually a complex structure with which the individual attempts to create a managed internal environment with a tolerable level of anxiety rather than feeling overwhelmed by anxiety of traumatic or panic proportions. The absence of a moderate level of perceived anxiety may be paradoxically experienced as a floating, falling, vulnerable, unguarded, passive-helpless state. The establishment of a constant level of manageable or tolerable anxiety or tension is described as having a channeling or organizing effect. It is associated with a temporary feeling of well-being, of being whole, of being "like a real person." It is a persistent, anachronistic attempt to erect a reliable stimulus barrier against the internal environment of the drives. In those individuals who early and over a long period of time experienced repeated breaching of the stimulus barrier, it is a manifestation of their organized effort to erect and maintain an effective and reliable barrier. If the tension can be kept as just an edge of excitement, the effect is pleasurable. If it is increased by a hostile, threatening, or challenging gesture from the outside, it becomes a distressing, anxious apprehension and results in a defensive reaction, often an angry or hostile outburst in an effort to restore or regain a sense of intactness.

The anxiety has rich connections with the pain-pleasure experiences of the individual. The anxiety of the chronic, free-floating, sustained type is so constructed as to ensure the pleasurable relief of tension and anxiety. This phase of the sequence is frequently transient and only fleetingly conscious. In some individuals the complex organization of the anxiety and relief is built into a diurnal rhythm. The anxiety is instituted on waking in the morning, is maintained steadily during the day with fleeting periods of relief associated with pleasure. There is a prolonged period of relief in the evening when the day's dangers, internal and external, have been survived, and there is finally a calm sense of security and safety in one's own room with the potential stimulation well controlled. These are often the night people who find it so difficult to relinquish this wakeful relative peace to go to sleep only to begin another anxious day the next morning.

Some of the long-term effects of the failure of the mothering person to provide reliable comforting and relief of tension can be recognized again in features of their object relations. They have a dread of relying on the object to provide relief of tension or pleasure, or of trusting in the possibility of experiencing mutual pleasure in the object relationship. Rather than being pleasurable, the sexual relationship is anticipated as dangerous, bringing fears of bodily damage and narcissistic injury. The sexual relationship is not experienced as a partnership or shared pleasure. It is predominantly self-centered. In the man, the orgasm and ejaculation in intercourse may be experienced as a loss, an irreversible ending, a depletion without prospect of restoration or renewal.

The object relationship as well as the indentification with a pathologically anxious parent are regularly powerful dynamic factors in the anxiety of these patients. Because of the shared experience of the anxiety and symptoms, these individuals have a large capacity for empathy and solicitude for the neurotic suffering of the parent. Ms. B. experienced a disturbance in her self image akin to depersonalization and had feelings of loss and mourning when her father had a remission of his severe phobic neurosis with depression which had incapacitated him for many years. Her reactions to his improvement were indicators of the extent to which the experience of her own neurosis constituted both an object tie and an identification with her father.

Reconstruction of the childhood experience of these patients points to complex causal connections between the qualities of nurturance in the mother-child relationship and the early somatic illness. This impression is corroborated by the observations of pediatricians and child developmentalists which are summarized in the following statement by Provence (1974):

> It is characteristic of the normally endowed infant in a pathogenic environment to react with disturbances in many aspects of development. Distortions of intellectual, social, and

emotional growth which characterize the badly nurtured infant have been amply documented. Moreover, because of poor nurturance he may also develop disorders of bodily function that involve any one or several organ systems. Disturbances of physical growth, of motility, of gastrointestinal and respiratory function and skin disorders are commonly encountered as reactions of poor nurturing. The particular set of reactions developed by such a normal infant will depend on many things, among them his biological makeup, the specific nature of the deprivation or trauma, and the phase of development in which adverse experiences occur [p. 160].

Since anxiety has such strong effects on the functioning of the ego in these patients as adults it is useful from the genetic point of view to examine the influence of anxiety on early ego development. Anxiety is regarded as an affect which is discharged into the body. In the mature person it is recognized as fear when it arises in connection with external danger. Ideally, the ego then institutes appropriate safety measures. When it arises in connection with internal dangers stemming from the instinctual drives, it normally operates as a signal function which activates the defensive capacities of the ego. With the return of the repressed and failure of the defenses, the ego is overwhelmed and the individual experiences involuntary, automatic anxiety. The level of effectiveness of the signal function and the quality and intensity of the involuntary automatic anxiety are characteristic for that person and are as difficult to change as the written signature. They have a long developmental history in the individual and are the resultant of complex interactions between endowment and nurturance which have the relation to one another of the factors in a complemental series.

Some of the endowment factors can be conceptualized as related very early in life to the effectiveness or threshold level of the stimulus barrier, to the innate rhythms of tension and discharge, which can be viewed as the balance between passivity and activity, and to the capacities for tolerating sustained tension states.

The experiential factors can be identified from the direct observation of infants and children and from reconstruction in the analysis of adults. Foremost among them is the effectiveness of the protective shield provided by the mother since the infant is relatively helpless before the stimuli which impinge upon him from both the external world and from his own body. In this sense the parent functions as an auxiliary ego for the child. Meeting these needs of the infant in a timely, effective, consistent manner is an important feature of Winnicott's "good enough" mothering, a concept which carries with it the implication that if the mother meets the child's needs to a reasonable degree, the child is able to adapt within limits to the individual qualities of the mothering. However, when the infant develops in the setting of a profoundly disturbed mother-child relationship, he or she suffers from deficits and distortions of the protective, stimulating, and organizing aspects of parental care. Since the parent serves as an auxiliary ego for a young child, a profound disturbance of the mother-child relationship can be understood as a failure of the auxiliary ego (Ferholt and Provence, 1976).

One of the effects of this failure is that the infant, who early on cannot be active to either internal or external stress, is unable to achieve gratifying discharge of tension without the aid or intervention of the parental auxiliary ego. With the poor nurturance of a disturbed mother-child relationship the infant endures, frequently and for extended periods of time, peaks of painful, unrelieved tension in connection with bodily functions (eating, sleeping, elimination). These are the pivotal experiences of anxiety which later are organized around phase-specific danger situations.

The illnesses which were frequent in the infancy and childhood of the patients I am referring to can be viewed as the consequence of the noxious effect of the environment in terms of mothering and object relations on an infant with specific vulnerabilities. For example, in Spitz's (1965) study of infantile eczema, the mothers had an infantile personality and betrayed hostility disguised as anxiety toward the child. They did not like to touch the child or care for him and deprived the child systematically of cutaneous contact. The child had a congenital predisposition for increased cutaneous responses, leading to increased cathexis of the psychic representation of cutaneous responses. Curiously, infantile eczema is a self-limited condition. A spontaneous cure usually occurs after the end of the first year when the child is no longer so passive and has progressed to directed activity. Then he is no longer so dependent on the contacts with mother. The respiratory and gastrointestinal disorders also bring with them repeated distress which exceeds the capacity of the adult to provide a protective shield adequate to forestall the traumatic effect.

Excessive anxiety in the context of poor nurturance can adversely affect the development and functioning of the ego. Toward the end of the first year, infants who have been in mother-child relationships with poor nurturance but with no evidence of organic deficits manifest behavior in the developmental testing situation which can be interpreted as indicative of delay or disturbance in the development of autonomous ego functioning. For example, they may have quantitative delays in specific areas but not across the board as in mental retardation. Some may show good competence in gross motor skills but not be able to use the skills to avoid something unpleasant, move away from danger, or move toward something gratifying. The competencies are not used in adaptation to daily life or to master anxiety as they are by a normal child. If the child meets with an obstacle, he may be severely frustrated or disappointed but does not use the functions which are developmentally available to him to reduce the anxiety (Provence, 1980).

One can draw a parallel between such a failure to respond appropriately to the perception of an external danger and the later failure of the neurotic prone to anxiety attacks to use anxiety effectively as a signal of danger from the drive derivatives. In each case the ego fails to employ capacities and functions available to it and responds instead in a fashion which indicates an intrasystemic antagonistic relationship between structuralized elements within the ego itself in which the ego does not make adaptive use of available functions.

The capacity to use anxiety effectively as a signal also has developmental roots in the mother-child relationship. Tolpin (1971) studied the developmental line of signal anxiety and traced hypothetically the intrapsychic steps by which the infant establishes the critical initial stages of what eventually becomes the structuralized signal function. She thought this occurred via the appropriately timed and consistent rescue by the mother at times of heightened tension and automatic anxiety. Tolpin starts, as did Freud (1926), with the assumption that the capacity of the infant to give the signal of anxiety is an autonomous given. This given, however, is guaranteed structuralization and effective operation only when the mother consistently and effectively carries out her role of anxiety reduction in response to the signal of distress from the child.

I would emphasize, however, that structualization does not insure effective operation. Features of the psychic organization may be elaborately structuralized but operationally ineffective or maladaptive. Indeed, as I have tried to show in the group of patients studied, the so-called automatic, involuntary anxiety becomes part of a highly structuralized subsystem in the ego with numerous connections to the instinctual and affective life of the patient as well as connections with defensive and autonomous functions of the ego. The anxiety attack and the prolonged anxiety state become parts of a complex, structuralized, affecto-motor, tension-discharge pattern generated and maintained by the ego for its own motivations.

Greenacre (1967) has drawn attention to the relationship between early trauma, high levels of tension and anxiety, and the qualities and intensities of aggression in the individual. Frequent experiences of prolonged frustration, tension, and anxiety with the object without adequate discharge have the effect of stimulating and intensifying the pain and aggression components in the pain-pleasure amalgam which is the nucleus of all satisfaction. One effect is to skew the pregenital psychosexual phases in the direction of their sadomasochistic content and to exert an influence toward fixation on the sadomasochistic aspects of pregenital sexuality. When this type of pain-pleasure amalgam meets with the fantasies and ideational content of the anal-sadistic phase and the separation-individuation process, one consequence is a markedly sadomasochistic organization of the personality. This becomes a central feature of the object relations in such individuals and sets the conditions and limitations of pleasure in their sexuality, casting it strongly in a polymorphous-perverse pattern.

Since we know that some of these developmental disturbances are reversible and that others, though not fully reversible, do not go on to psychopathology, what are the factors which influence the outcome? First, early experiences are more likely than later ones to have an effect similar to endowment or constitutional factors (Greenacre, 1967). This effect may operate in a manner analogous to the epigenetic principle in embryology which says that an injury or noxious influence at an early critical point in the development of an organ system has a greater effect on its subsequent development than an insult occurring when the organ system is more highly organized and structured. In this sense, the earlier the trauma, the more vulnerable the infant might be to subsequent potentially traumatic experiences. The poorly nurtured infants described earlier who were not able to integrate functions which were maturationally ready into their adaptive capabilities can be viewed as failing to make an integration at a vulnerable nodal point. This failure may then leave a permanent vulnerable structure in an alteration of the ego.

Focusing on the identifiable dramatic events tends to obscure those experiences which have a strain effect over a long period of time. This cumulative trauma or strain (Khan, 1963; Kris, 1956) may have a major source in the character and personality of the parents. Even though an early experience of traumatic potential may produce its effect partly because the parenting was not "good enough" in that situation, a persisting neurotic conflict, personality feature, or character trait of the parent may produce a repeated or continuing effect which tends to organize, structuralize, and elaborate the original responses to the trauma and contribute to the deformation of the ego.

A parental personality feature or character trait which has a repetitive or cumulative traumatic effect may in actuality have a double impact. As a feature of the child's experience it may exert an external traumatic effect and, through internalization and identification with the parent, it may be a continuing or interminable internal source of the same. The effectiveness of the mothering for satisfactory progress in development may improve when the child has left a developmental phase which is especially conflict-laden for the mother, eliciting hostility, aversion, or neglect. A later stage may be more gratifying to the mother and may not impinge as strongly upon her own neurotic conflicts (Coleman et al., 1953; Kris, 1962).

One of the striking features of the psychoneurotics with severe anxiety and numerous symptoms is their extreme feeling of helplessness and passivity toward their neurosis. This is in keeping with the general observation that the ego can be active and effective in recognizing and coping with problems and conflicts arising in the external world, while it remains passive, helpless, and easily overwhelmed in relation to the inner world of the drive derivatives. The same individual who may be capable of remarkable feats of organization and mastery in the external world may view himself as the passive, helpless victim of involuntary neurotic anxiety and symptoms, or may endure repeated suffering and self-damage from behavior determined by neurotic conflict, even though they are his own creation and are in the end preconsciously or consciously constructed.

The universal tendency toward alienation from the inner world, lack of responsibility for it, and helplessness and passivity toward it have a long developmental history. (In the psychoanalytic situation this tendency becomes a major source of resistance and one source of the negative therapeutic reaction.) From early infancy anxiety has close connections to the issue of activity and passivity. In the process of differentiating himself from the external world, the infant begins to be active to what is external but cannot be active to much of what is internal. This was one of the considerations which led Rapaport (1953) to propose his dual model of passivity and activity in which the passivity is viewed as the helpless-passive experience of tension and the passive-gratifying tension discharge. Activity is seen on the one hand as the defense against or the control of drive tension, which does away with passive helplessness in the face of drive demands, and on the other hand as the discharge of tension under the control of ego apparatuses by detour processes aiming to find the drive objects in reality. When the nature of the parenting is such that the child experiences frequent peaks of helpless-passive tension with insufficient or inept provision of opportunities for reliable and predictable relief or discharge of tension, the conditions are present for a developmental imbalance toward passivity and vulnerability to anxiety. The helpless-passive tension without relief is the anxiety attack of the infant. Again, research and clinical experience with infants and young children have made it possible to identify those children whom poor nurturance has left retarded in some areas of their development and whose future development is at risk because they are overbalanced toward passivity and are unable to muster sufficient activity for adequate coping and defense (Provence, 1974). Provence (1966) described a case in which infant observation, child analysis in the oedipal period, and follow-up at the age of 14 indicated that despite the mother's difficulty in meeting the child's need for comforting and relief of tension, the psychopathology predicted did not materialize because the child was able to maintain sufficient activity to institute adequate coping and defense measures.

With the profusion of anxiety and symptoms, old and new, the patients I am describing repeatedly re-create the neurosis in the course of the analysis. The symptomatic neurosis is re-created as a compromise formation when there is a confluence of the infantile conflicts with current conflicts which stimulate or reawaken the drives and their derivatives. Because the anxiety and symptoms overwhelm and paralyze the ego's function of self-observation, the analyst welcomes any opportunity to restore the functional capacity of the ego by analytic means, that is, without resorting to influence by authoritative reassurance or suggestion. One approach to this task is to focus analytic listening and attention on what takes place within the ego in the process of symptom formation. This means focusing on the intrasystemic conflicts and their effects on the functioning of the ego. For example, the ego is required to find a compromise solution between its relations with the external world, which requires the intactness of autonomous functions such as reality testing, cognition, and judgment, and its relations with the inner world of the drives which draw the ego in the direction of primary process functioning. The compromise arrived at with the formation of the symptom involves an infringement of these functions, especially where the reality has points of association with an old neurotic conflict which is currently revived, frequently in the transference. Then, by means of primary process mechanisms like condensation, displacement, and projection, the internal psychic reality is combined with the distorted external reality to make a seeming whole which passes the impaired ego's scrutiny with the aid of the overworked synthetic function. In this way the patient creates a split in the ego so that he lives in two realities side by side, with no apparent need to reconcile the logical and rational incongruities.

Anxiety and symptom formation have a complex relationship to the pain-pleasure amalgam and sequences in the individual. The pain components are very loudly in evidence in the dreadful, anxious affect and the images of illness, mutilation, suffering, and death which accompany them. When the superego has a major role in the neurotic conflict, feelings of guilt, the anticipation of shame and humiliation, and loss of love, of position, and of respect may be the chief sources of pain.

Besides the pleasure in the compromise gratification of the repressed instinctual wish in the symptom itself, some degree of pleasure is connected with the covert, erotized, passive homosexual fantasies in the male and the masochistic fantasies in the female. Another source of pleasure gain in the anxiety attack and the formation of the symptom is related to the split in the ego and the impairment of its autonomous functions which the patient carries out preconsciously. The preconscious motivation for instituting the split is to create a danger which serves as the necessary approximate substitute for the original danger. At the same time the patient knows that in actuality it is a false danger. Thereby, the pleasure gain connected with the eventual relief of the painful anxiety is assured. In a period of prolonged, intense anxiety, the pleasurable relief is usually brief and transient and frequently not in conscious awareness. It is immediately followed by another attack of anxiety, so that the ego is even less likely to perceive the motivation of gaining the assured relief.

I now turn to consider the implications of the impairment of ego functioning for technique. Communicating to the patient an awareness of how he or she selectively impairs autonomous ego functions in order to generate peaks of anxiety and form symptoms facilitates some shifts in the patient's psychic economy. The shifts occur mainly intrasystemically. With effective self-observation and reduction of antagonistic relations within the ego, the ego is less severely disrupted in dealing with drive derivatives. One effect is a greater feeling of self-control in the face of anxiety and neurotic symptoms. Anxiety begins to function more as a signal and not so overwhelmingly as a generated affect for which the patient feels no responsibility. One consequence is an enhanced feeling of self-control. Mr. A. described how he enjoyed the mastery of the anxiety. He likened it to the childhood experience of acquiring and using a skill. With the improved capacity for self-observation the patient can have a greater awareness of his defensive aims to defeat the analyst by falling back upon the insuperable tyrannical power of his anxiety and symptoms. With the reduction of the intensity of this resistance the patient may further work through conflicts which had already been under analytic scrutiny. Symptomatic behavior, previously regarded as outside the patient's control, can be recognized and experienced as having conscious or preconscious motivations. The employment of defenses which are more ego-syntonic is accompanied by a welcome feeling of being less vulnerable. The recognition of a larger role for personal motivation and the acceptance of an increasing share of responsibility for features of psychic life which are usually experienced passively are some of the accruements of a better intrasystemic integration of the ego.

This approach to technique is consonant with the effort which analysts have made since the introduction of structural concepts and ego psychology to integrate them with technique. Freud (1937) thought that the results of therapy depended on the thoroughness with which the replacement of repressions by reliable ego-syntonic controls was achieved. Hartmann (1951), stressing the continuing need to integrate theory and technique, expressed the view that with the introduction of ego psychology, unlike in other periods in the history of psychoanalysis, technique was lagging behind theory. He thought that technical progress might depend on a more systematic study of the various functional units within the ego. He pointed to the need for more detailed study of the intrasystemic correlations within the ego, e.g., the relation between the nonconflictual sphere and units of functioning within the ego that represent the countercathexes, the dealings with reality, the preconscious automatized patterns, or "that special functional control and integration that we know under the name of synthetic or better, organizing function"

(p. 145). He called for consistent scrutiny of intrasystemic synergistic and antagonistic relations and for differential consideration of various functions of the ego.

Gray (1981) also draws attention to what he calls the "developmental lag" in the evolution of technique for the analysis of neurotic conflict. He attributes the lag to the resistance analysts experience in fully assimilating and applying information that has been acquired about the importance of the ego in the therapeutic effectiveness of the psychoanalytic method. Gray even raises the question whether the lag is due to a biological limitation in the ego's capacity to perceive itself, rather than to a potentially resolvable resistance born out of intrapsychic conflict. Though he leans toward the latter, more optimistic view, Gray comes to the evocative conclusion that most of the obstacles the analyst encounters to making observations about the ego's defensive activity occur because of the gains to the *analyst* in not making them—gains ranging from libidinal satisfaction to relief from the analyst's own conflicts.

Loewenstein (1972), examining the concept of ego autonomy in relation to psychoanalytic technique, pointed out that the autonomous ego of the patient is the specific medium through which we observe the ego, id, and superego in the psychoanalytic situation and that the requirement of the basic rule accentuates the conflict between autonomous functions and defensive functions of the ego. Sterba (1934) dealt with the same issues in somewhat different terms in speaking of the therapeutic dissociation which is the fate of the ego in psychoanalysis and of the processes of dissimilation and assimilation in the ego which occur in analysis. The autonomous functions are the tools of the study of conflict in man, and these tools themselves become objects of the analyst's interest. Loewenstein observed that though the intrasystemic conflicts do not involve the same forces as the intersystemic conflicts, one can assume that the conflicts within the ego acquire a certain import or intensity.

If the analytic situation depends on the intactness of the autonomous functions of the ego, then it is steadily threatened or opposed by the process of splitting in the ego which is constantly operative, serves primarily a defensive function (Freud, 1938), and is a consequence of intrasystemic conflict. As Jeffrey Lustman (1977) summarized it in his study on splitting, Freud viewed splitting as a process which occurred in the ego, served the dominant purpose of defense, and resulted in behavior which could only be understood if one assumed the creation of separate, contradictory groups of mental representations within the psychic apparatus. Though Freud spoke explicitly of the process of splitting only in his unfinished 1938 paper, Lustman recognized an earlier statement of the idea in *The Ego and the Id* (1923), when Freud in effect spoke of splitting or disruption of the ego as a result of the different object identifications of the ego becoming cut off from one another by resistances. This effect was particularly evident in the cases I described.

Hartmann (1950) and Loewenstein (1956) pointed out that the defenses, acting independently, may result in an intrasystemic conflict between the defenses and the other functions of the ego which may disrupt autonomous functions of the ego such as thinking. Weiss (1967) proposed the view that during analysis the unconscious defenses are brought under the control of the conscious ego and thereby transformed from unconscious defense mechanisms to ego-syntonic control mechanisms and integrated into the ego, thus obviating the instigation of the intrasystemic conflict. Such an integration of unconscious defenses into the ego is the obverse of the tendency to splitting.

In summary, I have described a group of severe, chronic psychoneurotic patients with excessive anxiety and a profusion of symptoms. Anxiety has pervaded their character and the signal function is inadequately developed. Their vulnerabilities facilitate the formation of symptoms because of the relative ease with which autonomous functions of the ego can be selectively impaired. In addition to their roots in old and new conflicts, anxiety generation and symptom formation are psychic processes by which the individual can intensify psychic pain with the assurance of pleasurable relief in a continual struggle to master the ego's dread of being overwhelmed by traumatic anxiety. Analysis in these situations requires no modification of technique, but emphasizes the necessity of analyzing the intrasystemic antagonisms and conflicts in the ego with the aim of enhancing the autonomy of those functions which are the analyst's necessary allies in any analysis.

BIBLIOGRAPHY

COLEMAN, R. W., KRIS, E., & PROVENCE, S. (1953), The study of variations of early parental attitudes. *Psychoanal. Study Child*, 8:20–46.

FERHOLT, J. & PROVENCE, S. (1976), Diagnosis and treatment of an infant with psychophysiological vomiting. *Psychoanal. Study Child*, 31:439–459.

FREUD, A. (1965), Normality and pathology in childhood. *W.*, 6.

FREUD, S. (1923), The ego and the id. *S.E.*, 19:12–66.

―――― (1926), Inhibitions, symptoms, and anxiety. *S.E.*, 20:87–174.

―――― (1937), Analysis terminable and interminable. *S.E.*, 23:216–253.

―――― (1938), Splitting of the ego in the process of defence. *S.E.*, 23:275–278.

GRAY, P. (1981), "Developmental lag" in the evolution of technique for psychoanalysis of neurotic conflict. *J. Amer. Psychoanal. Assn.* (in press).

GREENACRE, P. (1941), The predisposition to anxiety. In: *Trauma, Growth and Personality*. New York: Norton, 1952, pp. 27–82.

―――― (1967), The influence of infantile trauma on genetic patterns. In: *Psychic Trauma*, ed. S. S. Furst. New York: Basic Books, pp. 108–153.

―――― (1971), *Emotional Growth*, 2 vols. New York: Int. Univ. Press.

HARTMANN, H. (1950), Comments on the psychoanalytic theory of the ego. *Psychoanal. Study Child*, 5:74–96.

―――― (1951), Technical implications of ego psychology. In: *Essays on Ego Psychology*. New York: Int. Univ. Press, 1964, pp. 142–154.

KHAN, M. M. R. (1963), The concept of cumulative trauma. *Psychoanal. Study Child*, 18:286–306.

KRIS, E. (1956), The recovery of childhood memories in psychoanalysis. *Psychoanal. Study Child*, 11:54–88.

―――― (1962), Decline and recovery in the life of a three-year-old. *Psychoanal. Study Child*, 17:175–215.

LOEWENSTEIN, R. M. (1956), Some remarks on the role of speech in psychoanalytic technique. *Int. J. Psychoanal.*, 37:460–468.

―――― (1972), Ego autonomy and psychoanalytic technique. *Psychoanal. Quart.*, 41:1–22.

LUSTMAN, J. (1977), On splitting. *Psychoanal. Study Child*, 32:119–154.

PROVENCE, S. (1966), Some aspects of early ego development. In: *Psychoanalysis—A General Psychology*, ed. R. M. Loewenstein, L. M. Newman, M. Schur, & A. J. Solnit. New York: Int. Univ. Press, 1966, pp. 107–122.

―――― (1974), Some relationships between activity and vulnerability in the early years. In: *The Child in His Family*, ed. E. J. Anthony & C. Koupernik. New York: Wiley, 3:157–166.

―――― (1980), Personal communication.

RAPAPORT, D. (1953), Some metapsychological considerations concerning activity and passivity. In: *Collected Papers*, ed. M. M. Gill. New York: Basic Books, 1967, pp. 530–568.

RITVO, S. & SOLNIT, A. J. (1958), Influences of early mother-child interaction on identification processes. *Psychoanal. Study Child*, 13:64–85.

―――― ―――― (1960), The relationship of early ego identifications to superego development. *Int. J. Psychoanal.*, 41:295–300.

SPITZ, R. A. (1965), *The First Year of Life*. New York: Int. Univ. Press.

SPRINCE, M. P. (1962), The development of a preoedipal partnership between an adolescent girl and her mother. *Psychoanal. Study Child*, 17:418–424.

STERBA, R. (1934), The fate of the ego in analytic therapy. *Int. J. Psychoanal.*, 15:117–126.

TOLPIN, M. (1971), On the beginnings of a cohesive self. *Psychoanal. Study Child*, 26:316–371.

WEISS, J. (1967), The integration of defences. *Int. J. Psychoanal.*, 48:520–524.

WINNICOTT, D. W. (1965), *The Maturational Processes and the Facilitating Environment*. New York: Int. Univ. Press.

Balance and Anxiety

ISIDOR SILBERMANN, M.D., F.A.C.P.

THE MIND AS A FUNCTIONAL SYSTEM, BEING CLOSELY LINKED TO THE body by the mental representations of our perceptions and experiences from within and without, is in perpetual flux. The multiple functions of the mind are powered by the drives, whose energies, as far as the mind is concerned, take shape as interrelated forces, thoughts, and affects. Freud's concept of a stimulus barrier, a protective shield against onrushing stimuli, is a *sine qua non* for our understanding of the functions of the mind. Freud (1950) assumed that the efforts of the psychic apparatus were, above all, directed toward keeping itself free, as far as possible, from stimuli, but that these efforts toward the maintenance of inertia were interfered with by the exigencies of life. Inertia he thought to be the primary function of the neurosystem.

In a dynamic system, however, where ceaselessly active forces create shifts and perpetual motions, absolute rest or permanent standstill cannot exist. The ruling principle in a dynamic system is "permanence of balance." It is the task of balance to harmonize opposing functions, to maintain them in a relatively stable relationship, and to keep their activities in equipoise. Balance is always of a temporary nature, precarious and labile; it is established, jarred, disrupted, and reestablished. Any grave disturbance of this function may have serious consequences. Pathology generally appears when the effort to re-create dynamic balance fails (Silbermann, 1961).

Equilibration is an inborn attribute, originally a function of the ego nucleus. It is not identical with constancy or stability. With maturation and development, the achievement and main-

---

Faculty, New York Psychoanalytic Institute.

tenance of equilibrium become a task of the ego, whose propitious growth and strength guarantee its appropriate functioning.

Man's deep-seated striving for balance shows its force far beyond his transitional sphere (Silbermann, 1979). He strives not only for equilibrium between body and mind, between his past and present, between fantasy and reality, between the unconscious and the conscious, but also between man and man, man and nature, man and God.

Balance has been extolled as the goal which man should seek by Lao-tzu, the Prophets, Pythagoras, Socrates, Plato, Aristotle, and many others. The Taoists symbolized the balance between active and passive, between female and male, etc., in their representation of the Yang and Yin as a circle divided *not* by a straight line but by a swinging moving line which creates two symmetrical parts in total equilibrium.

For both Freud and Spinoza, balance was necessary for health and contentment. Both suggested how balance could be achieved, how its fragmentation could be muted, how emotions could be harmonized with thoughts, and how man could make his unconscious and his conscious mind partners. Spinoza (1677) said that "balance and harmony exist in man only as long as he functions in accordance with Nature's unchanging laws. During the course of development, this harmony might become disturbed so that man is no longer able to grasp his own motivations and comprehend his wishes and fears" (p. 188). It was Spinoza's belief that development is resisted by the tendency to maintain previous conditions unchanged, which, if altered, will attempt to reestablish previous energy distribution (III, propos. 6–8).

Since maturation and development proceed in stages, it can be assumed that advancement from one phase to the next comes about by quantitative and qualitative changes in the distribution of energy. Whenever large quantities of exciting stimuli accumulate, the existing state of equilibrium is agitated and must give way to a new balance level, for which appropriate adjustments must be made.

Freud's discoveries concerning the structure and dynamic functions of the mind not only have given great impetus to psychiatrists, philosophers, and artists, but they have also inspired and encouraged many scientists to look with new vision at their fields of endeavor. On the other hand, I wonder whether the knowledge acquired by modern physicists might somehow assist us to develop additional new approaches to our own field of research, the mind. I find it of great interest, for instance, that the subatomic world and the mind share one essential common feature, i.e., there is never *total* rest in either; and in both, balances are always and continuously disrupted and reestablished.

In his remarkable book, *The Dancing Wu Li Masters,* Gary Zukav writes (1979): "The simple laws of conservation are derived from what physicists now believe to be the ultimate principles governing the physical world. They are the laws of symmetry." In the subatomic world there is never rest, "the particles do not just sit around, they are beehives of activity" (p. 240); there are constant interactions, disappearances, and re-creations of particles, collisions which may result in new configurations. The electrons, when exposed to increased energy, accelerate their wavelike motions and thus are thrown out of their ground state into the outer shells from which, however, they return to their home base when the energy supply subsides. During those trips they collide, explode, and also discharge the increased energy in the form of *visible* photons. This power play enables us to perceive what was "invisible" as a "visible" manifestation (p. 242).

The ego, too, is incessantly excited by stimuli from different sources—from the mind itself, the body, and the outside world.

These stimuli create shifts in energy distribution. Existing balances are disturbed and must be reestablished. As indicators of these cathectic shifts we experience affects (Spitz, 1965). Affect, then, is the experience of a balance variation, of the disturbance and the reestablishment of equilibrium.

Spinoza defined affects as "the modification of the body, whereby the *active power* of the said body is increased or diminished, aided or constrained, and also the *ideas* of such modifications" (p. 130; my italics). Of emotion he says: "Emotion is a confused idea, by the presence of which the mind is compelled to think of one thing rather than another" (p. 185).

For Freud (1950), the "wish" is an internal need, seeking discharge in movements that may be described as "internal change" or "expressions of emotion." Freud ascribes primacy in mental life to the affective processes. The core of an affect is the repetition of some significant experience; the affective state has become incorporated in the mind as the precipitate of a reminiscence. In 1894, Freud said that if someone with a disposition to neurosis attempts "to fend off an incompatible idea, he sets about separating it from its affect, then *that affect is obliged to remain in the psychical sphere*. The idea, now weakened, is still left in consciousness, separated from all association" (p. 51f.).

Following Novey's suggestion (1959), one might consider a developmental scale starting with the experiences of the newborn, its perceptions of tension increases and tension reductions, its inability adequately to regulate the resulting balance disturbance of the mind or to handle properly the overflow into physical manifestations. When the child advances in his development and maturation, when consciousness grows and thought and speech have ripened, only then can the experience of cathectic shifts or the affects become conscious experiences and be called "emotions" or "feelings."

In his undifferentiated state, up to the eighth month, the newborn, unable with his immature ego to experience feelings consciously, cannot by definition experience the emotions of pleasure or displeasure in the true sense of these words. However, the newborn reacts to tension increases or reductions with cerebral reflexes, in order to discharge the overload. Thus, the newborn has "affects" but not "emotions" or "feelings." Freud and many others asked if emotions can be unconscious. That question may be answered as follows: "Feelings" or "emotions" are connected with an idea and ordinarily are conscious; affects in their crudest form, as yet unconnected with thoughts, ordinarily are unconscious.

With regard to the factors that disturb balance, the following essential categories can schematically be distinguished:

1. Minor, incessant, wavelike shifts in mind and body within certain determined limits. I refer particularly to the shifts of balance due to the continous influx of stimuli through the sensory organs; from transitional spheres; from chemical and physiological changes; from various functional activities within the mind; from id, ego, and superego; from thoughts and emotions; from memories and suppressed thoughts; from the mind's self-fertilization with ideas; from transformed, tamed, and untamed drives.

All these processes in their daily course are developed and more or less regulated without stormy upheavals. They are mostly mute and cause relatively minor disturbances of equilibrium. Their mental representations are of a subliminal nature. However, if even these minor vacillations occasionally overstep their limits, the ego will set the pleasure-unpleasure mechanism in motion (Freud, 1926). *It will experience a warning in the form of mild anxiety.* As to the intensity of the anxiety, Freud asserts that there is undoubtedly a correspondence between the strength of the impulse and the intensity of the resulting anxiety.

2. Besides these uninterrupted, normal, functional shifts of balance, there are processes which gather momentum until a certain quantity is reached, thus forcing a *total* change of status and an alteration of the existing equilibrium. I refer to the stages of normal maturation and development which create not minor but *major* shifts, major perturbations of balance. These shifts, via their mental representations, are experienced by the ego as consciously disturbing emotions, as "feelings of anxiety."

3. Seemingly long-lasting high waves, *either in mind or body,* sensed as a constant onrush of stimuli which, via their mental representations, keep the ego's balance in continuous turmoil, are experienced by the ego as "pathological anxiety."

The second anxiety state may be called "threshold anxiety."

These threshold anxieties, in contrast to the third type or pathological anxieties, are of a temporary nature and are in a relatively short time replaced by feelings of well-being resulting from the experience of successful adaptation to a new level of equilibrium.

The advance to higher developmental stages can be hampered by many factors such as a defective ego nucleus, deficient mental transitional spheres, faulty ego development, a conflict-ridden, traumatized ego, a tendency to increased fragmentation, massive resistances, fixations, regressions.

A defective, immature, or conflict-laden ego seems to exhibit the tendency to retreat, to regress. Such an ego does not advance in the face of difficulties at a time when it anxiously anticipates emotional confusion resulting from the disruption of equilibrium. However, in regression, the forces pitted against each other remain restive and in conflict. Instead of new solutions and appropriate balances, the ego falls back on inappropriate and obsolete forms of equilibrium. Regression restrains the mind's expansion, deprives it of proper perspectives, and prevents the differentiation between the real and the imagined, the past and the present. Instead of embracing new challenges, a regressed mind roams around in the cobwebs and stale air of its own past.

Whereas the first and the continuous normal balance changes and balance restorations require energy within easily available limits, the second or threshold changes need larger amounts of mental energy to cross the thresholds and create a new equilibrium and new adaptations. The third category will require even greater amounts of ego energy to reestablish and, even if only for relatively short periods, to secure a balance. The ego, extremely labile, becomes too easily disrupted by frequent and rapid waves of stimuli. So enormous a demand on the ego leaves it and its defenses sapped of energy.

Freud (1926) said that in a concentration of cathexes on the psychic representations, the continuous nature of the cathectic process may produce a state of mental helplessness. He described anxiety as "the economic disturbance caused by an accumulation of amounts of stimulation which require to be disposed of. It is this factor, then, which is the real essence of 'danger'" (p. 137).

In these massive anxieties which betray violent experiences in the ego, the patient not only anticipates but actually experiences loss, e.g., of balance and strength. Thus, these anxieties are a combination of expectations of danger or trauma and an experience of a new loss. Such a state, as may be expected, will easily become the playground for the repetition of traumas. In addition, clinical observations have shown that the anticipation of danger and a replay of a trauma in severely affected patients are experienced *not* only as "pure anxieties" but also as anxieties mixed with depressive features.

The child after leaving his mother's womb, his muted environment, for a world filled with stimuli from everywhere must learn to adjust, step by step, to inner and outer conditions and changes. He must accept increasing inner tensions and frustrations previously unknown to him. Through his maturation and development, and through all the phases of childhood, adolescence, and maturity, he must keep his equilibrium between wishes and reality, between id strivings and demands of the ego and superego, without being disturbed by the accompanying balance shifts or by the connected experiences of brief anxieties.

Greenacre (1941) postulates that severe frustrations in the prenatal and early postnatal months leave an organic stamp on the makeup of the child: a genuine physiological sensitivity that heightens the *anxiety potential* and gives greater intensity to the anxieties of later life. Moreover, childhood traumatization or faulty ego anlage and ego development may add weight to the earliest agitating life experiences. In such cases minor and mostly well-tolerated anxieties may at any time grow beyond the acceptable; and the events encountered during growth may revive early traumas. For instance, while most women face their menarche and menstruations, pregnancy, and menopause without a sense of danger, some show disturbing neurotic or even psychotic symptoms (Silbermann, 1950).

All such events, enormous in their gravity, cannot be handled without a balance function, which makes it possible for the ego to utilize its defense functions and to discharge its mounting tensions in a way to permit the equilibrium to shift to and fro without being thrown out of gear. Without such well-equipped equilibration, man would fail; he could not reestablish his equipoise. The balance principle, its mechanism, is at its best when the ego is mature and strong, when it is not shaken by inner conflicts. Moreover, this vital function often shows signs of aging as the individual ages, or as he fails to achieve adaptation to the tasks of his later years.

From those who are able to express their feelings in words and gestures, we can learn how they experienced their sudden awareness of major balance disturbance in mind and/or body. They might describe the *beginning* of awareness in approximately these or similar terms: "I feel something strange, disturbing, bewildering. I feel somewhat confused, restless, and distressed. I don't know what it is, what is going on." Their faces often show perplexity and tension. At these brief moments when the awareness of something strange is not yet clearly formulated, there seems to be only an incipient feeling of anxiety, or "anxiety in *statu nascendi.*" Very quickly, however, out of the reservoir of hidden memories, thoughts emerge, attach themselves to the affects, creating a new combination of a still crude, vague affect and idea. By this connection—Brenner (1953) also mentioned that emotions are combined with thoughts—an affect advances from its crude to its transformed state of conscious "emotion" or "feeling." Accordingly, *affects* can be unconscious; however, *emotions or feelings,* through their linkage with ideas or conscious thoughts, are conscious experiences.

The mature ego can be expected to handle even somewhat graver shifts of balance appropriately. People with adequate ego strength, well-functioning mental transitional spheres, and ego functions without serious conflicts and impediments will not pathologically defend themselves against incoming stimuli. They will keep their minds open and receptive. Such an ego is not alarmed by slight tension increases; it does not feel threatened or endangered. It receives stimuli with a heightened expectation. Its longing for release of tensions, i.e., for pleasure, becomes the impetus for constructive and creative activities. An increase of tension is essential for creativity. Without it the artist and the scientist would be stifled and immobilized.

In contrast to those who dare to face the onrush of stimuli are those who feel intimidated and threatened by even small amounts of increased tensions, who usually call on inappropriate defenses, whose egos, instead of regulating and directing the stimuli into proper channels, admit defeat before coping means are exhausted. The weak ego is passive and gives free rein to many stimuli until the balance fails. It then experiences the resulting disruption of balance as anxiety. Not only has the ego failed to mobilize appropriate defenses and a discharge of the overload, but even after the anxiety attack the ego finds it difficult to recover from the shock of pain and distress.

The mnemonic system is the depository of all mental representations. If there is failure in maturation, this failure will reflect faulty threshold events. Such failure becomes the source of disturbing affects which scar the mind. Such a mind may become the breeding ground of complex pathology, with anxiety as the conscious experience of the disturbed equilibrium. The ego may be ill-prepared to handle fragmented thoughts or feelings, overcharged memories, fantasies, vibrating images, or shadows of the past. It will not be able to synthesize thoughts and affects, or to harmonize the id and the ego, or the unconscious and the conscious. The scarred mind will not arrive at a balance between fantasy and reality, between the past and the present, or between aggression and libido. Nor will it succeed in taming, modulating, neutralizing, and sublimating the drives and in "synthesis and fragmentation at their best" (Silbermann, 1961), and in the development and functioning of the mental transitional spheres; such a mind usually fails. A scarred mind fears tasting and testing. In contrast to the balanced mind, it trembles not with expectation, but with anxiety.

In dealing with the emotions, we encounter another serious problem, namely, the difficulty of putting them into words, and the related problems of interpreting their meaning, appreciating their intensity, or discovering the ideas connected with them. The ability to express one's feelings in words varies from person to person. Some use a plethora of words, some speak only a few words pregnant with meaning, some seem tongue-tied when feelings require verbal articulation. If a person says he suffers from anxiety, we know only that he refers to inner tensions, restlessness, discomfort, expectation of mishaps, oppressive moods, or the fear of anxiety-provoking agitation. Should one reply that he knows the other's feelings, the first one might say: "No, you cannot really know because I have so many perplexing feelings that it is impossible to express them." One of my patients, a painter, began his analysis with the following statement: "Words are not my vehicle for the expression of my emotions, but lines, forms, and colors are." Early in our work he spoke haltingly, with long pauses, rejected many of his words as inaccurate and imprecise. One day he brought some of his paintings to show how he expressed his feelings. When he looked at some of them, words started to flow more easily. He spoke of the meaning of the colors, of the warmth of the harmony, and of the coldness of his colors' disharmony. By using his pictures first as a bridge for articulating his emotions, before long he was able to proceed without them. But occasionally, whenever he felt verbally impeded, he sought help by drawing a quick sketch, saying, "Do you see what I mean?" Monet, so the story goes, felt near despair when he painted his water lilies. Even his genius, he seemed to believe, could not express the depth of his emotional experiences.

Affects become expressible only after the ego has developed the ability to perceive them consciously. The affects seem to be "id dwellers" at first, since they show various qualities of the id. Linear sequences do not exist, concepts of time and space are not valid, past and present are interchangeable, as are fantasy and reality. Even if affects become the content of the conscious ego and can thus be changed into emotions, they do not totally lose their id attributes. They exhibit entropy or a tendency to disorder. This may help to understand why thoughts overcharged with affects show features uncharacteristic of thinking, which shows order, logic, absence of contradiction and of ambiguity, and in which one thing is what it is and not something else at the same time. Referring to this complication, Spinoza describes thoughts contaminated by emotions as "impure," since feelings dim the clarity of thoughts and perturb their rationality. He also observes that this emotional admixture makes it possible to predict, only with probability, the different reactions of different people to identical stimuli. Such prediction is based not on objective but on subjective factors. For instance, the perception of a horse's footprints might put in motion chains of thoughts different in a soldier from those in a peasant (p. 143). He also stresses the importance of imagination in the creation of emotions.

Emotions as well as thoughts are sets of relationships. If we encounter what appears to be a simple or single feeling, we must consider it an indicator of a still hidden, larger conglomerate of correlations and combinations, making it even more difficult to translate the emotions into language and to capture all their shades of meaning and personal overtones.

The attempts by Locke, Wittgenstein, and others to solve the problem of purification of language could not succeed since no formula could be found to render language unpolluted by feelings which zigzag and are evasive, often totally without rhyme or reason. Since emotions are the *spiritus movens* of these difficulties, it might be helpful to pay attention to the coloration of words and to their emphasis and clarity. One may learn much from the construction and development of sentences, their speed of delivery, the softness or loudness of voice, the scarcity or abundance of verbiage, the resonance or emptiness of verbal formulations; and from errors and slips of the tongue.

I return once more to anxiety. Although the expected "performance anxiety" of the artist or scientist belongs to the group of anticipated danger anxieties, they reflect at the same time the spirit of the creative adventure, the challenge, and the need to utilize art or science for inspiration and enlightenment. This touch of anxiety is the élan vital of creative people and is as essential for their inspiration as oxygen for the flame.

When for pathological reasons the nearly incessant and overabundant influx of stimuli keeps the mental representations in constant agitation, the ego's equilibrium is threatened and anxiety is experienced. The proper equilibrium of the ego allows the production of balanced thoughts and feelings; the disruptions of balance will cause turmoil in the production of both.

I suggest that any grave disturbance of equilibrium is perceived as anxiety in degrees that range from very mild to very intense. There are *no* neurotic or psychotic manifestations—both are forms of balance turbulence—that do not show marked features of anxiety. The latter is the first announcement, the first alarm signal, the first indication of faulty equilibrium. Depending on the gravity of the agitation, the anxiety will "whisper or roar," last for shorter or longer periods. Serious balance disturbance is likely to become the fertile soil for a multiplicity of pathological symptoms. Since the literature is replete with reports of anxieties, their intricacies, their disturbing, even paralyzing features, I shall speak of only three patients with different degrees of balance disturbance caused by the influx of more than tolerable amounts of stimuli.

1. A woman whose analysis was terminated a long time ago returned for more analytic work. She had developed anxiety attacks which left her exhausted. These attacks occurred at home or at work without warning and without any reason obvious to her. She would suddenly feel inner trembling, discomfort, bewilderment; she said she had a sensation of losing ground, quickly followed by a feeling of danger and by fear of death. Comparing her previous depression with her present anxieties, she found the latter more upsetting and dramatic; and searching her mind, she was unable to find any reasons for her sudden "relapse." I recommended a thorough clinical checkup which determined that diabetes (hypoglycemia), accompanied by acute balance disturbance was at the bottom of her acute and spectacular symptoms. Treatment by an internist cured the attacks which were caused by disruption of her metabolic balance.

The course of these events may be outlined as follows: disruption of balance by a pathological physical process—formations of mental representations—overexcitation of the ego by a massive onrush of stimuli—attempts by the ego to master them—failure—major disruption of the ego's equilibrium, which the ego perceives with alarm and distress, with acute anxiety.

2. A patient wished to be analyzed in order to clarify events which puzzled him. Several times, while working at his desk, he suddenly felt a slight sensation, "too slight to be mentioned," of inner discomfort and restlessness, sensations which disappeared just as suddenly as they had come. However, a short time later, he found his secretary standing alarmed in his office. When he asked her what she was doing there, she informed him that he had cried out for help. He laughed and told her that she must have been dreaming. After similar bizarre occurrences, he was

advised to undergo psychoanalytic therapy. My previous work in neurology had acquainted me with the multitude of symptoms of brain tumors. A consulting neurologist confirmed my suspicions. Subsequently a meningioma was removed. So were the symptoms of anxiety and panic. In this case, only slight symptoms of anxiety were briefly sensed before the patient lost part of his consciousness.

Although balance disturbances occur in body and mind, the mind, as may be expected, is the major source of anxieties, as was the case in the next patient.

3. A man who, through psychoanalysis, had freed himself from a variety of obsessive-compulsive fantasies, many years later developed acute states of separation anxiety. These inhibited movement beyond certain limits. As long as he remained within his "territory," as long as he did not travel, he was free of symptoms and functioned efficiently. However, the thought of going beyond his safety boundaries threw him into a state of severe anxiety, with palpitations, sweating, and various other symptoms. In order to keep his ego free from the inundation of imagination, suppressed wishes, and memories, as well as rejected sexual desires, and in order to keep his fear of separation and loss of love under control, he had forced his ego into a state of "frozen equilibrium" and passivity. During our sessions, whenever he sensed that we were approaching repressed content, he would say: "I feel peculiar sensations, numbness, a sort of paralysis. My mind stopped dead. Nothing comes into it. I feel as if I was far away and as if your voice is coming from afar." These sensations were symptoms of his ego arrest, of his defense against the threat of failure in his ego's balance. They were the ego's response to imbalance.

SUMMARY

Anxiety is the experience of the ego's perception of a disturbance or disruption of its equilibrium.

Anxiety is the alarm which the ego sounds in its attempt to mobilize its defenses and discharge mechanisms in order to reestablish balance.

Anxiety may "whisper or roar," its quantity and quality may vary depending on the gravity of the stimuli and on maturation, development, and strength of the ego.

True anxiety is an affect combined with an idea, or a conscious emotion.

There is a stage in the development of "anxiety proper" which could be called "anxiety in *statu nascendi*." This is the preconscious experience of balance disturbances, of tension phenomena. These primary states, however, have not yet found their *firm* connections with thoughts and words; consequently they are still vague, difficult to grasp, bewildering, and hard to describe. When the combination with an idea is well established, the "anxiety proper" becomes more sharply focused and more easily formulated in verbal representations.

BIBLIOGRAPHY

Brenner, C. (1953), An addendum to Freud's theory of anxiety. *Int. J. Psychoanal.*, 34:18–24.
––––– (1974), On the nature and development of affects. *Psychoanal. Quart.*, 43:532–556.
Breuer, J. & Freud, S. (1893–95), Studies on hysteria. *S.E.*, 2.
Freud, S. (1894), The neuro-psychoses of defence. *S.E.*, 3:43–68.
––––– (1926), Inhibitions, symptoms and anxiety. *S.E.*, 20:77–175.
––––– (1950 [1895]), Project for a scientific psychology. *S.E.*, 1:283–397.
Greenacre, P. (1941), The predisposition to anxiety. In: *Trauma, Growth and Personality*. New York: Norton, 1952, pp. 27–82.
Locke, J. (1632), *Logic and Language*. Oxford: Blackwell, 1952.
Novey, S. (1959), A clinical view of affect theory in psycho-analysis. *Int. J. Psychoanal.*, 40:94–104.
Silbermann, I. (1950), A contribution to the psychology of menstruation. *Int. J. Psychoanal.*, 31:258–267.
––––– (1961), Synthesis and fragmentation. *Psychoanal. Study Child*, 16:90–117.
––––– (1967), Reflection on working through and insight. *Isr. Ann. Psychiat.*, 5:53–60.
––––– (1979), Mental transitional spheres. *Psychoanal. Quart.*, 48:85–106.
Spinoza, B. (1677), *Ethics*. New York: Dover, 1955.
Spitz, R. A. (1965), *The First Year of Life*. New York: Int. Univ. Press.
Wittgenstein, L. (1958), *Philosophical Investigations*. Oxford: Blackwell.
Zukav, G. (1979), *The Dancing Wu Li Masters*. New York: Morrow.

APPLICATIONS OF PSYCHOANALYSIS

"The Peasant Marey"

A Screen Memory

IZA S. ERLICH, M.S.W.

THE PURPOSE OF THIS PAPER IS TO LOOK BRIEFLY AT SOME UNCONscious mechanisms operative in Dostoevsky's little-known story "The Peasant Marey." My thesis is that the idyllic and idealized memory of a childhood episode in that story serves not only as a protective wall between the author and the unbearable reality of the Siberian prison but also as a screen memory covering some other, repressed, earlier experience or experiences.

In 1849, 28-year-old Dostoevsky was arrested and tried as a member of a clandestine radical organization. The young writer and his fellow conspirators were first sentenced to death, then the verdict was commuted to 9 years in Siberia, but the prisoners did not learn of the reprieve until a mock execution had been staged and they had actually faced a firing squad. This event and the years spent in Siberia changed the course of Dostoevsky's life and powerfully affected his beliefs.

In 1862, he described this harrowing period in the memoirs from *The House of the Dead,* a remarkably accurate rendition of his prison-camp experiences thinly disguised as memoirs of a fictitious convict. Some 15 years later Dostoevsky embarked on another largely nonfictional venture: a one-man monthly, *The Diary of a Writer,* which was filled with an amazing variety of

Assistant Clinical Professor, Department of Psychiatry; Staff Member, Division of Mental Hygiene Yale University Health Services;
Clinical Associate, Western New England Institute for Psychoanalysis.
A different version of this paper was presented at the 4th International Dostoevsky Symposium in Bergamo, August 1980.

material, topical articles, ideological essays, personal recollections, and short stories. "The Peasant Marey"—a cross between the two latter genres—appeared in this miscellany in 1876.

The first-person narrative takes the reader back to the setting of *The House of the Dead*.[1] The main ingredients of the story are as follows:

It takes place in a prison camp where 29-year-old Dostoevsky is incarcerated. It is Easter Monday. Convicts who are not working drink, curse, fight; some run amok; some lie half-dead on their bunks. Dostoevsky recoils in fear and disgust from "these wild orgies of the common people." On such days, he says, even the officials stayed away from the prison. "Blind fury" blazes up in his heart. He leaves the hut and, wandering aimlessly behind the barracks, meets a Polish political prisoner M——ski who "with flashing eyes and trembling lips [hisses] *'Je hais ces brigands!'*" (p. 100). Made uncomfortable by this echo of his own fury, Dostoevsky goes back to the barracks where he sees the drunken Tartar Gazin, beaten senseless by fellow convicts, lying on the floor. Dostoevsky makes his way to his bunk, lies down, and pretends to sleep; "no one," he says, "would bother a sleeping man." There is a parallel between the unconscious, no longer suffering, Gazin lying on the floor and Dostoevsky excaping into a daydream.

"By and by I did forget my surroundings and became imperceptibly lost in my memories. . . . These memories cropped up by themselves; I seldom evoked them consciously. It would begin from some point, some imperceptible feature, which then grew little by little into a complete picture, into some clear-cut and vivid impression. I used to analyse those impressions, adding new touches to an event that had happened long ago, and, above all, correcting it, correcting it incessantly" (p. 100f.).

Thus, Dostoevsky himself gives us an inkling of the psychological work he was involved in: first, a description of free association ("memories cropped up by themselves"); then corrections through secondary elaboration.

---

1. Dostoevsky frequently uses first-person narrative in his fiction, but in this instance he specifically emphasizes the autobiographical character of the incident.

As he seeks to escape from the unbearable reality, the day-dreamer recalls an idyllic childhood episode. The little boy's summer holidays are coming to an end. A cool and windy day makes him think of the dreaded winter and the impending return to Moscow. Like a day residue in the dream, the French utterance of the Pole, "*Je hais ces brigands!*" finds its counterpart in the memory of hateful French lessons. The boy eagerly runs toward "the fragrance" of nearby birchwoods. Suddenly, "amid the dead silence," he hears clearly the shout "Wolf! Wolf!" Panic-stricken, screaming, he rushes to the distant figure of a ploughing peasant whom at close range he recognizes as "our peasant Marey." Marey reassures the little boy that he was only dreaming: "Who ever heard of wolves in these parts?" he says. But the boy is still trembling all over: "the corners of my mouth were still twitching, and that seemed to strike him particularly. He quietly stretched out his thick finger with its black nail, smeared with earth, and gently touched my trembling lips. . . . I realised at last there was no wolf and that I had imagined the shout, 'Wolf! Wolf!'" As the boy, calmed, walks way, he turns once more to look at Marey. "I could no longer see his face clearly, but I felt that he was still nodding and smiling tenderly at me" (p. 103).

This image of a coarse-looking, but kindly and tender peasant allows the writer to look at the convicts with quite different eyes: "suddenly by some miracle all hatred and anger had vanished from my heart" (p. 105). He can now see in their shaven heads and branded faces the comforting face of the peasant Marey.

Thus, at 55, Dostoevsky writes of a memory which came to him when he was 29—a memory of an event that supposedly occurred when he was 9 years old. Like a Russian wooden doll within a doll within a doll, a memory contains a memory. I suggest yet another invisible doll in this structure, another memory, another event. To put it differently, it may be worthwhile to construe this account of the narrator's childhood experience as a screen memory.

In her paper on screen memories, Phyllis Greenacre (1949) speaks of those "isolated islands of recollection" marking the location of and representing "the lost continents of childhood experince" (p. 73). Reminiscent of single snapshots, screen memories do not fit into a more or less continuous stream of memory but stand apart by themselves. On analysis they often prove to cover some other forgotten event or events. Like daydreams and recollections with their inevitable selectiveness, distortions, and omissions, they contribute to a coherent picture of one's life not only as part of one's self representation but also as one's treasured possession, a biographical self image that becomes one's "personal myth" (Kris, 1956). Yet, screen memories are distinctive in that they are substitute memories, owing their emotional value not to their overt content but "to the relation existing between that content and some other, that has been suppressed" (Freud, 1899, p. 320). The memory of which we are aware is only a substitute, "the raw material of memory-traces out of which it was forged remains unknown to us in its original form" (p. 322).

Along with dreams, parapraxes, jokes, and neurotic symptoms, screen memories become a vehicle for the urge to express, and the need to repress, the unacceptable. In a setting of extreme anxiety one may develop what Fenichel (1927) calls "a hunger for screen experiences," which facilitate defensive use of later-occurring events to mold and reshape those already existing screen memories.

Screen memories can be easily distinguished from other memories by their telltale characteristics. There is a suddenness of recall, a seeming discrepancy between the intensity of affect and the insignificance of the content. There is also an apparent stagelike effect: the rememberer sees himself in child's shape and clothing and watches himself in a role of a child performer. These memories are usually marked by an unusual brightness, vividness, and sharpness of visual detail.

The childhood experience recounted in "The Peasant Marey" bears all the earmarks of a screen memory: we have here the sudden emergence of the memory in a moment of dire need; the richness, brilliance, and vividness of recall; the uncanny sharpness of detail; "All this came back to me all at once, I don't know why, but with an amazing accuracy of detail . . . now twenty years later in Siberia I suddenly remembered this meeting so distinctly that not a single detail of it was lost, which means of course that it must have been hidden in my mind without my knowing it . . . and came back to me suddenly when it was wanted" (p. 104).

With regard to another characteristic of screen memory, the relative insignificance of content as compared with its emotional charge, Dostoevsky does stress the powerful impact of the memory at the time of recall, but he leaves no doubt that the original event did not strike the child as all that important: "When I returned home from Marey that day I did not tell anybody about my 'adventure'. It was not much of an adventure, anyway. And besides, I soon forgot all about Marey. Whenever I happened to come across him now and then, I never spoke to him either about the wolf or anything else" (p. 104).

In the context of Dostoevsky's story the memory of this "nonadventure" performs a crucial overt function by creating a distance between the narrator and the raging rabble. The superimposed image of the peasant Marey offers Dostoevsky a different, more benign perspective on the hateful and menacing criminals. It also enhances the overall ideological thrust of *The Diary of a Writer* with its pervasive tendency to idealize the Russian peasant as a potential bearer of a higher truth and of genuine Christian values (see also Jackson, 1978). Significantly, "The Peasant Marey" follows immediately upon a descriptive entry, "On the Love of the People," which insists upon the inner beauty of the Russian people, buried like diamonds "under impassable alluvial filth" (p. 202).

One might wonder, incidentally, why such a crucial episode should have been omitted from *The House of the Dead* only to find its way into *The Diary of a Writer.*

While it would be of great interest to know more about the circumstances under which this memory surfaced, I have not come across any biographical information bearing on that issue. Yet two relevant factors may be mentioned. The narrator of *The House of the Dead* is, emphatically, not Dostoevsky: he is a reticent and wary man not given to dwelling on his past. It would be out of character for him to inject into a prison narrative a childhood memory. On the other hand, one of the explicit aims of *The Diary of a Writer* is that of creating an air of intimacy between the author and his audience. A personal recollection such as "Peasant Marey" fits such a pattern admirably.

I shall now consider some of the unconscious underpinnings of the narrative. The recollection has a fairy-tale ambiance (Kanzer, 1946)—the enchanting woods, the imagined wolf, the coarse-looking rescuer turned into a "kindly and almost womanly good fairy"—an ambiance which allows a transformation of a painful reality into a scene of joy and comfort. The image of an all-too-real brigand becomes split into a hallucinated bad wolf and a kindly consoling peasant.

I would suggest that a summoned recollection served not only as an antidote to the threatening feelings evoked by the occasion but also as a screen for some other earlier event of a "quite different" nature.

The drunken revelry of the criminals whom Dostoevsky describes as "crazed animals" evokes in a young writer a wide range of violent, conflicting emotions. Fear, revulsion, disgust, and rage—unwelcomed, but not repressed—form the overt ushering in of the story.

The hoarse, drunken songs, the excitement of the "wild orgies," the image of six strong peasants hurling themselves on Tartar Gazin, however, must have stirred not only fear and anger, but sexual excitement as well. I need hardly emphasize that in Dostoevsky's fictional universe violence and sexuality are closely intertwined. I called attention earlier to the similarity between the posture of the savagely beaten Gazin and that of the writer pretending to sleep. (The same Gazin, by the way, appears on the pages of *The House of the Dead* where he is depicted as an incarnation of evil, a sadistic child killer who lures children to remote spots, taunts them verbally, then cuts their throats!) Such similarity suggests a powerful identification with the victim. The scene may well have stirred up in Dostoevsky passive homosexual longings and sadomasochistic fantasies, not uncommon under such circumstances. Thus, the dreamy journey into the woodsy landscape of childhood allows the narrator to escape from the unbearable but acknowledged fear and rage as well as from unacknowledged erotic feelings.

The tale serves both to repress and to express a longing for submission to a powerful, coarse, and yet kindly and protective figure. The intense emotional charge of the narration is due to its dual function—of preventing a certain group of impulses from reaching consciousness while pushing other feelings to the fore as a substitute.

One can only speculate as to what kind of event lies buried under the kindly memories of Marey. In view of the nature of the arousal of this memory, I would posit that some sexual experience from very early childhood, both frightening and exciting, and possibly even touched with tenderness, lies behind this screen memory. Somebody real, rather than an imagined wolf, may at one time have frightened and excited the young boy.

The image of the wolf figures prominently in Russian fairy tales and was as easily available a target for Dostoevsky's infantile fears as for those of another famous Russian, the Wolf Man (Freud, 1918). Yet in some of the stories the grizzly wolf appears as a helper and rescuer expiating and correcting for some former misdeeds. It is of interest that not only Marey is given the same grizzled coloring as the wolf, but that the family watchdog is given the name "Volchok"—a diminutive of *Volk*—Russian for wolf: "with Volchok at my side I completely recovered my spirits" (103).[2]

We recall that Marey calms down the frightened lad by "quietly stretching out" his thick finger with its black nail smeared with earth and gently touching (the child's) trembling lips.

Putting aside the phallic, sexual, and masturbatory connotations of a thick finger, I am struck by the fact that typically an adult puts a finger on a child's lips, not so much to comfort, but rather to silence. Marey's gesture suggests, at least to me, "don't say anything, don't talk." This is very much in line with the previously quoted passage: "When I returned home from Marey that day I did not tell anybody about my 'adventure.'" The boy's reticence, like the twice-repeated motif of the thick finger smeared with earth, may be viewed as a telltale sign of another submerged event: Marey, or some other male figure for whom he stands, may have played the role of seducer. Child seducers need not be brutal; in fact, they often are quite gentle.

The meeting, we are told, took place in a secluded spot, in a deserted field with only God as a witness. "No doubt, anyone

2. I appreciate Dr. Stanley A. Leavy pointing this out to me.

would have done his best to calm a child, but something quite different seemed to have happened during that solitary meeting" (p. 104), says Dostoevsky. The question is: how different?

Even in the course of an analysis, reconstruction of a childhood event on the basis of dreams or screen memories is a chancy matter. What is fantasy and what is reality often remains an unsettled question, but in the analytic situation we work with a patient who can deny or corroborate our interpretations.

Obviously, Dostoevsky can neither repudiate nor confirm our guesses, reasonable as they may be. What we can draw on, in his absence, is his oeuvre with its amazing insight into the labyrinth of human impulses and its potential for mediated self-revelation.

Any student of Dostoevsky's is well aware of the writer's fascination with the murky world of child molesters. Nearly all of his major novels contain episodes having to do with seduction of a minor or at least intimations of such events.

In *Crime and Punishment,* this motif appears most blatantly in Svidrigailov's dream on the eve of his suicide. In *The Possessed,* it forms the core of Stavrogin's confession. In *The Idiot,* there are hints that Nastasia Filipovna was taken advantage of by her guardian. It is worth noting that in many of these situations a curious shift occurs: the corruptor appears to a deprived and frightened little girl as a rescuer or protector, while the child in her eagerness is suddenly seen as almost a seducer both inviting and repelling.

There is no plausible reason to believe that Dostoevsky himself was actually guilty of any such offense. N. Strakhov, a critic and publicist and erstwhile friend turned enemy, insinuated maliciously in a letter to Tolstoy that his great rival raped a little girl in a boathouse with the complicity of her governess (see Mochulsky, 1967). Freud unwittingly added to the credence of this innuendo by referring to Dostoevsky's "possible confession to a sexual assault upon a young girl" (1928, p. 178). Actually all that can be surmised is that an incident like that was related to Dostoevsky who intended to use it in *The Possessed* (Mochulsky, 1967).

Be that as it may, one might be tempted to assume that in the realm of erotic fantasies the writer's primary identification was with the sexual aggressor, with the victimizer rather than with the victim.

Yet, if my hypothesis that Dostoevsky was sexually approached as a very young child is valid, it is quite likely that he would identify as readily with an overpowered, frightened little girl, a humiliated target of sexual coercion. In the realm of the unconscious, the boundary between the sexes is fluid. The change of gender would only underscore the qualities of helplessness and passivity while allowing for the expression of submerged homosexual wishes.

Imaginative literature, like dreams, has the capacity to transform unconscious fantasies into conscious themes, making the unacceptable palatable, the frightening reassuring. Creative power allows a writer to become a master and reshaper of his fantasies.

Thus, an early traumatic sexual experience could become a "subtext" of an edifying tale as well as a subsoil for the seedy universe of the Svidrigailovs and the Stavrogins.

BIBLIOGRAPHY

DOSTOEVSKY, F. (1862), *The House of the Dead.* New York: Oxford Univ. Press, 1956.
———— (1876), The peasant Marey. In: *The Best Short Stories of Dostoevsky.* New York: Modern Library, n.d., pp. 99–105.
———— (1949), *The Diary of a Writer.* Santa Barbara & Salt Lake City: Peregrine Smith, 1979.
GREENACRE, P. (1949), A contribution to the study of screen memories. *Psychoanal. Study Child*, 3/4:73–84.
FENICHEL, O. (1927), The economic function of screen memories. In: *Collected Papers*, 1:113–116. New York: Norton, 1953.
FRANK, J. (1976), *Dostoevsky.* Princeton, N.J.: Princeton Univ. Press.
FREUD, S. (1899), Screen memories. *S.E.*, 3:303–322.
———— (1918), From the history of an infantile neurosis. *S.E.*, 17:3–123.
———— (1928), Dostoevsky and parricide. *S.E.*, 21:177–196.
JACKSON, R. L. (1978), The triple vision. *Yale Rev.*, Winter, pp. 225–236.
KANZER, M. (1947), Dostoevsky's "Peasant Marey." *Amer. Imago*, 4:78–88.
KRIS, E. (1956), The personal myth. In: *Selected Papers of Ernst Kris.* New Haven & London: Yale Univ. Press, 1975, pp. 272–300.
MOCHULSKY, K. (1967), *Dostoevsky.* Princeton, N.J.: Princeton Univ. Press.

The Domestic Dimensions of Violence

Child Abuse

RICHARD GALDSTON, M.D.

I SHALL DESCRIBE FINDINGS MADE IN THE COURSE OF WORK WITH 75 families, including 100 children who had been afflicted with child abuse, defined as the actual, or potential, serious physical assault of a small child by an adult. These families were studied between 1968 and 1978 in a project established to conduct research on the problem of the physical abuse of preschool children. The study was designed with the hypothesis that abusing parents who demonstrated some sign of a desire to become better parents could be involved in a therapeutic endeavor offering concurrent care and protection to their child and treatment for themselves. The Project consists of a therapeutic daycare facility for the children, the Parents' Centre, and an office from which to base the treatment of the parents. It was undertaken in collaboration with the Parents' and Children's Services of the Children's Mission.

This paper is limited to a consideration of the findings rele-

Principal Investigator of the Parents' Centre Project for the Study in Prevention of Child Abuse; faculties of the Boston Psychoanalytic Society and Institute and of Harvard Medical School.

This is a revised version of a paper presented at a symposium on the Violent Person, held by the Boston Psychoanalytic Institute on the occasion of its 45th Anniversary, May 19, 1978.

The W. T. Grant Fund provided support for the initiation of the Project.

vant to the psychodynamics of child abuse, particularly as these bear upon the domestic dimensions of violence. The important social, economic, historical, and racial aspects of the problem lie beyond its scope.

Among the varieties of violent experience to which man is heir, child abuse is unique. It is intimate, personal, within the family, and charged with emotions that are highly ambivalent. The intimacy of the attachment between abusing parents and their children is attested to by the fervor with which attempts to remove the child can be opposed by the very parents who have abused him. It is also demonstrated by the children who, even though they may cringe and flinch when their parents approach, will cry and cling anxiously to them when they move to leave.

The strength of this attachment in cases of child abuse renders management more complicated than in those cases where the parents are indifferent to the child. Such children are the victims of primary neglect or deprivation, rather than of physical assault, and their parents more willingly concede the need for their care, placement, or adoption. Parents and children who have been largely indifferent to each other can take their leave with little lost. They have suffered the chill of indifference rather than the warmth of wrath.

In the personal spectrum of human violence, child abuse lies midway between suicide and homicide. Its personal quality is attested to by the frequency with which the abusing parent complains that the child is persecuting him or her. The accusation that an infant cries deliberately to interrupt the parent's sleep, or that a toddler gets into things with malice aforethought bespeaks the extent to which these parents perceive their relationship with their child as personal. Their judgments of their child, hostile or laudatory, have a highly self-centered quality indicative of the degree to which the parents have identified themselves with the child as a part of their persons.

Child abuse is a family affair. Many of the mothers who have come to professional attention as a result of having abused their children demonstrate skill and patience in caring for other women's children. Several mothers whose abuse of their own children brought them under our care have gone on to work in other settings to provide excellent care for other women's children. One was honored as "Head Start mother of the year." It is the family aspect of the relationship, of being a parent to one's own child, that brings with it perceptions of the self that are intolerable. It is rare that an adult abuses a small child with whom he is unfamiliar. Child abuse appears to depend upon the domestic relationship for the elements of its etiology.

The ambivalent emotions with which abusing parents perceive their child are illustrated by their use of contradictory extremes in speech, dress, care, and demeanor. The term "monster" is the image employed most frequently by the parent. He or she is described as a "monster" bent upon persecuting the parent and the parent alone. This view often alternates with another version of the child as gifted with great promise and extraordinary talents, the whole described in language equally inappropriate to a young child whose developmental immaturity precludes any discernible competence for either good or evil.

The persistence of a high level of unconscious ambivalent attachment between parents and child appears to be a prime force in initiating a set of subsequent reactions which can be demonstrated to propagate violence as a prime mode of relating to other human beings. It is epitomized in conduct displayed by many of the children studied in the Parents' Centre Project. A little boy of 2 or 3 approaches another child or a child care worker and grabs her hand, bringing it toward his mouth. It is unknown whether that child will kiss that hand or bite it. No one knows what will happen; whether pain or pleasure will be the result of the child's actions. The possibility that his aggression might be delivered to others as violence has an intimidating effect upon them. Their response to being intimidated can vary in form and pattern, but the end result is the same: avoidance, in part or in whole, of the child who presents himself as the deliverer of the threat of ambivalence.

This child has two conflicting desires which he is unable to reconcile in a fashion predictable to himself or to others. The ambivalence about the desires he experiences in his mouth remains unmastered by him, and therefore lies beyond the knowledge of others. He is not responsible for the conduct of his jaws in relation to other persons. He does not know from one moment to the next whether he will kiss or bite the hand he takes, and others, as if heeding the adage about the sleeping dog, let him be. His abusing parents are in a similar position. They often do not know from one moment to the next whether they will kiss or hit the child whom they perceive alternately as a saint to be adored or a sinner to be exorcised.

The cumulative effect of such uncertainty erodes the willingness of others to relate to the child. The resulting isolation forces him to bear his ambivalence in solitude, a condition which the child cannot tolerate. This, in turn, leads to a mounting need to provoke others to interact in order to relieve him of the burden of cumulative tension from his unrequited longings. This condition renders the child highly liable to the eruption of tantrums, the massive and acute muscular discharge of the tension of ambivalence upon himself and whoever comes within his immediate vicinity.

An analogue to this sequence of insupportable ambivalence of desire can be observed among the parents of children who have been physically abused. They are prone to a similar impasse between the emotions of concomitant desires. They want, and they disallow their wants. They love and hate the same object at the same time, and they are unable to sort out these sentiments into a recognizable sequence for which they can accept responsibility. They have access to a wider range of persons and institutions with which to interact than is available to their children. Instead of having a tantrum, they tend to make a crisis, an acute emergency situation which compels other persons to interact with them. This has a comparable effect upon those who are drawn into their sphere of behavior. They, too, are intimidated and tend to withdraw beyond a range of involvement for fear of getting hurt. This leads to greater alienation and an increment in tension from frustrated desires.

The skill and energy with which these parents create crises in their lives have been prominent findings in this study. In many instances, their choice of mates appears to have been predicated upon a recognition of this talent for using each other as a partner with whom to form a coupling arrangement for the mutual sharing of the recurring tension of unconscious ambivalence. The couple forms a marriage of like minds locked together in a state of chronic chaos in which responsibility for who feels what about whom is never brought into the open view of consciousness. "When things got hot," as one father put it, "then I crank up my old chaos machine." The tension states of unacknowledged ambivalence lie beyond confrontation and remain inaccessible to mastery. Each partner relates to the state through reciprocal provocation derived from mutual ambivalence. Each partner leads the life of the other in a domestic exercise of sleight-of-hand, of which they are but dimly aware. The arrangement is innately liable to disintegration, truth having a natural tendency to out. Emotions, even when highly ambivalent, seek their own level. However, that leveling tendency runs counter to other requirements which the parents have imposed upon themselves, requirements dictated by the mutual need to conserve a system of avoidance.

It is as if these mates had chosen each other with a clause written into their vows of fidelity—that certain topics, thoughts, ideas, and sentiments were to be avoided within the context of their relationship. This phenomenon was demonstrated in an oft-repeated scene at the weekly meetings of the parents' groups. One or another parent launched into an impassioned and insightful description of the intrapsychic and interpersonal problems which afflict another member. Those same issues received no recognition when raised in relation to his and her own life. The avoidance is massive; not as a topic, but in relation to the self. It is not the idea, but the relevance of the topic to the person's own life that cannot be tolerated. Ideas such as the need to say "No" to demands, indications for toilet training, fears of sexual intercourse, and the longings to be taken care of receive detailed and thoughtful consideration in the context of the life of another, but are met as items inadmissible in the subject's own existence.

The Parents' Centre Project was designed for the concurrent study and treatment of parents and children afflicted with child abuse. It has enabled us to study these people as they struggle to contend with their desires and the troubles they encounter. By juxtaposing observations of the behavior of parent and child, we have attempted to understand how they influence each other.

The salient items can be subsumed under four headings as factors contributing to failure in the mastery of ambivalence and to the perpetuation of violence. The topics are discontinuity between the generations; prevalence of phobic ideation among the mothers; splitting and unmastered oral aggression; and a personal mythology of ghosts and monsters.

Some Factors Perpetuating Violence

DISCONTINUITY BETWEEN THE GENERATIONS

A rupture had broken the continuity between the generations of parent to child in all of the families in this study. None of the parents who abused their children was on equitable terms with his or her own parents. Either they had suffered a complete ending of communication with them, or they were locked in a struggle of hostile exploitative demands, each upon the other. This gap included physical and cultural estrangement or exploitation as well as a break in affective ties. Many of the parents had come from different parts of the country, leaving behind their own parents' values and traditions. Some were making an effort to supplant the void with a new life-style. Others fell into a routine of activity determined by contending with the recurring crises created by fights with welfare, social agencies, landlords, their mates, and their children. The estrangement from which the parents suffered spread to include their expectations for their future as well as memories of their past. Their fanciful dreams of future glory, spun with little regard for the requirements of reality, stood in striking contrast to the hard-headed cunning with which they met the demands of contending daily with the bureacracy of welfare and other public institutions. These parents were street-wise but home-foolish. They lived from day to day, cut adrift from their sense of their past without a feeling for continuity with their own lineage. They were unable to project a future for themselves or their children in any but the most whimsical of imagery. They were unable to direct their aggression in the service of their own desires, particularly in the domestic area.

PREVALENCE OF PHOBIC IDEATION

Phobic preoccupation with imagined dangers is a form of thought often expressed in cautionary warnings and avoidance behavior. It is difficult to measure its prevalence in different groups.

Fears, rational, irrational, and combinations of the two, dominated the mental content that these women shared in their group meetings and with their individual workers. Their world view was presented in extremes. They seized upon whatever reality afforded to confirm their fears. They ignored that which ran counter to the conviction that their fears were founded in external reality. They accumulated data to support their view of the world as fraught with danger from all sides, particularly from those desires that contained elements of sexuality or aggression. They provided their children with a view of the world as threatening, uncontested by access to alternative presentations that might have been available from grandparents, extended family, or broader social contacts. The dangers were repeatedly defined and localized as resident abroad, in the world outside. The streets, the neighbors, the blacks, the whites, the "them" were actively portrayed as menacing. What little safety there was, was said to be found at home with the mother. One mother said of herself and her child: "We're like a pair of marshmallows, each yelling to the other to put out the fire!"

These two factors, the rupture of relationships with their past and the prevalence of phobic preoccupation, greatly contribute to alerting a powerful sense of intimidation as the determinant of motivation and behavior in the daily conduct of life. Much of what was done or not done in the course of living occurred in relation to trouble, i.e., defensively to stay out of trouble, or violently to make trouble. This view of the day's events was so consuming that there was no room for entertaining recognition of the extent to which the family contributed to the creation of their own troubles by their own unmastered ambivalent aggression.

When one father was arrested for stealing a car parked in front of the local police station, or another found himself simultaneously hunted by both the police and his fellow criminals, or a mother was outraged that her social worker refused to support her falsification of her welfare status, the parents were too overwhelmed with the immediacy of their trouble to see that they had anything to do with its making. They defined their identities as victim, and their children joined them in this view.

The identity of self as victim living in historical isolation with a world view depicted in phobic imagery leaves little room for a sense of safety. What safety they could find derived from each other. For the children it rested with the parents, and for the parents in each other—despite all the evidence to the contrary. Despite drunken assaults by the men, slovenly neglect or abuse by the mothers, these relationships afforded the participants what sense of belonging they could find, and the relationship endured with a steadfastness that prevailed despite the stresses of urban living.

Children who grow up within this context impose a particular ordering to their perceptions of themselves and others. The study of their lives from birth to 6 years reveals a pattern of subordinating their own maturational needs to the priority of their parents' psychic requirements. Their mothers' phobias function as instructions to the children that they should fear the world outside and cling to their mothers as their only source of safety. The mothers' phobia specifies to their children that the mothers' perception of aggression as violence is so threatening that the mothers cannot stand it. If that fact needed further confirmation, the mothers' behavior with their men provides an object lesson for their children. Maternal phobia functions as a vector propagating to their children the experience that aggression carries with it the threat of violence, a danger which their mothers, who are their sole source of support and safety, cannot tolerate (Bowlby, 1973).

This attitude was demonstrated in many daily object lessons in which the child and mother lived out the mother's inability to endure the threat of her child's aggression. One mother repeatedly moved bric-a-brac about her living room in a vain effort to keep things out of reach to her 3-year-old daughter. Yet she never was able to tell the child directly that she did not want her to touch them.

Another mother complained of how hard it was for her to enter a store with her daughter because she felt compelled to buy the child whatever she wanted out of fear that if she refused, the child would make a scene and embarrass the mother. Another commented that she was afraid to expose her child to other children for fear that her daughter would see their toys, demand them for herself, and the mother would be unable to say "No."

Among younger children, toddlers just beginning to walk, the interaction with their mothers was marked by a description of their aggressiveness entirely out of proportion to the facts. The mothers spoke of their children as if they were menacing by their mobility. "Wild," "uncontrollable," "destructive," "attacking" were among the terms employed to characterize children barely able to toddle about. Usually these adjectives were used to modify the term "monster" as the epithet most favored in labeling their children. The monstrousness to which the mothers referred lay in their perception of the chilren's appetites. They responded to their children's early expression of aggression by either avoiding it through denial, disguise, dissimulation, or explaining it away as something else. Or they reacted in a retaliatory fashion with violent physical abuse, tangential and entirely out of proportion to the stimulus. Their punishments never fit the crime. Both of these patterns of response left the children with the same impression, i.e., that they were the bearer of dangerous aggression that was unmanageable by others and themselves in its potential for violence.

These children grow up in homes where they learn through their own experience and from the example of the adults who care for them that the use of aggression to attain satisfaction of desire is fraught with danger of violence to self and others. The gratification of wants as a consequence to the expenditure of effort remains a "rip off" attained at the expense of another, the victim. Aggression as work in the equitable service of desire lies beyond their experience. Eventually it becomes taboo. Whenever they get what they want, it brings with it the feeling that it was attained at the expense of another. Nothing can be gotten as *given to,* only as the result of someone having *given in* under duress.

This contamination of rewards with the taint of violence renders everything they get vaguely disappointing. Nothing ever can be earned as deserved. Nothing is ever enough, not because of insufficient quantity but because of the quality of having been stolen. These children are deprived of the experience of contentment, the equitable satisfaction of their own desires through their own efforts on their own behalf. They do not learn how to harness their aggression in the service of their desires. When they do get what they want, it appears to be either the result of luck, and therefore subject to equally fortuitous loss, or as the result of having violated another and therefore at the cost of a guilty conscience. Children growing up in homes in which aggression remains unmastered and intolerable to those upon whom they depend for their welfare cannot allow themselves to accept responsibility for their own aggression. It must be disowned, dissociated, and disposed of in order to guarantee their continued acceptability to their parents. This refutation of aggression can be achieved through inhibition of action, leaving the child a passive victim of his circumstance; it can be attained through denial and projection of responsibility for aggression onto others. With parents who live and teach the disownership and consignment of motivation to others, the stage is set for this lesson, the splitting of experience between the sensory and motor axes of behavior.

SPLITTING OF AMBIVALENCE AND UNMASTERED ORAL AGGRESSION

The verb to "split" was often used by the men studied in this project to describe their reaction to situations of stress in which they found themselves. "When things got too hot, I split the scene," as if by fleeing they could disown the inner tension from their ambivalence through abandoning the external circumstances. "We are all runners or losers!" declared one of the fathers. "Splitting the scene, taking off" becomes the externalized solution to an internalized problem. But, like their shadow, the scene goes with them only to be reestablished when they stop running.

This is the shadow of unmastered oral aggression (Abraham, 1924). Within this shadow, the potential for violence persists. It has a genealogy of its own which we have been studying in these families afflicted with child abuse and which we believe has relevance to the more general problem of the epidemiology of violence—the craving to get something for nothing.

In an article published in 1965 reporting on observations made within a hospital on children who had been physically abused and their parents, I stated that the forces contributing to the physical abuse of children bore no relation to spouse abuse. Time and further study have proven that statement to be mistaken. The contrary is the case: child abuse is a sign of a deeply sadomasochistic experience of the self as parent in relation to the mate.

Ten of the 68 mothers had confided to their workers at some point that they had seriously considered the murder of their mates; not as an abstract random thought, but as an act which they could visualize in their mind's eye. One woman told of keeping a knife under her pillow at all times, in case she decided to stab her mate. Another told of thinking that she might crush her man's skull as he lay in a drunken stupor. This woman had lived with the same man for over a decade in the hope that she could get him to marry her, after which she planned to divorce him. Another woman told of resisting the impulse to push her husband, invalided to a wheelchair by a back ailment, over a ledge. This woman subsequently ran off and left her husband, who then took part in the murder of a bus driver for which he was arrested and sentenced to prison.

At a group meeting, one of the mothers in the Project declared with a hint of pride, "We like our men to be mean, and if we can't find 'em mean, we make them mean." Another woman said of her man, "The nicer he is to me, the more I hate him." This predilection for mean men was demonstrated repeatedly. Known murderers, criminals, and cruel men were chosen and clung to, while reliable, devoted suitors were rejected as being "dull, not much fun." This persistent attachment to sadomasochistic relationships defied the best efforts of judges, social workers, or other authority figures at intervention. Despite broken noses, fractured jaws, repeated threats and assaults, these men and women clung to each other through thick and thin. When they did separate, the women found another man equally violent, or they attempted to return to live with or around their mothers. The men often turned to alcohol, violent crime, arrest, jail, or hospitalization.

Their men's meanness provided a fertile ground for the maintenance of mutual provocation to cruel and unusual harassment of each other, a process in which the abused child served as the go-between, an agent employed alternately by the assailant or the victim. The woman might use the child as a spokesman, attributing her own feelings to the child, causing the man to flare into anger and violence at the child or herself. Or the man, filled with feelings of inadequacy and guilt, might remonstrate with a child for the latter's alleged failings, punishing the child in his own stead, as a sacrifice to the pangs and demands of his own errant conscience.

The abused child remains in a position adjunct to the sadomasochistic relationship of the adults. He is an assistant to the assailant and/or the victim, a role which preempts his energies and precludes his options for his own growth and development. His identity becomes firmly embedded in the proposition that aggression subserves violence alone, leaving little room for learning the uses of aggression for growth, play, work, or education.

The consequences of the discontinuity between the generations, the mothers' phobic preoccupations, the tendency to split unconscious ambivalence, and unmastered oral aggression, all are propagated from the parents to the child within the vehicle of the sadomasochistic relationship which the parents maintain toward themselves and each other. It serves as a teaching aid for the child to learn through living with adults whose failure in the mastery of their oral aggression halters the child in his or her struggle to contend with this major issue of early development.

The tenacity with which these mates clung to each other against all odds suggests the presence of a deep abiding love, but a love of a special sort in which the exchange of mutual violations retains a prominent place. Indeed, the reports that the women gave of their men indicated that most of their energies were expended in trying to get the man to change in some major fashion, or in "fixing him" or "showing him" as punishment for his failure to change into what was wanted. Frustration and disappointment, rather than appreciation or pleasure, were the rule of their lives together. Despite, or perhaps *because* of this, they clung to each other with a deep attachment as both oppressor and oppressed.

Similarly, in other areas of their lives, the women revealed a strong, but deceptive will *not* to improve their lot. Despite apparent efforts to better their housing, vocational positions, or other aspects of their lives, job retraining, educational courses, and other programs usually came to naught, often with a striking success at "snatching defeat out of the jaws of victory," failing in the nick of time. The social landscape was littered with agencies and workers whose efforts at "uplifting their clients" resulted in nought. By actual count, one mother had 13 agencies actively involved in her behalf at the same time, none of which resulted in any discernible changes in her position. Yet later, when she was able to set her mind to it, this mother made a dramatic and enduring shift in her life, pulling herself together in a way that no one had been able to do for her.

One of the mothers in the Project who had demonstrated a genius at creating crises out of thin air presented her worker with a particularly acute, potentially painful, situation. As she recounted the desperateness of her straits, she burst into tears, to which her therapist responded by proffering some Kleenex. The woman turned in a towering rage, threw back the tissues, shouting, "Dammit, when I want your help, I'll ask for it. Don't you go trying to help me." Another mother threatened to quit the Project and remove her child when her demands for help in paying her overdue bills were granted. The need to be grateful was threatening to these women, and they avoided circumstances that might confront them with that expectation. They had "to bite the hand that fed them."

To attribute these and similar incidents to a need to suffer or to the enjoyment of masochism would not do the question justice. The need is not primarily to suffer; rather it is to experience the aggression and the affects mobilized by suffering from the frustration of desire. If the suffering is prematurely alleviated, the opportunity to experience their aggression and anger is removed and the parents are left choking on their own rage and unmastered aggression, driven on to find someone else with whom to be angry and with whom to fight.

This way of life, led along a course determined by the repetition of sadomasochistic relationships, could be attributed to the power of a compulsion initiated by the stimulus of a traumatic experience in early childhood. It could be assigned to the need for relief from the tension of pent-up aggression through the catharsis of instinctual discharge. Or it could be viewed as an adaptive attempt to establish a recapitulation of a set of developmental circumstances during which there had been a specific failure of maturation within the ego in its relation to the object world and to the formation of its superego.

I believe that the sadomasochistic behavior of these adults is the delayed consequence of a disordered weaning relationship in their childhood (Zetzel, 1953). The attitudes and actions characteristic of their sadomasochism bear striking resemblance to the behavior patterns of young children struggling to wean themselves from primary bonding to their mothers in their nursing relationship. The weaning child achieves the initiation of separation from that relationship through the equitable mastery of oral aggression, by joining his striated musculature to the service of his mouth and the appetites he experiences within. If the exercise of oral aggression goes unmastered, the weaning couple fails in the task and their relationship. The issue remains unsolved; primary bonding becomes transformed into chronic bondage, rather than separation-individuation.

Most of the mothers in the Project first brought their children to our attention when they were 12 months or older. In group and individual meetings, the mothers declared their love of being pregnant and of taking care of their infants. Histories of failure to thrive and other evidence of disordered primary bonding were absent, with few exceptions.[1]

The mothers' complaints about their children usually coincided with the onset of walking and talking. Then began their sense of outrage at the child for "being into everything and at me all the time, destroying everything," and, most often, that the child wouldn't listen to them. "He [or she] won't pay me no mind, won't do what he's told, and gives me back talk. He won't learn to eat what's put before him," was the explanation offered by two men who had forced children to sit at the table for hours on end. "He won't take 'no' for an answer."

The parents in our Project were unable to declare their desires squarely and to say "No" to themselves, or to their children, or their mates. Unable to say "No," they also could not say "Yes."

---

1. It is upon the basis of this and related observations that we have found it useful to distinguish between child abuse and primary neglect, deprivation, and exploitation, in the diagnostic nosology of the dysfunctions of early parenthood (Galdston, 1979).

They could grant themselves neither prohibition nor permission. All they could do for themselves was wallow in a mire of ambivalence, vacillating back and forth, seemingly adrift in a sea of circumstance.

Paradoxically, these parents, so wanting in the capacity to mobilize aggression to subserve their own personal wants, so prone to violence when confronted with their own desires, often proved determined and skillful workers when the task was in the service of another's wishes. In group meetings, mothers who could not say "No" to their own children, mates, or selves spoke with clarity and conviction about the need for other women to define the realities of limits within their families. Similarly, women, derelict in caring for their own children, proved to be excellent child care workers in settings outside of their home. These, and similar observations, suggest that, rather than an absolute failure in the mastery of aggression, these people are afflicted with an inability to use aggression in the service of the self; they cannot gratify their own desires by getting what they want for themselves through joining aggression to appetite.

Another set of observations pertaining to their choice of mates is relevant. Many of the women told of meeting their men as "pickups" in a bar or other public setting in an intensely felt impulsive act. "Love at first sight" is a common enough occurrence, but their first sight was never checked out against subsequent findings. These couples did not court. They did not get to know each other. Either they consummated and consolidated their relationships immediately, or rejected them out of hand.

Once established, the relationships ran their protracted sadomasochistic course, and terminated equally as abruptly, usually with a violent grand finale about which there seemed to be little remorse. As abruptly as they were "picked up," so were they "dropped," usually with the man being "thrown out." Nor was there any evidence of mourning at the loss; it was "out of sight, out of mind." More often, the mate was replaced with another chosen in the same manner.

A curious corollary to this pattern can be detected in the reactions of those who treated these people and their children. As their lives unfolded and we came to learn of their plights, at times it was difficult to take what we heard seriously. It all had the quality of a "soap opera," a certain unreality that bordered on the playful, a sort of "make-believe" that was vaguely amusing. That quality was abruptly shattered when the impact of their lives upon their children became apparent; then they came more to resemble Greek tragedies with an inexorable unfolding dictated by the observation that character is destiny.

In the initial design it was planned to include the men as active participants in the Parents' Centre Project. This never came to be. It took a while before it became apparent that the women did not want their men involved and did everthing possible to prevent it. They reported that the men refused, but when we did manage to make contact with some of them, they were surprised that we wanted to meet them and expressed a willingness to join in. The women seldom referred to their men as anything other than sources of aggravation. When they did speak of them, it was not as someone to whom they had a personal relationship, but rather as a third person singular, "him," or as a nicknamed figure, "Chico" or "Bootsie."

PERSONAL MYTHOLOGY OF GHOSTS AND MONSTERS

The parents' need to involve their child in their sadomasochism appears to arise out of a dynamic association between two symbols (May, 1975)—the monster, conspicuous in its prevalence; the ghost, conspicuous by its apparent absence. These symbolic representations of past and future bear a relationship that can be described as a personal mythology with conscious and unconscious features (San Martino and Newman, 1975).

"He [or she] is a monster!" was a phrase used by almost every mother to characterize her child at some point. The child might, when he was good, be very, very good, but when he was bad, she saw him as being a true monster.[2] This view of the child as a monster remained encapsulated, unaffected by the coexistence of other benign versions of the child, or by the comments of others. It represented a fixed idea (Solomon, 1962), sometimes

---

2. The word "monster" is defined as "an omen of things to come; something marvelous, a divine portent." It shares a Latin root with the word "Monstrance," the vessel in which the Host is exposed during the Roman Catholic ceremony. The monster contains a promise for the future.

more apparent, at other times, usually after a period of involvement in the Project, the image receded in the mother's mind, overlain by a more realistic recognition of her child.

In quality, the image appeared to reflect accurately the parent's appreciation of the developmental issues of oral aggression and the child's struggle for mastery. In degree, the picture of the child as monster was a gross caricature, an exaggeration all out of human proportion, depicting either an adult's view of a real monster, or the ghost of a child's vision of an adult.

As to the origins of ghosts,[3] we have little in the way of direct information. Few of the parents maintained active contact with their own parents. The discontinuity between the generations persisted. The memories of childhood they volunteered had a detached quality, removed from relevance to their present. The absence of a sense of personal continuity left their recollections of childhood as belonging to another person. When, on occasion, the recall of facts bestirred an arousal of emotion, the parent would abort the process with a comment, "Well, that's the way it was—tough; but I survived!" Most of what was recalled came in the aftermath of reenactment, with the recognition, "I did it to her just like they did to me . . . and I swore that I'd never do that to my kid . . . I was gonna be different!"

The parents' sense of being possessed by forces over which they had but feeble control was frequently acknowledged with an air of fatalism, as if there were nothing that could, or should, be done about it. "Well, that's just life in the big city." They were, as prisoners of the past with no idea of escape, resigned to a future for which their expectations were foreshortened.

Only in relation to their mates and to their children were they made acutely aware of being possessed by forces beyond their ken. Around their mates, there was little to offer, since the parents had usually chosen partners well-suited in reality to the roles of persecutor-victim. It was through their children that it was

---

3. The word "ghost," aptly employed by Selma Fraiberg et al. (1975), in "Ghosts in the Nursery," is defined as the "soul of a deceased person appearing in a visible form." It shares a root with the German word *Geist*, meaning fury, spirit. The derivatives are said to point to a primary sense, "to wound, tear, to pull to pieces."

possible, occasionally, to demonstrate the likelihood of ghosts from their pasts, deceiving the parent into seeing a monster where there was only a child, a "ghost" in the guise of a "monster."

What I said about ghosts from childhood is inferential, deduced as the most plausible explanation for the adults' view of their child as monster. On one occasion, we witnessed what certainly appeared to be a child in the process of making a ghost.

One afternoon at nap-time, the chief care worker was reading to a little girl while a little boy was listening in. The little girl interrupted the story to ask, "Did your momma read to you when you were little?" The worker responded, "Yes," adding that she loved to listen to her mother when she was a child. Then the little boy joined in, "Did your ma beat your butt when you was little?" When the worker told him, "No," the boy went on with mounting agitation. "Well my ma beats my butt, and when she does, why then I pinches her, and I kicks her, I bites her and cuts her up into little pieces and I chops off her head, and then I eats her up!" With that, he lapsed back into silence.

DISCUSSION

Many of the observations in this study point to the paradox of deeply ambivalent emotion as the basis for the longevity of attachment between mates and children, an attachment that endures for years, despite repeated violence, separations, and restorations. Their lives demonstrate an inextricable weaving together of aggressive and libidinal behavior that calls for some elaboration upon the dual instinct theory as a basis for understanding (Stepansky, 1977). Solnit's (1972) commentary on the relationship between the instincts outlines the issue: "we must realize that libido and aggression coexist, can almost never be viewed separately in the actual functional situation, have broad areas of overlapping, similar and converging functions, and still remain a psychic, metaphoric reference, best described as the demand the body and its functions make upon the mind" (p. 438).

The demands placed by their bodies upon their minds led the subjects of this study into lives of internal confusion and external chaos, chronically unable to get what they wanted without violence. Their failure to master the use of aggression in the service of personal satisfaction was most apparent within the domestic relationship of mate to the parent of a child during a particular phase of development. Generally, the mothers in the study reported satisfaction with their pregnancies and the first 6 to 9 months of their children's life. The onset of their complaints coincided with their children's growth out of infancy into active orality, in concert with the onset of rapidly increasing motor competence. This developmental period, characterized by Mahler (1972) as the practicing subphase, brought a marked change in the mothers' experience of their children.

The exaggeration and distortion with which the mothers described their children's behavior indicated the appearance of phobic ideation about the children's use of aggression toward the goal of separation-individuation. Their language and imagery were more fitting to an adult run amok. The "terrible 2's" became an era of "monstrous" behavior by children whose every expression of aggression was perceived by their mothers as a willful assault, aimed at destroying the maternal person through the force of insatiable demands delivered with ruthless energy.

This phenomenon illustrates the concept of projective identification, clinically delineated in the writings of Melanie Klein (1977). Having made the equation of the child's normal aggression with violence, the mothers then dealt with it as if it presented a real and immediate danger to be avoided and punished, but not prohibited. The meaningful prohibition of violence was conspicuously absent from the intercourse between these mothers and their children. The threat of abandonment and/or retaliation came to dominate the particulars of the mother-child relationship. The child was defined as one to be feared, and the mother's fear provided confirmation for the child's fear of aggression, his own and that of others.

It is difficult to epitomize the consequences of such an impasse in the child's efforts to master oral aggression within the aftermath of the weaning experience. It results in shifting recurring struggles about the direction of energy into aggression versus regression. If the child cannot pound the table, he tries to suck his thumb. If he cannot count upon being constrained while running, then he will run into a wall to be stopped. When the situation allows for neither aggression nor regression, then there follows a stoppage in ego development, a blight that leaves the child apathetic and atrophied both physically and emotionally. The children in this study presented initially with some variation upon this clinical picture (Fraiberg, 1968).

The treatment of these children rested upon the establishment of a relationship with a situation that defined their aggression as an item desirable and necessary to their being. The provision of objects, human and nonhuman, accessible to attack, with appropriate constraints upon violence, led to rapid restoration of growth in the development of their ego functions. This occurred even when there was little or no change in their parents' tolerance for their aggression. Although the parents usually complained about their children's growth, they did not remove them from the program. The rapid evolution of competence for emotional self-expression following upon their initiation of manageable aggression was a predictable sequence heartening to the observer.

A similar phase of phobic ideation appeared to have been a determining factor in the mothers' choice of men. Uniformly, they described them as "mean men" given to violent outbursts, usually precipitated by drink. The oft-repeated fight sequence began with one partner trying to get something from the other, usually without coming out and asking for it. The want went ungranted, and frustration became the basis for relating; one partner demanding without asking, not getting, and becoming angry and/or hurt, over and over until the point of violence was reached. Once mutual provocation had run its course to violent discharge, the tension between the partners subsided, only to recur. In several instances, a suitor offering what the women said they sought came into their lives, and met with their vigorous rejection. The loyal devotion with which the partners clung to each other suggests that frustration was an element essential to their relationship, precisely because it allowed for the containment of both libidinal and aggressive instincts without requiring the sustained effort to separate them out in daily living. The couples lived as "gluttons for frustration" in relationships that permitted them to express concurrently the behavioral derivatives of libidinal and aggressive instincts, without concern for integrity of self or appropriateness of circumstances.

The experience is exemplified in a story told by one of the mothers who attributed it to her husband. A man ordered his wife to prepare him two eggs for his breakfast—one was to be soft-boiled and the other fried. She dutifully complied and set them before him. He angrily threw them on the floor, shouting: "Dammit, you fried the wrong one!"

Our present understanding of the enduring devotion with which these men and women cling to a sadomasochistic mode of relating derives from this point. The fact that each cannot, or will not, give what the other wants, while standing for what they long for, provides the basis for their attachment. The partners need each other more for what they are *not,* than for what they are. The disparity between what is not, and what is longed for, offers a stimulus of challenge, to reconvene the symbolic representatives of the original parties, to establish again a weaning relationship of self-as-child with mate-as-mother. Through directing demands to unresponsive partners, the experience of oral frustration is reconstructed. The frustration of desires mobilizes oral aggression and the associated affect of disappointment and rage. Another opportunity to master the weaning experience is presented to the partners who have yet to learn how to get what they want through the exercise of aggression in the service of their hearts' desire. By trying to get "blood out of a stone," they have another chance to learn what they need to know about the realities of their desires, their choice of objects, and the nature of the energies within themselves for getting, instead of being given to.

The ways in which the parents related to themselves and their surroundings reflect perseveration of a form of thought and emotion which Modell (1968) and Solomon (1962) have described as the transitional object relationship. The persistence of this mode of relating appears in adulthood in a variety of clinical contexts and in daily life. Its manifestation in these couples has particular relevance to their need to direct their aggression against each other in a compulsive, repetitive, and frustrating fashion such that neither partner gets what he or she wants from the other.

Within the context of the transitional form of object relationship, the differentiation of actions derived from libidinal or aggressive impulses is not required. That the beloved be hurt, and that the victim continue to love the transgressor are needs acceptable to both parties. The partners remain stuck to each other within their failure to reconcile the instinctual basis for their emotional ambivalence; their inability to know the distinct qualities of their own aggression and love promotes their sadomasochistic behavior.

The issue of whether this results from the persistence of a unitary phase of undifferentiated psychic structure (Klein, 1932, 1957), or is the continuation of unresolved conflicts between two separate instinctual drives (Brenner, 1971; Hartmann et al., 1949; Parens, 1979) involves a set of unanswered questions that lie beyond the scope of this study. Whatever form the instincts may take in the prenatal and neonatal stages of being human, the service of adult love requires the masterful use of aggression to assure that the beloved is protected and cared for, rather than destroyed. Failure to sort out and differentiate the aggressive from the libidinal inclinations, and to bring them both under effective ego control jeopardizes the reproductive potential of the adult relationship.

Emergence of predictable knowledge of the distinct qualities of libidinal and aggressive inclinations begins in the aftermath of the weaning process when the child's knowledge of himself rests upon what Winnicott (1958) has described as the "mother's capacity to survive the instinctual moment and so to be there to receive and understand the true reparative gesture" (p. 24). The prevalence of phobic thoughts among the mothers studied made it impossible for them to survive the "instinctual moment" presented by their children's aggression. Whenever their children's aggression threatened to cross their path, they took leave of its reality through abandonment and/or punishment. Left to their own devices, such children remain ill-equipped to attain mastery in the developmental uses of aggression.

The plasticity of aggression during early development is such that circumstances impinging upon growth have a significant effect upon the ultimate disposition of the child's energies (Hartmann et al., 1949). Deficits in maternal protection coupled with repeated exposure to physical abuse during the period of 1 to 3 years of age appear to deprive the child of a major opportunity to master aggression in the service of the self. This study suggests the importance of providing psychotherapy for abusive mothers in the hope of reducing recurrent failure in the mastery of aggression that results in the propagation of violence from one generation to the next.

BIBLIOGRAPHY

ABRAHAM, K. (1924), The influence of oral erotism on character-formation. In: *Selected Papers on Psycho-Analysis*. London: Hogarth Press, 1927, pp. 393–406.

BOWLBY, J. (1973), *Attachment and Loss*. New York: Basic Books.

BRENNER, C. (1971), The psychoanalytic concept of aggression. *Int. J. Psychoanal.*, 52:137–144.

FRAIBERG, S. (1968), The origins of identity. *Smith Coll. Stud. Soc. Wk.*, 38:79–101.

———— ADELSON, E. & SHAPIRO, V. (1975), Ghosts in the nursery. *J. Amer. Acad. Child Psychiat.*, 14:387–421.

GALDSTON, R. (1965), Observations of children who have been physically abused. *Amer. J. Psychiat.*, 122:440–445.

———— (1975), Preventing the abuse of little children. *Amer. J. Orthopsychiat.*, 43:372–381.

———— (1979), Disorders of early parenthood. In: *Basic Handbook of Child Psychiatry*, ed. J. Noshpitz. New York: Basic Books, 2:581–593.

HARTMANN, H., KRIS, E., & LOEWENSTEIN, R. M. (1949), Notes on the theory of aggression. *Psychoanal. Study Child*, 3/4:9–36.

KLEIN, M. (1932), *The Psycho-Analysis of Children*. London: Hogarth Press.

———— (1957), *Envy and Gratitude*. London: Tavistock Publications.

———— (1977), *Love, Guilt, and Reparation and Other Works*. New York: Dell.

MAHLER, M. S. (1972), On the first three subphases of the separation-individuation process. *Int. J. Psychoanal.*, 53:333–338.

MAY, R. (1975), Values, myths and symbols. *Amer. J. Psychiat.*, 132:703–706.

MODELL, A. H. (1968), *Object Love and Reality*. New York: Int. Univ. Press.

PARENS, H. (1979), *The Development of Aggression in Early Childhood*. New York: Jason Aronson.

SAN MARTINO, M. & NEWMAN, M. B. (1975), Intrapsychic conflict, interpersonal relationship and family mythology. *J. Amer. Acad. Child Psychiat.*, 14:422–435.

SOLNIT, A. J. (1972), Aggression. *J. Ameri. Psychoanal. Assn.*, 20:435–450.

SOLOMON, J. C. (1962), The fixed idea as an internalized transitional object. *Amer. J. Psychother.*, 16:632–643.

STEPANSKY, P. E. (1977), *A History of Aggression in Freud* [*Psychol. Issues*, Mongr. 39]. New York: Int. Univ. Press.

WINNICOTT, D. W. (1953), Transitional objects and transitional phenomena. In: *Collected Papers*. London: Tavistock Publications, pp. 229-242.

_____ (1958), Psycho-analysis and the sense of guilt. In: *The Maturational Processes and the Facilitating Environment*. New York: Int. Univ. Press, pp. 15-28.

ZETZEL, E. R. (1953), "The depressive position." In: *Affective Disorders*, ed. P. Greenacre. New York: Int. Univ. Press, pp. 84-116.

Extreme Traumatization as Cumulative Trauma

Psychoanalytic Investigations of the Effects of Concentration Camp Experiences on Survivors and Their Children

ILSE GRUBRICH-SIMITIS

EARLY APPROACHES

IN *CIVILIZATION AND ITS DISCONTENTS* (1930), FREUD COMMENTS ON the subjective nature of extreme suffering with which in the final analysis it is not possible to empathize:

> No matter how much we may shrink with horror from certain situations—of a galley-slave in antiquity, of a peasant during the Thirty Years' War, of a victim of the Holy Inquisition, of a Jew awaiting a pogrom—it is nevertheless impossible for us to feel our way into such people—to divine the changes which original obtuseness of mind, a gradual stupefying process, the cessation of expectations, and cruder or more refined methods of narcotization have produced upon their receptivity to sensations of pleasure and unpleasure. Moreover, in the case of the most extreme possibility of suffering, special mental protective

The author, a member of the German Psychoanalytic Association, is in practice in Frankfurt/Main.

The original German version of this article appeared in *Psyche*, 33:991–1023, November 1979. Subsequent literature is not considered.

I am greatly indebted to Veronica Mächtlinger for her excellent translation.

devices are brought into operation. It seems to me unprofit-
able to pursue this aspect of the problem any further [p. 89].

Freud seems to have broken off his argument at this point
because he apparently considered these historical events too far
removed in time for further investigation to add anything to our
knowledge of the misery in our own society. No one, in 1929,
could have predicted the extremes of suffering which, 9 years
later, Freud himself was to escape only through emigration and
which have now come to be described by the word "holocaust."
The final unimaginability of these experiences, only one generation removed from ourselves, has been commented on by Elie
Wiesel (1975):

> Those who have not lived through the experience will never
> know; those who have will never tell; not really, not com-
> pletely. . . . The past belongs to the dead and the survivor does
> not recognize himself in the images and ideas which presum-
> ably depict him. . . . Auschwitz means death, total, absolute
> death—of man and of all people, of language and imagination,
> of time and of the spirit [p. 314].

Only poets such as Nelly Sachs, Immanuel Weissglas, and Paul
Celan may have been able to convey in language something of
the horror of which human beings proved themselves capable—
in the *realization* of a psychotic universe in the extermination
camps, a world unique in the technical perfection of its destructive apparatus, unique in the collective descent into an unimaginable primitivity of affect. Poems such as "Chorus of the
Survivors," "To Those Who Build the New House," "He," "Death
Fugue," "They Dug the Earth in Themselves," written during or
shortly after these events, contain in a condensed and en-
ciphered form all the internal and external elements later to be
discovered in analytic work with survivors and their children.

Fragmentary as these analytic findings may be, they should
not be allowed to be forgotten and should be extended. Not only
have they been collected with considerable delay, they seem to be
continually threatened by a new wave of repression, in spite of
the number of publications on this theme in the past 20 years.
Alexander and Margarete Mitscherlich (1960, 1968) have especially emphasized the need to resist the tendency to defend our-

selves against such insights. In this paper, therefore, I shall not only consider the present state of our knowledge and hypotheses concerning survivors and their children, but also examine the anxieties we experience when confronted with the repercussions of the concentration camps upon the inner world of the survivors and their children. These anxieties can be so overwhelming that they lead even psychoanalysts to withhold empathy and to deny the seriousness of such after effects.

The first descriptions of the world of the concentration camps and the very first attempts at a retrospective psychodynamic analysis appeared in the form of eyewitness reports in the 1940s and early 1950s, written by psychiatrically, psychologically, and sociologically trained authors who themselves had been imprisoned.[1] Today it seems self-evident that the psychic suffering of the survivors would persist after liberation in spite of a gradual return to an apparently normal daily routine; yet this insight was in fact achieved only very slowly over a period of many years. Traces of this struggle against tremendous resistance can still be found in the terminology originally used to describe the disturbances encountered. "Refugee neurosis" (Pedersen, 1948) was a preferred term or, even more euphemistically, "repatriation neurosis" (quoted by Eitinger, 1961). These terms implied that one was dealing with comparatively common adjustment problems resulting from a change of environment.

Paul Friedman (1948, 1949) was the first to point out that the psychic damage to the concentration camp survivors had been completely overlooked and that efforts at rehabilitation had been confined to material help. Physical survival was, however, no guarantee for psychic survival. In his clinical study of sur-

1. To mention only a few: Bondy (1943), Adelsberger (1947), Frankl (1947), Tas (1951); the latter also mentions attempts made together with the psychoanalyst Karl Landauer to work therapeutically with fellow prisoners in the camps. In *Der SS-Staat,* Kogon (1947) describes the social and organizational system of the concentration camp and also discusses the camp situation as an "Ecce homo mirror" in terms of a psychology of persecutor and victim. Bettelheim (1943, 1960) and Federn (1946) write from a psychoanalytic point of view, but Bettelheim uses his observations in Dachau and Buchenwald in 1938–39 to question the validity of the psychoanalytic model.

vivors who were reimprisoned in Cyprus in 1946 on their way to
Palestine, Friedman made important observations which were
confirmed only much later and elaborated on by others. The
typical symptoms he described were severe psychosomatic and
depressive reactions, sexual dysfunction, phobic states, flatness
of affect and emotional relationships, an "affective anesthesia"
(Minkowski, 1946), and survivor guilt. Metapsychologically,
Friedman diagnosed a severe impairment of the synthetic function of the ego and of reality testing. Adolescent prisoners
showed a marked retardation of their psychosexual development which Friedman related to conditions enforced on the
victims during their imprisonment: regression to infantile dependency, extreme intensification of narcissism, and a revival of
early castration anxieties evoked by the perpetual threat of
death. These early descriptions, which are still worth reading,
present us not only with the first formulations of the "survivor
syndrome" (Niederland, 1961) but also with the first intimations
of the countertransference problems met with in confrontation
with survivors.

Another early psychoanalytic investigation of the effects of
concentration camp imprisonment is the report of Anna Freud
and Sophie Dann (1951) on their observations on six orphans
from Theresienstadt who were sent to England in 1945.[2]

The Restitution Laws operating from the early 1950s as well as
their amendments in the following two decades led indirectly—
via the requirement for medical examinations to prove the damage to the petitioners' health and to assess the degree of reduction of earning capacity—to increased demands for scientific
information about the severe psychic injuries of many survivors.
In the first years, however, the psychiatric-neurological expert

---

2. The authors' relatively positive diagnosis at that time—that in spite of the
most severe traumatization during the pregenital developmental phases and
the fact that the children's first love objects were children of the same age, they
were in latency "neither deficient, delinquent nor psychotic" (p. 168), but
rather presented a picture of precarious normality—was later revised by Anna
Freud (1954). In puberty the children developed symptoms which necessitated
psychoanalytic treatment at the Hampstead Clinic. In this way a longitudinal
study became possible. See also Anna Freud (1960) as well as a detailed account
of the analysis of one such child as a young adult by Ludowyk Gyomroi (1963).

opinions acknowledged only disturbances which could be diagnosed in terms of neurological organic damage. This practice was dogmatically modeled on the then-prevailing psychiatric doctrine of the traumatic neurosis, developed among other reasons to explain the war neuroses of World War I. This approach was based on the assumption that even an extreme trauma, if it does not leave traces of organic structural damage, cannot in principle permanently affect behavior and emotional experience in a previously healthy individual. The theory held that where organic damage was not present, the cessation of the traumatic stimulus would in every case lead to a waning of the disturbances. Where this was not the case and the symptoms persisted, a diagnosis of "pension neurosis" or "tendency neurosis," which did not require compensation, was made. Moreover, petitioners were often subjected to techniques of examination which struck them as a continuation of the persecution and "selection" they had previously suffered. The survivors experienced these methods as secondarily traumatizing and stigmatizing and as producing a situation in which they felt themselves once more to be at the mercy of an omnipotent and arbitrary aggressor.[3]

Among the German physicians, however, some were influenced by the work of psychiatrists like Bastiaans, Eitinger, and Trautman. From the late 1950s onward, they attempted to set up the required examination in such a way that the claimant was regarded no longer as "an object to be judged" but rather as a human being with whom one could "enter into a conversation" (Jacob, 1961). They criticized the rigid scientific medical methods based exclusively on physical data, provided detailed phenomenological descriptions of the victims' emotional experiences, and developed specific assessment criteria and a more adequate nosology (see, e.g., Venzlaff's concept of "personality change through experience"). Finally, as the apocalyptic nature

3. Because most of the survivors were not living in the Federal Republic of Germany, foreign physicians were also charged by German consulates with the task of giving expert opinion. In 1963–64 Meerloo issued a warning to his colleagues not to hide behind the reflex hammer and confront survivors with a "cold, defensive wall of silence." Such an attitude could well lead to a strengthening of the survivors' already massive psychosomatic defenses.

and dimensions of the trauma under totalitarian terror were gradually recognized, theoretical progress as well as more humane practices ensued.[4]

PSYCHOANALYTIC OPINIONS ON EXTREME TRAUMATIZATION OF THE FIRST GENERATION

Although psychoanalysis was not considered, either by the psychiatrists or by the judges involved, to be an "authoritative method" (Eissler, 1963), psychoanalysts were also asked to give expert opinions. The almost stereotyped syndrome—described, e.g., as "chronic reactive depression" (Baeyer, 1958) or as "concentration camp syndrome" (this term originated in 1954; see Eitinger, 1961; Chodoff, 1963)—which some psychiatrists confronted with survivors gradually came to recognize was finally investigated psychoanalytically, only years after Friedman's isolated work. Kestenberg (1979) speaks of a "latency period"—in the sense of a distancing from the trauma—that had to be lived through before the analysts' own defenses were sufficiently permeable to permit the perception and examination of the horror connected with the disturbances of the survivors. Since the early 1960s, leading contributions have appeared, especially by Eissler (1963, 1967, 1968), Niederland (e.g., 1961, 1968a, 1968b), Krystal and Niederland (1968), and Hoppe (1962, 1964, 1965). Such initiatives were not confined to individual researchers. The aftermaths of concentration camp imprisonment have since then increasingly become a topic for psychoanalytic and psychoanalytically oriented congresses and symposia.[5]

4. Some of these authors should be mentioned for their meritorious work: Venzlaff (1958); Baeyer and his co-workers in Heidelberg (1958, 1964); the monograph *Psychiatrie der Verfolgten*, which has become a classic, also contains a comprehensive review of the literature); Paul and Herberg (1963).

5. To mention a few of the earliest such meetings: the Wayne State University Workshops on "The Late Sequelae of Massive Psychic Trauma" were held during 1963–65; the papers and discussions were later published in *Massive Psychic Trauma* (Krystal, 1968), which presents a summary of the views of psychoanalysts and psychoanalytically oriented psychiatrists. (See also *Psychic Traumatization*, edited by Krystal and Niederland [1971], which consists mainly of articles on extreme traumatization of concentration camp survivors, including an evaluation of two workshops held in 1968 by the American Psychoanaly-

It is not possible to comment on the by now very extensive literature on the "survivor syndrome" in any detail (see Hoppe's comprehensive review, 1971); nor do I intend to enter into the discussion of the psychoanalytic concepts of trauma and traumatic neurosis, which research on the "survivor syndrome" has revived. Rather, I want to describe and summarize the main characteristics of this syndrome, which most authors consider to be important and add some supplementary considerations. This will form a background to my discussion of the specific impairment of the parenting function in survivors, an impairment which results in the transmission of the trauma to the second generation. This is the problem with which we are confronted today, nearly 40 years later, as we begin to work analytically with the children of survivors.

Despite the great variety of clinical pictures ranging from psychosis through borderline structures and psychosomatic conditions to neurosis, a relatively clear-cut syndrome nevertheless can be discerned in survivors. This is probably primarily due to a certain uniformity in the extreme traumatization in the camps. By this statement I do not mean that even in this utmost horror, shades of difference did not exist. It made a difference whether one was imprisoned in Theresienstadt or in one of the extermination camps such as Auschwitz or Treblinka, or whether, within the camp, one had to exist in the death area or, e.g., in the workmen's barracks. However, it is the *combination* of extreme traumatic conditions in all concentration camps, the *realization of a psychotic universe,* that constitutes the essential difference between this and other forms of massive traumatization: the disruption of family ties and the loss of a familiar sociocultural environment; continuous separation anxiety; the witness-

---

tic Association on "Children and Social Catastrophe.") In 1966 Winnik led a symposium on "Psychiatric Disturbances of Holocaust ('Shoa') Survivors" for the Israel Psychoanalytic Society (see *Israel Annals of Psychiatry*, vol. 5, 1967; cf. also Winnik, 1967). After a colloquium chaired by Wangh, at the 24th International Psychoanalytic Congress in Amsterdam, several authors presented papers at a symposium on "Psychic Traumatization through Social Catastrophe" at the 25th International Psychoanalytic Congress in Copenhagen. These papers were published a year later in volume 49 of the *International Journal of Psycho-Analysis*.

ing of torture and murder; the perpetual helpless expectation of one's own violent death (by "selection," torture, starvation, forced labor, so-called "medical experiments," etc.); barbaric reinfantilization resulting from the prohibition of all individual initiative; annihilation of individuality (through the use of numbering and removal of all personal effects); elimination of privacy and demolition of shame barriers; the systematic abrogation of the principle of causality (no explanation was offered for events in the camps—there *was* no explanation); loss of the structuring dimension of time (no clocks or calendars); persistent experiences of debasement and degradation through being regarded as a member of a minority to be wiped out, as "vermin fit only to be exterminated"; being the object of systematic genocide.

An inversion of Freud's dictum of 1933 may best describe, in structural terms, the effect on prisoners of this global mental and physical assault: where ego was, there *id* shall be. Under the terror of the naked alternative Life or Death, all behavior became one-dimensional, unambiguous, entirely dictated by primary needs. More specifically, a drive regression to orality took place, in essence a shrinkage of libido to oral necessities in the interest of self-preservation. A displacement of libidinal cathexis from object to self representations, especially the body image, was the inevitable result. Continual external sadistic attacks led in the inner world of prisoners to progressive drive defusion and an anxiety-arousing remobilization of warded-off, infantile, sadomasochistic drive impulses.

The increased pressure from warded-off infantile wishes was additionally fostered by regressive changes in the *ego*, particularly in its defense organization. This was, so to speak, an unwelcome by-product, because these ego alterations had originally served the purpose of survival insofar as they led to a blunting of sensation and perception of traumatizing external stimuli. In this connection the defense mechanism of denial, albeit of a particular quality,[6] was of paramount importance. It proved

6. In his study of survivors of the Hiroshima bombing Lifton (1968) used the term "psychic closing-off"—which was later taken over to describe the typical defense of concentration camp victims.

most effective for survival in those prisoners who were able to combine this psychic "closing-off" of an unbearable external reality with an intense remembering of an idealized past and magical fantasying of a better alternative world—all this *without* becoming psychotic, in spite of the apparent similarity with the psychotic withdrawal from object representations and the erection of an alternative, hallucinatory, restitutive world.

A specific ego characteristic observed in survivors—Niederland (1968b) has called it "automatization of the ego" and Meerloo (1969) "robotization"—appears to be related to this global denial. These terms are used to describe an automatic functioning of the ego occurring, so to speak, at the periphery of the self, without accompanying affect. I conceive of this change in the ego-self organization as an ad hoc development of a "false self," albeit one with a genetic history different from that described by Winnicott (e.g., 1952). The gradual development of a shell of automatized ego functions can be thought of as an *armoring of the ego,* an adaptive achievement serving the purpose of coping with overwhelming anxiety. On the basis of Freud's second anxiety theory (1926), one would expect the adequate affective response of an ego confronted with persistent threats of death to be a continuous state of panic (automatic anxiety). Prisoners armored in the above sense were not overwhelmed, and anxiety situations could be perceived and dealt with psychically in terms of signal anxiety. It was only under these internal conditions that prisoners could—insofar as this was at all possible—remain capable of acting.[7]

Another centrally important defense mechanism was identification with the aggressor (A. Freud, 1936) who was seen to be omnipotent. This obviously functioned as an antidote to the permanent threat of impending "narcissistic depletion" (Eissler, 1968), despite enhanced narcissistic cathexis. "Narcissistic depletion" was dangerous to life because it could result in the so-called Mussulman stage—a gradual reduction to a sheer "reflex

7. This would correspond with Hillel Klein's observation (personal communication) that extreme traumatization (especially the sudden loss of love objects) had its most devastating effects when it occurred in the ghetto or immediately after arrival in the camps, e.g., during selection on the "ramp," *before* the ego had had time to armor itself through regression.

existence" which, through the almost complete withdrawal of self cathexes, inevitably ended in death.

This threat of narcissistic depletion was due not only to extended periods of deprivation of external narcissistic supplies, but to *superego* changes deriving from the massive assault on the prisoners' psyche. These consisted in a regression to archaic forms of superego functioning and led especially to grave changes in the *ego ideal*. The devalued enemy-image propagated by the persecutors and projected onto the persecuted insidiously established itself in the latters' ideal self. Paradoxically and tragically, this occurred by way of the very defense mechanism— identification with the aggressor—which was used originally to check the process of narcissistic depletion.

Among the symptoms which found delayed expression in many survivors were psychosomatic and hypochondriacal complaints, depression, a variety of anxieties and anxiety equivalents, sleep disturbances, repetitive nightmares (sometimes intruding into waking life in the manner of hallucinations), brooding preoccupations, feelings of unreality and depersonalization, changes in the body image, cognitive disorders, excessive irritability, restlessness, and outbursts of anger. On the other hand, one could observe apathy and paralysis of affects, an incapacity to relate to others in any but a dutiful way. After years of sheer survival from one day to the next, the future could no longer be conceived of as an extended period of time to be filled meaningfully. Time was frequently experienced as standing still. These manifestations of gross impairments in time perception went hand in hand with memory disturbances. There were extensive amnesias for the time before the persecution and frequent hypermnesias for particular camp experiences. Above all, life was overshadowed by the most severe feelings of guilt and shame for having survived at all, for having endured the humiliations and degradations, and for having tolerated the abandonment of previous superego and self-ideal demands.

Some of the psychic adaptations which during imprisonment could be regarded as necessary for survival were later often found to have resulted in irreversible structural damage. The extensive use of denial combined with an escape into an inner world of memories and fantasies, which were imperative to en-

dure camp conditions, interfered in normal daily life with reality
testing and coping. Enhanced libidinal cathexis of the body
image expressed itself after liberation as a hypochondriacal
preoccupation with bodily functions. The fact that many survivors later had the utmost difficulty in entering into spontaneous empathic relationships was probably due to the persistence
of these automatized ego functions, which have been characterized as an armoring of the ego. After all, it would not be
surprising to find that survivors unconsciously attempt to regulate their vulnerability to overstimulation, especially a repetition
of traumatic object loss, by a constant alertness, a readiness to
expect the worst, and an avoidance of intense cathexis of new
objects.

This inhibition of the readiness to cathect new objects also has
another source. It serves at the same time to maintain cathexis of
the lost objects. In analytically oriented treatments it has been
shown that survivors give up these earlier objects as finally and
irrevocably lost only when new objects gain in importance. This
maintenance of cathexis—a kind of immobilization of the lost
objects, which is characteristic of the inner world of many
survivors—can itself be fully understood only in the light of a
further pathogenic factor in the camps, i.e., the hindering or
total blocking of any work of mourning. Not only did many
victims witness the murder of relatives and friends; there were
no individual graves, no cathartic rituals—that is, no external
supports for introducing and carrying out the mourning process. Merely *showing* adequate horror, rage, and grief endangered one's own life. Under these circumstances the strong
aggressive impulses aroused in the persecuted against their persecutors could not be discharged, and the laborious work of
detaching cathexis from lost objects could not take place.[8] All

8. Psychoanalysts related the apparent symptom-free interval between liberation and the appearance of delayed aftereffects of imprisonment in many of
the survivors to this maintenance of the cathexis of lost objects as well as to a
refusal to give up hope of once more finding loved ones whose fate was not
known with any certainty. In order to establish a causal connection between
imprisonment and later mental disturbances, many of the investigators in the
restitution processes at first demanded that "bridging symptoms" be demonstrated. Only gradually did an understanding develop for the fact that overt

clinicians working with survivors agree that a severe pathology in dealing with aggressive drives is central to the survivor syndrome—a state of affairs which thwarts belated attempts at mourning and turns them into depression. Ubiquitous depressive moods, grave guilt feelings, paranoid anxieties, and psychosomatic complaints can be thought of as expressions of a chronic pathological form of regulating aggressive impulses through the use of defenses such as turning against the self, projection, and somatization.[9]

Some observations even support the view that the infiltration of the enemy-image into the structures of the superego and self ideal of the persecuted may persist and continue to direct and regulate behavior. Some survivors developed asocial characteristics after liberation, although such tendencies had not been observed either in their professional or personal life before traumatization. It was as though such survivors had continued to exist, as they were forced to in the camps, under the dictate of a corrupt value system, and in a lifelong identification with the aggressor were obliged, so to speak, to demonstrate the supposed truth of the persecutors' stereotype.[10]

It has repeatedly been emphasized that not all survivors became ill after liberation, that there is no obligatory correlation between having survived the concentration camp and the emergence of belated psychic aftereffects. Psychoanalysts too have again and again commented on the presumed impact of the pretraumatic personality with its specific stress tolerance[11] and

---

symptoms not seldom made their appearance only after years, when the defenses of the survivors against the full perception of their losses had become brittle and when what Wolfenstein (1957) has called their "postdisaster utopia" had been overtaken by reality.

9. Hoppe (1962) used the term "chronic reactive aggression" to describe some of his patients who instead showed alloplastic mechanisms of dealing with pent-up aggressive impulses.

10. Tanay (1968a) commented on the tendency in some survivors after liberation to choose "work situations of a masochist nature."

11. Wind (1971), e.g., suspects that a relationship exists between the capacity to survive and later recovery on the one hand, and the ability to actualize infantile masochistic drive impulses on the other. Other authors (among them Hoppe, 1962) consider it probable that obsessional and hysterical symptom

of the posttraumatic life experiences[12] on the outcome—whether psychic health or illness. It turned out to be a more or less chance factor, however, which proved decisive in determining whether or not mental disturbances developed. This lay in the question where, when, and to what extent the impact of the extreme trauma or a series of extreme traumas struck the individual. *Where* relates to the question: in which camp, or where within a particular camp, the survivor had been held prisoner; *when* refers to the ego state prevailing at the time of traumatization; this is not only the question of whether adaptive changes in the ego's defense organization, the armoring of the ego, had already taken place, but also at which stage in the individual's life cycle[13] the trauma occurred. The question *to what extent* applies to factors such as duration of imprisonment, the massiveness of the threat of death, sexual abuse, and loss of loved ones. The most extreme traumatizing factor appeared to be that of having experienced the murder of one's own children, i.e., the violent reversal of the natural order of dying which this represented. Eissler (1963), in his indictment of restitution procedures, poses the question in the title of his paper: "The murder of how many of one's children must one be able to tolerate without producing symptoms, to qualify for a 'normal constitution'?" He considers one interpretation of the Niobe myth to be that "the life of parents ends when they witness the death of their children." There are traumas under which any psychic structure must break.

Opinions on the question of the treatability of the psychic

---

neuroses or character disorders with their fixations at the anal and phallic developmental levels acted under camp conditions as a bulwark against too deep a regression to the oral level.

12. H. Klein (1971, 1973) believes that the environmental conditions in Israel seem to facilitate and encourage the reintegration of psychic structure in survivors; among these he lists the community life in the Kibbutz; holocaust monuments, and days of remembrance, which offer the opportunity for delayed, institutionalized, collective mourning; the possibility of projecting pent-up aggression onto a real external enemy. See also Winnik (1967) as well as the longitudinal studies of survivors in Norway by Eitinger (1975).

13. Some authors (among them Danto, 1968; Fink, 1968; Segall, 1974) hold the opinion that those survivors who experienced severe traumatization during adolescence were particularly gravely damaged.

disturbances of survivors and therapeutic prognoses differ very widely.[14] One reason for these differences appears to lie in the fact that different authors are talking about different groups of patients. Presumably this is a question which cannot be answered in generalized terms. Each case must be judged individually with reference to ego strength and severity of traumatization. Be that as it may, many authors are very skeptical and warn against too great a therapeutic enthusiasm, not least because of the strong masochistic defenses of survivors. In the view of these authors, an exceptionally fragile ego structure, a profoundly shattered basic trust, and the horror of the past to be remembered seem to indicate short-term, supportive, and counseling interventions. Others, however, report therapeutic successes with long-term uncovering treatments such as psychoanalysis and psychoanalytically oriented psychotherapy.

PSYCHOANALYTIC OPINIONS ON CUMULATIVE TRAUMATIZATION OF THE SECOND GENERATION

Rakoff, Sigal, and Epstein were the first to publish observations on the repercussions of the concentration camp experiences in families founded by survivors after their liberation. This paper tracing the impact on the second generation appeared in 1966, at a time when the children born immediately after the war were reaching adulthood.[15] The large number of children of survivors seeking psychiatric help, in comparison with control groups, had aroused attention in Montreal, which after 1945 had become a center for Jewish immigration. Psychiatrists distinguished two broad groups of symptoms in these patients: on

14. In the extensive literature on the survivor syndrome, the number of detailed case histories and of reports on psychotherapeutic work with such patients is strikingly small. See Hoppe (1965), Winnik (1967), Part VIII in Krystal (1968), Krystal (1971), Wind (1971), the case study of a psychotic patient by Nemeth (1971), and the impressive case history by Ludowyk Gyomroi (1963) already mentioned.

15. Several authors (among them Williams, 1973; Kestenberg, 1973) report that survivors seldom sought treatment for the developmental disturbances of their children because of their own overwhelming need to deny such problems. Indeed, parents often resisted attempts made by others to provide help. This meant that unless spectacular symptoms developed, patients of the second generation came into treatment only in adolescence or as young adults.

the one hand, apathy, depression, feelings of emptiness, and a specific lack of emotional involvement; on the other hand, "agitated hyperactivity." Clinical investigations of the family background revealed some of the features which were later repeatedly confirmed by more profound analytic studies, e.g., that a fragile and precarious family structure existed behind a façade of social and economic adjustment and that the psychic survival of the parents depended upon a special conformity of behavior in the children born after liberation. This meant that such children had no opportunity to develop an individual identity.[16]

In 1966 (at the already mentioned symposium of the Israel Psychoanalytic Society) Davidson too suggested that the effects of extreme traumatization continue into the second generation (Davidson, 1967). Winnik (1968) at the 25th International Psychoanalytic Congress reported for the first time on a psychoanalytic treatment of a patient born directly after the war. The patient's father had been imprisoned in a concentration camp before becoming a partisan fighter. Winnik explicitly raised the question whether parental disturbances resulting from extreme traumatization are transmitted to the children of survivors.

Once analytic attention had been directed toward this problem, extensive research activity soon developed not only in Canada and Israel but especially in the United States. Symposia were held,[17] continuous working groups set up,[18] ques-

16. Sigal and Rakoff have continued their investigations (see Sigal, 1971, 1972, 1973; Sigal and Rakoff, 1971; Sigal et al., 1973).

17. At both annual meetings of the American Psychoanalytic Association in May and December 1968, clinical experiences with children of survivors were described and opinions exchanged in the workshop "Children and Social Catastrophe." In 1970 a symposium organized by the International Congress of Child Psychiatry and the Association of Child Psychoanalysis took place in Jerusalem. Papers prepared for this meeting were subsequently published under the heading "Symposium: Children of the Holocaust" in Anthony and Koupernik (1973). In 1971 a further colloquium on "Children of Survivors" was arranged jointly by the American Psychoanalytic Association and the Association of Child Psychoanalysis (see Panel, 1974). Finally, workshops led by M. Bergmann, M. E. Jucovy, and J. S. Kestenberg were held in 1977 at the 30th International Psychoanalytic Congress in Jerusalem and in 1979 at the 31st International Psychoanalytic Congress in New York.

18. The "Group for the Psychoanalytic Study of the Effect of the Holocaust

tionnaires distributed,[19] and detailed case studies published.[20]

There is no doubt that in the beginning the expectation prevailed that in the second generation a clear-cut "survivor's child syndrome," comparable to the "survivor syndrome," would be discovered.[21] Although the various research programs have not yet published any final results, this expectation has evidently not been fulfilled. The clinical pictures seen in the second generation are even more diverse than those found in the first generation. The terrible uniformity and the physical violence which constituted part of the extreme traumatization of the parents play no part in the traumatization of the children. As a first approach to the problem I would like to suggest that the extreme traumatization of the first generation exerts its effect upon the second generation as a "cumulative trauma" (Khan, 1963).[22]

The observation that not all survivors developed psychic disturbances, and that these depended upon the nature and extent of the persecution suffered, applies equally to the children. Evi-

---

on the Second Generation," under the chairmanship of M. Bergmann, M. E. Jucovy, and J. S. Kestenberg, was founded in 1974 in New York in order systematically to investigate case material from analyses and analytically oriented therapy of children of survivors *and* of children of the persecutors (Kestenberg, 1977). A report on research programs and methods as well as first results and conclusions will be published soon. (I would like here to thank M. E. Jucovy and J. S. Kestenberg for allowing me to read their unpublished manuscripts and for the helpful discussions held with them and members of the group in Jerusalem and Sands Point, N.Y.).

19. See the summary report by Kestenberg (1974) on the questionnaire conducted in 1969–70 among members of the Association for Child Psychoanalysis.

20. E.g., Laufer (1973), Furman (1973), Lipkowitz (1973), and Kestenberg (1980). In the literature, reports on analyses and psychoanalytically oriented psychotherapies as well as on combined individual and family therapies have been published.

21. As recently as 1970, Barocas found a "striking resemblance" between the symptomatology of the survivors and that of their children and pleaded for a more careful examination of family dynamics.

22. It seems improbable that this process of transmitting the trauma to the next generation will stop once it has begun, unless children of survivors try to counterbalance the problems resulting from their cumulative traumatization either through seeking therapeutic help or by a compensatory choice of partner, thus providing their children with alternative possibilities of identification.

dently a correlation exists between the extent of extreme traumatization in the parents and the seriousness of the cumulative
trauma in the children. At the workshop at the 30th International Psychoanalytic Congress in Jerusalem (1977), several variables were discussed which seem directly to influence the degree
of psychic impairment in the second generation.[23] Severe disturbances with serious ego pathology emerged in children,
whose parents were *both* survivors of extermination camps and
had lost children in the holocaust. Another variable aggravating
disturbances in the second generation was the parents' inability
to talk to their children about their experiences (this evidently
correlates with the massiveness of their extreme traumatization)
or, if they were able to talk, could do so only by splitting off the
accompanying affect. Finally, the firstborn among the children
were particularly severely affected.[24]

Against the background of Winnicott's profound explorations
of the mother's caretaking functions, Khan (1963, 1964) has, in
his concept of the "cumulative trauma," described a particular
disturbance of the preverbal mother-child relationship. During
the period of greatest helplessness and dependence, at a time
when the earliest psychic structures are beginning to be established, the infant is at the mercy of the mother's capacity for
flexible empathy and her ability to function as an auxiliary ego
for his anaclitic needs, i.e., as a "protective shield" against the
infant's being overwhelmed by internal and external stimuli.
Khan's concept describes the pathogenic effects of the mother's
failure to fulfill this function. There is no question here of gross
violations of maternal caretaking, such as physical neglect or
actual desertion of the child. Khan is referring rather to externally inconspicuous failures of empathy which, over an extended period of time, silently and at first invisibly, exert a

23. Axelrod et al. (1980) describe similar variables in their study of patients
who were hospitalized in adolescence or as young adults.

24. This enhanced vulnerability of firstborn children applies especially to
those born very soon after liberation, i.e., where the birth of a new child was
part of a manic attempt by the parents to reconstitute the lost family and where
this occurred before a certain level of psychic reintegration—especially in the
mother—could possibly have been reached. H. Klein (1973) refers to the excessive anxieties of such mothers concerning their firstborn children.

cumulative traumatic effect. In these cases the child attempts, so to speak, to empathize with the mother, who is so essential for his survival and for the maintenance of his psyche-soma equilibrium. This imposes upon the child a persistent psychic and physical strain, which constitutes the trauma and leads to premature and selective ego development. The results, which become evident only in retrospect, are distortions of the ego (including the body ego), and consequently disturbances in psychosexual development.

Only detailed analytic case material could, of course, demonstrate convincingly how Khan's concept might be relevant to some of the psychic problems of the second generation: to the paralyzing feelings of alienation, apathy, and emptiness; the inability to set personal or professional goals or to know who one is and what one wants to be. Such analytic information would make it possible to elucidate the nature of the failure of empathy, specific in each case and lying beyond memory, by using reconstructions pieced together from the smallest details of the patient's repetitions of all the elements of the primary infantile situation, shown in the transference-countertransference manifestations. Reference to the psychic effects of extreme traumatization, as described in the preceding section, may at least help to understand why parental functioning in survivors should be impaired, in spite of their urgent conscious wish to have the children born after liberation.

Khan makes the assumption that the success of a mother's highly complex capacity to empathize with the changing needs of her infant and toddler depends upon her own state of relative emotional equilibrium which allows her to cathect the child libidinally with a moderate and caring intensity. This means that the mother's function as a protective shield will be only partially fulfilled, or not fulfilled at all, in those instances in which she is compelled to use her child for the satisfaction of her own pressing drive needs or when other reasons prevent her from optimally cathecting her child. Leaving aside the serious external difficulties and uncertainties of the postwar period, we may try to imagine the inner situation of those mothers who became pregnant shortly after liberation from a concentration camp, and consider several factors which would seriously interfere with an optimal cathexis and make empathic communication with a newborn baby extremely difficult: increased narcissism provoked by the constant threat of death; in terms of libidinal drives, the mothers' own strong needs to be cared for and mothered after years of living in an emotional emergency state; in terms of aggressive drives, the massive pent-up impulses of hate and revenge seeking an outlet; and finally, predominantly preconscious and unconscious reservations against the cathexis of new objects—whether as a prophylactic defense against renewed traumatic object loss or because, as a result of the lack of mourning, great drive quantities remain bound up in cathexes of representations of earlier lost objects.

However, of special importance may be the ego regression imposed by camp conditions, and the concomitant blunting of the capacity for perceiving external stimuli, a blunting that results from the sweeping use of the mechanism of denial. The irreversible "armoring of the ego" appears, in part, to be responsible for the lifeless, mechanical, and robotlike atmosphere which characterizes many survivor families. Whatever reservations one has about adultomorphic constructions, it is nevertheless possible to imagine that the state of the extremely traumatized mother—one in which she is psychically "closed off" and functions in an automatic manner—would be experienced by the child as an inability on his part to win the mother's interest for himself, as his being of no value to her; that is, until he begins to identify with the mother's automatized, virtually deadened ego and thus attains a deceptive feeling of attunement with her. One of the most frequent complaints of second-generation patients is that they can only function mechanically, that they are unable to experience themselves as being alive.

Finally, one must assume that a mother can adequately function as a protective shield only if her narcissism in regard to her maternal role is relatively intact—if she has a sense of certainty (which of necessity is based partly on illusory omnipotent fantasies) that she really *can* protect her child under all circumstances. It is precisely this sense of certainty, however, that is deeply shattered or even destroyed in mothers who have witnessed and lived through the murder of their children. Indeed, it is conceivable that *one* unconscious expectation which

extremely traumatized mothers attach to these later-born children is the restoration of their maternal narcissism and with it a
chance to *prove* that they are after all capable of preserving the
life of children they have created.

This radical theme of Life and Death also adds its weight to
other expectations with which survivors burden their later-born
children beyond the preverbal stage of the mother-infant dyad.
To mention a few of the missions through which the parents
obviously attempt to bind the children on *their* side of the
persecutor-victim schism that totally dominates their psychic
life: the children are expected to function for their parents
as a bridge to life, thereby, once more in a reversal of the
natural order of events, giving psychic birth to them, freeing
them from their inner deadness; to replace the lost, idealized
love objects by slipping, so to speak, into their interrupted biog-
raphies and start living where they left off; that is, in essence to
undo the murder of parents, siblings, children, relatives, and
friends; to return to the psychotic world of the concentration
camps as rescuers and ensure that this time the parents do not
emerge as damaged and humiliated victims; to avenge their parents for the crimes committed against them by acting out the
parents' defensively warded-off hate, or, as monuments, to bear
living witness to those crimes through their own unlived and
petrified lives; to demonstrate, through their very existence, the
generative capacity of their parents and thus give the lie to the
persecutors' intention to destroy a whole denigrated people; to
be a solace and comfort to their parents and help to ease the
oppressive feelings of shame and guilt, to lift the denial, and to
perform for them the work of mourning.[25]

25. That such delegations are not specific to survivors and their children but
rather are a universal phenomenon in any parent-child relationship is well
known from the work of the family therapists. In addition to the weight and
paradoxical nature of the missions, which often have a double-bind quality,
there is a particularly aggravating circumstance in the patients of the second
generation: born into a situation where whole families have been killed, they
grew up in relatively isolated, small family units. The possibility of alternative,
moderating identifications with grandparents and other relatives is missing, as
are visible signs (such as photographs and memory-related objects) of the earlier family history. (For information on the family dynamics in survivor families
see especially Graaf, 1975.)

While these themes recur in the analytic treatment material of second-generation patients, this content need not be present in the same form in the unconscious, preconscious, or conscious fantasies of the first generation. Communications of this kind coming from the parents will in any case be organized and laid down in the mental life of the children according to phase-specific drive wishes, ego needs, and anxieties.[26] During the separation-individuation stages as well as in the oedipal phase, whenever conflicts around differentiation and rivalry are involved, i.e., whenever the working through of aggressive impulses is necessary, the sadomasochistic polarization and splitting into perpetrator-victim, persecutor-persecuted may develop directly between parents and children, often with devastating sharpness. In this way, the severe disturbance in dealing with aggressive impulses—a disturbance central to the survivor syndrome—extends to include the new family and is handed down to the children.

Parents obviously feel compelled to suppress even appropriate aggressive impulses toward their children—for example, those required for limit setting, which is so essential for the formation of psychic structure—because all aggression is associated with guilt. In an atmosphere of anxious overconcern, the child is frequently overindulged and exposed to inconsistent discipline. Moreover, the parents also react with alarm to developmentally appropriate manifestations of aggression in their children whose attempts at differentiation and impulses of rivalry are perceived by the parents as being so potentially destructive because they additionally threaten the parents' own precarious defenses against bottled-up hate and revenge impulses dating from

26. Kestenberg (1979, 1980) has shown how the children, in a chronological order, i.e., according to the immediate phase-specific concerns of each drive developmental stage, are particularly receptive to the transmission of the main traumas in their parents' history of persecution, more specifically, to the distorting, pathogenic influence of the parental attitudes resulting from these traumas. For example, a mother whose main trauma lay in the danger of starvation may conceive of feeding her child in the oral phase as a matter of life and death and convey this to him. Or parents who are convinced that they survived only through their capacity for hard labor may transmit to the child, during latency, that only work is lifesaving and react with panic when the child finds the developmental transition from play to work difficult.

the period of persecution. Thus, learning to deal with conflicts and to come to terms with ambivalence is made especially difficult for the children; as a consequence they develop a predominantly archaic superego structure, which in turn may interfere with the achievement of drive fusion.[27]

Although the earlier expectation of a thoroughgoing parallel between the psychic disturbances in the first and second generation has not been confirmed, certain similarities in symptoms, fantasies, and defense structure, based on the children's identification with their parents, are nevertheless discernible. Patients of the second generation have reported nightmares whose content corresponds to that of typical survivor dreams. Complaints about an impaired sense of time—the experience that time is standing still, that there is no future—depression, a sense of alienation, and hypochondriacal fears are common to both parents and children. Survivor guilt in the parents toward the dead corresponds to a specific form of separation guilt which the children feel toward the parents: to begin to lead one's own life, to differentiate psychically from the parents means surrendering them to death. Even specific defenses, developed by the parents during the catastrophe, appear in patients of the second generation: besides a milder form of ego automatization one finds above all florid fantasy activity as a defense against external reality, the avoidance of intensive object cathexis, certain masochistic maneuvers, and a deep identification with the aggressor. The traumatic damage to parental omnipotence corresponds in the children to a pathogenic destruction of their infantile omnipotence, i.e., too early and too massive a frustration of the child's need for parental idealization.

Opinions with regard to diagnosis again differ widely. In spite of great diagnostic variability, however, most authors stress severe pregenital disturbances and character pathologies involving the ego/self in children of survivors. According to which concepts among the more recent theories of narcissism are

27. An inadequate integration of aggressive drive elements as one of the pathological consequences of the mother's failure to function as a protective shield has already been stressed by Khan (1963). Indeed, patients of the second generation frequently showed psychopathic and delinquent behavior in adolescence (Aleksandrowicz, 1973; Panel, 1974).

applied, the disturbances are thought of in terms of false self, schizoid character, basic fault, narcissistic personality or borderline syndrome. Several authors (Lipkowitz, 1973; Graaf, 1975) place the focal point of pathology in the separation-individuation phase, others (Axelrod et al., 1980) diagnose atypical schizophrenia. Kestenberg (1979) follows M. Oliner in regarding the disturbance as a kind of hysterical double identity, which may strike one as pseudoschizophrenic.[28]

These nosological characterizations, all of which were originally developed without reference to the children of survivors, add nothing to the question of specificity in such patients. In fact, several authors cast doubt on the suggestion that a specific factor exists (Lifton, 1968; Rosenberger, 1973; Aleksandrowicz, 1973). Sigal (1973, 1978) has stressed that even if the material from survivors' children were to divulge special contents and particular themes crystallizing around the concentration camp experiences and the persecution of their parents, this would not necessarily mean that anything "formally," structurally specific is implied. Sigal maintains that these patients do not differ basically from others who have grown up with parents who, for other reasons, were chronically *preoccupied* (e.g., because of alcoholism or a severe physical illness) and could therefore only inadequately respond to the needs of their children. Other authors (Kestenberg, 1979; H. Klein, 1973), however, plead for specificity.

Although Erna Furman's warning (1973)—that we know too little about the patients from the second and even less about those from the third generation to draw definitive conclusions—should still be taken to heart, there is nevertheless *one* fundamental fact that speaks for specificity: the fact which should again be considered that in the concentration camps a psychotic universe was *realized*. For the psychotic, the experience of the end of the world is the result of a radical displacement of cathexis and a breakdown of inner reality; for the survivors, it was a catastrophic *external* event which they *really* experienced.

---

28. In this paper Kestenberg also attempts a detailed metapsychological assessment in the form of a "survivor's child profile." See also Kestenberg (1980).

Their familiar world—the world of families, customary ways of thinking and feeling, value systems, institutions and traditions—literally perished. At a deeper psychic level, for those who witnessed the perpetration of atrocities of an unimaginable order of magnitude, worse than the worst imaginable oral-cannibalistic or anal-sadistic fantasies, under conditions in which all highly organized defense structures and mature superego demands had been destroyed, these events must have signified the downfall of the secondary process and the "seizure of power" by the primary process. This, in turn, could have been experienced as a state of being totally threatened from within, from one's own unconscious, i.e., as a sudden and catastrophic loss of faith in symbolic and sublimatory capacities as well as in the relative reliability of the distinction between internal and external reality—a state comparable perhaps to the structure-shattering effect of breaking the incest barrier. Aided by the regressive impairment of reality testing, already described, it is possible that for the first generation the boundary between fantasying and realizing has become blurred. This could mean that *one* expectation which extremely traumatized survivors attach to their later-born children might be to recover, through them, their faith in the secondary process and its ability to control and delay drive impulses.

For the children, however, this would constitute a further excessive paradoxical demand. How can they work through and come to terms with their own developmentally appropriate, object-directed death wishes and thereby make the basic discovery that their objects remain unharmed and are not destroyed? How can they learn that fantasies have an experimental character, an as-if quality, and are not in themselves dangerous—if the parents, tending as they do to confuse fantasy and reality, convey in their reactions that they *really* feel threatened by such aggressive impulses? This must finally lead in the children to the sealing off of all aggressive drives and their derivatives. The early conviction of the magical-destructive force of hostile wishes cannot be tempered in object relationships of this kind. Should such a mother unconsciously experience in the child the return of the aggressor and should the child share this fantasy, words such as: "If you don't stop you'll be the death of me" could be uttered to a defiant child in an atmosphere in which neither is certain whether the threat is to be taken literally, whether the terrible equation fantasying/verbalizing = realizing could not come true.[29]

Seen in this way, it is not surprising that in patients of the second generation a severe impairment of the ego function of reality testing and differentiation between fantasy and reality has frequently been found.[30] This uncertainty also applies to the historical reality in those patients whose parents cannot talk about their experiences of persecution. While I do not wish to go into technical details, *one* central feature in such analyses should be mentioned: in the long run it is possible to establish relatively stable ego boundaries only to the extent to which the patient is gradually able to calm his anguished brooding about his parents' past and thus be less at the mercy of the resulting acting out. This can be achieved through a step-by-step attempt to clarify exactly what the parents have suffered *in reality*[31]—in spite of the terrible nature of these experiences and however emphatically this knowledge of a fundamentally different experience will inevitably convey the feeling of being separate from the parents—to a much greater degree than in the usual generation gap.

This painful but necessary task can be encouraged by the analyst's confrontations; i.e., he must accompany and some-

29. It seems to me that Kestenberg (1979, 1980) attempts to denote this categorial uncertainty with her term "transposition." She describes as transposition an inner process which she considers specific to children of survivors, a psychic mechanism "beyond identification," through which the children transpose themselves into their parents' past in such a total way that they develop a pseudodelusionary feeling of having to orientate themselves in a double reality—that they are literally, at one and the same time, living in the parents' past and in their own present.

30. It is self-evident that this creates extra problems in treatment and leads to delays in the working through of fantasies arousing anxiety and shame.

31. Brody (1973) in her report on a patient whose father was able to avoid capture by the Gestapo and escape from Germany takes a similar view on the necessity of investigating the historical past. In this case, the father, who later suffered from a depression, could not speak about his flight and its accompanying circumstances. The son made use of fantasies of this flight in his oedipal conflicts in a way that—in the absence of reality information—was detrimental to his superego development.

times, indeed, be a step ahead of the patient in being prepared precisely and concretely to apprehend the horror of the parents' experience. It is important that both patient and analyst fundamentally accept the *reality* of the extermination camps, without dissociating the accompanying almost unbearable feelings of anxiety, horror and impotence, loathing, guilt, shame, and grief. This means that the analyst has to resist not only his natural need to protect himself but also the tendency, reinforced by his training, to bypass reality and to devote his attention, from the very beginning, to the patient's fantasies. It is only to the extent that the historical reality is ascertained that the patient will be able to approach his own inner and outer reality. Before this has been achieved it is not possible to assess in the analysis whether, when, and how the parents' persecutory experiences may be used for purposes of resistance.

SOME OF OUR ANXIETIES

The fact that among studies on the aftereffects of concentration camp imprisonment theoretical articles outnumber by far case histories or papers concerned with treatment may well reflect a general characteristic of the psychoanalytic literature. Nevertheless, the almost complete absence of comment on countertransference problems does seem to be a special feature of the survivor literature.[32] Broadly stated, the capacity to experience and reflect countertransference means being able, in manifold ways, to enter into trial identifications with the patient and consciously to keep one's own feelings in touch with the patient's

32. As far as I am aware, only one paper, Hoppe's "The Emotional Reactions of Psychiatrists When Confronting Survivors of Persecution" (1967), makes these problems the main subject of investigation. This article is, however, chiefly concerned with the emotional reactions of psychiatrists diagnosing survivors in connection with restitution claims as well as with the iatrogenic responses of those being examined; i.e., it is not a study of countertransference in a long-term therapeutic process (see, however, the final discussion of Hoppe's lecture). Brief references to countertransference are also to be found in the papers by Ludowyk Gyomroi (1963), Hoppe (1965), H. Klein (1968), Tanay (1968a), Wind (1971), Kestenberg (1974, 1979), and the Panel (1974). For a more detailed account of countertransference problems in the treatment of hospitalized patients, see Axelrod et al. (1980).

transference feelings, however archaic these may be. Special anxieties and attitudes, however, make this particularly difficult when one deals with the psychotic reality of the concentration camps and its aftermaths. These anxieties are not only evident in the analytic situation, but more generally are also responsible for the delay with which psychoanalysts turned their attention to the subject at all, as well as for the already mentioned tendency to withhold empathy and to belittle the seriousness of the damage when faced with relevant analytic material.

By the term "withholding of empathy" I mean the failure to attempt to empathize. I do not mean to imply that complete empathy with the totally unprecedented experiences of the "holocaust" is possible—an empathy of the kind that may well be successfully achieved when the circumstances and experiences involved relate to matters with which we are familiar. But even when the subjectivity of extreme suffering and the ultimate impossibility of empathizing with it (mentioned at the outset) must be accepted as a fact, this does not absolve us from the effort of trying to adopt the empathic-analytic attitude. In Germany the inhibition in doing so is presumably strengthened by feelings of shame and guilt, by the "narcissistic wound" of the Germans, described by Horkheimer (1961). The withholding of empathy is, however, not an exclusively German phenomenon. Several American authors, e.g., Tanay (1968b), Krystal and Niederland (1968, p. 341), have pointed to a "conspiracy of silence" between therapists and patients—an unspoken agreement not to talk about the horrors of the past. In conclusion, I would like to examine some of the reasons for these more general anxieties, or rather, to speculate about them, without specifically discussing the topic of countertransference—in which, of course, such anxieties play a significant part.

The anxiety is so overwhelming because of the very nature of the material, which forces our own archaic heritage into our preconscious, perhaps even conscious, awareness. In his significant contributions, Eissler explored psychoanalytically the reasons why psychiatrists concerned with restitution claims withheld their empathy. I would like to remind readers of two of these reasons, which are particularly relevant in the present discussion. One of these, according to Eissler (1963), has to do with our violent rejection of the insight that not only our bodies but also our psyche can be damaged, indeed, radically destroyed, by traumatic external events to which we, as adults, may be accidentally and helplessly exposed. The insight into the illusory nature of our belief in the autonomy of the psyche apparently represents a threat to the self and a narcissistic injury too severe to be accepted without fierce protest.[33] In 1967, Eissler eventually identified as the most offensive, the most unacceptable, and therefore the most profoundly repressed motive—a motive that one can only reluctantly express in words—a primitive tendency to despise the sufferer. This tendency conflicts with the demands of the superego and ideal self, which are rooted in Christian tradition and held to be unshakable. It seems that the old "pagan" attitude reasserts itself when we are confronted with survivors from concentration camps, individuals who have undergone suffering to such an extreme degree and still display such a "deficit of narcissistic self-cathexis."

Thus each of us experiences in and with himself that the ability to empathize with sufferers is a precarious cultural acquisition—a late phylogenetic achievement requiring continuous ontogenetic effort for its maintenance—and that the unconscious in its conservativism retains an archaic attitude of contemptuous rejection. In the last resort, the awareness of contemptuous impulses of this kind arouses in us feelings of anxiety and shame because they signify our own identification with the aggressor. After all, an open contempt for anything supposedly weak constituted a main feature of the Nazi ideology. On the other hand—contradictions present no problem to the unconscious—a vicious circle is set up in that the survivor too is unconsciously perceived as being identified with the aggressor, and this produces a further reason for withholding one's empathy. The very fact of survival appears to be experienced as a

33. In the "Holocaust" film the decisive playing down of reality no doubt consisted in demonstrating the physical vulnerability of the protagonists, who nearly all lost their lives, but met their death mentally intact, i.e., with an unchanged psychic structure (with the possible exception of Karl Weiss). This misrepresentation may, however, have been necessary, in Eissler's sense, in order to ensure the readiness of the spectators to identify and empathize with the characters.

verdict of guilt—as though having survived at all can only signify collaboration and nothing else but death through persecution be regarded unmistakably as a distancing from the persecutor. A rationally totally unfounded tendency to glorify the victims who died and to be suspicious of those who survived apparently exists in the unconscious.

The full force of the reality of the events which took place in the concentration camps can, when symbolically conveyed, still penetrate and reach us. The same regressive pull, although in an incomparably milder form, to which prisoners were exposed over years, may be triggered off in each of us, simply by hearing about what happened in the camps. Reaction formations, sublimations, mature superego structures may come under pressure, deeply repressed sadomasochistic drive impulses become activated. It is as though we too were to fall under the sway of the preambivalent split between persecutor and persecuted and—insofar as the "paranoid position" (M. Klein, 1934) represents a transitional constellation in all psychic structure formation—to catch a glimpse not only of the earliest stages of our drive development but also of our earliest ego organization. I refer here to the very beginnings of individuation, a time at which, according to Freud's concept of the "purified pleasure-ego" (1915), the earliest differentiations between self and not-self are made. This is achieved by way of primitive projective and displacement mechanisms, through which the self in formation relegates all unpleasurable experiences, whether originating in external or internal stimuli, to the "outside." These archaic layers of the ego offer, so to speak, a vulnerable working surface, without which group phenomena such as pathological prejudice, ethnocentricity, xenophobia, hence anti-Semitism and fascism, cannot be mobilized. Presumably these early precipitates in all of us already become activated by reports of what happened in the concentration camps. This is accompanied by a diminution of our sense of identity and contact with reality—to a more or less threatening degree determined by the history of our own infantile process of individuation and its corresponding fixations. The need to avoid this threat may bring primitive defenses into operation, similar in some ways, perhaps, to the spontaneous archaic defense maneuvers seen in confrontation with psychosis and perversion. In denying one's empathy to survivors and their children, one, so to speak, conveys to them: "I want nothing to do with all this; it is 'outside'; it is not-me"—and in this way the tragedy of their discrimination is prolonged.

It is, however, not only the mortifying insight, forced upon us by this glimpse into the earliest layers of the ego, that as members of the human species, under conditions of reduced reality perception and dominated by regressive defense mechanisms, we too in principle are capable of fascism—we are simultaneously thrown back upon and exposed to the extreme helplessness of the oral phase. It is conceivable that we have to defend ourselves so fiercely against the awareness of the utter defenselessness of the persecuted in the face of the deadly destructivity of the persecutors, not least because this perception arouses infantile anxieties or psychophysical anxiety equivalents that are normally buried under infantile amnesia. These anxieties belong to the earliest developmental stages in which our own physical and mental survival once depended literally upon the continuous presence of a good-enough, protecting object. It is as though, faced with the facts of the "holocaust" and from the viewpoint of this deep, preconscious matrix of perception, we retrospectively say to ourselves: "Such a catastrophe might also have been my fate, had I been deserted by my good object and instead been faced with an evil, destructive one; this thought is so unbearable that I cannot allow it to become part of me; I must turn my back on it and fight against those who want to burden me with it— turn them into scapegoats."

Thus: are we not in fact afraid that, in our trial identifications, we might experience, albeit in an incomparably weaker form, something of that which the survivors actually lived through? Faced with the reincarnation of complete barbarism, overwhelmed by industrialized mass murder and ultimately by the sheer futility of these events, are we not afraid of losing our own capacity libidinally to cathect life and the future and to maintain the belief in the realizability of integrating impulses of love and hate? To express this in terms of object relations theory: are we not afraid that we might suddenly lose contact with our good internal objects and in doing so forfeit an essential precondition for all progressive development—as if the mechanism of paranoia were to usurp reality and the bad internal objects were to be abruptly externalized and thus, in the form of external persecutors, were to be removed from the control of the self—a process which again could only result in panic anxiety.[34]

Even the few reasons mentioned here would be cause enough, for the purpose of evading anxiety and unpleasure, to lead to the avoidance of psychoanalytic confrontation with the aftereffects of concentration camp imprisonment in survivors and their children. One might then content oneself with the statement: this is a trauma and it ought not to be tampered with. What may seem to be a passive attitude is, however, active in its consequences. At the very least, the "derealization" and "psychic immobilism" that Alexander and Margarete Mitscherlich (1968) diagnosed in Germany as resulting from trauma-avoidance will be prolonged. In any case, no contribution would have been made to check the sinister and brutally decivilizing force which, because even decades later it continues ubiquitously to provoke splitting and projection, emanates relatively undiminished from the Nazi crimes. Not only in our work with patients is the achievement or reattainment of the "depressive position" the task to be accomplished.

Finally, it would be at variance with the tradition of psychoanalysis to place this trauma under a taboo. The essence and enlightening power of psychoanalysis consist, today as in the past, in taking everything of which human beings are capable— even the excesses of aggression—as a subject of investigation. This remains true, although such studies reveal shameful and terrifying insights into the fragile nature of our cultural achievements. Looked at in this way, the psychoanalytic discussion of the aftereffects of concentration camp imprisonment could be regarded as part of the "education to reality" which Freud demanded in *The Future of an Illusion* (1927). We might thereby train our ego function to develop and endure signal anxiety and thus register in good time those impending regressive intrapsychic changes which once ended in the "holocaust." Through the memory of this historical example we can no

34. See Fairbairn's considerations in "The Repression and the Return of Bad Objects" (1943).

longer pretend not to know to what horrors such inner developments may lead, given the particular political, social, economic, technical, and educational conditions prevailing in Germany at that time.

BIBLIOGRAPHY

ADELSBERGER, L. (1947), Psychoanalytische Beobachtungen im Konzentrationslager Auschwitz. *Schweiz. Z. Psychol.*, 6:124–131.

ALEKSANDROWICZ, D.R. (1973), Children of concentration camp survivors. In: Anthony & Koupernik (1973), pp. 385–392.

ANTHONY, E. J. & KOUPERNIK, C., eds. (1973), *The Child in His Family*, 2. New York: Wiley.

AXELROD, S., SCHNIPPER, O. L., & RAU, J. H. (1980), Hospitalized offspring of holocaust survivors. *Bull. Menninger Clin.*, 44:1–14.

BAEYER, W. V. (1958), Erlebnisreaktive Störungen und ihre Bedeutung für die Begutachtung. *Dtsch. med. Wschr.*, 83:2317–2322.

——— HÄFNER, H., & KISKER, K. P. (1964), *Psychiatrie der Verfolgten*. Berlin, Göttingen, Heidelberg: Springer.

BAROCAS, H. A. (1970), Children of purgatory. *Corr. Psychiat. J. Soc. Ther.*, 16:51–58.

BETTELHEIM, B. (1943), Individual and mass behavior in extreme situations. *J. Abnorm. Soc. Psychol.*, 38:417–452.

——— (1960), *The Informed Heart*. Glencoe, Ill.: Free Press.

BONDY, C. (1943), Problems of internment camps. *J. Abnorm. Soc. Psychol.*, 38:453–475.

BRODY, S. (1973), The son of a refugee. *Psychoanal. Study Child*, 28:169–191.

CHODOFF, P. (1963), Late effects of the concentration camp syndrome. *Arch. Gen. Psychiat.*, 8:323–333.

DANTO, B. L. (1968), The role of "missed adolescence" in the etiology of the concentration-camp survivor syndrome. In: Krystal (1968), pp. 248–259.

DAVIDSON, S. (1967), See Israel Psychoanalytic Society (1967), pp. 96–98.

EISSLER, K. R. (1963), Die Ermordung von wievielen seiner Kinder muss ein Mensch symptomfrei ertragen können, um eine normale Konstitution zu haben? *Psyche*, 17:241–291.

——— (1967), Pervertierte Psychiatrie? *Psyche*, 21:553–575.

——— (1968), Weitere Bemerkungen zum Problem der KZ-Psychologie. *Psyche*, 22:452–463.

EITINGER, L. (1961), Pathology of the concentration camp syndrome. *Arch. Gen. Psychiat.*, 5:371–377.

——— (1975), Jewish concentration camp survivors in Norway. *Isr. Ann. Psychiat.*, 13:321–334.

FAIRBAIRN, W. R. D. (1943), The repression and the return of bad objects. In: *Psycho-Analytic Studies of the Personality*. London: Tavistock, 1952, pp. 59–81.

FEDERN, E. (1946), Essai sur la psychologie de la terreur. *Syntèses*, 1:79–96, 99–108.

FINK, H. F. (1968), Development arrest as a result of Nazi persecution during adolescence. *Int. J. Psychoanal.*, 49:327–329.

FRANKL, V. E. (1947). *Ein Psycholog erlebt das Konzentrationslager*, 2nd ed. Wien: Verlag für Jugend und Volk.

FREUD, A. (1936), The ego and the mechanism of defense. *W.*, 2.

———— (1954), [Discussion:] Problems of infantile neurosis. *Psychoanal. Study Child*, 9:40–43.

———— (1960), Discussion of Dr. John Bowlby's paper [Grief and mourning in infancy and early childhood]. *Psychoanal. Study Child*, 15:53–62.

———— & DANN, S. (1951), An experiment in group upbringing. *Psychoanal. Study Child*, 6:127–168.

FREUD, S. (1915), Instincts and their vicissitudes. *S.E.*, 14:117–140.

———— (1926), Inhibitions, symptoms and anxiety. *S.E.*, 20:87–172.

———— (1927), The future of an illusion. *S.E.*, 21:5–56.

———— (1930), Civilization and its discontents. *S.E.*, 21:64–145.

———— (1933), New introductory lectures on psycho-analysis. *S.E.*, 22:5–182.

FRIEDMAN, P. (1948), The effects of imprisonment. *Act. Med. Orient*, 7:163–167.

———— (1949), Some aspects of concentration camp psychology. *Amer. J. Psychiat.*, 105:601–605.

FURMAN, E. (1973), The impact of Nazi concentration camps on the children of survivors. In: Anthony & Koupernik (1973), pp. 379–384.

GRAAF, T. DE (1975), Pathological patterns of identification in families of survivors of the holocaust. *Isr. Ann. Psychiatr.*, 13:335–363.

HOPPE, K. D. (1962), Verfolgung, Aggression und Depression. *Psyche*, 16:521–537.

———— (1964), Verfolgung und Gewissen. *Psyche*, 18:305–313.

———— (1965), Psychotherapie mit Konzentrationslageropfern. *Psyche*, 19: 290–319.

———— (1966), The psychodynamics of concentration camp victims. *Psychoanal. Forum*, 1:76–80.

———— (1967), The emotional reactions of psychiatrists when confronting survivors of persecution. *Psychoanal. Forum*, 3:187–196.

———— (1968), Re-somatization of affects in survivors of persecution. *Int. J. Psychoanal.*, 49:324–326.

———— (1971), The aftermath of Nazi persecution reflected in recent psychiatric literature. In: Krystal & Niederland (1971), pp. 169–204.

HORKHEIMER, M. (1961), Über die deutschen Juden. In: *Kritik der instrumentellen Vernunft*. Frankfurt a.M.: S. Fischer, 1967, pp. 302–316.

ISRAEL PSYCHOANALYTIC SOCIETY (1967), Psychiatric disturbances of holocaust ("Shoa") survivors. Symposium, held 1966 in Tel-Aviv. Summary in: *Isr. Ann. Psychiat.*, 5:91–100.

JACOB, W. (1961), Gesellschaftliche Voraussetzungen zur Überwindung der KZ-Schäden. *Nervenarzt*, 32:542–545.

KESTENBERG, J. S. (1973), Introductory Remarks [to Symposium: Children of the Holocaust]. In: Anthony & Koupernik (1973), pp. 359–361.

—— (1974), Kinder von Überlebenden der Naziverfolgungen. *Psyche,* 28:249–265.

—— (1977), Contribution to Panel: The psychological consequences of punitive institutions. In: *Humanizing America,* ed. J. Knopp. National Institute on the Holocaust: Temple University.

—— (1979), From psychoanalyses of children of survivors from the Nazi Holocaust (Parts I and II, in collaboration with M. Kestenberg). To be published in: *Psychoanalytic Explorations of the Effect of the Holocaust on the Second Generation,* ed. M. Bergmann & M. E. Jucovy. New York: Basic Books (in preparation).

—— (1980), Psychoanalyses of children of survivors from the holocaust. *J. Amer. Psychoanal. Assn.,* 28:775–804.

KHAN, M. M. R. (1963), The concept of cumulative trauma. In: Khan (1974), pp. 42–58.

—— (1964), Ego-distortion, cumulative trauma and the role of reconstruction in the analytic situation. In: Khan (1974), pp. 59–68.

—— (1974), *The Privacy of the Self.* New York: Int. Univ. Press.

KLEIN, H. (1968), Problems in the psychotherapeutic treatment of Israeli survivors of the holocaust. In: Krystal (1968), pp. 233–248.

—— (1971), Families of holocaust survivors in the kibbutz. In: Krystal & Niederland (1971), pp. 67–72.

—— (1973), Children of the holocaust. In: Anthony & Koupernik (1973), pp. 393–409.

KLEIN, M. (1934), A contribution to the psychogenesis of manic-depressive states. In: *Contributions to Psycho-Analysis.* London: Hogarth Press, 1948, pp. 282–310.

KOGON, E. (1947), *Der SS-Staat.* Stockholm: Bermann-Fischer.

KRYSTAL, H., ed. (1968), *Massive Psychic Trauma.* New York: Int. Univ. Press.

—— (1971), Review of the findings and implications of this Symposium. In: Krystal & Niederland (1971), pp. 217–229.

—— & NIEDERLAND, W. G. (1968), Clinical observations on the survivor syndrome. In: Krystal (1968), pp. 327–348.

—— ——, eds. (1971), *Psychic Traumatization.* Boston: Little, Brown.

LAUFER, M. (1973), The analysis of a child of survivors. In: Anthony & Koupernik (1973), pp. 363–367.

LIFTON, R. J. (1968), Observations on Hiroshima survivors. In: Krystal (1968), pp. 168–189.

LIPKOWITZ, M. H. (1973), The child of two survivors. *Isr. Ann. Psychiat.,* 11:141–155.

LUDOWYK GYOMROI, E. (1963), The analysis of a young concentration camp victim. *Psychoanal. Study Child,* 18:484–510.

MEERLOO, J. A. M. (1963–64), Neurologism and denial of psychic trauma in extermination camp survivors. *Amer. J. Psychiat.,* 120:65–66.

_____ (1969), Persecution trauma and the reconditioning of emotional life. *Amer. J. Psychiat.*, 125:1187–1191.

MINKOWSKI, M. E. (1946), L'anesthésie affective. *Ann. Med.-Psychol.*, 104:80–86.

MITSCHERLICH, A. & MIELKE, F., eds. (1960), *Medizin ohne Menschlichkeit.* Frankfurt a.M.: Fischer Taschenbuch Verlag, 3rd ed., 1978.

_____ & MITSCHERLICH M. (1968), Die Unfähigkeit zu trauern. München: Piper.

NEMETH, M. C. (1971), Psychosis in a concentration camp survivor. In: Krystal & Niederland (1971), pp. 135–146.

NIEDERLAND, W. G. (1961), The problem of the survivor. *J. Hillside Hosp.*, 10:233–247.

_____ (1968a), Clinical observations on the "survivor syndrome." *Int. J. Psychoanal.*, 49:313–315.

_____ (1968b), An interpretation of the psychological stresses and defenses of concentration-camp life and the late aftereffects. In: Krystal (1968), pp. 60–70.

PANEL (1974), Children of survivors. S. M. Sonnenberg, reporter. *J. Amer. Psychoanal. Assn.*, 22:200–204.

PAUL, H. & HERBERG, H. J., eds. (1963), *Psychische Spätschäden nach politischer Verfolgung.* Basel & New York: S. Karger.

PEDERSEN, S. (1948), Psychopathological reactions to extreme social displacements. *Psychoanal. Rev.*, 35:344–354.

RAKOFF, V., SIGAL, J. J., & EPSTEIN, N. B. (1966), Children and families of concentration camp survivors. *Canad. Ment. Hlth*, 14:24–26.

ROSENBERGER, L. (1973), Children of survivors. In: Anthony & Koupernik (1973), pp. 375–377.

SEGALL, A. (1974), Spätreaktion auf Konzentrationslagererlebnisse. *Psyche,* 28:221–230.

SIGAL, J. J. (1971), Second-generation effects of massive psychic trauma. In: Krystal & Niederland (1971), pp. 55–65.

_____ (1972), Familial consequences of parental preoccupation. Read at the Amer. Psychiat. Assn., Dallas.

_____ (1973), Hypotheses and methodology in the study of families of the holocaust survivors. In: Anthony & Koupernik (1973), pp. 411–415.

_____ (1978), Comment on J. S. Kestenberg's lecture: From psychoanalyses of children of survivors from the holocaust, Quebec.

_____ & RAKOFF, V. (1971), Concentration camp survival. *Canad. Psychiat. Assn. J.*, 16:393–397.

_____ SILVER, D., RAKOFF, V., & ELLIN, B. (1973), Some second-generation effects of survival of the Nazi persecution. *Amer. J. Orthopsychiat.*, 43:320–327.

TANAY, E. (1968a), Initiation of psychotherapy with survivors of Nazi persecution. In: Krystal (1968), pp. 219–233.

_____ (1968b), Discussion. In: Krystal (1968), pp. 196–197.

Tas, J. (1951), Psychical disorders among inmates of concentration camps and repatriates. *Psychiat. Quart.*, 25:679–690.

Venzlaff, U. (1958), *Die psychoreaktiven Störungen nach entschädigungspflichtigen Ereignissen.* Berlin, Göttingen, Heidelberg: Springer.

Wangh, M. (1967), Discussion [to K. D. Hoppe (1967)]. *Psychoanal. Forum,* 3:197–201.

―――― (1968), A psychogenetic factor in the recurrence of war. *Int. J. Psychoanal.*, 49:319–322.

Wiesel, E. (1975), For some measure of humility, *Sh'ma.* October 31, pp. 314–315.

Williams, M. (1973), Discussion. In: Anthony & Koupernik (1973), pp. 367–371.

Wind, E. de (1968), The confrontation with death. *Int. J. Psychoanal.*, 49:302–305.

―――― (1971), Psychotherapy after traumatization caused by persecution. In: Krystal & Niederland (1971), pp. 93–114.

Winnicott, D. W. (1952), Psychosis and child care. In: *Through Paediatrics to Psycho-Analysis.* London: Hogarth Press, 1975, pp. 219–228.

Winnik, H. Z. (1967), Further comments concerning problems of late psychopathological effects of Nazi persecution and their therapy. *Isr. Ann. Psychiat.*, 5:1–16.

―――― (1968), Contribution to symposium on psychic traumatization through social catastrophe. *Int. J. Psychoanal.*, 49:298–301.

Wolfenstein, M. (1957), *Disaster.* Glencoe, Ill.: Free Press.

Bibliographical Note

S.E.   *The Standard Edition of the Complete Psychological Works of Sigmund Freud,* 24 Volumes, translated and edited by James Strachey, London: Hogarth Press and the Institute of Psycho-Analysis. 1953–1974.

W.   *The Writings of Anna Freud,* 8 Volumes, New York: International Universities Press, 1968–1981.

Index